Postgenocide

Postgenocide

Interdisciplinary Reflections on the Effects of Genocide

Edited by

KLEJDA MULAJ

OXFORD
UNIVERSITY PRESS

OXFORD
UNIVERSITY PRESS

Great Clarendon Street, Oxford, OX2 6DP,
United Kingdom

Oxford University Press is a department of the University of Oxford.
It furthers the University's objective of excellence in research, scholarship,
and education by publishing worldwide. Oxford is a registered trade mark of
Oxford University Press in the UK and in certain other countries

First Edition published in 2021

Impression: 1

Published in the United States of America by Oxford University Press
198 Madison Avenue, New York, NY 10016, United States of America

British Library Cataloguing in Publication Data

Data available

Library of Congress Control Number: 2020948078

ISBN 978–0–19–289518–9

DOI: 10.1093/oso/9780192895189.001.0001

Printed and bound by
CPI Group (UK) Ltd, Croydon, CR0 4YY

Acknowledgements

I am indebted to Contributors to this volume for sharing their expert knowledge and for their supreme collegiality in the process of producing this work. I am genuinely grateful to the anonymous reviewers for Oxford University Press for their astute comments and suggestions which have helped in improving the content of the volume. At Oxford University Press, I am truly thankful to Andy Redman and Merel Alstein for finding merit in the idea of the volume and for their kind and professional encouragement during the review process and the revision of the manuscript. Most sincere thanks are due, too, to Jack McNichol for his superb guidance with the completion of this work and for his kind and timely replies to the many queries I sent his way. At the University of Exeter I have had the privilege of meaningful discussions on many themes covered in this volume with my students of 'War and Its Aftermath' (POL3168) and 'Conflict, Security, and Development in World Politics' (POLM084) modules. It is rewarding to be able to address more fully some of their questions in the chapters of this book. My deepest gratitude goes to my Family for their unconditional love and support.

Table of Contents

List of Contributors

Jobair Alam Assistant Professor of Law, Department of Law, University of Dhaka

Kevin Aquilina Professor of Law, Faculty of Laws, University of Malta

Christopher P Davey Adjunct Instructor of Political Science, Brigham Young University, Utah

Marcia Esparza Associate Professor of Sociology, John Jay College of Criminal Justice, City University of New York

Martine Louise Hawkes Research Fellow in Justice and Society, University of South Australia

Maureen S Hiebert Associate Professor of Political Science, Centre for Military, Security & Strategic Studies, University of Calgary

Tatevik Mnatsakanyan Lecturer in Diplomacy and International Governance, Loughborough University London

Klejda Mulaj Senior Lecturer in International Relations, Department of Politics, University of Exeter

Rajika L Shah Deputy Director of the Center for the Study of Law & Genocide and Adjunct Professor, Loyola Law School, Loyola Marymount University, Los Angeles

Christopher Soler Senior Lecturer in Law, Faculty of Laws, University of Malta, and State Advocate

Andrew Wallis Independent Political Scientist, Historian, and Investigative Journalist

1
Introduction
Postgenocide: Living with Permutations of Genocide Harms

Klejda Mulaj

Opening Remarks

Genocide—one of the gravest crimes known to humankind—remains a challenging phenomenon to understand and explain academically and a serious problem to address in policy terms. Its recurrence reflects failure of political will to prevent. The large-scale human suffering caused by genocide demonstrates the failure to protect. And persistent challenges to recovery and healing, and difficulties to re-imagining life anew—in its aftermath—show ideational and material inadequacies to rebuilding. These failures however have led to persistent efforts to understand, explain, interpret, and re/act to the tragedies of genocide; that have produced a body of knowledge that is expansive and multi-disciplinary ranging from criminology, history, law, politics, sociology, philosophy, and cultural and indigenous studies.

Indeed, the existing body of knowledge on genocide has offered a valuable contribution to casting light on important questions on this heinous crime encompassing matters of etymology; etiology of genocide; politics, history, and sociology of genocide; laws of genocide; responses to genocide; gender and genocide; and a broad range of literature on case-specific and comparative studies.[1]

[1] Representations of these works include Donald Bloxham and A Dirk Moses (eds), *The Oxford Handbook of Genocide Studies* (OUP 2010) (hereafter Bloxham and Moses, *The Oxford Handbook of Genocide Studies*); Douglas Irvin-Erickson, *Raphael Lemkin and the Concept of Genocide* (University of Pennsylvania Press 2017) (hereafter Irvin-Erickson, *Raphael Lemkin*); Berel Lang, *Genocide: The Act as Idea* (University of Pennsylvania Press 2016) (hereafter Lang, *Genocide*); Irving Louis Horowitz, *Taking Lives: Genocide and State Power* (Transaction Books 1980); Leo Kuper, *Genocide: Its Political Use in the Twentieth Century* (Yale University Press 1981); Claudia Card and Armen T Marsoobian (eds), *Genocide's Aftermath: Responsibility and Repair* (Blackwell 2007) (hereafter Card and Marsoobian, *Genocide's Aftermath*); Joyce Apsel and Ernesto Verdeja (eds), *Genocide Matters: Ongoing Issues and Emerging Perspectives* (Routledge 2013); Adam Jones, *The Scourge of Genocide* (Routledge 2014); Frank Chalk and Kurt Jonassohn, *The History and Sociology of Genocide: Analysis and Case Studies* (Yale University Press 1990); Martin Shaw, *War and Genocide: Organized Killing in Modern Society* (Polity Press 2003); Thomas W Simon, *The Laws of Genocide* (Greenwood Publishers 2007); William Schabas, *Genocide in International Law: The Crime of Crimes*, 2nd edn, (CUP 2009) (hereafter Schabas, *Genocide in International Law*); Zygmunt Bauman, *Modernity and the Holocaust* (Polity Press 1989); Scott Straus, *The Order*

Klejda Mulaj, *Introduction* In: *Postgenocide*. Edited by: Klejda Mulaj, Oxford University Press (2021). © The Several Contributors. DOI: 10.1093/oso/9780192895189.003.0001

Despite the wide-ranging literature intensified particularly since the 1990s in the wake of mass atrocities in the former Yugoslavia, Rwanda, Darfur, and elsewhere, the scourge of genocide is not necessarily either fully understood or fully researched in all its complex aspects. Moreover, the respective disciplinary studies on genocide 'speak' only in limited ways to genocide studies in other disciplines. In addition, not unlike the study of war, the study of genocide is frequently undertaken in instrumental, strategic terms—ie, as a relation between means and ends—overlooking thus the capacity of genocide violence for communication and for being a generative force, a mechanism for change.

This volume advances existing knowledge of genocide scholarship by addressing in an interdisciplinary fashion a set of crucial—yet insufficiently explored—questions that delve on the effects of genocide in the postgenocide era. These effects vary from socio-political and legal responses to genocide; to meaningful, scholarly interpretations of genocide and other mass atrocities; to legal scholars' scrutiny of the efficacy of the genocide law and prospects of its enforcement; to genocide's impacts on the victims' communities and their efforts for recognition and redress; to genocide's effect on the communities of perpetrators and their attempts to denial and revisionism; to initiatives of world leaders (perceived) to make up for their failures to launch intervention and stop mass killing; to the (re)construction of genocide narratives via the display of personal objects of victims in museums, galleries, and archives.[2]

In seeking to unpack effects of genocide in the postgenocide era, the chapters in this volume examine: how the law contributes to advancing genocide knowledge; how international criminal courts and tribunals develop standards of responsibility and prosecute genocide perpetrators and with what effect; how victim groups transition to a postgenocide society; what are the uses of genocide in postgenocide setting; how are memory and denial of genocide constituted and reiterated; how are genocide narratives constructed and contested in postgenocide settings; and how postgenocide may provide an umbrella term for studying genocide and mass violence more broadly—by expanding and complementing some of the existing approaches in terms of processes, actors, identities, and narratives involved. In dwelling on these themes, our chapters aim to interrogate prevalent assumptions in genocide scholarship and limits thereof with the view of going beyond them in thought and action.

of Genocide: Race, Power, and War in Rwanda (Cornell University Press 2006); Timothy Longman, *Memory and Justice in Post-Genocide Rwanda* (CUP 2017); Lara J Nettelfield and Sara E Wagner, *Srebrenica in the Aftermath of Genocide* (CUP) 2014 (hereafter Nettlefield and Wagner, *Srebrenica*).

[2] The above listing of genocide effects is neither hierarchical nor all inclusive. It is a reflection of the themes covered in this volume.

Postgenocide

It is appropriate to note at the onset the meaning of the term 'postgenocide' in the context of this volume. Postgenocide may be conceived to suggest an approach to study genocide and its effects after mass killing has ended. The purpose of this subsection is not to provide a strict definition of postgenocide, because a more in-depth insight of this term can be gained from reading the ensuing chapters. But it is incumbent to begin by offering some clarity on the meaning of postgenocide for the purposes of the analyses presented in this book—and the suggested possibilities that engagement with postgenocide might afford to genocide scholars of various disciplinary backgrounds.

The initial instinct might be to consider the 'post' in postgenocide in temporal terms, signifying a period or era 'after' genocide has come to an 'end'. In fact this is a common conception in the existing genocide scholarship. For instance, the Holocaust Museum treats each instance of genocide that it presents in four parts: Background, Violence, Response, Aftermath.[3] Other studies have conceived aftermath in temporal terms, although not exclusively so;[4] studies which can be distinguished from the present volume in that they address singular cases and/or aspects of aftermath such as memory and belonging. This volume, in contrast, broadens and deepens concerns about the aftermaths of genocide—effects of genocide since the inception of genocidal killing. In this spirit, the ensuing chapters consider legal recourse after the fact with particular reference to challenges of criminalizing state responsibility for genocide and punishing this crime via internationalized courts and tribunals; the role of law in enabling postgenocide recovery via restitution; and more generally, how affected people deal with that deadly experience; how victims' communities react to, and resist, denial and revisionism; and how survivors strive for recognition, redress, and recovery of their identities; in addition to casting light upon some formerly opaque, overlooked cases. In doing so our chapters explore what several disciplines—such as law, political science, sociology, and ethnography—bring to bear on genocide scholarship and help rethink existing assumptions in the field.

It bears emphasizing that the meaning of *aftermath* is more complex than the initial instinct of temporal understanding of the *term* might suggest, although *its* definition is not an easy task. Scholars who have studied and written on the effects of genocide have been candid about challenges of defining 'after' and 'aftermath'.

[3] United States Holocaust Memorial Museum, 'Aftermath: Unity, Reconciliation, and Justice' <https://www.ushmm.org/genocide-prevention/countries/rwanda/case-study/aftermath/unity-reconciliation-justice> accessed 1 July 2020.

[4] See, for example, Karen Auerback, *Aftermath: Genocide, Memory and History* (Monash University Press 2015); Lerna Ekmekcioglu, *Recovering Armenia: The Limits of Belonging in Post-Genocide Turkey* (Stanford University Press 2016); Hannah Grayson and Nicki Hitchcott (eds), *Rwanda Since 1994: Stories of Change* (Liverpool University Press 2019).

They ask how do we arrive at 'the intellectual demarcation of the transformation of a post-conflict to a normalized state?' Do we delineate time in the wake of violent ruptures in calendrical milestones of years past and/or anniversaries marked? Or, do we pay attention to social time and processes?[5] Contemporary liberal interventions in war-torn countries of Bosnia, Kosovo, Afghanistan, and Iraq have worked with the idea of fast track repair set out on significant milestones such as a swift return to the rule of law, internationally monitored elections within months of the initiation of the peace treaty, stabilization of currency, rebuilding of armies and police forces, and so on. Liberal interventions in the aftermath of bloodshed have tried to be economic with time which in turn has condensed processes that demand long periods to materialize.

In his book *After Evil*, Robert Meister situated his analysis in 'a time between times, when evil has ended but before justice has begun. There is, *ex hypothesi*, still time before a leap into justice and still a danger of relapse into evil of the past.'[6] A temporal understanding of 'post' in postgenocide indicates the *transitional* character of the events and processes in the aftermath of genocide. The chapters in this collection show that although effects of genocide are long-term, addressing them is still in a transitional phase in Meister's sense that they (ie, genocide effects) remain grounded in a time between times, when justice has not yet been attained and there is still danger in relapsing back into evil. The temporal meaning of 'post' in postgenocide can therefore imply the time it takes to produce the desired change, or the rate at which change occurs, concomitant with the claims and counterclaims pertaining to (real and imagined) realities of genocide.[7]

Furthermore, concern with (the rate of) change implies a preoccupation with the question what does it mean for a great evil—such as genocide—to be over and done with?[8] 'Post' in postgenocide therefore cannot have merely a temporal meaning. This volume suggests that paying attention to meanings and social processes inherent in the 'post'—ie, processes and their meanings that follow genocide—affords high explanatory purchase. Reflecting of this conceptual advancement, 'potgenocide' rather than 'post-genocide' is used throughout this book. It is to the consideration of processes that follow genocide that our chapters make a prime contribution.

It bears noting at this juncture that postgenocide shares a certain affinity with 'postcolonial'. Just like postcolonial does not signify the era 'after' colonialism came to an end, so postgenocide does not signify merely the time period 'after' genocide but rather the *effects* of genocide in shaping realities of societies subjected to cruelty of this heinous crime. Postcolonialism suggests that the world has been

[5] Refer, for instance, to Nettelfield and Wagner, *Srebrenica* (n 1) 28.

[6] Robert Meister, *After Evil: A Politics of Human Rights* (Columbia University Press 2011) 10 (hereafter Meister, *After Evil*).

[7] ibid 14.

[8] ibid.

moulded by colonialism.[9] Similarly postgenocide suggests that the era following the genocidal killing is shaped by genocide. Furthermore, analysis of the ensuing chapters share with postcolonial literature a sensitivity to the role of knowledge not merely as a 'mirror' which represent the 'real', but as a force that shapes what is out there.[10] In addition, postgenocide shares with postcolonial the assumption that identities are constituted via multifarious—unequal even coercive—exchanges which impact all actors involved.[11] Just like hierarchical exchanges impact both the colonized and colonizers, so unequal and coercive exchanges between architects and perpetrators of genocide, on the one hand, and genocide survivors, on the other hand—ranging from direct violence of genocide, to court cases, to various processes of denial and remembrance—touch both communities of victims and perpetrators in significant ways. Identities are not fixed either in time or in place. They are shaped discoursively in dialogue and contestation with the Other, a theme explored in Parts II and III of this volume.

Because more often than not genocide happens in the midst of war, there is also a certain affinity between postgenocide and postwar (or postconflict)—both in the temporal and processual understanding of 'post'. This is so because timewise postgenocide, postwar, and postconflict overlap as in the cases of the Holocaust, Rwanda, Srebrenica, and other genocides, and also because the effects of genocide—just like the effects of war/armed conflict—shape lives of people and societies subjected to them long after peace agreements are signed.[12] This is not to suggest, however, that genocide is war and vice versa, unless one refers to a total, apocalyptic (nuclear) war. Despite overlaps, conceptually, 'postwar' and 'postconflict' can be conceived to be broader than 'postgenocide' in terms of the multitude of effects and processes involved.

[9] For postcolonialism see Sanjay Seth (ed), *Postcolonial Theory and International Relations: A Critical Introduction* (Routledge 2013) (hereafter Seth, *Postcolonial Theory*); Shampa Biswas, 'Postcolonialism' in Tim Dunne, Milja Kurki, and Steve Smith (eds), *International Relations Theories: Discipline and Diversity* 4th edn (OUP 2016).

[10] Sanjay Seth, 'Postcolonial Theory and the Critique of International Relations' in Seth (ed), *Postcolonial Theory*, (n 9) 28.

[11] This is an assumption that manifests itself also in other processes such as for instance postconflict state building under the auspices of international actors. These have been considered in Klejda Mulaj, 'On State Building and Wicked Problems: Stateness, Nationhood, and Mimicry' (2019) 56 (2/3) International Studies 129–146.

[12] Armed conflict and war are very complex processes of violent contestations. Any definition of these two terms cannot do justice to their full meaning. For the sake of drawing attention to their scale difference, nonetheless, it might be useful to note a common held differentiation: 'Armed conflict' takes place where there is a clash between two or more parties, normally one thereof being a state, parties which in their contest use armed force as a result of which no fewer than twenty-five deaths result within one year. An armed conflict qualifies as war when 1,000 battle-related deaths are incurred in one year. See Uppsala University's Department of Peace and Conflict Research, 'Definition of Armed Conflict', < https://pcr.uu.se/research/ucdp/definitions/#Active> accessed 1 July 2020. No claim is made here that the above definitions reveal much about dynamics or war/s and armed conflict/s. Nor space allows to discuss such dynamics here.

Reflecting on twentieth-century struggles, Robert Meister has observed that participants in such struggles 'imagined a future consensus on what evil was . . . If a struggle over the *meaning* of evil is the moral template for war, then consensus on the *fact* of evil is what it would mean for this war to end'.[13] It is not, nonetheless, as Meister suggests, that '[t]he wars of the twentieth century ended with consensus on both the fact and evil of genocide'.[14] Indeed, in many 'endings' of twentieth-century wars, consensus on the fact and meaning of 'evil' was not so clear-cut, such as, for instance, the Balkan Wars of 1912–1913, and 1990s; manifestation/s of the Second World War in the territories of the former Socialist Federal Republic of Yugoslavia (referred to as Yugoslavia); Wars in the Congo (1996–1997 and 1998–2003), Ethiopia (1974–1991), and Eritrea-Ethiopia (1998–2000). However, Meister is right in his observations of the ending of the Second World War with reference to the Holocaust. There is consensus on both the fact and evil of this genocide. Denying the Holocaust has become not only a factual disagreement about the past, but also a way to challenge a prevailing consensus in the meaning of good and evil.[15] General consensus, nonetheless, on the fact and evil of genocide is not necessarily prevalent outside the archetypal case of the Holocaust. Genocide denial in other cases remains common, as chapters in the second part of this volume demonstrate. Moreover, although in a given genocide the distinction between perpetrator and victim may appear clear, such distinction in all genocides is not set in stone. Furthermore, in struggles involving same actors in varying time periods, the roles of perpetrators and victims have shifted or become blurred.[16]

This volume suggests that postgenocide can be posited as a new approach to critically rethink the study of genocide and its effects. The ensuing chapters may be considered to be what Hannah Arendt called thought-events, that is, scenes of 'battlegrounds' between forces-as-ideas of the past and (an emerging) future mediated by the author who situated between these forces—in the now—gives battle to both of them. The past—as Arendt noted—is not merely 'a burden man has to shoulder and of whose dead weight the living can or must get rid in their march to the future. In the words of Faulkner, 'the past is never dead, it is not even past. [The] past . . . presses forward, and it is . . . the future which drives us back into the past'.[17]

In line with an interconnected understanding of past and future, the 'post' in postgenocide signifies not only the era 'after' genocide came to an 'end', but the entire period following the inception of genocide. Our chapters unpack ways in which the period after genocide killing has ended is affected by genocide itself.

[13] Meister, *After Evil* (n 6) 6. Emphasis in original.

[14] ibid 6–7.

[15] ibid 7.

[16] Refer to René Lemarchand, 'Introduction', in René Lemarchand (ed), *Forgotten Genocides: Oblivion, Denial, and Memory* (University of Pennsylvania Press 2011) 5; and Christopher Davey's Chapter 12 in this volume.

[17] Hannah Arendt, *Between Past and Future: Eight Exercises in Political Thought* (Penguin Books 1954) 10–11 (hereafter Arendt, *Between Past and Future*).

The critical rethinking of the study of genocide via the postgenocide lens will be a long-term undertaking. This volume cannot be all inclusive of the very broad aspects of postgenocide themes. It does nonetheless offer a renewed beginning to that undertaking.

The De/Stabilized Meaning of 'Genocide'

The readers of this book will realize that our contributions go beyond questions of definition and etymology. It is necessary, however, to highlight briefly in this introduction the evolution of the concept of genocide, its overlaps with closely related offences—crimes against humanity, ethnic cleansing, and war crimes—and contentious issues pertaining therein. Overcoming problems of non-universal definitions requires, at a minimum, knowing the contestations involved.

Contemplation of the term 'genocide' and its interpretations have long preoccupied scholars of various disciplines, not least law, politics, and sociology. Despite extensive scholarly considerations agreement on a universal definition of genocide has not been achieved. The Jewish-Polish jurist, Raphael Lemkin, who coined the term 'genocide' in the winter of 1942, was interested to document accounts of crimes perpetrated by the Nazis against the Jewish people and other minority groups in the course of the Second World War. His observations of this war led Lemkin to conclude that wars in the twentieth century were not fought merely between states for the purposes of territorial control, but rather by states against populations with the view of shaping identities of the targeted people as was the case of the Nazi regime in Germany, which was waging war to obliterate targeted civilian populations, primarily Jews.[18]

Up till this time, states were considered to be the basic units of international law. It was accepted that states can commit crimes against one another and that no state should interfere in the policies of another with regard to treatment of people living within one state's territory. The Nazi regime justified its policies towards the German Jews under the cover of internal legality. Hence, for Lemkin, minorities such as Jews were afforded no protection in international law, since the ruling government believed it could do as it wished to the Jewish people.[19] Lemkin attached fundamental value to group identity for the sake of culture and civilization, and also for the lives of members of the group/s as well as the existence of groups themselves. For him, 'the engine of all human creativity was the possibility of living in a plural world animated by diversity, to allow for the free exercise of subjectivity, and to allow individuals to experience different subjective positions'.[20] Because the

[18] Raphael Lemkin, *Axis Rule in Occupied Europe* (Columbia University Press 1944). Irvin-Erickson, *Raphael Lemkin* (n 1) 1, 12.

[19] Refer to Lang, *Genocide* (n 1) 20, and for a longer treatment of this theme his Chapter 6.

[20] Lemkin, cited in Irvin-Erickson, *Raphael Lemkin* (n 1) 247.

architects and perpetrators of genocide aim to deprive humanity of the richness stemming from group identities, genocide can be considered a crime against all mankind.[21]

Lemkin and other distinguished figures such as René Samuel Cassin, John Peters Humphrey, Hersch Lauterpacht, and Eleanor Roosevelt—were part of a movement dedicated to reconfiguring human rights institutions and humanitarian law after the Second World War.[22] Their work laid the ground for the 1948 United Nations Convention on the Prevention and Punishment of Genocide which entered into force in 1951 (hereinafter referred to as 'the Genocide Convention' or 'the Convention'). Article II of this Convention, defines genocide as:

> acts committed with *intent* to destroy, in whole or in part, a national, ethnical, racial or religious group as such: (a) Killing members of the group; (b) Causing serious bodily or mental harm to members of the group; (c) Deliberately inflicting on the group conditions of life calculated to bring about its physical destruction in whole or in part; (d) Imposing measures intended to prevent births within the group; (e) Forcibly transferring children of the group to another group.[23]

This is the most widely accepted definition of genocide in the courts of law and academia. Despite being criticized on many grounds, as elaborated below, it is to the Convention that most scholars and legal experts refer in identifying genocide. According to the above definition, genocide is a group-based crime. It is a sociopolitical process undertaken with the intent to destroy human groups in whole or in part. One noticeable aspect of the evil of genocide is that it involves twofold murder, or a double murder, that is, killing at two levels: (i) murder of individuals as a means to (ii) the destruction of the group. But it is the second level—destruction/murder of the group—that is a feature of genocide which distinguishes it from both individual murder and mass murder.[24] Genocide is more than mass murder due to its key feature of special intent (or *dolus specialis*), that is, the mental factor—known in juridical terminology as *mens rea*—to destroy in whole or in part, a national, ethnic, or religious group, as such.[25] The special intent (*dolus specialis*) that genocide perpetrators entertain towards group destruction is a key feature that distinguishes genocide from other related crimes, namely 'ethnic cleansing', 'crimes against humanity', and 'war crimes'.

[21] ibid 234.
[22] ibid 1.
[23] United Nations, 'UN Convention on the Prevention and Punishment of Genocide, 1948', <https://treaties.un.org/doc/Publication/UNTS/Volume%2078/volume-78-I-1021-English.pdf> accessed on 1 July 2020.
[24] Lang, *Genocide* (n 1) 22, 51.
[25] Schabas, *Genocide in International Law* (n 1) Chapters 4 and 5.

Whilst war crimes 'address the criminal conduct of a perpetrator toward an immediate protected object', crimes against humanity 'address the perpetrator's conduct not only towards the immediate victims but also towards the whole of humankind'.[26] War crimes are committed in the course of armed conflicts. Therefore, they are closely related to a military campaign or battle; they tend to form part of a military operation plan. Crimes against humanity may be committed in armed conflict or in a time of peace.[27] What distinguishes crimes against humanity from ordinary crimes such as murder or rape is their intrinsic gravity.[28] Although crimes against humanity are considered to be more serious offences than war crimes, in their many deliberations, the International Criminal Tribunal for the former Yugoslavia (ICTY) and the International Criminal Tribunal for Rwanda (ICTR) have ruled that war crimes committed on a systematic and large scale amount to crimes against humanity.[29] In general, even when the material element is the same, the mental element of the category of war crimes is of a lesser magnitude than that pertaining to crimes against humanity.[30]

Intent is the main distinction between genocide and ethnic cleansing. The contributing factor to this difference consists in the fact that whilst the intent of genocidaires is the destruction of the targeted group, the intent of ethnic cleansers is—primarily—the forced displacement/uprooting and dispossession of the targeted group. On its part, the world court has concluded that notwithstanding this distinction, there exist cases where ethnic cleaning may form part of the material element of the crime of genocide. A case in point is when measures are adopted with the intent to destroy a targeted group rather than remove that same group from the land territory it occupies.[31] When a community with a territorially

[26] ICTY, *Prosecutor v Dražen Erdemović*, Joint Separate Opinion of Judge McDonald and Judge Vohrah, IT-96-22-A (Appeals Chamber, 7 October 1997) para 21 <www.icty.org/x/cases/erdemovic/acjug/en/erd-asojmcd971007e.pdf> accessed 1 July 2020 (hereafter ICTY, *Prosecutor v Dražen Erdemović*). As this ICTY chamber noted in the same paragraph: 'Crimes against humanity are especially odious forms of misbehaviour and in addition form part of a widespread and systematic practice or policy. Because of their heinousness and magnitude they constitute egregious attacks on human dignity, on the very notion of humaneness.'

[27] Hersch Lauterpacht proposed that the Nuremberg Tribunal used the notion of 'crimes against humanity' to criminalize extermination of four million Jews and Poles in occupied Poland as an act of killing individuals as part of a systematic plan. Lauterpacht worked in tandem with Lemkin to advance a rights-based approach to international law, conceptualizing two crimes that lie at the foundation of the present global international legal regime. Irvin-Erickson, *Raphael Lemkin* (n 1) 2–3. See also Philippe Sands, *East West Street: On the Origins of Genocide and Crimes Against Humanity* (Weidenfeld & Nicolson 2016) xxi, xxviii.

[28] Payam Akhavan, *Reducing Genocide to Law: Definition, Meaning, and the Ultimate Crime* (McGill University 2012) 73 (hereafter Akhavan, *Reducing Genocide to Law*).

[29] ICTY, *Prosecutor v Duško Tadić*, Judgment in Sentencing Appeals, Separate Opinion of Judge Cassese, IT-94-1A and IT-94-1A *bis* (Appeals Chamber, 26 January 2000) para 16 (hereafter ICTY, *Prosecutor v Duško Tadić*); ICTY, *Prosecutor v Dragoljub Kunarac*, IT-96-23 and IT-96-23/1-A (Appeals Chamber, 12 June 2002) paras 171–172; ICTY, *Prosecutor v Goran Jelisić*, IT-95-10-A (Appeals Chamber, 5 July 2001) para 82; ICTR, *The Prosecutor v Jean-Paul Akayesu* ICTR-96-4-T (Trial Chamber, 2 September 1998) para 470; ICTY, *Prosecutor v Mirjan Kupreškić*, IT-95-16-T (Trial Chamber, 14 January 2000) paras 698–704.

[30] ICTY, *Prosecutor v Duško Tadić* (n 29) paras 12 and 14.

[31] ICJ, *Bosnia and Herzegovina v. Serbia and Montenegro* [2007] ICJ Rep 2007 (I) at 190.

bounded culture is intentionally and forcefully uprooted—as a consequence of which individual members cannot maintain the cultural and social ethos of their community—then the latter will suffer deprivations and harms characteristic of the crime of genocide.[32] Hence, cultural genocide. Some legal scholars have insisted on the separation of the crime of ethnic cleansing from genocide.[33] Others argue that ethnic cleansing should be incorporated under the umbrella of the crime of genocide.[34] Despite these two diverging views, there is wide agreement that ethnic cleansing is a crime against humanity.

Between genocide and crimes against humanity, the former is the most atrocious. From a criminal pyramidal perspective, genocide is at the apex, rather than crimes against humanity and war crimes.[35] This is evinced by the fact that the international community has sought to prohibit and punish this crime by allocating a singular international treaty—the United Nations Convention on the Prevention and Punishment of the Crime of Genocide—to this horrendous crime rather than including it within the list, or as part, of crimes against humanity such as in the Nuremberg Principles and the Draft Code of Offences Against Peace and Security.[36] Scholars are of the view that genocide is an aggravated form of crime against humanity.[37] That the statute of the International Criminal Court refers to 'genocide' separately from 'crimes against humanity' (and also 'war crimes' and 'the crime of aggression') suggests that for drafters and 122 state parties to the Rome Statute, '"genocide" would not be adequately addressed by the rubric of "crimes against humanity", whether because it is outside the latter's purview or because even if it were covered there, the act itself is sufficiently radical to warrant its independent characterization'.[38]

A wide body of case law uses the notion of gravity of crimes—or otherwise referred to as hierarchy of crimes—in justifying sentences for various crimes, the principle of proportionality thus shaping the punishment of crimes. The concept of gravity—that certain crimes are so heinous that demand international action—has

32 Mohammed Abed, 'Clarifying the Concept of Genocide', in Card and Marsoobian (eds), *Genocide's Aftermath* (n 1) 47–48.

33 For instance Schabas, *Genocide in International Law* (n 1) 225.

34 Refer for example to Larry May, *Genocide: A Normative Account* (CUP 2010) 1, 19 (hereafter May, *A Normative Account*). May argues for a deflated idea of genocide. For him genocide 'is not morally unique in its horrendousness, and it is not the crime of crimes' p 20.

35 Mark Drumbl, 'Prosecutor v. Radislav Krstić: ICTY Authenticates Genocide at Srebrenica and Convicts for Aiding and Abetting' (2004) 5(2) Melbourne Journal of International Law 434–50.

36 Akhavan, *Reducing Genocide to Law* (n 28) 81.

37 Lang, *Genocide* (n 1) 58. This was also Lemkin's view. Refer to Irvin-Erickson, *Raphael Lemkin* (n 1) 3, 13.

38 Lang, *Genocide* (n 1) 56. The Rome Statute refutes William Schabas' proposal for 'crimes against humanity' to replace 'genocide'. For a compelling critique of Schabas' proposal refer to Lang, Chapter 4. The list of parties to the ICC Statute can be found at United Nations, 'Rome Statute of the International Court' <https://treaties.un.org/pages/ViewDetails.aspx?src=TREATY&mtdsg_no=XVIII-10&chapter=18&lang=en> accessed 1 July 2020.

been central in rationalizing the international community's decisions to establish a highly selective criminal law regime in the form of the international criminal tribunals and more recently the International Criminal Court (ICC).[39] The ICTR jurisprudence has pointed out that 'some criminal behaviours are more serious than others ... [T]he effective gravity of the offences committed is the deciding factor in the determination of the sentence: the principle of gradation or hierarchy in sentencing requires that the longest sentences be reserved for the most serious offences'.[40]

Support for a hierarchy between war crimes and crimes against humanity—in particular genocide—is not uniform, nonetheless. Jurists and law practitioners such as Antonio Cassese, James Crawford, Patricia Wald, and Dianne Marie Amann have argued in favour of the notion of hierarchy of crimes,[41] whereas others like Mohamed Shahabuddeen and Larry May have argued to the contrary.[42] That several Appeals Chamber judges from the ICTY who challenged the notion of hierarchy of crimes came to sit on the ICTR Appeals Chamber explains the subsequent juridical pronouncements thereupon.[43] Some judgments have produced contradictory interpretations of the hierarchy of crimes. For instance, in the ICTY's *Erdemović* Appeals Judgement, the majority of the Appeals Chamber adhered to the idea of the hierarchy of crimes in relation to crimes against humanity versus war crimes.[44] However, in the ICTY's Tadić case judge Shahabuddeen rejected a hierarchy between war crimes and crimes against humanity.[45] Similarly, at the ICTR, the *Akayesu* judgment of 1998 disagreed with the notion of hierarchy of crimes.[46] Such non-uniform judicial interpretations remain active spaces where effects of genocide are felt in the postgenocide era. They also show that there cannot always be a sharp divide between interpretations of genocide and crimes against humanity.

[39] Margaret M deGuzman, 'Gravity and the Legitimacy of the International Criminal Court' (2009) 32 Fordham International Law Journal 1400–1465.

[40] ICTR, *Prosecutor v Nahimana, Barayagwiza and Ngeze*, ICTR-99-52 (Appeals Judgement, Appeals Chamber, 28 November 2007) para 1060.

[41] For instance, ICTY, *Prosecutor v Duško Tadić* (n 29); International Law Commission (1994) 1 *Yearbook of the International Law Commission* 214 para 21 referring to the view of James Crawford; ICTY, *Prosecutor v Goran Jelisić*, IT-95-10-A (Appeals Chamber, Partial Dissenting Opinion of Judge Patricia Wald, 5 July 2001); Diane Marie Amann, 'Group Mentality, Expressivism, and Genocide' (2002) 2(2) International Criminal Law Review (hereafter Amann, 'Group Mentality').

[42] For instance, ICTY, *Prosecutor v Duško Tadić*, Judgement in Sentencing Appeals, Separate Opinion of Judge Shahabuddeen, IT-94-1A (Appeals Chamber, 26 January 2000) (hereafter ICTY, *Prosecutor v Duško Tadić*); May, *A Normative Account* (n 34) 19–20.

[43] Akhavan, *Reducing Genocide to Law* (n 28) 84.

[44] ICTY, *Prosecutor v Dražen Erdemović* paras 23–27.

[45] ICTY, *Prosecutor v Duško Tadić* (n 42).

[46] ICTR, *The Prosecutor v Jean-Paul Akayesu*, ICTR-96-4-T (Trial Chamber, 2 September 1998) para 470.

The critique of the Convention's legal definition of genocide goes beyond the disconcerted interpretations of hierarchy of crimes, and overlaps between genocide and crimes against humanity. Being much scrutinized, the legal definition of genocide is criticized also on various other grounds from questioning the existence of groups (and hence genocide itself); to narrowly focusing on only four protected groups (national, ethnical, racial, and religious) thus excluding other biological, cultural, or political groups; to the adoption of a high threshold of genocidal intent.[47] Moreover, the legal definition in the Convention does not provide for the emerging role of violent non-state actors (VNSAs) in the context of transformation or disintegration of state sovereignty, and the potential of VNSAs for committing genocide.[48]

Despite encountered challenges, the ongoing evolution of the idea of genocide charted briefly above demonstrates the sustained influence of this idea and its increased effects in legal and political spheres. The very existence of the Genocide Convention—certain ambiguities, even inconsistencies notwithstanding—and the frequency with which scholars and policy makers refer to it suggest that the meaning of genocide is stabilized both at the international and national levels. However, concomitantly with this apparent stability there has also been sustained criticism, or a pushback, to the detriment of the concept of genocide as defined in the Convention from those who seek to deflate the meaning of genocide and collapse it within the umbrella of crimes against humanity,[49] and others who seek added clarity to the existing legal definition of genocide with the view to rendering the Convention better suited to reflect changes that have taken place in the seventy-two years since its adoption and therefore strengthening genocide law to cater for the realities of the twenty-first century, including new destructive processes that may account as novel forms of genocide.[50] The Convention itself does not forbid alterations, and amendments can contribute to maximizing the stability of the idea of genocide and its related laws. The ongoing debates on the meaning of genocide, its interpretations and applicability in certain settings, and possibility of the Convention's amendments are demonstrations of the socio-political effects of genocide in postgenocide setting.

[47] Refer for instance to May, *A Normative Account* (n 34); Ann Curthoys and John Docker, 'Defining Genocide' in Dan Stone (ed), *The Historiography of Genocide* (CUP 2008); *Frank Chalk*, 'Redefining Genocide' in George J Andreopoulos (ed) *Genocide: Conceptual and Historical Dimensions* (University of Pennsylvania Press 1997). For a compelling critique of May's questioning of the existence of groups in the genocide setting refer to Lang, *Genocide* (n 1) chapter 4.

[48] Alyson J K Bailes and Daniel Nord, 'Non-State Actors in Conflict: A Challenge for Policy and for Law' in Klejda Mulaj (ed), *Violent Non-State Actors in World Politics* (Hurst and Columbia University Press 2010).

[49] For instance, May, *A Normative Account* (n 34); and Schabas, *Genocide in International Law* (n 1).

[50] For instance, Lang, *Genocide* (n 1); Kevin Aquilina and Klejda Mulaj, 'Limitations in Attributing State Responsibility under the Genocide Convention' (2018) 17(1) Journal of Human Rights 123–139 (hereafter Aquilina and Mulaj, 'State Responsibility').

Permutations of Genocide Harms

The evil of genocide generates multiple harms and security challenges that necessitate serious considerations of this crime from policy, humanitarian, and scholarly perspectives. Considering what distinguishes genocide from other atrocities, what makes genocide the specific evil that it is, Claudia Card has suggested that it is social death that distinguishes genocide from other mass murders.[51] Central to genocide, social death involves major loss of social vitality, loss of identity, and a serious loss of meaning for one's existence. 'Social vitality is destroyed when the social relations—organizations, practices, institutions—of the members of the group are irreparably damaged or demolished'.[52] The injustice of genocide is an evil because it inflicts such high levels of harms to victims that makes their lives—and deaths—indecent and unbearable. When a group with a distinct identity is made a target of genocide, its survivors are left with a weaker heritage, tradition, and intergenerational bonds. The harms of genocide do not pertain merely to physical death in very large scale, but also to social death, in Card's sense, because genocide attacks social connections and social contexts that make dying bearable and life meaningful.[53]

Nevertheless, Larry May has opined that genocide involves primarily what he calls 'status harm', in that when the group to which individuals belong is destroyed, those (individuals) who become deprived of group membership lose status in terms of their protection of human rights. He contends that the 'status harm' (not social death) is the basis of the harm of genocide. May rejects the idea that genocide causes harm to the international community by adversely affecting all of humanity.[54] His thoughts are implicitly grounded on a dichotomy between group and individual rights. 'The harm of destroying a social group is that individuals suffer a significant loss in that their group identity is destroyed'.[55] Furthermore, May contends that genocide 'leaves the individual group member without recourse to claim his or her rights as a human, and sometimes without resources even to understand who he or she is. Understood in this way, genocide is not primarily a harm to the group but to the individual person'.[56] This interpretation contradicts the conception of genocide as a group crime—destruction of group identity being a defined feature of genocide. Indeed, in the most widely held meaning of the term, without

[51] Claudia Card, 'Genocide and Social Death' (2003) 18(1) Hypatia 63 at 63, 65 (hereafter Card, 'Genocide and Social Death'). For a philosophically grounded discussion of Card's argument refer to essays in Card and Marsoobian (eds) *Genocide's Aftermath* (n 1).

[52] Card, 'Genocide and Social Death' (n 51) 73.

[53] ibid 63, 73. This is completely compatible with Lemkin's view and the importance and value he attached to group identities for the sake of vitality of humanity. Refer to Irvin-Erickson, *Raphael Lemkin* (n 1) 234, 246.

[54] May, *A Normative Account* (n 34) 10–11.

[55] ibid 18.

[56] ibid 71.

reference to the group, genocide ceases to be the specific evil it is. The claim that genocide can be treated 'as a crime primarily that harms individuals, not primarily as a harm to the groups that are targeted themselves'[57] is problematic. A dichotomy of group and individual rights in the context of genocide, even more so primacy of individual harm to group harm, does not have much of an analytical and/or persuasive value. Genocide violates both group and individual rights to a barbaric extent. The suffering of the group and its individual members are interconnected and even reinforcing. Hence the notion of twofold murder or double murder—explained above—is a key feature of genocide.

Moreover, groups subjected to genocide are rarely exterminated completely. Even in the most malicious attacks, thankfully, there are surviving victims who manage to go on living and preserve and further develop cultural traditions of their group. Whilst May realizes the latter fact, he overlooks the performative effects of genocidal violence, its generative powers and capacity to act as a mechanism for survival and change. Key here is transferability of the material power of genocide—not least death and suffering—to (contests over) memory, remembrance and laws of genocide, and, crucially, re-imagining, re-understanding, and re-experiencing political community in the postgenocide setting. Genocide may be conceived as violence that destroys bodies and material culture, violence that attacks elements of being and understanding group (and individual) identity. Its aftermath gives way to surrogate contests (surrogate, because there are no dead or injured bodies as in genocide) via which genocidal violence is delegitimized and contested by survivors' communities and (sometimes) re-interpreted and justified by the community of perpetrators. It is via these surrogate contests that populations affected by genocide begin to re-imagine life anew, and engage in re-constitutive processes of their identity and political community.[58] The experience of suffering and loss in genocide provides additional meaning to the value of life and identity of the surviving groups and peoples.

Genocide is a fatal attack on the dignity and security of groups and their individual members subjected to such attack. The harms of genocide are directly a function of security infringements at all analytical levels: the individual, group, national, regional, and international. But, the harms of genocide are not contained only to groups and individuals subjected to this heinous crime within borders of a given country. Indeed, harms of genocide rapidly spread across state boundaries to destabilize entire regions and, in many ways, affect the entire world. Refugee exoduses across adjacent states' boundaries are amongst the most visible effects, but refugee movements can spread across, and amongst, continents too. Heightened genocide effects—including refugee movements—capture public discourse,

[57] ibid 75.

[58] Klejda Mulaj, 'Violence of War, Ontopology, and the Instrumental and Performative Constitution of the Political Community' (2018) 44(1) Review of International Studies 70–71, 77.

inducing policy makers to consider their responses. The diplomacy at the United Nations (UN) and the North Atlantic Treaty Organization (NATO) in relation to suffering incurred in the genocide in Bosnia and the accompanying War (1992–1995) and crimes against humanity in Kosovo in the second half of the 1990s produced unique interventions to—belatedly—stop further human suffering there, which have not been replicated in humanitarian crises that followed in the Middle East, Africa, and Asia. Hopes raised by the adoption of the Responsibility to Protect (R2P) principle by the UN members at the 2005 World Summit have been dashed in the face of the ongoing wars in Syria, Libya, as well as the exodus of the Rohingya from Myanmar.[59] Lessons of Bosnia and Kosovo have not been learned outside the European continent. The failure of the international community to intervene means that large scale death and anguish of innocent people continue and that entire regions are destabilized. Moreover, the ongoing maltreatment of Syrian, Libyan, and Rohingya civilians show that warfare has not been tamed. Violence of war remains central to genocide and human suffering.

A common trait of genocide is that it usually takes place during war. Moreover, the state is frequently involved in the commission of this heinous crime. A review of the genocides perpetrated during the modern era indicates that genocide has been aimed at defenceless civilians during an intra- or inter-state war with the genocidal acts organized, encouraged and officially sanctioned by the highest echelons of the state.[60] Indeed, more often than not, states have been the main perpetrators of genocidal violence, genocide being a display of state monopoly of power, and a negative expression of state power.[61] Moreover, the clout of war has been conducive to state's genocide denial even as genocide has been planned, before it [ie, war] began, and in the course of its execution.[62] In point of fact, genocidal governments have systematically utilized military force for the purposes of genocide. It is curious that despite active state involvement, no state has been ever held criminally accountable for committing genocide.[63]

Harms of genocide on societies do not cease when a peace deal is reached to terminate fighting. Clearly, the consequences of genocidal violence extend beyond the genocide itself. There are long-term physical, psychological, and social effects with which survivors have to grapple on a daily basis for the rest of their lives. Particularly harsh is the suffering of victims of gender-based violence and

[59] For an analysis of R2P in the context of the Rohingya crisis see Jobair Alam's Chapter 5 in this volume. For deficiencies of R2P as a response to genocide refer to Roland Paris, 'The "Responsibility to Protect" and the Structural Problems of Preventive Humanitarian Intervention' (2014) 21(5) International Peacekeeping 569–603.

[60] Refer for instance to L Edward Day and Margaret Vandiver, 'Criminology and Genocide Studies: Notes on what might have been and what could be' (2000) 34(1) Crime, Law and Social Change 44.

[61] Paul Bartrop, 'The Relationship between War and Genocide in the Twentieth Century: A Consideration' (2002) 4(4) Journal of Genocide Research 519–32.

[62] Refer to Part II of this volume.

[63] Refer to Kevin Aquilina's Chapter 2 in this volume.

children born of rape who live with traumas in destitution and face long-term stigmatization.[64] Moreover, there are purposeful uses of genocide in the postgenocide era, sometimes coupled with new forms of identity politics, and at other times—as in the case of genocides against aboriginal peoples—coupled with seemingly 'neutral' politics detached from genocide which inadvertently overlooks the genocidal past.[65] More often than not, denial of genocide enables the perpetrators' community and their leaders to eschew responsibility and sometimes to challenge the legitimacy of the postgenocide political order.[66] Contrasting opinions of victims and offenders about genocide underpin contested claims for identity, legitimacy, and political authority and hinder the development of a harmonious society and the achievement of durable peace. Noticeable venues where these competing views are channelled pertain to efforts to pursue accountability for the perpetrators and recognition of suffering and justice for genocide survivors and their communities. These constitute distinct spaces where effects of genocide continue to be felt in times of peace ensuing the bloodshed.

Inadequate Responses, Ir/Reconciliation

Amongst the various responses to genocide none fares worse than prevention, as the massive loss and suffering incurred in so many genocides attest. There are many complex reasons for failure to prevent genocide ranging from disagreement on whether a given situation qualifies as genocide (and the broader the definition used, the wider such disagreement); to the (unrealistic) expectation that the forces (intent to) perpetrating the crimes—frequently belonging to, or aided by states—cease their atrocities and protect the victims (as currently in Myanmar); to the (proverbial) lack of political will of the international community to intervene; to open disagreements at the highest international body tasked with the maintenance of global peace and security, the UN Security Council (UNSC). In a recent contribution on the duty to prevent genocide, John Heieck has argued that the permanent members of the UNSC have a special duty to prevent genocide, which may include use of force as last resort.[67] Moreover, adhering to the intent requirement of the Convention's genocide definition sufficiently narrows the cases where the execution of such duty is required.[68] Heieck offers a noble suggestion that

[64] See, for instance, Amy E Randall (ed), *Genocide and Gender in the Twentieth Century: A Comparative Survey* (Bloomsbury 2015); Charli Carpenter (ed), *Born of War: Protecting Children of Sexual Violence Survivors in Conflict Zones* (Kumarian Press 2007); Siobhan K Fischer, 'Occupation of the Womb: Forced Impregnation as Genocide' (1996) 46(1) Duke Law Review 91–133.

[65] Refer to Chapter 11 by Maureen Hiebert and Chapter 9 by Martine Louise Hawkes in this volume.

[66] For elaborations on this point refer to Chapter 6 by Tatevik Mnatsakanyan, Chapter 7 by Klejda Mulaj, and Chapter 8 by Andrew Wallis in this volume.

[67] John Heieck, *A Duty to Prevent Genocide* (Edward Elgar Publishing 2018) Chapters 1 and 2.

[68] ibid Conclusion.

permanent members of UNSC refrain from exercising the veto when the Council considers genocide prevention.[69] This is a laudable recommendation. It is questionable, nonetheless, whether the permanent five are willing to give up such an exclusive right central to their exercise of power and protection of their manifold vested interests. It is because of the erratic record of the UNSC, that it can be said that the duty to prevent genocide and save strangers facing annihilation in faraway places is an imperfect duty. This is so due to the agency condition, because there is no universal agreement on the agent which is capable and willing to perform that duty each time the threat of genocide raises its head.[70] Even when use of force to stop genocide has led to some qualified positive outcomes—as in Bosnia and Kosovo—state practice of use of force for humanitarian purposes remains ridden with controversies.[71]

The evil in genocide is so stark that it has been said that it resonates with 'the darkest of humanity's inhumanity'.[72] But that some good has come out of efforts to end, prevent, and understand this evil should not be overlooked. For instance, Berel Lang has opined that a concurrent event with conceptualization of genocide and its expression in legal and moral discourse has been the emergence of 'group-rights', the notion that groups have the right to exist, to be groups. The recognition of genocide as a group crime, and of group-rights as a condition of morality and (aspiration of) justice following the Second World War have been closely related occurrences. Group-rights are a consequence of group-wrongs. 'And at the beginning of that beginning, genocide'.[73] The emergence of minority rights after the First World War and its related jurisprudence in the interwar period and then the Holocaust in the Second World War converged in the adoption of the UN Genocide Convention. Efforts to grant the concept of genocide a prominent place in legal, political, and public discourse subsequently culminated in the operations

[69] ibid 214.

[70] Refer to Kok-chor Tan, 'The Duty to Protect' in Terry Nardin and Melissa S Williams (eds), *Humanitarian Intervention* (New York University Press 2005) especially 86, 96.

[71] Of the genocide responses considered in this volume, international military intervention has been omitted. In addition to space restrictions, this is done for the following reasons: (1) foreign military interventions to end genocide—referred to also as humanitarian intervention—are very rare operations as mass deaths of Rwandans, Darfuris, Syrians, and the Rohingya, amongst others, attest. (2) Even when they take place in response to mass atrocities—including genocide—international military interventions are intertwined with the (non-humanitarian) interests of intervenors. Moreover, such operations do not 'end' mass atrocities in a processual sense. (3) Despite being a rare occurrence, international armed intervention to end mass killing is covered comprehensively in the existing literature. (4) As a means of response to mass violence—including genocide—foreign military interventions tend to overlook 'the embeddedness of mass killing in their local contexts and exaggerate the impact and influence of external actors'. Alex J Bellamy, 'When States Go Bad: The Termination of State Perpetrated Mass Killing' (2015) 52(5) Journal of Peace Research 565. See also Alex J Bellamy, 'Military Intervention' in Bloxham and Moses (eds), *The Oxford Handbook of Genocide Studies* (n 1); Taylor Seybolt, *Humanitarian Military Intervention* (OUP 2007); Klejda Mulaj, 'Dilemmas of Reacting to Mass Atrocities: Humanitarian Intervention to End Violent Conflict in Western Balkans' (2001) 7(2) Democracy and Security.

[72] Irvin-Erickson, *Raphael Lemkin* (n 1) 237.

[73] Lang, *Genocide* (n 1) 28–29. Citation in page 29.

of the ICTY and ICTR, and the Rome Statute and the formation of the ICC.[74] Although the Genocide Convention does not mention rights—either individual or collective—its text is underpinned by a commitment to rights doctrine which can be inferred also by Lemkin's writings.[75]

Legal responses to genocide represent a positive—though incomplete—aspect of efforts to counter this crime. Such responses have broken new grounds in terms of both policy and scholarship, and also arguments justifying them. These responses serve as useful lenses for examining postgenocide as the first part of this book demonstrates. Retrospective legal interventions in response to genocide and/or mass atrocity are commonly justified on deterrent and retributive grounds. A third rationale that has emerged of late comes under the banner of expressivism—the idea of performativity of re/action to this crime—although the later attracts less attention than deterrence and retribution, and consequently has not made much inroads in social sciences despite being of direct relevance to them.

Deterrence is frequently invoked as a rationale for the work of international courts and tribunals. The United Nations Security Council implicitly upheld a deterrence rationale when establishing ICTY and ICTR under Chapter VII of the UN Charter.[76] As a justification for the sentencing of extraordinary international crimes (also referred to as core crimes), deterrence rests on the assumption that the punishment of a perpetrator will reduce the probability that another person in the same circumstances will offend in the future—not least because of the fear of getting punished.[77] Deterrence may take two forms, namely specific and general. The former impairs the freedom of a perpetrator (by means of a sentence) whereas the latter presumes that the punishment of a perpetrator will inhibit likely wrongdoers.[78] Although conceived to be central to international criminal law, the empirical and theoretical purchase of deterrence is viewed with scepticism. Despite some scattered reference to the merits of specific deterrence, no discernable general deterrent effect has been proffered yet.[79] Atrocity has continued to occur following the creation of inter/national criminal tribunals and recently the establishment of the International Criminal Court.

Unlike deterrence whose focus is on society, the primary focus in retribution lies with the individual offender, albeit a focus on the victims is noticeable, too. The idea of retribution is rooted in philosophical thought. Immanuel Kant suggested that retribution implies that the criminal perpetrators ought to be punished

[74] ibid 37.

[75] ibid 53. Irvin-Erickson, *Raphael Lemkin* (n 1) 20–24.

[76] Margaret M deGuzman, 'Choosing to Prosecute: Expressive Selection at the International Criminal Court' (2012) 33(2) Michigan Journal of International Law 265–320, at 307.

[77] Mark A Drumbl, *Atrocity, Punishment, and International Law* (CUP 2007) 16, 169 (hereafter Drumbl, *Atrocity*).

[78] Diane Marie Amann, *Group Mentality* (n 41) 115.

[79] Drumbl, *Atrocity* (n 77) 16–17; Akhavan, *Reducing Genocide to Law* (n 28) 63.

because they deserve it.[80] Retribution as the dominant rationale for the punishment of extraordinary crimes, does not view the criminal as simply a small cog in a social engineering process but rather as an end in itself, as an actor deserving of condemnation.[81] Nonetheless, there is disconnect between the desired effects of criminal sentencing, on the one hand, and the retributive (and deterrent) aspirations, on the other.[82] This disconnect is a function of various factors from political interference in the judicial process, to limited resources assigned to judicial institutions which pursue criminal accountability, to procedural flaws emanating from inadequate legal provisions, to ambiguous judicial interpretations. Together they undermine the capacity of retribution—in particular ensuring lack of proportionality for very serious international crimes, including genocide.[83]

Justifications for international criminal prosecutions transcend the determination of guilt or innocence of the accused. This belief pertains to the symbolic function of criminal trials—that is to the messages that trials, verdicts, and punishments send to the present defendants and to potential criminals. Such a belief is central to expressivism as a rationale for justification of punishment of extraordinary crimes.[84] Expressivism is grounded on the view that actions carry meanings, hence they are expressive. Mark Drumbl has opined that unlike retribution and deterrence, which respectively punish because the perpetrator deserves punishment or because potential perpetrators are likely to be deterred, the expressivist punishes to strengthen public's faith in rule of law.[85] The performance aspect of storytelling in the form of authoritative judicial pronouncements has high expressive value—both when narration pertains to the big fish, leaders and propagandists of atrocity, and to the small fry, the foot soldier, and facilitator. For expressivists, punishment promises to educate future generations about the effects of genocide and other serious crimes, and generates moral consensus on the repudiation of these crimes.[86] Although expressivism as justification for criminal prosecution is emphasized less than deterrence and retribution, there is no incompatibility between the three. Implicit in these three rationales is a close relationship between,

[80] Immanuel Kant, *The Philosophy of Law: An Exposition of the Fundamental Principles of Jurisprudence as a Science of Right*, translated from the German by W Hastie (Clark 1887).

[81] Drumbl, *Atrocity* (n 77) 150.

[82] ibid; Aquilina and Mulaj, 'State Responsibility' (n 50); Maria Elander, 'The Victim's Address: Expressivism and the Victim at the Extraordinary Chambers in the Courts of Cambodia' (2013) 7(1) The International Journal of Transitional Justice, 95–115, (hereafter Elander, 'The Victim's Address').

[83] As Hannah Arendt aptly noted, the harm of genocide is so great that terms of imprisonment can never be retributively proportionate. 'The Nazi crimes ... explode the limits of the law; and that is precisely what constitutes their monstrousness. For these crimes, no punishment is severe enough'. Hannah Arendt's Letter to Karl Jaspers (17 August 1946) in Lotte Kohler and Hans Saner (eds), *Hannah Arendt and Karl Jaspers, Correspondence 1926-1969*, translated from the German by Robert Kimber and Rita Kimberm (Harcourt Brace Jovanovich Publishers 1992) 54.

[84] Drumbl, *Atrocity* (n 77) 17–18; Elander, 'The Victim's Address' (n 82) 100.

[85] Drumbl, *Atrocity* (n 77) 173.

[86] ibid 17.

or transferability of, what goes on within the courtroom and beyond it.[87] In addition, the rationales of retribution, deterrence and symbolism—in the operations of inter/national criminal tribunals' response to mass atrocity—convey the important message that law is a facilitator of justice, even if the later cannot be (fully) achieved.

Fulfilment of objectives of international criminal tribunals depend on enforcement, the record of which is not inspiring. For many decades after the Nuremberg trials, international criminal law was not enforced by the international community.[88] The absence of international enforcement has sapped legal expressions embodied in the Genocide Convention and other human rights treaties. The primacy of sovereignty and strategic and political considerations of resourceful states have led to a very erratic record of indictments proffered.[89] In turn, the problem of enforcement coupled with international criminal tribunals' resource constraints have ensured selectivity of prosecutions and consequently selective sentencing of wrongdoers.[90] In the two most recent cases of genocide—Rwanda (1994) and Srebrenica, Bosnia (1995)—the ICTR found that fifty-two cases and the ICTY found six cases of accused persons, respectively, acted with the intent to commit genocide. These deliberations were made in response to the Rwandan genocide that brought about the death of over 800,000 Tutsi in just over three months and the Srebrenica genocide which claimed some 8,000 lives of Bosnian Muslim men and boys in just a week.[91] Therefore, the amount of retribution exacted has been restricted and hence the notion of proportionality has incurred a serious stretch. Lastly, although criminal trials have put the emphasis not only on the accused but also on victims' witnesses, the courts' shaping of victims' messages—its expression—has been limited. As Maria Elander points out 'the court cannot hold the complexity of victimization'. The court '[c]annot listen (to all)'. It 'can only accommodate *some* victims, recognize *certain* vulnerabilities. While some victims become the objects of devotion, others must remain unnoted, repressed, ungrieved and confined to the unconscious'.[92] Due to these operational and structural challenges the inter/national criminal courts and tribunals suffer performative shortfalls.

Perhaps the complexity of victimization is more tightly held by truth and reconciliation commissions (TRCs) wherein victims may recount their victimization

[87] Mark Osiel, *Mass Atrocity, Collective Memory, and the Law* (Transaction Publishers 2000) 293.
[88] Amann, 'Group Mentality' (n 41) 116.
[89] Refer to Chapter 2 by Kevin Aquilina and Chapter 4 by Christopher Soler in this volume.
[90] Indeed, the reach of international criminal law has attached to only a small number of perpetrators, whereas many perpetrators as well as organizations and even states are dispensed of responsibility.
[91] The Tutsi figures from <https://unictr.irmct.org/en/genocide> accessed 1 July 2020. For the events at Srebrenica in July 1995 see United Nations, 'Report of the Secretary-General Pursuant to General Assembly Resolution 53/35: The Fall of Srebrenica' (United Nations, 15 November 1999) <https://www.refworld.org/docid/3ae6afb34.html> accessed 1 July 2020. National courts in both Bosnia and Rwanda continue to try criminal suspects.
[92] Elander, 'The Victim's Address' (n 82) 114.

without being impeded by procedures of criminal trials.[93] It should be noted nonetheless that use of TRCs as a response to genocide remains limited, unlike the case of crimes against humanity. Truth commissions have been established by various governments since 1970s to investigate serious breaches of human rights by their predecessors such as in Argentina, Canada, Chile, Côte d'Ivoire, El Salvador, Guatemala, Liberia, South Africa, Sri Lanka, etc.—not all of which have ended in success. TRCs are 'political sites of contestation over material and symbolic resources'.[94] Their capacity to deliver justice and restitution is disputed. Indeed, it is debatable whether TRCs—and other victim-centred approaches such as official apologies, reparations, and memorials—can bring 'much desired voice, empowerment, and healing to those who endured physical and structural violence'.[95] Even in the context of South African Truth and Reconciliation Commission—held by some as an original response to mass atrocity—many survivors and families of the deceased tortured victims have protested against amnesties offered by this commission to perpetrators of past atrocities.[96] Leila Nadya Sadat has opined that amnesties undermine both justice and truth and therefore are unsatisfactory responses to genocide/mass atrocities. Moreover, truth commissions may undermine accountability when they are set up by unrepentant governments in order to manipulate public opinion abroad or at home.[97] This is the case of the Commission of Truth and Reconciliation in Yugoslavia established in 2001 by President Vojislav Koštunica—a long-term critic of the ICTY who has 'consistently treated indicted Serb war criminals as patriots'.[98] In setting up this—nominal—truth commission in the aftermath of genocide at Srebrenica, Bosnia, a genocide which Mr Koštunica denies, he was not interested in giving voice to victims. Indeed, the commission was staffed by Serbs only, most of whom held strong nationalist views. In fact the commission had no intention to pursue real investigation as it never conducted interviews or held any hearings.[99] The primary aim of this TRC was to influence public opinion in Western countries, receive foreign aid in times of economic

[93] Elizabeth Kiss, 'Reflections on Restorative Justice' in Robert I Rotberg and Dennis Thompson (eds), *Truth v. Justice: The Morality of Truth Commissions* (Princeton University Press 2000) 70–74.

[94] Onur Bakiner, *Truth Commissions: Memory, Power, and Legitimacy* (University of Pennsylvania Press 2010) 3.

[95] ibid 10 and 223. See also Rajika Shah's Chapter 3 in this volume.

[96] Refer, for instance, to John Dugard, 'Reconciliation and Justice: The South African Experience' (1998) 8 Transnational Law and Contemporary Problems 286–87.

[97] Leila Nadya Sadat, 'Universal Jurisdiction, National Amnesties, and Truth Commissions: Reconciling the Irreconcilable' in Stephen Macedo (ed), *Universal Jurisdiction: National Courts and the Prosecution of Serious Crimes under International Law* (University of Pennsylvania Press 2004) 193–213 at 198 (hereafter Sadat, 'Universal Jurisdiction').

[98] Diane Orentlicher, *Some Kind of Justice: The ICTY's Impact in Bosnia and Serbia* (OUP 2018) 234. An opponent of Slobodan Milošević's transfer to The Hague, Mr Koštunica has openly declared that '[t]here is no solid evidence suggesting that Serbs committed any war crimes'. Petar Luković, *Serbia's New Capital* (*Institute for War and Peace Reporting Tribunal Update* No. 219, 5 May 2001).

[99] Priscilla Hayner, *Unspeakable Truths: Transitional Justice and the Challenge of Truth Commissions* (Routledge 2011) 252–53.

hardship, and diminish pressure for cooperation with the ICTY.[100] Therefore, the utilitarian rationale of this so-called truth commission nullified from its inception truth-seeking aspirations implied in its title. Although, in principle, truth commissions can provide a public platform for victims or their families to narrate their stories and have their suffering acknowledged, they cannot be an alternative to punishment.[101] In responding to serious violations of human rights truth commissions, like reparations, can complement—but not replace—legal accountability, which remains a high aspiration of international justice.[102]

Reconstruction of the relationship between communities of perpetrators of past atrocities and those of victims/survivors is a very challenging and long-term undertaking.[103] Efforts to deal with past atrocities are a noticeable feature of many postgenocide societies. Yet these efforts are simultaneously laudable, inadequate, and incomplete. They suggest that justice remains an impenetrable (hence aporetic) 'experience of impossible'.[104] Moreover, the postgenocide aspiration of reconciliation—as a complete healing of traumas of victims and perpetrators grounded on a universal understanding of past atrocities—may be unachievable. As it can be observed from any case of post/genocide, a theological reconciliation conceived as a process of deep ontological transformation of both the perpetrators and victims is unrealistic.[105] Perhaps a more realistic goal might be the coexistence of victims' communities and those of perpetrators in an irreconcilable mode grounded on commitment for mutual respect and denunciation of resort to violence as a means to resolving disputes. Rather than demanding the theological fraternity and deep ontological transformation of victims and perpetrators, respect requires that the experience of victims and survivors be recognized, and that the political, social, and economic marginalization be minimized in order for social and economic standing to become roughly equal across society. Moreover, respect reflects the ability to see the Other as a dignified human being with moral worth. Furthermore, respect promotes social interactions that induce tolerance and trust in democracy.[106]

[100] This commission was intended to operate on a three years' mandate (2001–2004). The dissolution of the former Yugoslavia in 2003, marked the end of this commission as it could not rely on an office that no longer existed, namely the President of Yugoslavia. In the two years of its existence this TRC neither held hearings nor conducted interviews.

[101] Sadat, 'Universal Jurisdiction' (n 97) 198.

[102] On reparations see Rajika Shah's Chapter 3 in this volume.

[103] Refer, for instance, to Chapter 9 by Martine Louise Hawkes, Chapter 10 by Marci Esparza, and Chapter 11 by Maureen Hiebert in this volume.

[104] Jacques Derrida, 'Force of Law: The "Mystical Foundation of Authority"' in Drucilla Cornell, Michel Resenfeld, and David Gray Carlson, *Deconstruction and the Possibility of Justice* (Routledge 1992) 3–67 at 16.

[105] For theological views on reconciliation refer to Desmond Tutu, *No Future Without Forgiveness: A Personal Overview of South Africa's Truth and Reconciliation Commission* (Doubleday 2000); and Miroslav Volf, *Exclusion & Embrace: A Theological Exploration of Identity, Otherness, and Reconciliation*, Revised and Updated (Abingdon Press 2019).

[106] Refer to Ernesto Verdeja, 'A Normative Theory of Reparations in Transitional Democracies' in Card and Marsoobian, *Genocide's Aftermath* (n 1) especially 179.

The Chapters

The ensuing chapters are exercises on how to think about postgenocide. Their analyses manifest the author's experience of reflecting on the effects of genocide from viewpoints of various disciplines—mainly law, politics, sociology, history, and ethnography. Like any collection of papers, this book could have contained more or fewer contributions without necessarily altering its character. All chapters like in 'a musical suite, are written in the same or related keys'.[107] It is the chapters' topic that determines their sequence. The first part of the book unpacks how the law and legal responses to genocide serve as useful lenses for examining the aftermaths of this crime. The second part of the book reflects on issues of genocide denial and remembrance with particular reference to Turkey and Armenia, Serbia and Bosnia, and Rwanda. The third part of the book sheds light on issues of postgenocide identities, memory and irreconciliation with special focus in indigenous communities in Australia, Canada, and Guatemala. The chapters do not offer definite solutions to the problems they unpack, but seek to clarify issues and present reasoned pathways for confronting specific questions.

One key pillar of the postgenocide space consists of legal responses to genocide and laws that ground such responses. Kevin Aquilina's Chapter 2 shows that although more often than not, states are parties in a genocide enterprise, the centrality—and responsibility—of states for genocide does not receive attention commensurate with the severity of the problem. His chapter highlights the failure of the international community to hold states criminally responsibility for genocide. Underscoring difficulties at proving state criminal responsibility for genocide, this contribution compares and contrasts individual criminal responsibility and state criminal responsible for genocide. Whereas in the former case the matter has been dealt with by domestic and international criminal courts and tribunals, in the latter sense there is no international judicial authority which can try states for criminal responsibility. Aquilina observes that the state enjoys far more privileges than the individual and from an examination of international criminal law of genocide and practice, concludes that states are virtually untouchable. His analysis suggests, however, that non-state corporate criminal liability, and how this institute has evolved in international law, may provide some transferable lessons for state responsibility for genocide. With this view it considers the forms of criminal punishment inflicted upon a legal person and identifies in addition thereto other penalties which can be inflicted upon states for criminal responsibility. Considering stumbling blocks at finding states criminally responsible and liable, Aquilina highlights the nexus between individual responsibility and state responsibility, and the failures of international genocide law in establishing state responsibility for genocide.

[107] Arendt, *Between Past and Future* (n 17) 15.

Whilst state primacy is frequently challenged in the discipline of International Relations (IR), this is rarely the case in the law of genocide and its praxis. Yet, as this chapter suggests, there are actions that the international community can take to punish those states criminally responsible for genocide. This is imperative for the promise of 'never again' to be given a chance to materialize.

Assessing the role of law in enabling postgenocide healing with particular reference to restitution, Chapter 3 by Rajika L Shah considers how effective law is as an instrument in the toolkit of postgenocide responses. Her analysis pays close attention to restitution and compensation in the postHolocaust setting. She shows that while Holocaust survivors and their heirs have worked towards achieving some degree of restitution from Germany and other actors complicit in the crimes, obtaining restitution for other genocide victim groups has been a challenge. Indeed, none have been able to replicate the success of the Holocaust restitution movement. Yet, since the Holocaust, international and domestic law have increasingly required compensation for the victims of mass atrocities. In exploring the factors which condition whether any restitution is achieved, Shah finds that there is no uniform application of law. As a result, the ability of law to adequately address the need for restitution to genocide survivors is an open, and disturbing, question. She argues nonetheless that restitution and compensation measures are necessary, though not sufficient, in order for any transitional justice process to be both meaningful and as complete as possible. Without recognition and redress for the staggering amounts of property typically lost or stolen in a genocide, the (aspired) reconciliation that allows survivor groups to not only acknowledge the past but transcend it will remain frustratingly elusive.

Christopher Soler's contribution of Chapter 4 evaluates the record of the prosecution and punishment of the crime of genocide by internationalized courts and tribunals. It unpacks the effects of the criminal sanction, generally the incarceration of perpetrators, against the fulfilment of the responsibility to protect. His chapter commences by unmasking the challenges in the prosecution of genocide which are intrinsic in the very nature, features, and characteristics of the crime itself. His analysis explores the extent to which genocide has been prosecuted and punished by various internationalized courts and tribunals. These include the *ad hoc* international criminal tribunals—primarily the ICTY and the ICTR—the International Criminal Court (ICC), and the hybrid criminal tribunals. He shows how the nascent quasi-prosecutorial model can sow the seeds for the delivery of criminal justice before the right place (the *forum conveniens*) and at the right time, notwithstanding the prospect of a delayed execution thereof. Soler argues that the international community should strive to prosecute and punish genocide as a matter of principle irrespective of side effects the prosecution itself may trigger at national, regional, or international levels. He advocates 'justice for its own sake', an expression that distinguishes the inherent value of prosecutions from their presumed social effects.

In Chapter 5, Jobair Alam reflects on the worst state-led prosecution of a minority group in our times, which amounts to genocide, namely the Rohingya. Based on relevant conventions related to atrocity crimes and decisions of international criminal tribunals and courts, including the ICC, as well as other scholarship on the Responsibility to Protect (R2P), his chapter examines the atrocity crimes committed against the Rohingya under international criminal law (ICL) and the application of R2P thereupon. Alam suggests that such atrocities are constitutive of violations of *jus cogens* which warrants *obligatio erga omnes*. Accordingly, the perpetrators can be brought to justice under national, international and universal jurisdictions, which, nonetheless, has not yet been undertaken. Given the failure of ICL mechanisms, Alam then argues that the normative foundations of the R2P and its preventive aspects provide valuable tools for intercepting mass atrocity crimes. The Rohingya—who face direct and structural violence at the hands of the Myanmar State—need protection from these crimes by the action of the international community. The distinctiveness of his chapter lies in that it explains how insular national politics can undo the gains made by the international community in upholding the distinctiveness of humanitarian claims through the application of the R2P. Despite three major challenges associated with the application of the R2P—namely, the flawed idea of sovereignty as responsibility in Myanmar, the statelessness of the Rohingya, and the Association of Southeast Asian Nations' (ASEAN's) contextual application of the R2P—Alam concludes that the international community must fight impunity for *erga* crimes otherwise it may further undermine the dignity of the victims (the Rohingya) and risk an unsafe global society where moral claims are subordinated to legalisms.

Opening the second part of the book, Tatevik Mnatsakanyan (Chapter 6) begins by observing that, although critical International Relations scholarship offers rich explorations on 'sovereignty', 'subjectivity', and 'violence', such scholarship has not yet been brought to bear on the study of genocide and its effects. Her chapter aims to fill this gap by bringing critical IR to bear on sociological/historiographical literature on genocide denial. The Armenian genocide serves a *via media* for exploring a wider theoretical and political concern, namely: what can genocide and genocide denial reveal about 'sovereignty', 'subjectivity', and 'violence', and thereby, about postgenocide and possibilities for resistance? Mnatsakanyan argues that denials should be examined in close relationship with the unfolding of the genocide itself. She pursues this claim via a two-pronged framework, *conjunctural* and *relational*, inviting attention to heterogeneous and contradictory forces in a historical conjuncture, and to the relational production of political processes. She argues that denials were not only integral to, but *generative* of, the Armenian genocide. Reflecting on the implications of her analysis for postgenocide—the state of the political in Turkey today—Mnatsakanyan contends that without treating denials as generative, as the conditions of possibility for the genocide, it is futile to attempt to understand postgenocide denials, and begin to imagine alternatives to current politics.

In her reflections on genocide denial and identity politics in postgenocide Bosnia, in Chapter 7 Klejda Mulaj demonstrates how the genocide discourse remains active in the efforts to construct, or contest, the Bosnian polity and its political community. Her chapter contributes to a deeper understanding of the relationship between genocide and the fragile peace in genocide's aftermath. It shows how representations of genocide affect, and sometimes undermine, the constitution of peace and the cohesion of the political community. Her chapter can be read also as an interpretation of how violence of war permutates in times of peace. Mulaj observes that in Bosnia, recognition of genocide and its denial are part of a broader struggle over pertinent issues of identity, authority, legitimacy, and security, mediated by competing frameworks on the use of force in the course of war. This broader struggle—expressed by diverse viewpoints of the Bosnian Muslims and Serbs on the above mentioned issues—constitute an intense contest over the re-imagination of the Bosnian political community that have produced serious fractures in national unity. At present, Bosnia's political community is fractured both from without due to the denial of genocide by the Serbs and the latter's contestation of war narratives that underpin dominant interpretations of genocide, and from within, amongst other factors, due to failures to fully recognize and address the needs of victims—women and men violated in the course of genocide and war, and children borne of rape. Misrecognizing victims, failing to recognize their suffering and provide redress, produces for them a form of social subordination which is directly responsible for their disconnect with the community of the nation which ought to embrace them. For so long as the suffering of genocide victims is not fully recognized and meaningfully redressed, their recovery and integration in the postgenocide political community will remain incomplete, with detrimental repercussions for Bosnia's national unity.

Considering several mediums of denial of the genocide against the Tutsi in Rwanda, Andrew Wallis in Chapter 8 argues that if unchallenged, such denial has the potential to threaten future positive judicial, political, and economic outcomes for the country and its people. His chapter charts the proponents of denial, which began contemporaneously with the crimes themselves. In exile from August 1994, the genocidal interim regime 'rebranded' itself to the international community to downplay guilt, avoid prosecution and obtain support for its ultimate aim—a return to power in Kigali. This grouping, heavily based within former francophone and Flemish supporters (legal, political, Church, diplomatic, media, non-governmental organizations ('NGOs')), has since used a campaign of disinformation, disassociation and false narratives to confuse and threaten truth. Wallis assesses how the failure of international criminal justice—at the ICTR and in states such as France, UK, Belgium, and the Vatican—have wittingly and unwittingly assisted denial. He contends that the denial campaign has become more strident during recent years; it has widened to deflect not just blame and guilt from the perpetrators onto Rwanda's President Kagame, but targets undermining Rwanda's foreign aid and political/diplomatic wellbeing. Denialists, Wallis suggests, have been assisted by the international community's failure to respond to denial in a consistent manner: while Holocaust negation is widely condemned, denial of the Rwandan genocide is poorly understood, often tolerated, and in some cases actively encouraged by NGO/media/state actors for opaque political reasons.

The third part of the book contributes to discourses of postgenocide identities, memories, and ir/reconciliation. Martine Hawkes' Chapter 9 explores the role of museums, galleries, and archives in constructing a history of genocide through the personal objects they collect and display, and the ways in which these objects are mobilized to give physical shape to particular narratives. Her chapter presents these institutions as being reflexive, in the sense that they do not simply mirror the world but also produce what we know about particular histories and people. She suggests that the role museums, galleries, and archives play in producing public knowledge of genocide is particularly apparent in the power they hold over what an institution will collect or keep, what it will not collect or keep and which story it will tell through the arrangement and description of these objects. The personal objects, removed from their original setting, stand not only in the context of a collection but also in the broader political and ideological context of the construction of the narrative of the genocide. In exploring how narratives of genocide are constructed, Hawkes focuses on the objects taken through the genocide of Aboriginal people in Australia. These are objects which, stolen through genocide, are most often *not* mobilized in memory of that genocide or even with this provenance recorded. They are retained through an assumption of the right to retention that is not so different from the colonial logic of value that informed the original 'collection' of these objects, as well as of the land of Australia itself. These objects—Hawkes argues—can tell us much about the power that institutions hold over both the retention of the objects and of the narrative that they will (or will not) be used to tell. However, in the materiality of these objects, there is the potential to understand something about them that takes us beyond their institutional mobilization. In their materiality, an unbroken connection to Country is demonstrated which can emphasize how these personal objects came into collections while contributing to the work of dismantling the retention or display of personal objects that reproduces the genocide trauma.

In Chapter 10, Marcia Esparza suggests that whereas scholars and activists have examined different aspects of causes and processes of the genocide against the Indigenous Maya community in Guatemala (1981–1983), its aftermath continues to be under-represented in the literature seeking to integrate Latin America to the larger discussion of genocide. This gap obscures the lingering effects and long-term repercussions of extreme forms of state violence, as well as the reality of resistance by Maya communities. She examines the role played by local archives in decolonizing dominant narratives, which silenced Indigenous Maya resistance against state violence in the wake of genocide in Guatemala in the early 1980s. In this sense, the recovery and preservation of local archives (maintained by Indigenous communities), as opposed to national archives, can reveal alternative memories of resistance to state violence. Esparza considers what presentations of genocide in local archives suggest for the framing of current identities and understanding of indigeneity, and whether local archives might promote intra-community and national reconciliation in the context of persisting genocide legacies. Her analysis seeks to demonstrate that a postcolonial and critical memory studies approach can be helpful in understanding how local human rights archives may be seen as tools of resistance, because they challenge national narratives based on genocidal rhetoric. This 'genocidal rhetoric' refers to a narrative of hatred against Indigenous peoples, who were criminalized by the state during the Cold War years in Guatemala. Local archives reveal that far from being only passive victims, or perpetrators, these rural communities resisted in part through the archival act itself as they built up their own historical material and used it not only to legally challenge the state, but also to formulate alternative narratives of Indigenous resistance and political identities.

Contemplating prospects for reconciliation after cultural genocide in Canada, Maureen S Hiebert begins Chapter 11 by noting that the Canadian Truth and Reconciliation Commission report calls for the Canadian government and (settler) Canadians to acknowledge the painful past of the Indian Residential Schools (IRS) (1890s–1990s) and to chart a new nation-to-nation(s) relationship with Canada's indigenous peoples. She argues that, while the report has raised awareness among non-indigenous Canadians of this shameful episode in Canadian history, the discourse around reconciliation replicates unequal power dynamics between indigenous and non-indigenous people endemic in Canadian politics and society. This in turn portends a reconciliation process that will do little to foster a genuinely new, and equal, relationship between the two communities. There are certainly non-indigenous Canadians who are more than willing to take a hard look at the nation's past, but this is not a dominant orientation. Hiebert contends that the selective listening of the residential schools story is grounded in a constructed identity that paints Canada and (non-indigenous) Canadians as an inclusive, tolerant society that genuinely embraces multiculturalism and whose past is not marked by the worst aspects of other western nations: slavery, segregation, and Indian Wars at home, or overseas empires and foreign adventurism abroad. This self-conception has led various levels of government to emphasize the idea of reconciliation as a process by which settler colonialism is conceptualized as a closed historical event that is now firmly in the past. There is little acknowledgement that the logic and structures of settler colonialism, which as the TRC notes amounts to cultural genocide, are still foundational to contemporary Canadian politics, law, economy, and society. As such, reconciliation is understood to be about performing rituals of atonement and recognition, rather than a thorough-going process of power redistribution. These rituals include the increasingly common practice of acknowledging the indigenous nations and tentative moves by educational institutions to teach a more in depth and accurate version of indigenous history. Although necessary for reconciliation, Hiebert argues that these are steps without tangible costs. They do not involve the redistribution of land or the devolution of real political power, which can bring more economic, social, and political parity for Canada's indigenous nations.

In the concluding Chapter 12, Christopher P Davey explores agendas for further postgenocide research, with particular reference to the following questions: How are the intersections of the geopolitical order, warlordism, climate change, and resource exploitation changing what we think about genocide and use of this term? What is the impact of this nexus on identities in postgenocide? His chapter considers how genocide violence might be framed through the lens of postgenocide. Davey suggests that postgenocide can be expanded as an approach to studying mass violence occurring beyond the usual framing of state violence and intent. He contemplates, from a world-systems view, the relationships that violence on a very large scale has to resource exploitation, global warming, warlordism, and crises-ridden states. Actors within this paradigm of mass violence can be varied and generally labelled as militarized without necessarily a particular state-based authorization. Davey's analysis considers identities in postgenocide as fluid and layered between victim and perpetrator experiences. This conception is explored using a variety of cases where the above mentioned relationships and dynamics are present, including some of those already highlighted in the proceeding chapters of this book. Use of postgenocide is not an attempt to broadly redefine genocide. It is to emphasize an approach where legal and historical views on genocide are complemented in capturing the above intersections, and takes into account recent developments—including those in climate violence research. In doing so Davey seeks to illuminate the concept of postgenocide so that it could be applied to other conflicts involving mass violence beyond formal states and traditional conceptions.

PART I

THE LAW AND RESPONSIBILITY FOR GENOCIDE

2

Challenges to Criminalizing State Responsibility for Genocide

Kevin Aquilina

Introduction

In terms of responses to the heinous crime of genocide, humankind seems to be living in historic times. The United Nations Convention on the Prevention and Punishment of the Crime of Genocide ('the Genocide Convention' or 'the Convention')[1] has celebrated its seventy-second anniversary. The International Criminal Tribunal for Rwanda (ICTR) wound up on 31 December 2015 and the International Criminal Tribunal for Former Yugoslavia (ICTY) concluded its task on 21 December 2017[2]—their pending cases being taken over by the International Residual Mechanism for Criminal Tribunals.[3] The International Criminal Court (ICC), established in 2002, as of 2019 has 124 Member State parties thereto although it still has to hold its first genocide trial case. However, there is no doubt that the Genocide Convention, much that its drafters aspired for, has not achieved its aim of preventing and punishing the crime of genocide universally. Article 1 of the Genocide Convention states that: 'The Contracting Parties confirm that genocide, whether committed in time of peace or in time of war, is a crime under international law which they undertake to prevent and to punish'. Yet many cases of genocide unfolded during the last seven decades, notwithstanding the efforts of the international society of states to outlaw this crime such that genocide has become an enduring problem of our time.[4] Although genocide continued during

[1] United Nations Convention on the Prevention and Punishment of the Crime of Genocide (opened for signature 9 December 1948, entered into force 12 January 1951) 78 UNTS 277.

[2] For cases before the International Criminal Tribunal for Rwanda, see International Residual Mechanism for Criminal Tribunals, 'The Cases' <https://unictr.irmct.org/en/cases> accessed on 18 May 2020, and for cases before the International Criminal Tribunal for Former Yugoslavia, see International Residual Mechanism for Criminal Tribunals, 'Cases' <https://www.icty.org/en/cases> accessed on 18 May 2020.

[3] The ongoing cases of the United Nations International Residual Mechanism for Criminal Tribunals are available at <https://www.irmct.org/en/cases> accessed on 18 May 2020.

[4] Refer to Uğur Ümit Üngör, 'Genocide, an Enduring Problem of our Age' in Uğur Ümit Üngör (ed), *Genocide: New Perspectives on its Causes, Courses and Consequences* (Amsterdam University Press 2016) 11. For a list of various cases of genocide post-1948, see Antonio Cassese, *Human Rights in a Changing World* (Polity Press 1994), especially 79–80 (hereafter Cassese, *Human Rights*). On the history of genocide see, Nigel Eltringham and Pam Maclean (eds), *Remembering Genocide* (Routledge

Kevin Aquilina, *Challenges to Criminalizing State Responsibility for Genocide* In: *Postgenocide*. Edited by: Klejda Mulaj, Oxford University Press (2021). © The Several Contributors. DOI: 10.1093/oso/9780192895189.003.0002

this period, most perpetrators have not been apprehended and punished. Nor has state criminal responsibility for genocide been affirmed. Unsuccessful attempts have been made in the past to declare genocide an international crime of state.[5] Suffice it to mention here the failed British amendment[6] to the then draft Genocide Convention to include state criminal responsibility, and the International Law Commission's botched proposal[7] to add state criminal responsibility to its draft articles on state responsibility.[8] More recently, with the international crime of aggression being defined in the ICC Rome Statute, 'the definition of the crime itself requires the ICC to make a determination of state responsibility as a prerequisite for the finding of individual responsibility for the commission of the crime'.[9] Hence, 'with aggression, the focus on the state persists in that the court has *first* to pronounce on state responsibility, and only after it has done that can it proceed to determining individual guilt or innocence'.[10] Given that very few of the individual perpetrators have been called to justice, the Convention cannot be acclaimed to be

2014); and René Lemarchand (ed), *Forgotten Genocides: Oblivion, Denial, and Memory* (University of Pennsylvania 2011). For a discussion of prosecution and punishment of genocide in a postgenocide setting by international courts and tribunals, see Christopher Soler's Chapter 4 in this volume.

[5] For a discussion of such unsuccessful instances, see Nina HB Jørgensen, *The Responsibility of States for International Crimes* (OUP 2003) 28 (hereafter Jørgensen, *Responsibility of States*).

[6] Anja Seibert-Fohr, 'State Responsibility For Genocide Under The Genocide Convention' (hereafter Seibert-Fohr, *State Responsibility for Genocide)* in Paola Gaeta (ed), *The UN Genocide Convention: A Commentary* (OUP 2009) 369–70; Jørgensen, *Responsibility of States* (n 5) 35–41. See also Saira Mohamed, 'A Neglected Option: The Contributions of State Responsibility for Genocide to Transitional Justice' (2009) 80 University of Colorado Law Review 332–40 (hereafter Mohamed, 'Neglected Opinion'). Another defeated attempt, also at the United Nations, to amend Article IV of the Convention 'to provide for State responsibility and liability for damages and restitution' was made in 1985. See United Nations Economic and Social Council, Commission on Human Rights, Sub-Commission on Prevention of Discrimination and Protection of Minorities, *Review of Further Developments in Fields in which the Sub-Commission has been concerned*, Draft resolution submitted by Mr Deschênes and Mr Mubanga-Chipoya, Doc. E/CN.4/Sub.2/1985/L.15, 26 August 1985.

[7] Kevin Aquilina and Klejda Mulaj, 'Limitations in attributing state responsibility under the Genocide Convention' (2018) 17(1) Journal of Human Rights 126 (hereafter Aquilina and Mulaj, 'Limitations'); Anja Seibert-Fohr, *State Responsibility for Genocide* (n 6) 350. For the *travaux préparatoires* of draft article 19 on international crimes and international delicts, see International Law Commission, *Yearbook of the International Law Commission 1976: Report of the Commission to the General Assembly on the Work of its Twenty-eighth Session*, Vol II, Part II (United Nations 1977) 95.

[8] International Law Commission, (hereafter 'ILC') draft articles on Responsibility of States for Internationally Wrongful Acts 2001, adopted by the ILC at its 53rd session, 2001, in *Report of the International Law Commission on the Work of its Fifty-third Session*, UN GOAR, 53rd Sess., Supp. No 10, UN Dic. A/56/10, Chapter IV.E.1 (2001). For a commentary on the ILC's draft articles, see James Crawford, *The International Law Commission's Articles on State Responsibility: Introduction, Text and Commentaries* (CUP 2002) (hereafter Crawford, *International Law Commission* (n 8)); and Marco Sassòli, 'State Responsibility for Violations of International Humanitarian Law' (2002) 84 International Review of the Red Cross 401.

[9] Dapo Akande and Antonios Tzanakopulos, 'The Crime of Aggression in the ICC and State Responsibility' (2017) 58 Harvard International Law Journal 34 (hereafter Akande and Tzanakopulos, 'The Crime of Aggression'). As to individual criminal responsibility under the Rome Statute, see Gerhard Werle, 'Individual Criminal Responsibility in Article 25 ICC Statute' (2007) 5 Journal of International Criminal Justice 953.

[10] Akande and Tzanakopulos, 'The Crime of Aggression' (n 11).

a success story albeit the pious intentions of the United Nations, complying states, and human rights activists.

A key aspect of the Convention's success deficit pertains to attributing criminal responsibility for genocide to states, despite the oft-heard proclamation that genocide is 'the crime of state'.[11] Leslie Green opines 'that this offence is not one likely to be perpetrated as a matter of private enterprise. It requires the instigation, connivance, collusion or acquiescence of state authority'.[12] Without state support it is virtually impossible for *genocidaries* to conceive, plan, prepare, instigate, and fulfil conclusively their criminal act. At the same time, without state support it is impossible to make the Convention more efficient to prevent, stop, and punish genocide. This is because although in the last seven decades various inroads have been made in the criminalization of genocide perpetrated by individuals, very little progress has occurred in relation to state criminal responsibility. Indeed, contrary to the case of individual criminal responsibility, not even one state has ever been convicted by an international court or tribunal for the crime of genocide. Nor is it likely to be ever the case under obtaining international criminal law. There is thus a mismatch between state criminal responsibility and individual criminal responsibility for genocide. As Antonio Cassese aptly put it: 'states have consistently shied away from the notion that they themselves might be held criminally responsible for genocide. In their view, states as international subjects may not commit *crimes* proper: they can only incur state liability for *internationally wrongful acts*'.[13] It seems therefore inappropriate to apply criminal law categories to state conduct. As a matter of fact, Cassese criticized the International Court of Justice (hereafter 'ICJ' or 'the Court') for 'sitting, as it were, on two stools, by combining public international law and criminal law categories'.[14] Although, more often than not, genocide is a state sponsored crime, the state as the crime's principal remains unpunished whilst the state's accomplices—the individuals who are the material executors of the crime—occasionally get punished. Indeed, the Genocide Convention is mainly concerned with prosecution of individual perpetrators.[15] We are therefore faced with a puzzle: on the one hand, without the connivance of the state genocide cannot materialize, on the other hand, 'the view that States can commit genocide in the sense of "State crimes" finds little support'.[16] It offends human rights activism and

[11] One of the first authors to refer to genocide as 'the crime of state' is Pieter Drost. See Pieter N Drost, *The Crime of State: Penal Protection for Fundamental Freedoms of Persons and Peoples. Book II—Genocide: United Nations Legislation on International Criminal Law* (A.W. Sythoff 1959).

[12] Leslie C Green, *Essays on the Modern Law of Warfare* (Transnational Publishers, Inc 1985) 240. James Crawford concurs: 'In practice only State agencies are likely to have the means to commit the crime of genocide, although there is no such link as a matter of definition.' See also Crawford, *International Law Commission* (n 8) 19; and Mohamed, 'Neglected Opinion' (n 6) 331.

[13] Antonio Cassese, 'On the Use of Criminal Law Notions in Determining State Responsibility for Genocide' (2007) 5 Journal of International Criminal Justice 875.

[14] ibid 881.

[15] Refer to William A Schabas, *Genocide in International Law: The Crime of Crimes* (CUP 2009) 491.

[16] ibid 446.

the liberal tradition that *genocidaire* states manage to shun away from the responsibility they carry for the occurrence of such a grave crime.

Paola Gaeta makes the case that states are prohibited from committing genocide in terms of customary international law[17] and that this constitutes also a rule of *jus cogens*.[18] Nonetheless, the Convention strictly speaking—as opposed to customary international law and *jus cogens*—'does not impose upon contracting states themselves the obligation not to commit genocide, but rather restricts itself to laying down obligations for contracting states in criminal matters'.[19] Yet, the ICJ has to be commended for adopting, in relation to Article 1 of the Convention, a liberal construction.[20] This is so because, although the Convention's text does not expressly prohibit states from engaging in committing genocide, they are nonetheless obliged by Article 1 aforesaid 'to prevent and punish genocide'. The ICJ has therefore progressively developed the wording of the Convention when it held that:

> It would be paradoxical if States were ... under an obligation to prevent ... [the] commission of genocide by persons over whom they have a certain influence, but were not forbidden to commit such acts through their own organs, or persons over whom they have such firm control that their conduct is attributable to the State concerned under international law. In short, the obligation to prevent genocide necessarily implies the prohibition of the commission of genocide.[21]

In the ICJ's view, it is paradoxical to oblige a state to prevent genocide whilst at the same time not debarring its organs from committing genocide themselves. Although, arguably, the Court was reading into the wording of Article 1 of the Convention, it however did not develop its reasoning concomitant thereto by concluding that there is also state criminal responsibility for genocide. The criminal aspect of the Convention has been construed by the Court to apply limitedly to

[17] Paola Gaeta, 'On What Conditions Can a State Be Held Responsible for Genocide?' (2007) 18(4) The European Journal of International Law 632 (hereafter Gaeta, 'State Responsible for Genocide'). On the meaning of genocide in customary international law, see Patrick Thornberry, *International Law and the Rights of Minorities* (Clarendon Press 1991) 101 (hereafter Thornberry, *Rights of Minorities*).

[18] Antonio Cassese maintains that once 'genocide has become part of *jus cogens* or peremptory law ... two or more states cannot legitimately conclude agreements providing for acts or measures of genocide. Cassese, *Human Rights* (n 4) 79. The ICJ has also recognized the peremptory norm nature of the prohibition of genocide as being 'assuredly the case'. See *Armed Activities on the Territory of the Congo (New Application: 2002) (Democratic Republic of the Congo* v. *Rwanda), Jurisdiction and Admissibility (Judgment)* [2006] ICJ Reports 6 at 32 para 64. See also Thornberry, *Rights of Minorities* (n 17) 95; and Sam Clearwater, 'Holding States Accountable for the Crime of Crimes: An Analysis of Direct State Responsibility for Genocide in Light of the ICJ's 2007 Decision in Bosnia v Serbia' (2009) 15(1) Auckland University Law Review 1 at 4, n 16 and n 17 (hereafter Clearwater, 'Holding States Accountable').

[19] Gaeta, 'State Responsibility for Genocide' (n 17) 632.

[20] ibid.

[21] International Court of Justice, *Application of the Convention on the Prevention and Punishment of the Crime of Genocide (Bosnia and Herzegovina v. Serbia and Montenegro) (Judgment)* [2007] ICJ Reports (I) para 166 (hereafter *Bosnia v Serbia*).

individuals, not to states.[22] In sum, according to the ICJ, the Genocide Convention gives rise to dual responsibility: individual criminal responsibility for genocide and civil state responsibility for genocide.[23] However, it is the contention of this contribution that 'state responsibility' should be understood in the public international law, not in the criminal law, sense; that is, the only responsibility which a state can be held accountable for is civil responsibility, what the International Law Commission refers in Article 2 of its draft articles to as 'international wrongful acts'.[24] Not all authors share the Court's interpretation of the Convention. For Gaeta, the Genocide Convention mandates states 'to prevent the commission of genocide as an instance of individual criminality, regardless of whether these acts are committed by state officials belonging to any state'.[25] Further, the difficulties inevitably encountered to determine 'whether a state possesses the *dolus specialis* of genocide, or the debate concerning whether or not the crime of genocide can be committed only when there is a state policy or campaign of genocide' are representative and contribute to an ongoing discussion.[26] However, a critical, yet insufficiently considered, question is whether state criminal responsibility is distinguishable from individual criminal responsibility and, whether a state can be held criminally responsible for genocide?

This chapter addresses this posited question by arguing in favour of criminalizing state responsibility for genocide in a postgenocide context even though this is not the position currently at law. It does so after it briefly surveys how international criminal law has developed initially, following the International Military Tribunal's judgment finding for individual criminal responsibility for genocide.

22 ibid paras 168–169. This is in line with the statement of the International Military Tribunal (hereafter 'IMT') that 'crimes against international law are committed by men, not by abstract entities and only by punishing individuals who commit such crimes can the provisions of international law be enforced'. See *Trial of the Major War Criminals Before the International Military Tribunal, Nuremberg, 14 November 1945-1 October 1946. Official Documents*, Vol 1 (International Military Tribunal 1947) 223. Anja Seibert-Fohr observes that: 'The IMT's famous pronouncement [cited above] ... was intended to explain that individuals could be held accountable despite the fact that at that point in time international law had been primarily concerned with state obligations. It was not the intent of the IMT to negate state responsibility'—Anja Seibert-Fohr, *State Responsibility for Genocide* (n 6) 369–70.

23 For this distinction, see Clearwater, 'Holding States Accountable' (n 18) 4–22, and André Nollkaemper, 'Concurrence between Individual Responsibility and State Responsibility in International Law' (2003) 52 International and Comparative Law Quarterly 615 (hereafter Nollkaemper, 'Individual Responsibility and State Responsibility').

24 The latest 2001 set of Articles adopted by the International Law Commission considers an international wrongful act of a state to materialize when an act or omission '(a) is attributable to the State under international law; and (b) constitutes a breach of an international obligation of the state'. For a commentary on this Article, see Crawford, *International Law Commission* (n 8) 81–85.

25 Gaeta, 'State Responsibility for Genocide' (n 17) 635.

26 ibid. See also Andrew B Loewenstein and Stephen A Kostas, 'Divergent Approaches to Determining Responsibility for Genocide: The Darfur Commission of Inquiry and the ICJ's Judgment in the Genocide Case' (2007) 5 Journal of International Criminal Justice 845–50; P-M Dupuy, 'International Criminal Responsibility of the Individual and International Responsibility of the State' in A Cassese, P Gaeta, and JRWD Jones (eds), *The Rome Statute of the International Criminal Court: A Commentary*, Vol II (Oxford University Press 2002) 1096; André Nollkaemper, 'Individual Responsibility and State Responsibility' (n 23) 633.

It takes stock of the developments in this area of the law pursuant to the adoption of the Convention in 1948 which has seen progress occurring in international criminal law not only in relation to individual criminal responsibility through the creation of international courts and tribunals to adjudicate genocide such as the ICTR, ICTY, and ICC in addition to prosecution of the crime of crimes at domestic level, but also through the elaboration of new concepts such as that of the joint criminal enterprise, the widening of command responsibility in relation to military and paramilitary groups, and the extension of corporate criminal responsibility to other non-state legal persons for crimes even if, admittedly, such widening of international criminal law has so far not covered the crime of state of genocide. It then follows the unfolding events in international criminal law in relation to violent or otherwise non-state actors' corporate criminal liability, and moving in the direction—in parallel within municipal law—to penalize corporate criminal liability. It argues that the next natural step is to hold states not only civilly responsible for genocide but even criminally. The ICJ, notwithstanding the negative response it received from commentators in relation to its *Bosnia v Serbia* judgment[27] for being timid and for having shied away at establishing state criminal responsibility, must nonetheless be credited with making a very bold step for a court which tends to uphold state sovereignty beyond reasonable limits when it affirmed that the duty to prevent genocide comprises the duty not to commit genocide. Indeed, one has to bear in mind, in this context, what Cassese refers to as 'the principle propounded since the late 1890s by the positivist school whereby in the international community "all that was not prohibited was by this mere fact permitted". This is merely another way of saying that freedom of states (or sovereignty) was the fundamental feature of the international community'.[28] The chapter thus serves to identify the hurdles which the international community still has to address in order to square the circle and move on from attributing state criminal responsibility for genocide to physical persons to juridical persons in the form of states as well. This notwithstanding, the Convention does have positive attributes, deterrence apart, which cannot be brushed aside lightly.

State Criminal Responsibility *versus* Individual Criminal Responsibility for Genocide

There is an unresolved, protracted, debate as to what the state is and how best to define the state. In legal literature, it is frequently stated that the state does not exist except as a legal fiction. Further, the will of the state is nothing but a manifestation of the will of constitutionally 'responsible rulers, [and] public officials'—to use the

[27] *Bosnia v Serbia* (n 21).
[28] Antonio Cassese, *International Law in a Divided World* (Clarendon Press 1986) 169–70.

wording of Article IV of the Convention—and their agents who represent, control and direct the state at a given moment in time. In so far as responsibility is concerned, international law distinguishes between state responsibility and individual responsibility. There is therefore a dual responsibility at law. State criminal responsibility for genocide is distinct from individual criminal responsibility for genocide. Nevertheless, the two concepts are not mutually exclusive but complementary in nature. Arja Seibert-Fohr maintains that '[i]ndividual criminal responsibility and state responsibility do not replace each other. Neither do they compete. They belong to different areas of international law which complement each other in a common desire to effectuate primary norms of international law, such as the prohibition of genocide'.[29]

State responsibility leads to civil liability being the product of a wrongful act (of genocide),[30] whilst individual responsibility brings about criminal liability. Both the state and an individual have the responsibility, that is, the duty, stipulation or obligation, to prevent and desist from committing the crime of genocide. Whilst this prescription is clear for individuals from a reading of Articles IV, V, and VI of the Convention, the same cannot be said for states. Nevertheless, the ICJ has held that this stipulation applies also to states.[31] But once genocide is committed, repercussions will devolve upon the state and the individual/s for having failed to carry out their lawful duties. So whilst both a state and an individual may be responsible for genocide, they are not both liable to the same degree for the postgenocide effects or consequences of their action or inaction (for genocide can be one of commission or omission; 'omission' implying the non-taking of preventive measures which will therefore allow the crime to happen). The corollary of this argumentation is that the liability of a state and that of an individual do very well vary from each other due to the diverse juridical nature of both persons, the first legal and fictional, the second physical and real.

On the international plane, there is no judicial body which can find a state both criminally and civilly liable or an individual both criminally and civilly liable. The practice in international law is to find criminal liability for individuals and civil liability for states with different judicial bodies taking cognizance of such litigation/prosecution. In so far as individual criminal responsibility is concerned, the international courts and tribunals extant in the past and current ones have been established only to try and punish individual criminal responsibility. This is, of course,

[29] Anja Seibert-Fohr, *State Responsibility for Genocide* (n 6) 373.

[30] Amabelle C Asuncion coins the expression 'civil genocide' to cover states as distinct from individuals. See Amabelle C Asuncion, 'Pulling the Stops on Genocide: The State or the Individual?' (2010) 20(4) The European Journal of International Law 1206.

[31] Saira Mohamed comments on this point as follows: 'Conceding that Article I "does not *expressis verbis* require States to refrain from themselves committing genocide," the Court found that, "taking into account the established purpose of the convention, the effect of Article I is to prohibit States from themselves committing genocide."' Mohamed, 'Neglected Opinion' (n 6) 347. See also Clearwater, 'Holding States Accountable' (n 18) 4–22.

not the case with domestic law where an accused person may be tried for the crime of genocide before a court of criminal jurisdiction for criminal liability and before a separate court of civil jurisdiction for civil liability emanating from the wrongful act of genocide. In so far as international law is concerned, states are brought to justice only from a civil law perspective before the ICJ and there is no concomitant form of criminal liability for states before the ICC or any other competent criminal tribunal which can be attributed thereto.

An examination of the practice of diverse international courts and tribunals established to decide genocide cases—such as the ICTR, ICTY, ICC, and ICJ—indicates that at an international law level state responsibility is limited only to civil liability and that the standard of proof which has to be satisfied to find an infringement for genocide goes well beyond the high standard of proof beyond reasonable doubt allowed for individuals in criminal prosecutions.[32] This means that the standard of proof at international civil law to establish state responsibility is higher than the standard of proof at international criminal law to establish individual responsibility. This contrasts and mars with the situation at domestic law where in the case of civil liability, even if an organ of the state happens to be the defendant, a lower standard than proof beyond reasonable doubt is applied, that is, one based on a balance of probabilities. In addition, 'proof beyond a reasonable doubt does not mean proof beyond a shadow of a doubt'.[33] Yet the ICJ applies a higher standard both than a balance of probabilities and proof beyond reasonable doubt as it requires 'proof by fully conclusive evidence'. As argued elsewhere: '[i]n so far as the ICJ is concerned, it had established its standard of proof in the Corfu Channel Case ... The ICJ's standard of proof requires a threefold test to be met. It has (1) "to constitute decisive legal proof," (2) to be "conclusive evidence," and (3) once "[a] charge of such exceptional gravity against a State [is made, it] would require a degree of certainty that has not been reached here"'.[34] By slavishly applying this sky-rocketing near-to-impossible standard of proof to ground state responsibility for genocide, the Court has become hostage of its own past pronouncements: it has placed itself in a juridical impossibility to prove decisively, conclusively, and

[32] Normally proof beyond reasonable doubt is the standard adopted both by domestic and international criminal courts and tribunals. But the same cannot be said for the standard of proof of a balance of probabilities in national and universal law for the ICJ has adopted its own incongruent standard which favours state sovereignty to the detriment of state responsibility. See Dermot Groome, 'Adjudicating Genocide: Is the International Court of Justice Capable of Judging State Criminal Responsibility?' (2007) 31 *Fordham International Law Journal* 932–35 (hereafter Groome, 'Adjudicating Genocide'); and Kristen Hessler, 'State Sovereignty as an Obstacle to International Criminal Law', in Larry May and Zachary Hoskins (eds), *International Criminal Law and Philosophy* (CUP 2010) 39 (hereafter May and Hokins, *International Criminal Law*).

[33] King's Bench Division, *Miller v. Minister of Pensions* [1947] 2 All ER 372, [1948] LJR 203, 91 Sol Jo 484, 177 LT 536, 63 TLR 474.

[34] Aquilina and Mulaj, 'Limitations' (n 7) 131; Berglind Halldorsdottir Birkland, 'Reining in Non-State Actors: State Responsibility and Attribution in Cases of Genocide' (2009) 84 New York University Law Review 1641–42.

certainly that genocide can be perpetrated by a state. In other words, such an astronomical standard of proof evinces the covert application of state immunity from punishment in the case of genocide when the perpetrator is a state.

Furthermore, whilst there are several decided cases in relation to criminal liability for genocide committed by individuals, the same cannot be said for civil liability for genocide perpetrated by states even though the convicted *genocidaires* might well happen to be citizens and officials of the particular state allegedly responsible for genocide. One cannot therefore contemplate an attribution of criminal responsibility by association of a convicted *genocidaire* with the state which s/he served as a responsible ruler or public official during the period when genocide took place.

Although the Genocide Convention holds both a state and an individual liable for genocide, criminal responsibility is ascribed only to an individual. The state has more of a civil liability to answer for such as that of being condemned to pay punitive damages, or of an international responsibility such as that of taking preemptive measures to prevent genocide. What exists in domestic and international law to punish corporate criminal liability does not apply to the criminal activity of a state even though a state is a corporation in its own right: it might have more powers, responsibilities, functions, decision-makers, resources, etc, but its structure is similar to that of a body corporate. So why should corporate criminal liability not extend to a state committing the crime of genocide in the same way that a corporation can be found guilty of committing any criminal offence recognized by international law?

Artificial Non-State Legal Persons: Can they Commit Genocide? The Case of Corporate Criminal Liability

In law, there are non-physical artificial persons to which legal personality is ascribed. Such is undoubtedly the case of the state. But there are other contenders such as ships and aircrafts which, though *stricto jure* are more appropriately classified as things (*res*) rather than persons, still enjoy legal personality. These *res*—like the state—are afforded legal personality, and are considered objects of the law and nationals of a state. They enjoy rights and duties as individuals do. Under international law, these *res* are subject to civil and criminal law liability. Sanctions can be imposed upon them for their criminal wrongdoing and civil wrongful acts. Like the state they are inanimate objects but their will is manifested through a human person in the same way that state action is determined by the human mind. Another instance of a non-physical person enjoying legal personality is the body corporate. Even such bodies corporate enjoy rights and obligations at law and have their own separate and distinct legal personality from their human agents so much so that in national law there are provisions in laws regulating corporate criminal responsibility and individual criminal responsibility. In the opinion of this writer, there should be no reason why what applies to these *res* should by analogy not apply to the state in so far as criminal responsibility is concerned.

Legal persons come in different forms and guises. Both national criminal law and international criminal law allow for corporate criminal responsibility. At the moment of writing, national criminal law regulating corporate criminal liability is on the increase. Yet it cannot be said to be universal though with the internationalization of corporate criminal responsibility, domestic criminal law is being updated accordingly. Guy Stessens clarifies that 'it was only after the Second World War that the criminal law came to recognise the concept of corporate criminal liability'.[35] Yet not all states regulate corporate criminal responsibility. Joanna Kyriakakis refers to a number of countries 'that do not provide for corporate criminal liability. These included Brazil, Bulgaria, Luxemburg, the Slovak Republic, Greece, Hungary, Mexico, Sweden, and the Ukraine'.[36] In common law jurisdictions, Celia Wells reports, that there 'has been a gradual expansion in the common law of corporate criminal liability, both of the range of offences a corporation is capable of committing and in the means by which an offence is imputed. There are now very few offences which a corporation cannot commit'.[37] Corporate criminal responsibility has also infiltrated within the penal laws of civil law jurisdictions as Günter Heine observes:

> A large group of countries established corporate criminal liability (amongst others the Netherlands [1976], Norway [1991], Iceland [1993], France [1994], Finland [1995], Belgium [1999], draft law of the Slovak Republic [2000], draft law of Turkey [2000], incorporated corporate sanctions *sui generis* (Spain [1995], Sweden [1986], draft law of Switzerland [1998], Korea, Japan) or enacted non-criminal corporate sanctions (Germany, Portugal, draft law of Italy 2000, draft law of Poland 2000, draft law of Bulgaria [2000].[38]

[35] Guy Stessens, 'Corporate Criminal Liability: A Comparative Perspective' (1994) 43 International and Comparative Law Quarterly 493. See also Joanna Kyriakakis, 'Corporations and the International Criminal Court: The Complementarity Objection Stripped Bare' (2008) 19 Criminal Law Forum 117–18; and Jørgensen, *Responsibility of States* (n 5) 72–79.

[36] Joanna Kyriakakis, 'Corporate Criminal Liability and the ICC Statute: The Comparative Law Challenge' (2009) LVI Netherlands International Law Review 342. For a list of arguments levelled against prosecuting corporations for genocide, see Michael J Kelly, *Prosecuting Corporations for Genocide* (OUP 2016) 179–92 (hereafter *Prosecuting Corporations*).

[37] Celia Wells, *Corporate Liability Rules in the Common Law Jurisdictions of Australia, Canada, England and Wales, New Zealand and the United States*, Organization for Economic Co-operation and Development, Directorate For Financial, Fiscal and Enterprise Affairs, Committee on International Investment and Multinational Enterprises, Working Group on Bribery in International Business Transactions (CIME) (OECD 2000) 9.

[38] Günter Heine, *Corporate Liability Rules in Civil Law Jurisdictions*, Organization for Economic Co-operation and Development, Directorate For Financial, Fiscal and Enterprise Affairs, Committee on International Investment and Multinational Enterprises, Working Group on Bribery in International Business Transactions (CIME), (OECD 2000) 2.

Thus, it is no surprise that corporate criminal liability is developing universally win international criminal law. Harmen van der Wilt distinguishes between corporate and individual criminal responsibility when he observes that 'it is more appropriate to present the corporation as an autonomous agent who can be held responsible for the consequences of its policy, irrespective of any determination of the blameworthiness of the individual employees'.[39] This deduction stems of course from the juridical personality which a body corporate enjoys that is separate and distinct from that of its directors, managers, owners, employees, contractors, or agents. But is corporate criminal responsibility an institute of domestic criminal law only, or is it recognized also by international criminal law? Mohamed Mattar replies in the affirmative listing a number of international treaties which include a provision on corporate criminal liability thereby indicating that the latter is not an unknown, even though still in evolution, institute of international criminal law:

- the United Nations Convention Against Transitional Organized Crime, Article 10 ('Liability of legal persons')
- the Council of Europe Convention on Action against Trafficking in Human Beings, Article 22 ('Corporate liability')
- the Organisation for Economic Co-operation and Development Convention on Combating Bribery of Foreign Public Officials in International Business Transactions, Article 2 ('Responsibility of Legal Persons')
- the Council of Europe Criminal Law Convention on Corruption, Article 18 ('Corporate liability')
- the Council of Europe Convention on the Protection of the Environment through Criminal Law, Article 9 ('Corporate liability')
- the United Nations International Convention for the Suppression of the Financing of Terrorism, Article 5 (although this Convention does not have a marginal note, or *chapeau*, for its provisions, Article 5 thereof deals with corporate criminal liability)
- the United Nations Convention on the Law of the Sea, Article 137, paragraph 3 (which refers to 'natural or juridical person') and
- the Convention on Civil Liability for Oil Pollution Damage, Article 1, paragraph 2 (the definition of 'person' means 'any individual or partnership or any public or private body').[40]

[39] Harmen van der Wilt, 'Corporate Criminal Responsibility for International Crimes: Exploring the Possibilities' (2013) 12 Chinese Journal of International Law 73 (hereafter van der Wilt, 'Corporate Criminal Responsibility').

[40] See Mohamed Mattar, 'Corporate Criminal Liability: Article 10 of the Convention Against Transnational Organized Crime' (2012) 66(1) Journal of International Affairs 108–09; Volker Nerlich, 'Core Crimes and Transnational Business Corporations' (2010) 8 Journal of International Criminal Justice 896–97; and Kelly *Prosecuting Corporations* (n 36) 49; Joanna Kyriakakis, 'Prosecuting Corporations for International Crimes: The Role of Domestic Criminal Law' in May and Hoskins, *International Criminal Law* (n 32) 112.

This enumeration is not intended to be a comprehensive one as several other instances come to mind.[41] Such is the case of the following four:

- the Council of Europe Convention on the Prevention of Terrorism, Article 10 ('Liability of legal entities')
- the Convention on International Civil Aviation, Article 17 ('Nationality of aircraft'), which accords nationality to aircrafts
- the United Nations Convention on the Law of the Sea, Article 91 ('Nationality of Ships') which bestows nationality upon ships and
- the Protocol on the Statute of the African Court of Justice and Human Rights (as amended by the Malabo Protocol),[42] Article 46C ('Corporate Criminal Liability').

The trend is that corporate criminal liability is spreading its roots in international criminal law and slowly but surely is being adopted by the international community as an instrument to punish corporations in breach of international law. The more corporate criminal liability develops in international criminal law, the more will be states' acceptance, recognition, and implementation thereof in domestic law.

Typology of Legal Persons: The State as a Legal Person

Legal persons may, in turn, be sub-classified under broad categories. They can be in the forms of private corporations, ships, and aircraft. Private corporations can be further sub-divided into companies, cooperative societies, partnerships (civil or commercial), foundations, civil society organizations (such as trade unions, employer organizations, chambers of commerce, etc), and voluntary organizations (which may be philanthropic, charitable, cultural, educational, etc). There are also private military armies,[43] paramilitary groups and militias which would fall under the legal person category and, as evidenced from past genocide experiences, these

[41] Harmen van der Wilt, for instance, comments upon the French botched attempt to include a provision regulating corporate criminal liability in the Rome International Criminal Court Statute. Harmen van der Wilt, 'Corporate Criminal Responsibility' (n 39) 46–47. The full text is available at United Nations, *United Nations Diplomatic Conference of Plenipotentiaries on the Establishment of an International Criminal Court, Rome, 15 June–17 July 1998, Official Records, Reports and other documents*, Vol III (United Nations 2002) 251–52.

[42] This Protocol is not yet in force. In this respect, Gerhard Werle and Moritz Vormbaum comment that: 'One of the most important innovations of the Annex to the Malabo Protocol, compared to the ICC Statute and other international criminal tribunals' statutes, is the inclusion of a provision on corporate criminal liability for international crimes.' Gerhard Werle and Moritz Vormbaum (eds.), *The African Criminal Court: A Commentary on the Malabo Protocol* (T.M.C. Asser Press 2017) 151 (hereafter Werle and Vormbaum, *African Criminal Court*).

[43] Regis Bismuth, 'Mapping a Responsibility of Corporations for Violations of International Humanitarian Law Sailing Between International and Domestic Legal Order' (2010) 38(2) Denver Journal of International Law and Policy 204 n 6.

military forms of legal persons have lent more than a helping hand in the commission of genocidal atrocities cashing out profits therefrom. Violent non-state actors[44] and liberation movements[45] also candidate themselves as juridical persons. All these artificial persons—howsoever designated or classified, whether legal or illegal, whether national or multinational—can be complicit in the offence of genocide. In addition, the question whether an entity is corporate or unincorporate is normally left to be regulated by domestic (rather than international) law and not all municipal laws, where extant, regulate entities in the same way. For instance, there are states which request mandatory registration for non-voluntary organizations and civil society associations, whilst other states do not.

The state is one such legal person. It is an abstract entity, a legal fiction, a creature of the law. Yet it still has its own institutions which act independently from each other and have an existence of their own. The state is more in the nature of a group of companies, a corporate group, with a parent company and subsidiary companies. Within the context of genocide, the preferred definition of a 'state' is that of Theda Skocpol: 'a set of administrative, policing and military organisations headed, and more or less well coordinated, by an executive authority'.[46] The Montevideo Convention on Rights and Duties of States of 26 December 1933 (hereafter 'the Montevideo Convention') unequivocally considers the state to be a 'person' as evidenced from the text of Article 1: 'The state as a person of international law should possess the following qualifications: (a) a permanent population; (b) a defined territory; (c) government; and (d) capacity to enter into relations with the other states.' Therefore, from the international law perspective, the state is a legal person, although of course there can be both *de jure* and *de facto* organs of the state in operation and also unrecognized states in the world such as the Turkish Federated State of Cyprus and others[47] as well as failed, collapsed or weak states. In the words of Article 3 of the said Montevideo Convention: 'The political existence of the state is independent of recognition by the other states.' Recognition, therefore, does not constitute statehood, even though states should strive for it as they have to interact with the international community. The state has quite a lot in common with other legal persons (notably private corporations, ships, and aircraft). For instance, both the state and non-state legal persons may derive benefits from genocide both during and after its occurrence. Through the commission of genocide, these legal persons draw 'economic benefit from their massacres by taking over the victims' goods, businesses, and other activities',[48] including their land.

[44] Klejda Mulaj (ed), *Violent Non-State Actors in World Politics* (Columbia University Press, 2010).
[45] Ingrid Detter, *The International Legal Order* (Dartmouth Publishing Company 1994) 134–35.
[46] Theda Skocpol, *States and Social Revolution: A Comparative Analysis of France, Russia and China* (CUP 1979) 29. See also Aquilina and Mulaj, 'Limitations' (n 7) 125.
[47] For a discussion of the cases of unrecognized states, see John Dugard, *Recognition and the United Nations* (Grotius Publications Limited, 1987) 81–122.
[48] Antonio Cassese, *Human Rights* (n 4) 72. On the corporation as an atrocity contributor, see Michael J Kelly, *Prosecuting Corporations* (n 36) 15–48.

Nevertheless, there are also differences amongst legal persons. States enjoy state immunity, though there are exceptions here as well such as in the case of commercial transactions where the state acts *jure gestionis* not *jure imperii* when performing sovereign acts.[49] In the case of genocide, Article IV of the Convention clarifies that: 'Persons committing genocide ... shall be punished, whether they are constitutionally responsible rulers, public officials, or private individuals'. This constitutes 'a reason to depart from the normal principle of company law not to pierce the veil of corporate identity'[50] once exceptional circumstances warrant such course of action. Piercing the corporate veil for liability purposes is not only prohibited as a rule but, in this case, should be mandated. States, at international law, are the primary actors and have full liberty of contracting: they decide which treaties ought to apply to them or not and to what extent, through the law of treaties' institutes of reservations and declarations. This is not the case for other non-state persons (and natural persons as well). Moreover, states do defend their turf through Article 2, paragraph 7, of the United Nations Charter by erecting a barrier for the international community to interfere in their own domestic affairs.[51]

Civil Reparations for a Wrongful Act of State

At the other end of the responsibility spectrum there is reparation for a wrongful act of state—a delict—which has to be distinguished from a penal sanction for breach of a criminal law which an international criminal court can inflict upon a state.[52] Whilst an international criminal court such as the ICC should have its jurisdiction extended to try states for criminal responsibility for genocide (and this could also be extended to other core crimes included in the ICC Rome Statute and other crimes enumerated in the Malabo Protocol to the Statute of the African Court of Justice and Human Rights), the ICJ already possesses and has applied in the past civil reparations against a state for a wrongful act. Article 31, paragraph 1, of the ILC's Articles on state responsibility provides that: 'The responsible State is under an obligation to make full reparation for the injury caused by the internationally

[49] Christopher H Schreuer, *State Immunity: Some Recent Developments* (Grotius Publications Limited 1988) 10–43.

[50] ibid 120. One of the difficulties met by prosecutors is 'the determination of the specific mode of liability the respective leader has incurred in criminal liability for the crimes charged in the indictment'. Héctor Olásolo, *The Criminal Responsibility of Senior Political and Military Leaders as Principals to International Crimes* (Hart Publishing 2009) 2.

[51] This provision reads as follows: 'Nothing contained in the present Charter shall authorize the United Nations to intervene in matters which are essentially within the domestic jurisdiction of any state or shall require the Members to submit such matters to settlement under the present Charter; but this principle shall not prejudice the application of enforcement measures under Chapter VII.'

[52] For reparations refer to Haig Khatchadourian, 'Compensation and Reparation as Forms of Compensatory Justice' in Claudia Card and Armen T Marsoobian, *Genocide's Aftermath: Responsibility and Repair* (Blackwell Publishing Ltd 2007) 147–65.

wrongful act.' Essentially reparations come, in terms of Article 34, in three forms: 'Full reparation for the injury caused by the internationally wrongful act shall take the form of restitution,[53] compensation and satisfaction, either singly or in combination, in accordance with the provisions of this chapter'. The three forms of reparation—restitution, compensation and satisfaction—are defined by the ILC Articles on state responsibility in Articles 35, 36, and 37 thereof. According to the Permanent Court of International Justice, it is 'a principle of international law that the breach of an engagement involves an obligation to make reparation in an adequate form. Reparation therefore is the indispensable complement of a failure to apply a convention and there is no necessity for this to be stated in the convention itself'.[54]

Compensation is a remedy of a lesser form than restitution whilst satisfaction is the most lenient of all three civil punishments which can be inflicted upon a state. There is therefore a hierarchical difference in so far as severity of punishment is concerned amongst the three civil law measures. What is important to the argument of this chapter is that all these three penalties can be contemplated distinctly from the criminal sanctions above listed so as to ensure that one and the same penalty is not inflicted for both the civil and the criminal actions. Indeed, the penalty must be commensurate not only to the injury suffered, whether under international criminal or civil law, but also to the nature of the action, that is, whether the action is for international state criminal responsibility or civil responsibility for an internationally wrongful act. Further, both the criminal action and the civil action should be allowed for genocide committed by one state (other legal person, violent non-state actor, or individual) against another state (its other legal persons, violent non-state actors, or individuals) as well as when genocide is perpetrated against the state's own inhabitants, without recourse to any external element and irrespective of whether mass migration occurs from that state to neighbouring states. In other words, state criminal responsibility for genocide has to extend to all forms of genocide, irrespective of the territory where it is committed. Needless to say, the same argument applies to the civil action for state responsibility for genocide.

[53] Restitution is equivalent to the Roman law concept of *restitutio in integrum*. In another judgment, the ICJ held that: 'reparation must, as far as possible, wipe out all the consequences of the illegal act and reestablish the situation which would, in all probability, have existed if that act had not been committed. Restitution in kind, or, if this is not possible, payment of a sum corresponding to the value which a restitution in kind would bear; the award, if need be, of damages for loss sustained which would not be covered by restitution in kind or payment in place of it—such are the principles which should serve to determine the amount of compensation due for an act contrary to international law.' Permanent Court of International Justice, *Case Concerning the Factory at Chorzów (Claim For Indemnity) (Merits)*, 13 September 1928, Series A, No 17, Publications of the Permanent Court of International Justice 47. On restitution in enabling postgenocide recovery, refer to the contribution of Rajika L Shah, Chapter 3 in this volume.

[54] Permanent Court of International Justice, *Case Concerning the Factory at Chorzów (Claim For Indemnity) (Jurisdiction)*, 26 July 1927, Series A, No 9, Publications of the Permanent Court of International Justice 21.

Criminalizing State Responsibility for Genocide and Its Attendant Implementation Difficulties

Ian Klabbers opines that 'states can only be held responsible for internationally wrongful acts—that is, acts that are somehow committed in violation of an international obligation incumbent on the state'.[55] That a state can commit crimes is affirmed by the UN International Convention on the Suppression and Punishment of the Crime of *Apartheid*, 1976, which in Article 1, paragraph 2, contemplates state criminal responsibility: 'The State Parties to the present Convention declare criminal those organizations, institutions and individuals committing the crime of *apartheid*.'[56] Indeed, telling are the words in Article 46C of the Protocol on the Statute of the African Court of Justice and Human Rights (as amended by the Malabo Protocol) which, under the heading of 'Corporate Criminal Liability', contains a provision distinguishing between two types of legal persons: states and non-states. Article 46C reads, in relevant part, as follows: 'For the purpose of this Statute, the Court shall have jurisdiction over legal persons, with the exception of States.'[57] The Malabo Protocol aforesaid is clearly recognizing that there are state legal persons and non-state legal persons and that, therefore, the state (although exempted from the provisions of this Protocol) is a legal person. But, the state is considered a superior legal person due to the attribute of sovereignty. This attribute exempts states from taking up responsibility for the worst crimes known to human kind, genocide included. Indeed there is a close relationship between genocide, on one hand, and historical (re)production of sovereignty, on the other; (re)production which frequently involves genocidal violence and its denial.[58]

As noted above, a state's protection from intervention is enshrined in the UN Charter (Article 2, paragraph 7). The Montevideo Convention, though earlier in time than the Charter, also has a (wider) provision to this effect in Article 8: 'No state has the right to intervene in the internal or external affairs of another.' Those states which happen to be permanent members[59] of the Security Council have an added advantage through the casting of the veto which prohibits non-interference not only in their own domestic affairs but even in those of their allies: 'Decisions of the Security Council on all other [non-procedural] matters shall be made by an

[55] Jan Klabbers, *International Law* (CUP 2017) 139.

[56] United Nations, International Convention on the Suppression and Punishment of the Crime of Apartheid (opened for signature 30 November 1973, entered into force on 18 July 1976) 1015 UNTS 245. 245. On the state as a corporation, see Jørgensen, *Responsibility of States* (n 5) 78–79.

[57] Werle and Vormbaum, *African Criminal Court* (n 42) 251.

[58] On the relationship between historical (re)production of sovereignty and denial, refer to Tatevik Mnatsakanyan's Chapter 6 in this volume.

[59] Article 23, paragraph 1, of the United Nations Charter provides that: 'The Security Council shall consist of fifteen Members of the United Nations. The Republic of China, France, the Union of Soviet Socialist Republics [now Russia], the United Kingdom of Great Britain and Northern Ireland, and the United States of America shall be permanent members of the Security Council ...' United Nations, United Nations Charter (1945) 1 UNTS XVI.

affirmative vote of nine members including the concurring votes of the permanent members.'[60]

For a state to be held responsible for the commission of a crime, international law must state so. Otherwise the principles *nullum crimen sine lege* and *nulla poena sine lege* may be pleaded. A state can incur criminal responsibility for genocide, in the same way that an individual may attract criminal responsibility for genocide only if a law says so. This is nothing but the application of the rule of law at an international level. Hence, there has to be a clear rule of international law which ascribes criminal responsibility to a state, *qua* state, rather than *qua* individuals who form the will of that state. At the moment of writing this is not the case in international law as Article IV of the Genocide Convention does not encompass states but only 'constitutionally responsible rulers, public officials and individuals'. In so far as the first two categories of persons are concerned, they are still punished *qua* individuals rather than as representatives of a state. This is not the case with corporate criminal responsibility where an individual is charged both in an individual capacity for individual criminal responsibility and as a representative of a corporation and if the said individual is found guilty then the corporation is also punished in addition to the individual. Article IV of the Convention provides for nothing of the sort as what it does is to exclude outright the possibility for responsible rulers and public officials from pleading state immunity thereby running scot-free from any form of punishment for genocide. Even the Rome Statute does not contain a provision on state criminal responsibility for genocide even if this treaty is of more recent vintage entering into force less than two decades ago when compared to the Genocide Convention of seventy-two years ago.

The difficulty with a state being found guilty of committing genocide is to identify who is the actual perpetrator of the crime. Furthermore, the state has a very intricate and complex structure raising the question who represents the will of the state. In addition, the state may be acting through its own officials or through agents who or which have no connection thereto such as when militias are recruited to commit genocide in lieu of the regular armed forces of that state[61] or where recourse is had to paramilitary groups[62] who are commissioned to do a job on behalf of the state and who act quite independently from the command structure of the

[60] ibid Article 27 paragraph 3 of the United Nations Charter.

[61] Take the case of the Interahamwe militia in Rwanda and the Janjaweed militia in Sudan. For a study of state responsibility for militias' genocide crimes, see Matthew H Charity, 'Criminalized State: The International Criminal Court, the Responsibility to Protect, and Darfur, Republic of Sudan' (2011) 37 Ohio Northern University Law Review 77–89. On the responsibility to protect, refer to Chapter 5 by Jobair Alam in this volume.

[62] This is, for instance, the case of Arkan's Tigers in Bosnia and the Scorpions in the Srebrenica massacre. Narissa Kashvi Ramsundar clarifies that 'international law is limited in the extent to which it addresses State responsibility for the commission of atrocities committed by armed groups who rely on considerable levels of State support'. See Narissa Kashvi Ramsundar, *State Responsibility for Support of Armed Groups in the Commission of International Crimes* (Brill Nijhoff 2020) 2 (hereafter Ramsundar, *Support of Armed Groups*).

commissioning state. Sometimes it might also be difficult to establish whether a state exists or not and whom to indict in such cases such as with failed states where there is no official government in place or where the official government does not control the whole territory and insurgents, rebels, separatists, or terrorists might have effective control and command of a particular state territory. History is replete with examples of this nature.

Perhaps the major stumbling block in establishing the criminal responsibility of a state is the *dolus specialis* required for the commission of the crime. How can it be proved that a state had such a special intent? The best form of evidence of a state's *dolus specialis* manifests itself in a genocidal plan drawn up and approved by the leadership of a state. Depending on the constitutional organs of a state, such leadership might be an executive President, a Cabinet of Ministers, a dictator, a parliament, etc. What is important is that such genocidal plan is approved by the competent state authority with constitutional functions entrusted with decision-making powers. Ideally, evidentially, the plan should be reduced to writing and published officially as it is more easily ascertainable in that way. Yet if it is written but not published, the *dolus specialis* might still be proved even though through a lengthier process. Two examples which can be cited in this respect, both from Germany, relate to the Jews and the Hereros. The Final Solution was Nazi Germany's declared policy on the execution of the Jews.[63] As to the Herero's, an 'Extermination order' issued by German General Lothar von Trotha in their regard constituted 'an explicit written declaration of intent to commit genocide'.[64] The fact that the decision to commit genocide is not published means that it is still languishing in a government file or record even though one might have difficulties to get access thereto as Bosnia had when Serbia was exhibiting only redacted official documents before the ICJ and the international court voluntarily desisted from ordering the production of the unabridged documents.[65] If, on the

[63] See Christopher R Browning, *The Origins of the Final Solution: The Evolution of Nazi Jewish Policy, September 1939-March 1942* (Heinemann 2004) in particular Chapter 9, 'The Final Solution from Conception to Implementation' 374–415; Aly Gőtz, *Final Solution: Nazi Population Policy and the Murder of the European Jews* (Arnold, 1999) in particular Chapter 11, 'Elements of the Decision to Carry out the Holocaust' 243–63 and Chapter 12 'The Murderers' Postscripts' 264–72; and Steve Hochstadt (ed), *Sources of the Holocaust* (Palgrave Macmillan 2004) 5.

[64] See David Olusoga and Casper W Erichen, *The Kaiser's Holocaust: Germany's Forgotten Genocide* (Faber and Faber Ltd 2000) 150. The text of General von Trotha's proclamation reads as follows: 'I, the Great General of the German troops, send this letter to the Herero . . . The Herero people must leave the land. If they do not do this I will force them with the Groot Rohr [Cannon]. Within the German borders every Herero, with or without a gun, with or without cattle, will be shot. I will no longer accept women and children, I will drive them back to their people or I will let them be shot at. These are my words to the Herero people. Signed: The Great General of the Mighty Kaiser, von Trotha', in David Olusoga and Casper W Erichen 149–50.

[65] In his dissenting opinion, Vice-President Judge Awn Shawkat Al-Khasawneh stressed that: 'In the first place, the Court was alerted by the Applicant to the existence of "redacted" sections of documents of the Supreme Defence Council of the Respondent. Regrettably, the Court failed to act although, under Article 49 of its Statute, it has the power to do so. It is a reasonable expectation that those documents would have shed light on the central questions of intent and attributability'—Dissenting Opinion of Vice-President Al-Khasawneh, *Bosnia v Serbia* (n 21) para 35.

contrary, the genocidal plan is unwritten, then it is harder to establish genocide occurrence, though not necessarily impossible. A plurality of events pointing in that direction should possibly allow a court to establish genocidal intent more so if it orders the defaulting state to file the document in court or, should the state fail to do so, appoints a court expert to have access to all the defaulting states' documents and archives in order to attempt to trace and search for such document or evidence of such plurality of events in pointing in the direction of a tacit genocidal state policy. This procedure is not, however, supported by court practice.[66] Dermot Groome maintains that in the absence of proof of a genocidal plan, 'pattern evidence could be used to establish the existence of a genocidal plan only if that evidence excludes all other possibilities', yet pattern evidence had been disregarded by the ICJ marking 'an important methodological departure from the ICTY trial chambers, which have endorsed the importance of such evidence'.[67]

Should no court proceedings have been instituted, a genocidal plan may still be ascertained in a postgenocide setting following the establishment by the Security Council of a Commission of Inquiry whose task would be that of ascertaining whether there is a *prima facie* case of genocide. The UN Secretary General, the General Assembly and any UN Member State should be empowered to lodge such a request with the Security Council and, once made, a Commission of Inquiry should be appointed promptly. The Commission should not take more than a very short period of time from its appointment to deliver its initial report to the Security Council and, unless proof to the contrary is adduced against the *prima facie* commission of genocide, the UN Member State shall be presumed to have perpetrated genocide. It would be at this stage that following the determination of such constructive perpetration of genocide, the UN Security Council and the ICC Prosecutor should take measures to suppress genocide whilst the ICJ should issue by way of a preliminary measure an order for the cessation of the wrongful action immediately upon the decision being taken to establish such Commission of Inquiry. There is indeed nothing innovative in this procedure as the ICJ has already acceded to a request for provisional measure to prevent genocide in *The Gambia v Myanmar*.[68] Should the ICJ order not be respected, the Security Council should order the imposition of sanctions. Importantly, when the Security Council considers cases of genocide, the permanent members should, by way of international

[66] *Bosnia v Serbia* (n 21) para 206.

[67] Dermot Groome, 'Adjudicating Genocide' (n 32) 943. See also Ademola Abass, 'Proving State Responsibility for Genocide: The ICJ in *Bosnia v. Serbia* and the International Commission of Inquiry for Darfur' (2008) 31 Fordham International Law Journal 898–902; and Robin M Smith, 'State Responsibility and Genocidal Intent: A Three Test Approach' (2016) 34 Australian Year Book of International Law 97–118.

[68] Application of the Convention on the Prevention and Punishment of the Crime of Genocide (The Gambia v Myanmar) (Order), 23 January 2020 <https://www.icj-cij.org/en/case/178> accessed 29 May 2020.

custom, abstain from exercising their veto if that would amount in the ICJ's guidance and determination to the presumed continuation of genocidal acts.[69]

Another impelling issue needing addressing is of a procedural nature. What happens if genocide is not committed interstate, that is, genocide is not carried on by one state against targeted people/s residing in another state, but by a state against a group of people within its own territory? Which judicial organ will try that state once, in all probability, the domestic courts or forces of law and order might not have the necessary clout to prosecute and/or convict their own state leaders? Marko Milanović raises a number of issues in this respect:

> Non-injured states could claim from the responsible state, *inter alia*, the cessation of the wrongful act and the specific performance of its international obligation, and could even ask the Court to issue provisional measures, however unlikely it may be that a genocidal state would actually abide by such measures. Non-injured states cannot claim compensation as a form of reparation to themselves, as no damage was caused to them, but they might be able to claim compensation on behalf of the victims of the responsible state, possibly by setting up a compensation fund for which the non-injured state could act as a trustee. Article 48(2)(b) of the ILC Articles does seem to allow for a claim by a non-injured state for reparations in the interest of the beneficiaries of the *erga omnes* obligation, but this was admittedly done in progressive development of the law.[70]

In the case of interstate genocide, which will be the international judicial organ to try a state for criminal responsibility for genocide? The ICC complementary principle[71] should not apply in those cases where the ICC Prosecutor entertains serious doubt that the rights of victim states or victim persons will not be respected in national courts which might be controlled by a judiciary appointed by, and still sympathetic to, the outgoing *genocidaire* regime.

[69] For proposals for change of the Genocide Convention, see Benjamin Whitaker, *Revised and updated report on the prevention and punishment of the crime of genocide*, United Nations Economic and Social Council, Commission on Human Rights, Sub-Commission on Prevention of Discrimination and Protection of Minorities, E/CN.4/Sub.2/1985/6, 2 July 1985, paras 69–91.

[70] Marko Milanović, 'State Responsibility for Genocide' (2006) 17(3) The European Journal of International Law 564.

[71] Jann K Kleffner explains the principle of complementarity as denoting 'that the [International Criminal] Court is only to exercise its jurisdiction if States remain wholly inactive vis-à-vis ICC crimes or, in case States investigate, prosecute and adjudicate cases, if they prove to be unwilling or unable to do so genuinely. According to the principle of complementarity, in other words, national courts retain primary competence to exercise jurisdiction over core crimes. They are envisaged to take pride of place and constitute the first line of defence in the fight against impunity. The ICC, on the other hand, is supposed to function as a "permanent reserve court", which steps in when effective national suppression of ICC crimes is absent'. Jann K Kleffner, *Complementarity in the Rome Statute and National Criminal Jurisdictions* (OUP 2008) 4.

State Criminal Responsibility and Liability

State criminal liability is being used here as an extension of the concept of corporate criminal liability, to apply it to the state. The latter, after all, is a body corporate even though distinct from other corporations encountered in domestic criminal law (be it a company, a foundation, local governmental authority, public corporation, etc). In reality, all bodies corporate—like the state—are legal fictions. In law they do not have a physical existence of their own even though state agents do exist in the person of responsible rulers and public officials (hereafter 'state officials') who take decisions in the name, and on behalf, of the state. These state officials constitute the mind and the will of the state they represent. So although legally speaking the state is one thing and its officials another, in reality there is quite of an intimate relationship between the two. Of course, as in company law, sometimes it is not possible to know exactly who is representing the will of the company at a certain determinate moment in time as there might be several directors, managers, etc, involved. So all such officers have to be indicted to answer for their alleged criminal activity on behalf of the body corporate in question and then the court of criminal jurisdiction will have the arduous task of selecting those bearing responsibility. As to the state—which has a more elaborate system of government—once again, it might not be exactly clear who has devised, approved, ordered, and executed the criminal action—as different persons might be responsible in the decision-making and execution processes and at different times and levels of responsibility. For, to a certain extent, notwithstanding its complexity, the state is made up of individuals who are leading (the high ranking state officials) and those who are following (the low ranking state officials and the citizenry).

When the criminal act is conducted by or on behalf of the state, it is done through various players. It could be through an agent of the state not necessarily entrusted with carrying out that conduct (as when the state official involved has taken the initiative him/herself without complying with orders dispensed by the control and command structure of the state's organs), when complying with the state's organs orders s/he has exceeded his/her mandate, or when the state official is simply following orders conveyed by his/her respective control and command structure. So even in the case of state responsibility for genocide, the position tends to be complicated and difficult to first establish responsibility and then liability. State liability has to vary from individual criminal liability because whilst a physical person convicted of the crime of genocide may be imprisoned, the state may not, for there is no state to arrest, handcuff, detain, and imprison. The state as a physical *persona* simply does not exist. There can be other forms of punishment more appropriate to a legal person than to a physical person such as inflicting a monetary fine; confiscating the instrumentalities and proceeds of crime; imposing payment of a monetary fine corresponding to property the value whereof corresponds to the proceeds of crime; temporary or permanent closure of an undertaking or establishment (such as a weapons or chemical gas factory) used for illegal purposes; freezing or seizing of any funds used or allocated for the purpose of committing a crime; and freezing or seizing of proceeds derived from a criminal offence.

The questions arising from the above considerations that need to be posed at this juncture are the following: (a) can a state be found responsible for genocide from a criminal perspective? and (b) if this is so, what punishment may be meted out in such a case? The answer to both these questions is in the negative. It is affirmative in so far as civil responsibility is concerned but negative as to criminal responsibility because there is no international court or tribunal which can declare a state responsible for the crime of genocide. Here lies the problem in relation to the criminal responsibility of the state, first and foremost, and in relation to the criminal liability of the state, secondarily. Unless there is an international court or tribunal which can find a state criminally responsible for genocide, there is no international institution which can convert that responsibility into a liability and pass on to punish the state for commission of the crime of genocide. The conclusion, in answer to both above questions, is that at the current state of play, a state cannot be found criminally responsible for genocide, nor may its criminal behaviour attract any criminal liability. A state, *qua* state, is immune from criminal punishment from genocide. This leaves a state open only to a declaration of civil responsibility and civil liability for genocide. A very worrying factor indeed!

From the above analysis it can be deduced that there are other stumbling blocks which will ensure that a state is not punished for having committed genocide within its territory ranging, inter alia, from sovereignty, non-interference by the international community in domestic affairs, lack of an international court or tribunal to try for criminal responsibility for genocide committed by a state, highly onerous rules of procedure, blind respect for state secrecy in the provision of information by way of evidence, granting of amnesties to top officials of the state from prosecution, excessively high standards of proof, imposition of nearly insurmountable standard of proof to find against a state for genocide.

It appears that the main difficulty which exists between individual responsibility and state responsibility is that of establishing a nexus between the state agent who has perpetrated genocide on its behalf. Normally, the state agents in question are Presidents, Prime Ministers, ministers, and senior public officials, including military officers. There is also the genocide plan, written or intended, and state policy which has to be arrived at via the same route that international customary law is discerned.

On the contrary, it should be noted that the 'ICTY had rejected the ICJ's "effective control" test and established a much lower standard (overall control)[72] for

[72] International Criminal Tribunal for Former Yugoslavia, *Prosecutor v Tadić (Appeals Judgment)*, IT-94-1-A, A Ch (15 July 1999) paras 120-162 (hereafter *Prosecutor v Tadić*). For the distinction between the ICJ's 'effective control' and the ICTY's 'overall control' see, in particular, paras 124–125, 131–132, and 137.

determining state responsibility in situations of "aiding and assisting".[73] Also, this tribunal developed the joint criminal enterprise doctrine[74]—controversial as it might be[75]—which introduced a threefold categorization of collective crime[76] contributing to establishing a basis for genocidal convictions. So whilst the ICTY was moving in the direction of making individuals responsible for genocide through adopting a more prosecution friendly interpretation of its Statute, the ICJ implemented a more state-centric construction of the Genocide Convention to the detriment of genocide victims thereby protecting state immunity instead.

Inroads in State Immunity Supporting the Case for State Criminal Responsibility

Sovereign immunity metamorphosed over time. In antiquity, the supreme and absolute sovereign monarch—subsequently replaced by the modern state (hence 'state immunity')—enjoyed a divine right of kings, could do no wrong, epitomized the state (*l'état c'est moi*) and was unshackled by law (*princeps legibus solutus est*—'the Prince is not bound by laws'). This notwithstanding, sovereign immunity witnessed a progressive encroachment thereupon: although the attribute shifted from that associated with the sovereignty of one person (the king, despot or monarch) to extend to that of the head of state and other government officials and agents, it mellowed down over time from absolute to restrictive immunity. As one author put it, '[t]he history of the law of State immunity is the history of the triumph of the doctrine of restrictive immunity over that of absolute immunity. The accomplishment of this triumph, on the plane of international law, has been a slow, gradual and incremental process'.[77] From what was originally conceived and worked out in practice as an unaccountable despot, the state has, as evidenced from past history, been constrained to shed some of its unfettered dominance, even if not yet to the desired level concomitant with post-Second World War international law and international relations' values of peace, democracy, human rights, rule of law, good governance, accountability, and transparency. State immunity is one such antiquity

[73] Mark Gibney, 'Genocide and State Responsibility' (2007) 7(4) Human Rights Law Review 764. *Prosecutor v Tadić* (n 72) is a relevant case in this respect.

[74] For a history of this doctrine, see Allison Marston Danner and Jenny S Martinez, 'Guilty Associations: Joint Criminal Enterprise, Command Responsibility, and the Development of International Criminal Law' (2005) 93(1) California Law Review 102–17.

[75] For criticisms of this doctrine, see, for instance, Jens David Ohlin, 'Three Conceptual Problems with the Doctrine of Joint Criminal Enterprise' (2007) 5(1) Journal of International Criminal Justice 69; Cliff Farhang, 'Point of No Return: Joint Criminal Enterprise in Brđanin' (2010) 23(1) Leiden Journal of International Law 137–64 especially n 1 at 137.

[76] These three categories are set out by Kai Ambos, 'Joint Criminal Enterprise and Command Responsibility' (2007) 5 Journal of International Criminal Justice 159 at 160.

[77] Xiaodong Yang, *State Immunity in International Law* (CUP 2012) 6 (hereafter Yang, *State Immunity*).

relic that still manifests itself in public international law where a government enjoys limited immunity from being sued for wrongdoing. In this privileged position, the state issues commands free from any external supervisory authority, such as a judicial body, unless it elects to divest itself, out of its own volition, of this historic, anachronistic and illiberal exemption bequeathed unto itself. This principle owes its rationale to sovereign equality of states, where domestic courts are powerless to exercise jurisdiction over foreign states: *par in parem non habet imperium* ('equals have no sovereignty over each other'). This notwithstanding, absolute sovereign immunity has been dented through the emergence of cracks and crevices that are incrementally redirecting, even if at a slow pace, sovereign immunity law within the fold of post-Second World War international law values. This has been achieved through laboriously negotiated treaty provisions and progressive case law.

Treaty Law

Arguably the two most important treaties that have dented state immunity are:

(a) the Council of Europe Convention on State Immunity of 16 May 1972[78] that made inroads into state immunity even though: (i) it is concerned with private law disputes between individuals and states; (ii) has failed to attract widespread support; and (iii) does not extend to criminal proceedings; and
(b) the United Nations Convention on Jurisdictional Immunities of States and Their Properties of 2 December 2004,[79] which, although (i) not yet in force, and (ii) does not also extend to criminal proceedings, nonetheless, recognises several areas where state immunity cannot be claimed and to which states party to that convention will renounce. These exceptions to state immunity are in relation to commercial transactions; contracts of employment; personal injuries and damage to property; ownership, possession and use of property; intellectual and industrial property; participation in companies or other collective bodies; ships owned or operated by a state; and arbitration agreements.[80] This convention—like the previously mentioned one—constitutes an important pointer in a desired direction.

In addition, another universally recognized limitation to state immunity comes in the form of *acta jure gestionis* as distinct from *acta jure imperii*: '*Acta jure gestionis* are private, commercial, or non-sovereign acts, whereas *acta jure imperii* are

[78] ETS No. 74.
[79] United Nations General Assembly Resolution A/RES/59/38.
[80] Part III, Articles 10 to 17 of the United Nations Convention on Jurisdictional Immunities of States and Their Property (opened for signature 2 December 2004, not yet in force).

public, governmental, or sovereign acts'.[81] When the state engages in economic—as opposed to political—activities, immunity is scaled down from absolute to relative and the state can be sued for wrongdoing.

Hazel Fox and Philippa Webb correctly observe that a 'foreign State is not subject to the criminal proceedings of a national court of another State by reason of substantive law than procedural immunity . . . By reason of its independent status, the foreign State cannot be subjected to such prosecution by the forum State or its officials nor punished by way of fine, penalty, or imprisonment'.[82] Nonetheless, the Nuremburg trials rejected Head of State immunity: 'The principle of international law, which under certain circumstances, protects the representatives of a state, cannot be applied to acts which are condemned as criminal by international law. The authors of these acts cannot shelter themselves behind their official position in order to be freed from punishment in appropriate proceedings.'[83] Moreover, the International Military Tribunal—as the Nuremberg Tribunal was properly designated—added that: 'He who violates the laws of war cannot obtain immunity while acting in pursuance of the authority of the state, if the state in authorizing action moves outside its competence under international law.'[84] This principle was subsequently enshrined in Principle III of the Principles of Nuremberg which proclaimed that: 'The fact that a person who committed an act which constitutes a crime under international law acted as Head of State or responsible Government official does not relieve him from responsibility under international law'[85] and reflects Article 7 of the Charter of the International Military Tribunal. Since the Nuremburg trials, this principle has been incorporated into subsequent international criminal law instruments such as in Article 7(2) of the Statute of the ICTY, Article 6(2) of the Statute of the ICTR, Article 27(2) of the Statute of the ICC, and Article 6(2) of the Statute of the Special Court for Sierra Leone. Moreover, the United Nations' International Law Commission is currently developing draft articles on immunity of state officials from foreign criminal jurisdiction and is proposing in draft article 7 that state immunity should not apply to the following crimes under international law: '(a) crime of genocide; (b) crimes

[81] Edward Chukwuemeke Okeke, *Jurisdictional Immunities of States and International Organizations* (OUP 2018) 99.

[82] Hazel Fox and Philippa Webb, *The Law of State Immunity* (OUP 2015) 21–22.

[83] Secretariat, International Military Tribunal, *Trial of the Major War Criminals Before the International Military Tribunal: Nuremberg 14 November 1945—1 October 1946, Official Documents*, Vol 1 (International Military Tribunal 1947) 466.

[84] ibid.

[85] International Law Commission, *Formulation of Nürnberg Principles*, Document A/CN.4/22, Report by J Spiropoulos Special Rapporteur, 12 April 1950, *Yearbook of the International Law Commission*, Vol 2 (United Nations Publications, 1950) 182 <https://read.un-ilibrary.org/international-law-and-justice/yearbook-of-the-international-law-commission-1950-vol-ii_cc800c08-en#page187> accessed on 20 January 2018.

against humanity; (c) war crimes; (d) crime of *apartheid*; (e) torture; (f) enforced disappearance.'[86]

From the above, it is evident that absolute state immunity has incurred cracks and crevices. However, state immunity remains absolute more in the political than in the economic sphere. Indeed, whilst, as have been seen in relation to treaty law, absolute sovereign immunity has not been impacted in the political sphere to the extent of the economic sector, there are also inroads to state immunity in the political arena that have developed both by treaty law and case law. Treaty law has dented head of state immunity through the Nuremberg Principles for, when heads of state or former heads of state loose immunity, that privation weakens the claim to absolute immunity by the state. By hitting heads of state, former heads of state and state officials, one is in effect targeting the might of the state. Further, once draft article 7 aforesaid is approved and comes into force, then the political sphere will suffer a severe backlash—perhaps the most striking one that it has not yet endured to date—whereby state immunity would not be permitted to be pleaded in the case of the most heinous crimes established by International Criminal Law that humanity has ever witnessed; this should hopefully act as an effective deterrent against the perpetration of such crimes by state actors. Case law, like treaty law, is also moving in this direction.

Case Law

Case law is sounding the death knell of the state immunity vestige where states, their leaders and their representatives claim immunity from judicial process.[87] The ICJ in the *Democratic Republic of Congo v Belgium* judgment[88] opined that a Head of State could be prosecuted before an international tribunal and does not enjoy immunity from prosecution for international crimes. It recognized four exceptions to immunity by an incumbent or former state official: (1) these officials may be tried by their own domestic courts in terms of domestic law; (2) their immunity may be waived by their own government; (3) former state officials may be tried by a foreign court in respect of acts committed prior or subsequent to their period of office in respect of acts committed during that period of office in a private capacity; and (4) both incumbent and former state officials may be subject to criminal proceedings before certain international criminal courts, where they have jurisdiction as is the case of the International Criminal Court.[89]

[86] International Law Commission, 'Seventh report on immunity of State officials from foreign criminal jurisdiction, Report by Concepción Escobar Hernández, Special Rapporteur' (International Law Commission, 18 April 2019) <https://undocs.org/en/A/CN.4/729> accessed on 20 January 2018.

[87] For a discussion of such cases see Yang, *State Immunity* (n 77) 12–22.

[88] *Case Concerning the Arrest Warrant of 11 April 2000 (Democratic Republic of the Congo v. Belgium)* [2002] ICJ Reports 3.

[89] ibid para 61.

The House of Lords Pinochet case[90] of 25 November 1998—that decided that a former head of state did not enjoy immunity from criminal prosecution for acts of torture committed when head of state—demonstrates than even the law pertaining to head of state immunity has shifted from absolute to qualified immunity. Whilst heads of state enjoy immunity from criminal prosecution when in office, and former heads of state for non-criminal acts performed in an official capacity, the latter succumb to divestiture of such immunity when, as head of states, they perpetrated criminal acts.

A final noteworthy case that can be cited is of Charles Taylor, a former President of the Republic of Liberia indicted for war crimes and crimes against humanity, who pleaded sovereign immunity to criminal proceedings before the Special Court for Sierra Leone. The Appeals Chamber thereof held that 'the principle seems now established that the sovereign equality of states does not prevent a Head of State from being prosecuted before an international criminal tribunal or court'.[91]

Bruce Broomhall makes the case that the Nuremberg principles should be extended to state immunity: 'For reasons flowing from the Nuremberg principles, immunity should be irrelevant for the same reason that superior orders or prior legality under national law are irrelevant. To acknowledge claims of immunity would in effect allow States to choose whether or not their agents would be responsible under international law, making regular enforcement (the rule of law) all but impossible.'[92] Furthermore, if state sovereignty, in line with post-Second World War values particularly that of democracy, is interpreted to mean—as W Michael Reisman[93] posits—'popular' sovereignty rather than 'ruler' sovereignty, then the whole edifice upon which state immunity is constructed shifts. For Kofi Annan state sovereignty is being redefined: 'When we read the [United Nations] Charter today, we are more than ever conscious that its aim is to protect individual human beings, not to protect those who abuse them.'[94] Hence there is a transmutation in how state sovereignty is now conceived: 'States are now widely understood to be instruments at the service of their peoples, and not vice versa.'[95]

[90] House of Lords, *Bartle and the Commissioner of Police for the Metropolis and Others, Ex Parte Pinochet*, R v. [1998] UKHL 41; [2000] 1 AC 61; [1998] 4 All ER 897; [1998] 3 WLR 1456 (25th November, 1998); *Pinochet, Re* [1999] UKHL 52 (15 January 1999); *Bartle and the Commissioner of Police for the Metropolis and Others, Ex Parte Pinochet; R v. Evans and Another and the Commissioner of Police for the Metropolis and Others, Ex Parte Pinochet*, R v. [1999] UKHL 17 (24th March, 1999).

[91] Special Court for Sierra Leone, *Prosecutor v. Charles Ghankay Taylor (Appeals Judgment)* 31 May 2004, SCSL-2003-01-I A Ch (31 May 2004).

[92] Bruce Broomhall, *International Justice and the International Criminal Court: Between Sovereignty and the Rule of Law* (OUP 2003) 128.

[93] W M Reisman, 'Sovereignty and Human Rights in Contemporary International Law' in G H Fox and B R Roth (eds), *Democratic Governance and International Law* (CUP 2000) 243.

[94] K A Annan, 'Two Concepts of Sovereignty' (1999) 352 *The Economist* 49.

[95] ibid.

The above inroads into state responsibility point in the direction for making a sound case for rendering states criminally liable in a postgenocide milieu. By applying the principle of analogy, the argument favouring civil liability of states can be extended to their criminal liability. By surveying the progressive development of public international law in relation to state immunity law, the erosion of state immunity is manifest through various measures adopted in the past. A convincing case can be made that since the enunciation of Nuremberg Principle III, and its adoption in subsequent treaty law, sovereign immunity has been stripped away as a defence against criminal liability for political leaders of states when, prior thereto, it was accepted as a complete defence; conventional law has developed such that absolute state immunity has metamorphosed into a qualified state immunity whilst rendering the state criminally accountable; case law is adopting a narrower construction of state immunity; corporate criminal liability is gaining acceptance for artificial entities and, as states are themselves artificial entities, they should, by analogy, be subject to the same rules of criminal responsibility; and, finally, bearing in mind the ICJ's Bosnia decision that states can commit genocide, all these should lead to strengthening the argument that states should therefore also be subject to criminal liability for 'the crime of crimes'.

Conclusion

This chapter contributes to an ongoing academic and policy debate on how best to respond to mass atrocity in a postgenocide setting, with particular reference to state responsibility for genocide. In academic circles it is widely acknowledged that genocide is uniquely a crime of state. Indeed, realistically speaking, it is a crime the perpetration whereof necessitates state support—whether directly or indirectly, covertly or overtly, totally or partially. Being a crime of state, it should not suffice to punish only a handful of responsible leaders and state officials who devised and supervised the implementation of genocide. All responsible persons should be punished, be they physical persons, corporations, violent non-state actors and others, whether as principals, co-principals, accomplices and co-accomplices, instigators, and conspirators, more so that they would have somehow benefited from its perpetration. However, this is still not enough to assuage the incalculable harm occasioned to the well-being of the affected targeted group, humanity as a whole, and to international peace and security. The state which conceived, planned, took preparatory measures, instigated, conspired, fomented, covered up, aided, abetted, executed, and benefitted from genocide should not go unpunished. As argued above, there is almost always an inevitable state connection in the perpetration of this crime. Yet, although there is a dual responsibility for genocide—state and individual—those states which commit, aid or abet genocide are not shouldering their criminal responsibility *qua* the main culprit of the crime which to date continues to enjoy absolute unconditional immunity from prosecution and punishment before the International Criminal Court and can be effectively carried out by a state with criminal impunity.

Despite serious political, legal, and procedural challenges, this chapter has argued in favour of state criminal responsibility for genocide and against state immunity for this crime. International Law has evolved considerably since the adoption of the Genocide Convention. Relevant factors have been the establishment of the ICTR, ICTY, and ICC with their attendant interpretations of international genocide law; the ICJ pronouncing itself on the Convention by way of advisory and contentious jurisdictions; the ILC drawing up its draft articles on state responsibility; the international community recognizing corporate criminal liability; the evolution of the concept of joint criminal enterprise; the application of the concept of command responsibility by the ICJ and the ICTY; the recognition of a dual responsibility for genocide;[96] developments in treaty law and case law limiting absolute state responsibility; and a series of inroads into state responsibility. Thanks to all these and other slow but sure developments, states are recognizing that genocide is a crime of state. What is important at this juncture is that the international community of states moves on from such recognition to holding genocidal states liable not only for a civil wrongful act of genocide but, more importantly, for state criminal responsibility for genocide. Unless and until this is done, genocide will not be successfully outlawed but will continue to linger on causing much suffering and hardship to humankind, as well as hefty resources will have to be spent by the international community to provide redress and contribute towards rebuilding. Genocide, after all, is not only the crime of state but also an affront to the rule of law and to human dignity, on which the whole edifice of international human rights law is constructed. The international community is running out of time to do the right thing—to criminalize state responsibility for genocide. It should implement what it has postponed for so long and pass on to approve, as promptly as possible, and bring into force imminently draft article 7 of the United Nations International Law Commission's draft articles on immunity of state officials from foreign criminal jurisdiction thereby denying state immunity in the case of genocide (and other serious international crimes). In the same way that a corporation is not allowed to hide its corporate guilt for the perpetration of a criminal offence behind its directors, managers, and other high-ranking employees, the state should not continue to be allowed to hide its corporate guilt

[96] This has been specifically acknowledged by the ICJ: 'The Court observes that that duality of responsibility continues to be a constant feature of international law.' International Court of Justice, *Bosnia v Serbia* (n 21) para 173.

behind a few state rulers and officials. The problematic application, or lack thereof, of the Genocide Convention over the past seven decades clearly points out that it is high time that it be revisited, *inter alia*, to extend it to cater for state criminal responsibility for genocide. This is necessary if the promise of 'never again' is to be turned into an effective policy.

3

The Role of Law in Enabling Postgenocide Recovery

Assessing the Importance of Property Restitution

Rajika L Shah

> [P]art and parcel of every genocide is theft.[1]

Introduction

In the aftermath of genocide or mass atrocity, the priority for survivors is to seek safety, shelter, and a means of supporting themselves and any remaining members of their families and former communities. Uprooted from their homes, driven away from everything familiar, and lacking in all but the most basic resources, they do what they can to rebuild their lives out of the tatters and trauma that remain. It is likely to be years, decades, or even generations before they can realistically imagine attempting to recover property taken during the genocide. By that point, written records may be lost or destroyed, individuals with firsthand knowledge of what was lost may have died, and families may no longer have ties to their home place.

As they struggle to regain a semblance of their previous normality, survivors, neighbouring states, and the international community grapple with the immense needs and challenges of holding perpetrators accountable, compiling an accurate and detailed evidentiary and historical record, rebuilding torn communities, and moving forward on a more stable footing. As victim groups and societies struggle to move forward, the question of restitution—specifically, restitution (or compensation) of real and personal property stolen, lost, or destroyed during genocide—plays a vital role in the process of transitional justice. Without recognition and redress specifically for the staggering amounts of property typically lost or stolen in a genocide, the aspiration for reconciliation that allows survivor groups to not only acknowledge the past but transcend it—transforming loss, pain, and anger into

[1] Michael J Bazyler, *Holocaust, Genocide, and the Law: A Quest for Justice in a Post-Holocaust World* (OUP 2016) 153 (hereafter Bazyler, *Holocaust, Genocide, and the Law*).

Rajika L Shah, *The Role of Law in Enabling Postgenocide Recovery* In: *Postgenocide.* Edited by: Klejda Mulaj, Oxford University Press (2021). © The Several Contributors. DOI: 10.1093/oso/9780192895189.003.0003

new growth—can remain frustratingly slow, even elusive. Reparative justice is thus 'both a moral and legal imperative'.[2]

Law is a seemingly powerful tool that can deliver at least 'some measure' of justice.[3] The international law of reparations requires states to make full amends to one who suffered a legal injury due to the state's internationally wrongful acts.[4] Restitution, and compensation where restitution is not available, is a core form of reparations. While traditionally this law applied only as between states, modern international human rights law is widely understood to have modified these obligations to include substantive and procedural remedial duties owed by states towards individuals.[5]

The fundamental assumption underlying these laws is that they apply to all uniformly and equally. Unfortunately, restitution, in full or in part, is not available to all. Whether a particular claimant is able to obtain restitution, and how much, is heavily dependent on a variety of factors which may include nationality, date, and location of the atrocities, intervening changes in the law, and political will. Major challenges arise with respect to the forum, scope of claims, and identification of victims and victim groups, not to mention availability of funds. Certain property claims may be included within the scope of a mass claims compensation scheme, but typically not the full range of property losses which can include real property, insurance claims, bank deposits, looted assets, artwork, and cultural objects, and household goods.[6] Domestic property claims made in litigation are subject to wide disparities in treatment due to individual differences in factual circumstances, as well as an array of legal doctrines that present hurdles for plaintiffs to overcome. Internationally, states may, but often do not, espouse the individual claims of their nationals in a state-to-state dispute. International human rights law expressly seeks to hold states accountable for their unlawful actions towards individuals, including their own nationals, but depends on the existence of a competent tribunal capable of providing and enforcing an effective remedy. International criminal law has

[2] Carla Ferstman and Mariana Goetz, 'Introduction' in Carla Ferstman and Mariana Goetz (eds), *Reparations for Victims of Genocide, War Crimes and Crimes against Humanity: Systems in Place and Systems in the Making* (2nd edn, Brill Nijhoff 2020) 5.

[3] Michael Marrus, *Some Measure of Justice: The Holocaust Era Restitution Campaign of the 1990s* (University of Wisconsin Press 2006) (hereafter Marrus, *Some Measure*); Ernesto Verdeja, 'A Normative Theory of Reparations in Transitional Democracies' in Claudia Card and Armen T Marsoobian (eds), *Genocide's Aftermath: Responsibility and Repair* (Wiley-Blackwell 2007) 166 (hereafter Verdeja, 'Normative Theory').

[4] Case Concerning the Factory at Chorzów (Claim for Indemnity) (*Germany v Poland*) (Merits) [1928] PCIJ Series A, No 17 (hereafter *Germany v Poland*).

[5] See, eg, Theo van Boven, 'Victims' Rights to a Remedy and Reparation: the United Nations Principles and Guidelines' in Carla Ferstman and Mariana Goetz (eds), *Reparations for Victims of Genocide, War Crimes and Crimes against Humanity: Systems in Place and Systems in the Making* (2nd edn, Brill Nijhoff 2020) 23; Richard Falk, 'Reparations, International Law, and Global Justice' in Pablo de Greiff (ed), *The Handbook of Reparations* (OUP 2006) 484–85 (hereafter Falk, 'Reparations').

[6] Arturo J Carrillo and Jason S Palmer, 'Transnational Mass Claim Processes (TMCPs) in International Law and Practice' (2010) 28(2) Berkeley J Intl L 343, 404–06.

moved towards victim-centred remedies including a right to compensation, most prominently at the International Criminal Court ('ICC'). However, many questions remain as to when compensation will be awarded, whether it can or should cover property claims, and how it will be funded.

The ability of law to adequately and fairly address the need for restitution to genocide survivors is thus open to question. Has law failed in its capacity to deliver justice? These shortcomings are widely acknowledged, at least among experts working in these fields.[7] At least one historian, commenting broadly on 'the gap between the universalistic rhetoric of legalism and the reality of ongoing impunity for certain states and mass murderers with the right connections to other powerful states and interests', has depressingly concluded that law is unlikely to have 'the remotest qualifying influence over the desperate pursuit of group and state interest'.[8] Indeed, it has been suggested that perhaps little more can reasonably be expected.[9]

This chapter, in recognizing the centrality of property theft to victims' lived experience of genocide and assessing the state of law and legal mechanisms requiring restitution and compensation in the postHolocaust setting, is more hopeful. It argues that, since the Holocaust of the Second World War and largely as a result of the success of sustained Holocaust restitution efforts in the decades since the Second World War ended, international and domestic law have increasingly required restitution for the victims of mass atrocities. Though developments in the law may be slow-moving, compensation for injuries and restitution of property taken during genocide are now considered vital components of transitional justice mechanisms.[10] Further, while there is undoubtedly more progress to be made in universalizing the availability, coverage, and rate of restitution following a mass atrocity, it is also clear that restitution as a legal requirement is increasingly the norm. There is, in fact, significant movement towards greater material accountability by those

[7] Luc Walleyn, 'The Role of Victims' Lawyers in Reparation Claims' in Carla Ferstman and Mariana Goetz (eds), *Reparations for Victims of Genocide, War Crimes and Crimes against Humanity: Systems in Place and Systems in the Making* (2nd edn, Brill Nijhoff 2020) 386 (hereafter Walleyn, 'Role of Victims' Lawyers') ('And yes, very few cases lead to any real reparation'); Falk, 'Reparations' (n 5) 484 (stating that the human right to an effective remedy 'tends to be unavailable where it is needed most'); Naomi Roht-Arriaza, 'Reparations in the aftermath of repression and mass violence' in Eric Stover and Harvey M Weinstein (eds), *My Neighbour, My Enemy: Justice and Community in the Aftermath of Mass Atrocity* (CUP 2004) 121 (hereafter Roht-Arriaza, 'Reparations') (affirming that 'few reparations have actually been paid to victims of war crimes and human rights abuses in the wake of mass violence').

[8] Donald Bloxham, 'Milestones and Mythologies: The Impact of Nuremberg' in Patricia Heberer and Jürgen Matthäus (eds), *Atrocities on Trial: Historical Perspectives on the Politics of Prosecuting War Crimes* (University of Nebraska Press 2008) 279–80.

[9] Agnes Heller, 'Rights, Modernity, Democracy,' in Drucilla Cornell et al (eds), *Deconstruction and the Possibility of Justice* (Routledge 1992) 355, 360 (hereafter Heller 'Rights') ('[I]f everyone is born free, everyone has to be equal before the law and receive maximum protection under the law.... Yet equal and maximum protection under the law and equal access to power are never completely realized.').

[10] See Verdeja, 'Normative Theory' (n 3) 170; Basic Principles and Guidelines on the Right to a Remedy and Reparation for Victims of Gross Violations of International Human Rights Law and Serious Violations of International Humanitarian Law, Commission on Human Rights, UN Gen Assembly, UN Doc A/RES/60/147 (Annex) (16 December 2005) (hereafter Basic Principles).

who bear responsibility for or are complicit in the perpetration of genocide. This movement, though flawed, has succeeded in providing victims and survivors with a growing and necessary arsenal of legal tools to obtain redress—and, as a result and perhaps even more crucially, with the accompanying sense that their losses, and their suffering, matter.

Property Theft Accompanying Genocide is Itself a Form of Genocide[11]

Victims of genocide and other mass atrocities indisputably have individual claims for their own personal injuries and for the loss of the lives of their loved ones. However, they also have claims for the property losses that accompany the atrocities.

Individual claims for restitution exist against both state and non-state actors. The claims may be directed at: (1) those who directly perpetrated the genocide or mass atrocity; (2) those who aided and abetted or facilitated the genocide or atrocity in some way; and (3) those who took no direct or indirect participation in the genocide or atrocity but nevertheless benefited from it by virtue of having received, purchased, or come into possession of property taken during the genocide or atrocity.

Postatrocity property losses typically include both personal and real property. Personal property losses can run from the mundane, such as household items, to valuable assets including agricultural livestock, insurance policies, bank accounts, or safe deposit boxes. Real estate losses are frequently devastating and may be the most difficult on which to recover; it is often the case that full documentation is lacking, there are subsequent inhabitants, or the state has taken over the property.[12] Whatever they consist of, these property losses are far from trivial. Not only do such property losses deprive the victims of their tangible assets—indeed, perhaps all their material wealth—at a time when they are most in need of resources, but they also rob victims of an essential sense of identity and self.[13]

At least one influential US court has recognized the centrality of property takings to the commission of genocide. In 2016, in *Simon v Hungary*, the US Court of Appeals for the District of Columbia explicitly held that property takings

[11] Portions of this section build on the author's previous work in Rajika L Shah, 'The Making of California's Art Recovery Statute: The Long Road to Section 338(c)(3),' (2017) 20 Chapman L Rev 1, 5–8 (hereafter Shah, 'Art Recovery'); and Michael J Bazyler and Rajika L Shah, 'The Unfinished Business of the Armenian Genocide: Armenian Property Restitution in American Courts,' (2017) 23 Southwestern J Intl L 223, 232–35 (hereafter Bazyler and Shah, 'Unfinished Business').

[12] Michael J Bazyler et al, *Searching for Justice After the Holocaust: Fulfilling the Terezin Declaration and Immovable Property Restitution* (OUP 2019) (hereafter Bazyler et al, *Searching for Justice*).

[13] Bazyler, *Holocaust, Genocide, and the Law* (n 1) 153–55.

themselves—apart from any murders—constitute a form of genocide.[14] The *Simon* plaintiffs were fourteen elderly Holocaust survivors originally from Hungary. They sued the Republic of Hungary and its state-owned Hungarian railway for having collaborated with the German Nazis in 1944–45, during the waning months of the Second World War, to perpetuate the deportation and extermination of nearly half a million Hungarian Jews.[15] Because the plaintiffs sued Hungary and a Hungarian state agency, jurisdiction over the defendants was governed exclusively by the Foreign Sovereign Immunities Act ('FSIA').[16] Unless one of the enumerated exceptions was met, the general rule applied and the foreign sovereign and the state railway would be immune from suit in US courts. The relevant exception in *Simon*, commonly known as the 'takings' or 'expropriation' exception, holds that a foreign sovereign and its related entities are not immune from suit in US courts if '[1] rights in property [2] taken in violation of international law are in issue and [3] that property or any property exchanged for such property is present in the United States' in connection with a specified commercial activity with a US nexus.[17]

The *Simon* plaintiffs' property-related claims for conversion and unjust enrichment satisfied the first element of the exception, and the state-owned railway did not dispute that it engaged in the requisite US-based commercial activity.[18] Thus, the key issue in *Simon* was whether plaintiffs' property had been 'taken in violation of international law'. Because there was no dispute that genocide itself violated international law, the court began its analysis by determining whether the alleged property takings '[bore] a sufficient connection to genocide that they amount to takings in violation of international law'.[19]

The *Simon* plaintiffs alleged a three-step governmental policy designed to inflict maximum destruction, carried out in the space of just three months. First, Hungarian Jews were targeted in a persecution campaign that included travel and certain clothing bans, bans from eating in restaurants or using public pools, and the requirement that every Jew wear the yellow Star of David.[20] Second, Jews were forced into cramped, unsanitary ghettos, and had their clothing removed. All of their property was systematically inventoried and confiscated by Hungarian officials going door to door.[21] Third and finally, Jews were rounded up and marched to the railways, all their remaining belongings confiscated, and they were transported

[14] *Simon v Republic of Hungary*, 812 F3d 127, 142 (D.C. Cir. 2016) (hereafter *Simon v Hungary*). Just as this chapter went to press, the U.S. Supreme Court granted a petition for writ of certiorari on a later ruling by the D.C. Circuit in *Simon*. 2020 WL 3578676 (Mem) (U.S. 2 July 2020) (No. 18-1447).

[15] ibid 134. The *Simon* plaintiffs brought causes of action for property loss, including conversion and unjust enrichment, as well as personal injury and international law claims.

[16] See *Argentine Republic v Amerada Hess Shipping Corp*, 488 US 428, 434 (1989) (stating that the FSIA is 'the sole basis for obtaining jurisdiction over a foreign state in our courts').

[17] 28 USC § 1605(a)(3).

[18] *Simon v Hungary* (n 14) 142, 147.

[19] ibid 142–43.

[20] ibid 133.

[21] ibid.

to Nazi death camps (primarily Auschwitz-Birkenau in German-occupied Poland) under the direction of Nazi mastermind Adolf Eichmann, where they were virtually all murdered upon arrival.[22]

As the above makes clear, widespread property confiscation was not merely incidental to the extermination of Hungarian Jews, it was part and parcel of an integrated plan to destroy the group, its way of life, and its culture.[23] The court accordingly held that 'the pivotal acts constituting genocide' as alleged in *Simon* 'are those set out in subsection (c) of the definition' of genocide as found in the Convention for the Prevention and Punishment of the Crime of Genocide ('Genocide Convention'), adopted by the United Nations in 1948 and entered into force in 1951.[24]

In other words, the property takings alleged by plaintiffs were intended to 'deliberately inflict … on the group conditions of life calculated to bring about its physical destruction in whole or in part'.[25] The court's view on this point was unambiguous: the property taken from Hungary's Jews did more than 'finance Hungary's war effort' and was not merely incident to the ghettoization of the Hungarian Jews.[26] Rather, the 'systematic, "wholesale plunder of Jewish property"' by Hungarian and German authorities was intended to deprive Jews of the resources they needed to survive as a people; the property was taken for the very purpose of ensuring the destruction of Hungary's Jews.[27] As a result, the international law violation required to establish the court's jurisdiction under the FSIA's takings exception was not the uncompensated expropriations, but rather genocide itself.[28]

In agreeing with the plaintiffs, the *Simon* court confirmed and further articulated the conclusion reached by the US Seventh Circuit Court of Appeals four years earlier in another case involving the theft of property of Hungarian Jews during the Second World War.[29] In *Abelesz v Magyar Nemzeti Bank*, the federal appellate court

[22] ibid 133–34.

[23] ibid 134.

[24] ibid 143. The Genocide Convention set forth for the first time a legal definition of genocide and criminalized genocidal activity, whether committed in peacetime or during war. Article II of the Convention defines genocide as:

> [A]ny of the following acts committed with intent to destroy, in whole or in part, a national, ethnical, racial or religious group, as such:
>
> (a) Killing members of the group;
> (b) Causing serious bodily or mental harm to members of the group;
> (c) Deliberately inflicting on the group conditions of life calculated to bring about its physical destruction in whole or in part;
> (d) Imposing measures intended to prevent births within the group;
> (e) Forcibly transferring children of the group to another group.

Convention on the Prevention and Punishment of the Crime of Genocide (opened for signature 9 December 1948, entered into force 12 January 1951) 78 UNTS 277, Art II.

[25] *Simon v Hungary* (n 14) 143.

[26] ibid.

[27] ibid (some internal formatting omitted).

[28] ibid 145.

[29] *Abelesz v Magyar Nemzeti Bank*, 692 F3d 661 (7th Cir 2012).

explained that acts of thievery such as 'the freezing of bank accounts, the [establishment of] straw-man control of corporations, the looting of safe deposit boxes and suitcases brought ... to the train stations, and even charging third-class train fares to victims being sent to death camps' is both a 'ghoulishly efficient' means of financing the rounding up and deportation or incarceration of the targeted group, and an 'integral part' of the genocide.[30]

Moreover, two years later in 2018 the DC Circuit further affirmed and expanded its fundamental holding in *Simon*. In *Philipp v Germany*, the court held—over Germany's strenuous objections—that 'seizures of art may constitute "takings of property that are themselves genocide".'[31] In doing so, the court recognized the myriad ways in which property takings, and particularly the taking of valuable items of cultural property, can form an integral part of genocide—even when they occur at early stages before mass killings take place.

The collection of art at issue in *Philipp* was known as the Welfenschatz, 'a unique collection of medieval relics and devotional art' composed of several dozen pieces that had for generations been housed in a German cathedral.[32] A Consortium of Jewish art dealers purchased the Welfenschatz in 1929 and shortly thereafter, after selling some of the pieces, stored the remainder of the collection in an Amsterdam warehouse.[33] After experiencing 'catastrophic economic hardship', persecution, and physical hardship, in 1935 the Consortium sold the Welfenschatz to the German state of Prussia, of which Hermann Goering was prime minister, for 'barely' 35 per cent of its value, and fled the country.[34]

The court explicitly acknowledged that:

> By seizing businesses' inventory—like the other economic pressures alleged in the complaint, such as the 'boycott of Jewish-owned businesses,' and 'exclu[sion]' of Jews from certain professions—the Nazis 'dr[ove] Jews out of their ability

[30] ibid 675. As fully stated by the court:

> Genocide, the complaints here clearly imply, can be an expensive proposition. Expropriating property from the targets of genocide has the ghoulishly efficient result of both paying for the costs associated with a systematic attempt to murder an entire people and leaving destitute any who manage to survive. The expropriations alleged by plaintiffs in these cases—the freezing of bank accounts, the straw-man control of corporations, the looting of safe deposit boxes and suitcases brought by Jews to the train stations, and even charging third-class train fares to victims being sent to death camps—should be viewed, at least on the pleadings, as an integral part of the genocidal plan to depopulate Hungary of its Jews. The expropriations thus effectuated genocide in two ways. They funded the transport and murder of Hungarian Jews, and they impoverished those who survived, depriving them of the financial means to reconstitute their lives and former communities.

[31] *Philipp v Germany*, 894 F3d 406, 411 (DC Cir 2018), *cert granted*, 2020 WL 3578677 (Mem) (U.S.2 July 2020) (No 19-351).

[32] ibid 409.

[33] ibid.

[34] ibid.

> to make a living,' and thereby, in the words of the Genocide Convention, 'inflict[ed] ... conditions of life calculated to bring about [a group's] physical destruction in whole or'—at the very least—'in part.'[35]

Further, there was no reason not to consider the forced sales of art imposed by the Nazis—characterized by a 'pretense' of negotiations, 'purchases' from 'powerless counterparties', and the impossibility for Jewish dealers to sell their art on the open market—as genocidal takings.[36] That these takings occurred during 'earlier steps' of the Holocaust characterized by 'isolation and expropriation' rather than the later 'ghettoization and deportation' was irrelevant because the genocide occurred in steps beginning as early as 1933.[37]

Finally, in a discussion with perhaps the most far-reaching implications, the court directly connected the takings with a genocidal intent to destroy. Holding that, as in *Simon*, the takings evidenced a desire 'to deprive [German] Jews of the resources needed to survive as a people', the court noted allegations that the Welfenschatz was 'historically, artistically and national-politically valuable'—an 'iconic' collection of German 'Aryan' heritage which was appropriated by Nazis who regarded the Consortium as 'state's enemies' for owning it.[38] Once the prominent and successful Consortium members were made vulnerable, 'Prussian interest in the Welfenschatz was ... revived'.[39]

These conclusions comport with victims' sense of why property takings are at the core of genocidal activity, and place property claims at the heart of any effort to restore victims to wholeness. Though *Simon* and *Philipp* were decided in the context of the Holocaust, the experience is virtually universal. Every victim group experiences mass private and communal property takings during genocide, and often as a form of genocide itself.[40]

[35] ibid 412 (internal citations and some formatting omitted).

[36] ibid.

[37] ibid 413.

[38] ibid 413–14.

[39] ibid.

[40] In a telling illustration of both the precariousness and importance of law in providing avenues for redress, these important rulings in both *Simon* and *Philipp* now hang in the balance; just as this chapter went to press, the U.S. Supreme Court agreed to review both cases on petitions filed by Hungary and Germany respectively. *Republic of Hungary v Simon*, 2020 WL 3578676 (Mem) (U.S. 2 July 2020) (No. 18-1447); *Federal Republic of Germany v Philipp*, 2020 WL 3578677 (Mem) (U.S. 2 July 2020) (No 19-351). The jurisdictional issue is at the core of the petitions, as are questions of international comity—a doctrine of prudential abstention in which the courts of one nation, in recognition of the legislative, executive, and judicial acts of another nation, may decline to hear a case notwithstanding the existence of valid jurisdiction.

Full Reparation Requires Recognition of Both Material and Moral Injury

In international law, restitution is considered a form of reparation, which includes both restitution and compensation.[41] As stated by the Permanent Court of International Justice in the seminal Chorzów Factory case in 1928: 'The essential principle contained in the actual notion of an illegal act ... is that reparation must, as far as possible, wipe out all the consequences of the illegal act and reestablish the situation which would, in all probability, have existed if that act had not been committed.'[42] The court required '[r]estitution in kind, or, if this is not possible, payment of a sum corresponding to the value which a restitution in kind would bear'.[43] This widely followed theory of reparation—which was affirmed by the UN General Assembly in the (nonbinding) 2005 Basic Principles and Guidelines on the Right to a Remedy and Reparation for Victims of Gross Violations of International Human Rights Law and Serious Violations of International Humanitarian Law ('Basic Principles')—is focused on restoring the injured party to the *status quo ante* and is not concerned with the consequences or cost of reparation to the wrongdoer.[44] Though it may provide a form of remedial justice, it has been criticized as embodying nothing more than a popular assumption rather than resting on any 'positive argument', as well as resulting in 'absurd notions of compensation' that limit potential compensation for, eg, descendants of victims who suffer their own forms of inherited loss but cannot be said to have themselves been injured by the primary atrocity.[45]

Modernly, a state's international obligation to make reparation for internationally wrongful acts encompasses both material and moral injuries caused by such acts.[46] Material damage is here defined as 'damage to property or other interests of the State and its nationals which is assessable in financial terms'.[47] Moral damage, on the other hand, 'includes such items as individual pain and suffering, loss of

[41] There are a wide range of reparations measures that go beyond these remedies, such as the establishment of clinics or medical monitoring, remembrance, memory, and education initiatives, and the creation or strengthening of national mechanisms to combat impunity. Martha Minow, *Between Vengeance and Forgiveness: Facing History after Genocide and Mass Violence* (Beacon Press 1998) 3–4, 92–93 (hereafter Minow, *Vengeance and Forgiveness*). Though these measures may play an important or even essential role in postgenocide transitional justice, this chapter focuses exclusively on restitution and compensation as specific forms of reparation.

[42] *Germany v Poland* (n 4) 47. This has been described as the 'counterfactual conception of compensation'. See, eg, Rodney C Roberts, 'The Counterfactual Conception of Compensation' in Claudia Card and Armen T Marsoobian (eds), *Genocide's Aftermath: Responsibility and Repair* (Wiley-Blackwell 2007) 166 (hereafter Roberts, 'Counterfactual').

[43] Roberts, 'Counterfactual' (n 42) 166.

[44] Basic Principles (n 10) para 19.

[45] Roberts, 'Counterfactual' (n 42) 134–43.

[46] Draft Articles on the Responsibility of States for Internationally Wrongful Acts, Intl L Commn, with Commentaries, 53 UN GAOR Supp (No. 10) at 43, UN Doc A/56/10 (3 August 2001) (hereafter Draft Articles) Art 31; Basic Principles (n 10) para 18.

[47] Draft Articles (n 46) Commentary to Art 31 at (5).

loved ones or personal affront associated with an intrusion on one's home or private life'.[48] International law recognizes that moral damage, as defined thus, may not be readily susceptible to restitution or financial compensation, and to that extent requires what is known as satisfaction.[49] Satisfaction may take the form of, *inter alia*, 'acknowledgement of the breach, an expression of regret, a formal apology or another appropriate modality', and is considered an exceptional remedy—often symbolic.[50] In this way, satisfaction reflects what some have called 'reparative justice' (as a form of 'corrective justice')—justice that provides 'a way of vindicating the dignity of those who are wrongfully injured' and 'so far as possible forces injurers to recognize, acknowledge, and honor their victim's rights'.[51]

In the case of genocide or other mass atrocity, the need for satisfaction as a form of reparation is acute—and, indeed, may be the only form of reparation many survivors and their descendants either seek or are willing to accept.[52] The failure to honour such claims—or worse, the outright denial that the wrong even occurred—is often cited as a crucial factor preventing victim groups from fully participating in social, economic, and civic life postatrocity and in perpetuating intergenerational trauma. It makes sense, then, that 'any theory of reparations must include both material and symbolic components' if it is to have any hope of moving the affected groups closer toward reconciliation, inclusivity, and healing.[53]

These two forms of reparation, the material and the moral, are thus inextricably linked. As will be seen below, the ability of law to achieve restitution for property losses incurred during genocide is often, though not always, a function of wrongdoers' willingness to acknowledge a moral responsibility.

Holocaust Restitution: A Model of Success[54]

Following the Second World War, the world Jewish community made reparations for a variety of wartime injuries a priority.[55] Holocaust restitution efforts continued for the next seventy years, and included restitution for both Jews and other victim groups.[56] These remarkable efforts led to compensation totalling more than $100

[48] ibid.

[49] ibid Commentary to Art 36 at (1); ibid Art 37(1).

[50] ibid Art 37(2); ibid Commentary to Art 37 at (1), (3).

[51] Haig Khatchadourian, 'Compensation and Reparation as Forms of Compensatory Justice' in Claudia Card and Armen T Marsoobian (eds), *Genocide's Aftermath: Responsibility and Repair* (Wiley-Blackwell 2007) 148, 155.

[52] Walleyn, 'Role of Victims' Lawyers' (n 7) 386; Roht-Arriaza, 'Reparations' (n 7) 130.

[53] Verdeja, 'Normative Theory' (n 3) 166, 178–82.

[54] For further reference or discussion of these points, see also Bazyler and Shah, 'Unfinished Business' (n 11) 235–40.

[55] Marrus, *Some Measure* (n 3) 65.

[56] See Carol Kino, 'Stolen Artworks and the Lawyers Who Reclaim Them' *New York Times* (New York, 28 March 2007) H28.

billion in today's dollars from successive German governments alone for individual and community-based payments.[57] Austrian, French, and Dutch government or government agency payments, together with various Holocaust restitution litigation settlements, total at least another $2 billion.[58]

Holocaust restitution was accomplished through three succeeding waves of activity.[59] During the first period of postHolocaust restitution, immediately after the war, the Allied countries focused on recovering and returning assets stolen by the Nazis throughout Europe, including but not limited to stolen Jewish property.[60]

The second period began in 1949, when sovereignty was restored to Germany after the Allied occupation.[61] The major event in this period was a 1952 bilateral treaty between Germany and Israel known as the Luxembourg Agreement, named after the location where the treaty negotiations took place. Under the Luxembourg Agreement, West Germany (but not East Germany), formally known as the Federal Republic of Germany ('FRG'), agreed to make payments to the new state of Israel over the following decade.[62] The treaty also included a provision for lifetime payments to individual Holocaust survivors living in the West (Jewish survivors living behind the Iron Curtain were not covered) for the duration of their lives.[63]

The third period began in the 1990s and focused on restitution litigation in US courts.[64] Its purpose was to tackle the 'unfinished business' of the Holocaust by seeking to hold accountable private actors and state agencies for the benefits they received as a result of Nazi persecution of both Jews and non-Jews.[65] This included restitution of unreturned bank deposits, the largest portion from Swiss banks; payments arising from insurance policies taken out by Jews from European insurance companies and never paid; and compensation made by German multinational

[57] Statement of the Hon J Christian Kennedy, Special Envoy for Holocaust Issues, 'America's Role in Addressing Outstanding Holocaust Issues': Hearing Before the House of Representative's Committee on Foreign Affairs, Subcommittee on Europe, 110th Cong. 8, Serial No. 110-110 at 5 (3 October 2007) (hereafter Kennedy Hearing); see also Susan Slyomovics, *How to Accept German Reparations* (University of Pennsylvania Press 2014) 23 (noting that 'Germany has created the largest sustained redress program, ... a landmark process that set into motion a global legal transformation in how abuses by a state may be evaluated') (hereafter Slyomovics, *German Reparations*).

[58] Kennedy Hearing (n 57) 5–6.

[59] See Bazyler, *Holocaust, Genocide, and the Law* (n 1) 155.

[60] ibid 155–57.

[61] ibid 158–60.

[62] ibid, 158; see also Agreement between the State of Israel and the Federal Republic of Germany and the State of Israel (signed 10 September 1952, entered into force 25 March 1953) 162 UNTS 205, Art III (hereafter Germany-Israel Agreement).

[63] Germany-Israel Agreement (n 62) Art III.

[64] Bazyler, *Holocaust, Genocide, and the Law* (n 1) 161.

[65] Stuart E Eizenstat, *Imperfect Justice: Looted Assets, Slave Labor, and the Unfinished Business of World War II* (PublicAffairs 2003) (hereafter Eizenstat, *Imperfect Justice*); John Authers and Richard Wolffe, *The Victim's Fortune: Inside the Epic Battle over the Debts of the Holocaust* (HarperCollins 2002); Robert A Swift, 'Holocaust Litigation and Human Rights Jurisprudence' in Michael J Bazyler and Roger P Alford (eds), *Holocaust Restitution: Perspectives on the Litigation and Its Legacy* (New York University Press 2006) 50; Marrus, *Some Measure* (n 3) 20–21.

corporations and the German state to still-living individuals who laboured as slaves for these companies during the war.[66]

A number of individual lawsuits were also specifically directed toward compensation for the loss of stolen art. The most famous of these cases is *Altmann v Republic of Austria*,[67] a case that went all the way to the United States Supreme Court and was dramatized in the 2015 feature film, 'Woman in Gold', but there have been several others.[68] The record of success of these cases is mixed, and many were dismissed on technical grounds. These dismissals prompted Congress in 2016 to pass the Holocaust Expropriated Art Recovery Act ('HEAR Act').[69] Recognizing the difficulties facing claimants in US courts seeking to recover Holocaust-era stolen art, the HEAR Act extended the statute of limitations in all United States courts—state and federal—on such claims to six years following actual discovery of 'the identity and location of the artwork or other property' and 'a possessory interest of the claimant in the artwork or other property'.[70] The goal was to give effect to the longstanding US policy of restitution of Holocaust-era stolen property, as expressed in the Terezin Declaration and Washington Principles, among others, as well as to ensure that such suits are adjudicated on the merits and not tossed out on limitations grounds.[71]

The Holocaust restitution movement and accompanying litigation that began in the late 1990s led to multibillion dollar settlements with Swiss banks, French banks, and the state railway, the Dutch railway, Austrian companies, German companies, and multiple European insurance companies for their roles in facilitating and/or benefiting from the massive thievery that took place as European Jews were being persecuted and then murdered.[72] Perhaps most strikingly, the Holocaust restitution movement achieved unprecedented recognition by Germany of the state's financial responsibility for the crimes committed during the Holocaust. Ultimately, though the total amounts paid out fall far short of the restoration value of all property losses—and clearly there is no amount of money that can compensate for the lives lost and injuries suffered—the Holocaust restitution movement can be considered successful.

[66] Eizenstat, *Imperfect Justice* (n 65) xiii; Michael J Bazyler, *Holocaust Justice: The Battle for Restitution in America's Courts* (New York University Press 2003) 323.

[67] *Altmann v Republic of Austria*, 541 U.S. 677 (2004).

[68] See, eg, *Cassirer v Thyssen-Bornemisza Collection Foundation*, Civil Minutes—General (Judgment), Case No CV-05-3459 (CD Cal, 30 April 2019); *Von Saher v Norton Simon Museum of Art at Pasadena*, 897 F3d 1141 (9th Cir 2018), cert denied, 139. 2616 (20 May 2019); *Museum of Fine Arts, Boston v Seger-Thomschitz*, 623 F3d 1 (1st Cir 2010); *Konowaloff v Metropolitan Museum of Art*, 702 F3d (2d Cir 2012); *Malewicz v City of Amsterdam*, 517 F Supp 2d 322 (DDC 2007); *Detroit Institute of Arts v Ullin*, No 06-10333, 2007 WL 1016996, at *1 (ED Mich, 31 March 2007); *Toledo Museum of Art v Ullin*, 477 F Supp 2d 802 (ND Ohio 2006).

[69] Pub L 114–308, 114th Congress, HR 6130 (22 USC § 1621 note) (16 December 2016).

[70] ibid § 5(a).

[71] ibid § 3.

[72] Bazyler, *Holocaust, Genocide, and the Law* (n 1) 161–68; see also Kennedy Hearing (n 57) 5–6; see generally Marrus, *Some Measure* (n 3).

PostHolocaust Challenges to Enforcement

One major question is whether the success experienced by the Holocaust restitution movement can be replicated in other contexts, or whether it was unique to that particular set of historical, legal, and political circumstances. To date, while there has been substantial development in legal standards and mechanisms enabling postatrocity restitution, no other genocide survivor group has achieved anywhere near similar results.

US-based Litigation

Following the success of the Holocaust restitution movement, by the mid-2000s there was much reason for optimism regarding mass atrocity restitution lawsuits filed in American courts.[73] Not surprisingly, a wide range of other victim groups also attempted to achieve redress through lawsuits in US courts, hoping for similar results.[74]

Perhaps the most well-known of these are the Armenian genocide restitution cases. The Armenian genocide civil suits explicitly followed the Holocaust civil litigation model. The Armenian genocide restitution movement began with insurance litigation filed in California federal courts against New York Life Insurance Company and French insurance company AXA.[75] Both companies did business in Ottoman Turkey, where they had sold insurance policies to the Ottoman Armenians during the early years of the twentieth century, but had never paid on these policies. These initial Armenian suits were successful, reaching separate settlements totalling nearly $40 million.[76] However, none of the successive Armenian suits for financial crimes—the return of looted assets, bank deposits, and insurance claims against different companies—resulted in a positive outcome. Suits against the Republic of Turkey and Turkish state banks for compensation resulting from the unlawful expropriation of Armenian real property during the

[73] Michael J Bazyler, 'From "Lamentation and Liturgy to Litigation": The Holocaust-Era Restitution Movement As a Model For Bringing Armenian Genocide-Era Restitution Suits In American Courts' (2011) 95 Marquette L Rev 245; Bazyler, *Holocaust, Genocide, and the Law* (n 1) 153–83.

[74] See, eg, *In re World War II Era Japanese Forced Labor Litigation*, 114 F Supp 2d 939, 940 (ND Cal 2000) (suit brought by Korean 'comfort women'); *Balintulo v Ford Motor Co*, 796 F3d 160 (2d Cir 2015); *Balintulo v Daimler A.G.*, 727 F3d 174, 175 (2d Cir 2013); *Khulumani v Barclay Nat'l Bank Ltd*, 504 F3d 254, 255–256 (2d Cir 2007) (suits against multinationals arising out of their business activities in apartheid South Africa); *In re African-American Slave Descendants Litigation*, 471 F3d 754 (7th Cir 2006) (claims by African-Americans for reparations against the US government and American companies involved in slavery arising from the American slave era).

[75] See 'Turkey Sued in California Over Armenian Genocide' *Reuters* (30 July 2010) <http://www.reuters.com/article/us-usa-turkey-genocide-idUSTRE66T5LH20100730> accessed 28 June 2020.

[76] ibid.

genocide also failed—after a long, nearly unprecedented six-year wait while the federal appellate court debated its decision, also on statute of limitations grounds.[77]

Descendants of survivors of what is sometimes called the 'first' genocide of the twentieth century, which was perpetrated by Germany starting in 1885 and escalated into an all-out campaign of extermination between 1904 and 1909 against the Herero and Nama peoples in southwestern Africa, now Namibia, have filed numerous lawsuits in US courts also following the Holocaust restitution model. Two initial suits filed in the mid-2000s against German companies that allegedly benefited from the genocide followed the financial crimes model, while a third suit filed in 2017 sought compensation directly from Germany.[78] Again, all were dismissed on technical grounds. Germany's consistent position in the litigation was that it was under no legal obligation to make reparations to the Herero and Nama since no such obligation existed at the time of the events.[79] In recent years, perhaps fuelled in part by a 1985 report from the UN Economic and Social Council's Commission on Human Rights concluding that a genocide did occur, Germany has entered into direct settlement negotiations with the Namibian government in a tacit acknowledgment of at least a 'political–moral' obligation.[80]

Survivors of the genocide in Darfur and mass atrocities in other parts of Sudan also have attempted to obtain redress from the French banking giant BNP Paribas for its complicity in the atrocities. In 2014, the bank pled guilty in the United States to criminal activity in violation of US sanctions and federal and state law in processing billions of dollars of US dollar-denominated oil transactions on behalf of the Sudanese government.[81] The 2016 suit, filed in New York, alleged that the bank's unlawful activity allowed Sudan to fund the genocide and purchase the arms and weapons it used to commit atrocities. In a rare victory for plaintiffs, the federal appellate court held that the suit could not be dismissed on the basis of the act of state doctrine, which forbids US courts from sitting in judgment on the valid acts of a foreign sovereign, because acts of genocide, ethnic cleansing, and other mass atrocities alleged by plaintiffs could never be considered valid in international law.[82] The court further held that plaintiffs' claims were not time-barred and could

[77] See *Bakalian v Central Bank of Turkey*, 932 F3d 1229 (9th Cir 2019).

[78] *Rukoro v Federal Republic of Germany*, 363 FSupp3d 436 (SDNY 2019); *Herero People's Reparations Corp v Deutsche Bank, AG*, 370 F3d 1192, 1193 (DC Cir 2004); *Hereros ex rel Riruako v Deutsche Afrika-Linien Gmblt & Co*, 232 F App'x. 90, 93 (3d Cir 2007).

[79] 'US judge dismisses Namibian genocide claims against Germany' *DW.com* (7 March 2019) <https://p.dw.com/p/3EdCN> accessed 25 June 2020 (citing German legal representative Ruprecht Polenz that 'we've always said that it's not a legal but a political-moral issue').

[80] Daniel Pelz, 'Namibians losing patience over German slowness to act on genocide claims' *DW.com* (9 May 2018) <https://p.dw.com/p/2xQIp> accessed 25 June 2020.

[81] 'BNP Paribas Agrees to Plead Guilty and to Pay $8.9 Billion for Illegally Processing Financial Transactions for Countries Subject to U.S. Economic Sanctions', Press Release, US Dept of Justice, Office of Public Affairs (30 June 2014) <https://www.justice.gov/opa/pr/bnp-paribas-agrees-plead-guilty-and-pay-89-billion-illegally-processing-financial> accessed 25 June 2020.

[82] *Kashef v BNP Paribas SA*, 925 F3d 53, 60–62 (2d Cir 2019) (hereafter *Kashef v BNP Paribas*).

proceed.[83] Only time will tell if the suit is ultimately successful. However, even if plaintiffs ultimately prevail and BNP Paribas is required to pay compensation to the victims, the claimant class is limited to Sudanese individuals lawfully residing in the United States as refugees or asylees, and does not extend to those still living in Sudan or neighbouring regions.[84] A previous suit brought against Canadian oil and gas giant Talisman Energy, Inc, for its alleged role in aiding and abetting the Sudanese government in committing atrocities in southern Sudan, was dismissed after years of litigation.[85]

Much of the difference in outcome between the settlements achieved by Holocaust victims and the failure to obtain redress by other groups of victims is reflected in the difference in approach and attitude of the defendants: while Germany and German companies ultimately expressed remorse for the Holocaust and sought to move past that difficult chapter in their history by laying the outstanding claims to rest, different political considerations and pressures are at play in these other situations. For example, Germany has resisted acknowledging its actions against the Herero and Nama as genocide,[86] and Turkey steadfastly refuses to recognize the massacres of the Armenians as a genocide.[87] Sudan's long-running president Omar al-Bashir, the architect of the country's worst atrocities over decades of conflict whose arrest warrants from the International Criminal Court have been outstanding since 2009, was ousted from office in April 2019; it remains to be seen whether the interim ruling coalition government will either prosecute him domestically or turn him over to the ICC for prosecution.[88]

In addition, with respect to the Armenian and Herero/Nama lawsuits the length of time that passed between the events at issue and the claimant litigation was a major contributing factor; the same time concerns did not apply in the Sudanese-BNP Paribas litigation largely because the suit was filed shortly after the bank's admitted criminality was made public.[89]

It is also the case that none of the Holocaust restitution lawsuits, most filed as class actions, ever reached trial; the ones that did succeed were the result of

[83] ibid 62.

[84] ibid 57.

[85] *Presbyterian Church of Sudan v Talisman Energy, Inc*, 582 F3d 244 (2d Cir 2009).

[86] See *Herero People's Reparations Corp v Deutsche Bank, AG*, 370 F3d 1192, 1193 (DC Cir 2004); *Hereros ex rel Riruako v Deutsche Afrika-Linien Gmblt & Co*, 232 F App'x 90, 93 (3d Cir 2007).

[87] See, eg, 'The Events of 1915 and the Turkish-Armenian Controversy over History: An Overview' Republic of Turkey Ministry of Foreign Affairs <http://www.mfa.gov.tr/the-events-of-1915-and-the-turkish-armenian-controversy-over-history_-an-overview.en.mfa> accessed 25 June 2020.

[88] See 'Omar al-Bashir: Sudan's Ousted President' *BBC News* (14 August 2019) <https://www.bbc.com/news/world-africa-16010445> accessed 25 June 2020. As of this writing, one person wanted in connection with the situation in Darfur (Sudan) is in the custody of the International Criminal Court. Ali Muhammad Ali Abd–Al-Rahman ('Ali Kushayb'), suspected of war crimes and crimes against humanity in Darfur between 2003-04, voluntarily surrendered to ICC custody on 9 June 2020. Many hope that this development signals renewed vigour in the Darfur prosecutions, and perhaps is a first step in bringing Bashir to the ICC.

[89] *Kashef v BNP Paribas SA* (n 82), 62–63.

negotiated settlements between the parties. Many were dismissed outright on technical grounds: statute of limitations, political question, lack of subject matter jurisdiction, and *forum non conveniens*.[90] These same defences, and others—international comity, foreign affairs preemption, act of state doctrine—have successfully been used by defendants in numerous cases seeking restitution or compensation for losses during genocide.[91]

Diplomatic Protection under International Law

International law presents similarly challenging circumstances for claimants seeking restitution for property losses incident to genocide or other mass atrocities. Because states and not individuals are the primary subjects of international law, many processes grounded in international law operate only at the state-to-state level. Traditionally, individuals seeking reparations from a foreign state could seek redress under the doctrine of diplomatic protection. Pursuant to this 'elementary principle of international law', the state of the individual's nationality could espouse the claims and pursue remedies on the individual's behalf, either through diplomatic channels or in an international judicial setting.[92]

This bedrock principle lies at the heart of a number of international mechanisms. The International Court of Justice ('ICJ'), the judicial organ of the United Nations, has jurisdiction to hear disputes only between states.[93] Though there have been several instances in which states have brought claims on behalf of their nationals before the ICJ, they are relatively rare and, not surprisingly, typically involve political considerations as to when the espousing state will agree to take up its individual national's cause. These can include the type and gravity of injuries suffered, importance of the damage suffered not only to the individual but to the home state itself, relationship between the home state and the defendant state, and difference in political orientation and/or legal systems of the two states.[94] To date, no state has been willing to bring claims before the ICJ on behalf of its own nationals against another state where the individual harm resulted from genocide or other mass atrocity.

[90] See *In re Holocaust Victim Assets Litigation*, 105 F Supp 2d at 140–42; *Simon v Hungary* (n 14) 132 (holding that federal courts do not have jurisdiction over claims for personal injury or death against a foreign sovereign).

[91] For further reference or discussion of these points, see generally Shah, 'Art Recovery'; Bazyler and Shah, 'Unfinished Business' (n 11) 240–41, 243.

[92] The Mavrommatis Palestine Concessions (*Greece v United Kingdom*) (Judgment) [1924] PCIJ (ser B) No 3, at 12.

[93] Statute of the International Court of Justice (opened for signature 26 June 1945, entered into force 24 October 1945) 3 Bevans 1179, 59 Stat 1031, Art 34(1).

[94] Wilhelm Karl Geck, 'Diplomatic Protection' in *Max Planck Encyclopedia of Public International Law* (1987) 1062 (hereafter Geck, 'Diplomatic Protection').

The doctrine of diplomatic protection has proved somewhat more useful for genocide victims seeking reparations through direct state-to-state negotiations. The armistice agreements and the 1947 Paris Peace Treaties that ended the Second World War each included clauses requiring the protection, return, and/or compensation of property. Several European countries also entered into a large number of bilateral claims settlement agreements, both with the United States and with each other, that addressed compensation for property confiscated during the war, property confiscated due to nationalizations after the war, or both.[95] Typically, these bilateral agreements provided for a lump-sum payment by one nation to the other nation in full settlement of all claims of one state's nationals against the other state—regardless of whether the settlement amount was sufficient to provide full satisfaction of all the claims.

Indeed, though these bilateral settlement agreements resulted in payments totalling hundreds of millions of dollars—a significant payout for individuals who otherwise would have had little to no opportunity to press their claims directly, or at all—they were far from perfect. None of the postwar lump sum settlements were large enough to pay 100 per cent of valid claims, and many recipients had to accept a small fraction of the total percentage of their claims; when a state has espoused a claim, it is entitled to settle that claim for any amount of money or no money at all, even as against the wishes of the claimant.[96]

Other limitations included whether the claimant had continuously held citizenship of the payee state from the time the property was confiscated until the date of the claim—a challenging requirement in the face of so much movement of people across borders before, during, and after the war, and certain date limitations—particularly in the case of many Eastern European countries that became communist after the war.[97]

International Human Rights Law

One of the most revolutionary advances in postwar international law is the development of human rights law. As a body of law expressly established to hold states accountable directly to individuals, through which states pledged to protect and respect a wide spectrum of fundamental rights, human rights law promised to end impunity for states that committed atrocities against their own citizens. It thus

[95] See generally Bazyler et al, *Searching for Justice* (n 12); Richard B Lillich and Burns H Weston, *International Claims: Their Settlement by Lump Sum Agreements* (University Press of Virginia 1975); Burns H Weston et al, *International Claims: Their Settlement by Lump Sum Agreements, 1975-1999* (Transnational Publishers 1975).

[96] Geck, 'Diplomatic Protection' (n 94) 1058.

[97] See generally Bazyler et al, *Searching for Justice* (n 12) (summarizing bilateral claims settlement agreements with and among the forty-seven countries signatory to the Terezin Declaration, pledging to restitute property confiscated during the Second World War).

held out the hope that individuals were now empowered by law to hold their own governments accountable for human rights abuses committed against them, and seek compensation for such abuses. However, enforcement of human rights norms is spotty and dependent on state consent, making meaningful compensation for death, injuries, and property losses incurred in mass atrocities largely illusory.

Though each of the major multilateral international human rights treaties establishes a Committee tasked with monitoring implementation by states parties, only some allow for the relevant Committee to hear individual petitions regarding alleged violations and award pecuniary compensation.[98] Moreover, states' acceptance of a Committee's competence to hear such petitions is voluntary and must typically be given through signature on a separate optional protocol or by submitting an affirmative declaration. None of the Committees' views are legally binding on the states to whom they are directed.

Regional human rights regimes are similarly limited by the scope of state consent, and by geographic reach.

The American Convention on Human Rights (ACHR) sets forth a complex system of competence as between the Inter-American Commission and Court to review individual petitions alleging violations of the treaty. All individual petitions must first be filed with the Commission, but states may opt out of the jurisdiction of either the Commission or the Court, or both.[99] Moreover, individuals may not apply directly to the Court.[100] One of the most important players in the Inter-American system, the United States, has signed but not ratified the ACHR; though the Commission hears individual petitions and issues reports regarding the United States, the United States does not recognize them as binding in any way and has not accepted the jurisdiction of the Court.

The African Commission on Human and Peoples' Rights is not expressly empowered to hear individual complaints.[101] Communications not from Member States can be considered, but only if they meet a fairly stringent set of procedural

[98] These are the First Optional Protocol to the International Covenant on Civil and Political Rights (opened for signature 19 December 1966, entered into force 23 March 1976) 999 UNTS 171 (ICCPR); International Convention on the Elimination of All Forms of Racial Discrimination (opened for signature 21 December 1965, entered into force 4 January 1969) 660 UNTS 195 (CERD); Convention against Torture and Other Cruel, Inhuman or Degrading Treatment or Punishment (opened for signature 10 December 1984, entered into force 26 June 1987) 1465 UNTS 85 (CAT); Optional Protocol to the Convention on the Elimination of All Forms of Discrimination against Women (opened for signature 10 December 1999, entered into force 22 December 2000) 2131 UNTS 83 (CEDAW); Optional Protocol to the Convention on the Rights of Persons with Disabilities (opened for signature 30 March 2007, entered into force 3 May 2008) 2518 UNTS 283 (CRPD); and International Convention for the Protection of All Persons from Enforced Disappearance (opened for signature 6 February 2007, entered into force 23 December 2010) 2716 UNTS 3 (CED).

[99] American Convention on Human Rights (opened for signature 22 November 1969, entered into force 18 July 1978) 1144 UNTS 123, Arts 45, 62.

[100] ibid Art 61.

[101] African Charter of Human and Peoples' Rights (opened for signature 27 June 1981, entered into force 21 October 1986) OAU Doc CAB/LEG/67/3 rev. 5, (1982) 21 ILM 58, Art 45.

and substantive requirements that clearly allow for political intervention at any number of points in the process.[102] The more recently established African Court of Human and Peoples' Rights can only hear cases brought by the Commission, by states parties that lodged a complaint at the Commission or against whom such a complaint was lodged, by a state party whose citizen is the victim of a human rights violation, and by African intergovernmental organizations.[103] Only eight states have signed on to the Court's jurisdiction, severely limiting the geographic and substantive scope of its review.[104]

The European human rights system contains more protections to ensure that judgments of the European Court of Human Rights are carried out. The Committee of Ministers of the Council of Europe, composed of the foreign ministers of each Member State or their permanent representatives, may supervise execution of the final judgment and, if found to be lacking, refer the situation back to the Court for a determination of whether the Member State has failed to fulfil its obligation to abide by the Court's judgments.[105] These measures were designed to create both legal and political incentives for compliance in advancement of the ultimate goal of universality, and are the most robust among the regional mechanisms. Even at the European Court, however, universality is elusive. From 1959, the first year of its establishment, through 2018 the Court found at least one violation in 84 per cent of the judgments it has ever delivered.[106] While recent reforms have enabled a large number (2,000+) of cases requiring ongoing supervision of execution by the Committee of Ministers—many of which involved ongoing violations—to be closed, significant questions remain as to the ability of Council of Europe mechanisms to achieve sustainable reform in a number of substantive areas and countries.[107]

Asia, which has the highest human population in the world, is also the only major region without any formal human rights treaty or mechanism whatsoever. On 18 November 2012, Association of Southeast Asian Nation ('ASEAN') Member States issued the ASEAN Human Rights Declaration ('AHRD') together with the Phnom Penh Statement on the Adoption of the AHRD. As there is no judicial or

[102] ibid Arts 55–59.

[103] Protocol to the African Charter on Human and Peoples' Rights on the Establishment of an African Court on Human and Peoples' Rights (opened for signature 9 June 1998, entered into force 25 January 2004), Art 5.

[104] Activity Report of the African Court on Human and Peoples' Rights (AfCHPR) 1 January–31 December 2018, EX.CL/1126(XXXIV), <http://www.african-court.org/en/images/Activity%20Reports/Activity%20report%20January%20-%20December%20%202018.pdf> accessed 25 June 2020, at 1.

[105] Convention for the Protection of Human Rights and Fundamental Freedoms (opened for signature 4 November 1950, entered into force 3 September 1953) 213 UNTS 222, 312 ETS 5, Art 46.

[106] Overview 1959-2018 ECHR, European Court of Human Rights (March 2019), at 3 <https://www.echr.coe.int/Documents/Overview_19592018_ENG.pdf> accessed 25 June 2020.

[107] Supervision of the Execution of Judgments and Decisions of the European Court of Human Rights 2018: 12th Annual Report of the Committee of Ministers, Council of Europe, Committee of Ministers (April 2019), at 7–9.

quasi-judicial body to hear individual complaints under the AHRD, it is difficult to know how these rights would be interpreted in practice in the Southeast Asian context. Though there is an ASEAN Intergovernmental Commission on Human Rights, it remains a government-driven body with an overall mandate for strategic planning to promote and protect human rights in the ASEAN region at the governmental and regional level.[108] There is no formal enforcement mechanism.

It is easy to become disillusioned with the patent lack of universality evident in modern human rights enforcement. It can clearly be seen in this body of law, perhaps more than any other, that geographic location and nationality of the victim are largely determinative of outcomes. For all that remains to be done in bridging those gaps, however, the advances that have been made are not insignificant—indeed, quite the opposite. The number of states that continue to resist the responsibility of human rights obligations vis-à-vis their own citizens is far less today than it was even twenty-five years ago. As flawed as human rights mechanisms may be, the movement in the international system is towards greater inclusion, not less. Though we may have only imperfect solutions to offer victims and survivors, it is clear that other bodies of international law are continuing to look for creative ways of bridging the gaps.

International Criminal Law

International criminal law has increasingly recognized that it may have a vital role to play in providing restitution to victims of mass atrocities. Beginning with the Nuremberg and Tokyo trials following the Second World War, international criminal tribunals have focused almost exclusively on prosecutions. The International Criminal Tribunal for the Former Yugoslavia ('ICTY') and International Criminal Tribunal for Rwanda ('ICTR') recognized the need for robust victims' and witnesses' units at the tribunals to provide protection, facilitate communication with the tribunal, and offer counselling and trauma services to those severely affected by the events, but largely avoided issuing orders for restitution.[109]

The Rome Statute of the ICC went quite a bit further. The Statute requires the Court to 'establish principles relating to reparations to, or in respect of, victims, including restitution, compensation and rehabilitation'.[110] In doing so, the Court may also 'determine the scope and extent of any damage, loss and injury to, or in respect

[108] 'About AICHR' AICHR ASEAN Intergovernmental Commission on Human Rights, at <https://aichr.org/about-aichr/> accessed 25 June 2020.

[109] Christine Evans, *The Right to Reparation in International Law for Victims of Armed Conflict* (CUP 2012) 91.

[110] Rome Statute of the International Criminal Court (17 July 1998, entered into force 1 July 2002) UN Doc A/CONF 183/9 (hereafter Rome Statute), Art 75(1).

of, victims'.[111] Thus, the Court is empowered to make reparations orders directly to or on behalf of victims of the crimes it prosecutes.[112]

Importantly, however, the Rome Statute empowers the Court to make restitution orders only against individual defendants—it 'does not deal with any issue relating to States' responsibility, either in the sense of sanctioning the State for the benefit of the individual victim, or in respect of issuing orders against the State'.[113] Moreover, no reparations award can issue unless the defendant has been criminally convicted, and only to the extent that the conviction encompasses the harm for which reparations are ordered.[114]

As of this writing, the Court has ordered restitution or reparations in three cases, against defendants Thomas Lubanga Dyilo (USD 10 million),[115] Germain Katanga (USD 1 million),[116] and Ahmad Al Faqi Al Mahdi (EUR 2.7 million).[117] These amounts are nowhere near sufficient to fully satisfy each potential individual claim for property restitution, and indeed it seems very unlikely that the Court would order individual awards for mass property theft incident to genocide versus collective claims as a form of symbolic or commemorative award.[118]

Another key question is where the money to pay victims will come from.[119] Most defendants at the ICC claim indigency, and those who do not—such as high-level government officials or heads of state—have likely found ways to hide or shield their personal assets.[120] Though the Rome Statute established a Trust Fund for victims and their families, out of which reparations orders may be paid, it is not automatically funded.[121] According to the Statute, any 'money and other property collected through fines or forfeiture' may be transferred to the Trust Fund, but whether such fines are paid or forfeiture is made is also dependent on the state

111 ibid.

112 ibid Art 75(2).

113 David Donat-Cattin, 'Article 75' in Otto Triffterer (ed), *Commentary on the Rome Statute of the International Criminal Court: Observers' Notes, Article by Article* (2nd ed, Beck/Hart 2008) 1400.

114 See *Prosecutor v Lubanga* (Judgment on the appeals against the 'Decision establishing the principles and procedures to be applied to reparations' of 7 August 2012 with Amended order for reparations (Annex A) and public annexes 1 and 2) [2015] ICC-01/04-01/06-3129, paras 65, 99; Carla Ferstman, 'Reparations at the ICC: The Need for a Human Rights Based Approach to Effectiveness' in Carla Ferstman and Mariana Goetz (eds), *Reparations for Victims of Genocide, War Crimes and Crimes against Humanity: Systems in Place and Systems in the Making* (2nd edn, Brill Nijhoff 2020) 450 (hereafter Ferstman, 'Human Rights Based Approach').

115 *Prosecutor v Lubanga* (Public redacted Judgment on the appeals against Trial Chamber II's 'Decision Setting the Size of the Reparations Award for which Thomas Lubanga Dyilo is Liable) [2019] ICC-01/04-01/06 A7 A8.

116 *Prosecutor v Katanga* (Public redacted Judgment on the appeals against the order of Trial Chamber II of 24 March 2017 entitled 'Order for Reparations pursuant to Article 75 of the Statute') [2018] ICC-01/04-01/07 A3 A4 A5.

117 *Prosecutor v Al Mahdi*, (Public redacted Judgment on the appeal of the victims against the 'Reparations Order') [2018] ICC-01/12-01/15 A.

118 Ferstman, 'Human Rights Based Approach' (n 114) 457–61.

119 See Sam Garkawe, 'Victims and the International Criminal Court: Three Major Issues' (2003) 3 Intl Crim L Rev 345, 364 (hereafter Garkawe, 'Victims').

120 ibid.

121 Rome Statute (n 111) Arts 75(2), 79.

of the individual defendant's finances.[122] Other potential sources of funding include the Assembly of State Parties, direct funding from the Court's own budget, or voluntary contributions from public or private sources.[123] The latter is potentially problematic in that it raises the possibility that a donor might set conditions on payment of restitution, though clear and strict donation guidelines from the Assembly of State Parties could ameliorate the problem.[124]

Moreover, if victims are paid restitution but the source of the funds is not the proximate wrongdoer, that removes much of the moral force of restitution as a form of atonement and may fuel—rather than abate—the sense that restitution is not 'enough'.[125] Theories of distributive justice may favour the notion of a collective 'redistribution of economic resources with the goal of enhancing the livelihood of victims so that they may realistically pursue their life plans',[126] or even that victims have an economic human right to live with 'moral integrity' and thus there is an obligation to make reparations to those who suffer 'regardless of who or what is responsible for the situation in which' they find themselves.[127] In any event, to date, only a few million dollars has been dedicated to restitution and reparations at the ICC, compared with the more than $1.5 billion that has been spent on investigations and prosecutions.[128] Given the vastly higher sums that would be needed in order to make the victims whole, as required in international law, the prospects for meaningful restitution and compensation for victims at the ICC seem dim.

Conclusion

In the wake of terrible events such as genocide, survivors and observers experience a range of deep emotional, spiritual, and moral responses, swiftly followed by calls for justice.[129] The process of transitional justice is broadly conceived as 'a society's attempts to address a legacy of large-scale past abuses, including through measures like trials, truth commissions, and the full range of reparations' including but not limited to financial compensation.[130] In the post-Second World War period,

[122] ibid Art 79(2); Garkawe, 'Victims' (n 119) 365.

[123] Garkawe, 'Victims' (n 119) 365–66.

[124] ibid 366.

[125] Slyomovics, *German Reparations* (n 57) 24 (noting that 'offenders who pay money to resolve murder cases constitute a clear and public admission of guilt to the surrounding society').

[126] Verdeja, 'Normative Theory' (n 3) 173.

[127] Rhoda E Howard-Hassmann, *Reparations to Africa* (University of Pennsylvania Press 2008) 167–68, 184.

[128] Luke Moffett, 'Reparations at the ICC: Can it Really Serve as a Model?' (Justiceinfo.net, 19 July 2019) <https://www.justiceinfo.net/en/justiceinfo-comment-and-debate/opinion/41949-reparations-at-the-icc-can-it-really-serve-as-a-model.html> accessed 25 June 2020.

[129] Minow, *Vengeance and Forgiveness* (n 41) 4.

[130] Bruce Broomhall, *International Justice and the International Criminal Court: Between Sovereignty and the Rule of Law* (OUP 2003) 189; Annie R Bird, *US Foreign Policy on Transitional Justice* (OUP 2015) 1 (citing Charles W Kegley et al, *American Foreign Policy: Patterns and Process* (Cengage Learning 2003) 17).

international law has increasingly recognized that restitution for the material losses that occur in genocide is a required component of any such programme.

Establishing state and/or individual liability for the losses—determining who is responsible to pay restitution—is often a challenge, and legal processes and procedures for ensuring restitution are inadequate and incomplete. There is no single explanation for why this is; rather, as this chapter has suggested, much depends on the context, historical circumstances, political will, existence of a tribunal or agency with competence to make a restitution award, and availability of sufficient funds. Though successes do occur, the reality for many survivors and their heirs is that law, while necessary, is not yet sufficient. In the words of two prominent scholars and legal practitioners, 'while *full* restitution and compensation is the international standard, a *fraction* of restitution is often what is ultimately offered and accepted'.[131]

However, this should not be reason for despair. Many more avenues for potential redress are available to victims today than existed even a few decades ago. The growing insistence on postconflict restitution in international soft law—including not only the Basic Principles, but also the Terezin Declaration[132] and the Pinheiro Principles[133]—signals an awareness among states that they cannot avoid full responsibility for their action or inaction. It is true that there are 'no tidy endings following mass atrocity'.[134] Law is not, nor can it be, a panacea. And, as implied in this chapter, there is no one response to genocide which can provide final closure or complete accountability for its barbaric acts. But there also can be no doubt that, of the many approaches needed to respond to the unbearable loss and suffering incurred in genocide, law is essential to enable a modicum of recovery and healing.

[131] Michael J Bazyler and Kristen L Nelson, 'Holocaust Property Theft and Restitution: The Right to an Effective Remedy under Article 8 of the Universal Declaration of Human Rights' in Carla Ferstman and Tony Gray (eds), *Contemporary Human Rights Challenges: The Universal Declaration of Human Rights and its Continuing Relevance* (Routledge 2019) 103 (emphasis in original).

[132] Forty-seven countries issued the Terezin Declaration in June 2009 on the site of the Terezín concentration camp in the Czech Republic. By endorsing the Terezin Declaration, these nations agreed to continue and enhance their efforts to right the economic wrongs that accompanied the genocide committed against European Jews and other groups persecuted during the Holocaust (Shoah, in Hebrew). The Terezin Declaration and its companion document, the 2010 Guidelines and Best Practices for the Restitution and Compensation of Immovable (Real) Property Confiscated or Otherwise Wrongfully Seized by the Nazis, Fascists and Their Collaborators during the Holocaust (Shoah) Era between 1933 and 1945, endorsed by forty-three countries, focuses in substantial part on the treatment of immovable (real) property restitution.

[133] Principles on Housing and Property Restitution for Refugees and Displaced Persons, Commission on Human Rights, UN Economic and Social Council, UN Doc E/CN.4/Sub.2/2005/17 (28 June 2005).

[134] Minow, *Vengeance and Forgiveness* (n 41) 102.

4
Postgenocide Justice? Assessing the Prosecution and Punishment of Genocide by Internationalized Courts and Tribunals

Christopher Soler

This chapter deals with legal remedies consisting in the prosecution and punishment of genocide by internationalized courts and tribunals. In adherence to the notion of 'postgenocide' adopted in this volume, the following analysis conveys the idea that recourse to legal mechanisms constitutes an important aspect of the effects of genocide in its aftermath. Moreover, the truth-finding exercise sows the seeds for the formation of a body of knowledge, the appreciation and understanding of which impacts realities of effected societies which are frequently constrained to confront the phenomenon of genocide. To this extent the chapter also 'advances existing knowledge of genocide scholarship'.[1]

Judicial institutions are active spaces where the crime of genocide is prosecuted and punished. The following analysis appraises the contributions made by internationalized courts and tribunals in a postgenocide context. It examines the functions that were performed by such courts and tribunals, together with the effects of the tasks they undertook, with reference to key decisions which were delivered by these institutions. The judicial institutions in question include the *ad hoc* international criminal tribunals, namely the International Criminal Tribunal for the Former Yugoslavia (ICTY) and the International Criminal Tribunal for Rwanda (ICTR), the International Criminal Court (ICC), and the hybrid criminal tribunals. Particular attention will be given to the ICC so that the chapter be more forward-looking and constructive. The analysis begins by unmasking the exceptional nature of genocide and revealing how its peculiar nature can affect the impact of *dicta* delivered by internationalized courts and tribunals. My analysis

[1] Klejda Mulaj, 'Introduction: Postgenocide: Living with Permutations of Genocide Harm', Chapter 1 in this volume 2 (hereafter Mulaj, 'Introduction: Postgenocide: Living with Permutations of Genocide Harm').

Christopher Soler, *Postgenocide Justice? Assessing the Prosecution and Punishment of Genocide by Internationalized Courts and Tribunals* In: *Postgenocide*. Edited by: Klejda Mulaj, Oxford University Press (2021).
DOI: 10.1093/oso/9780192895189.003.0004

focuses on considerations related to seeking justice in a postgenocide setting, that is, exclusively *post factum*.

It should be premised that the relationship between law and justice can be peculiar. Being value-driven, justice can be conceived in different ways.[2] The overlapping use of 'law' and 'justice' is exposed in the designation of Courts either as 'Courts of Law' or 'Courts of Justice'. The law entails a system of formalized regulation[3] whereas justice refers to the desired effect of the application, execution and implementation of the law within communities, institutions, and states. Justice is more complex than law, although the latter can be rather challenging when positive law is confronted with natural law, because it may possess elements of subjectivity. In the context of this chapter, law is conceived to enable the aspired postgenocide justice.

Plotting Genocide: Some Underlying Assumptions

In order to assess the prosecution and punishment of genocide, it is necessary to understand the extraordinary dynamics of this crime. A main feature of core crimes, that is crimes subject to the jurisdiction of the ICC—namely genocide, crimes against humanity, war crimes, and crimes of aggression—is that they are forms of what Röling calls 'system criminality'.[4] Besides involving a plurality of offenders and an *auctor intellectualis* pulling the strings,[5] these crimes are peculiar in shape, size, and texture. Although there are structural similarities between some core crimes, such as between genocide and the crime against humanity of persecution,[6] the crime of genocide is unique in many ways. Its singularity is not only important as a matter of fact, but it engenders some practical consequences. I will show how challenges to prosecute genocide which are faced by the territorial state, being the *forum conveniens*, are intrinsic in the very essence and nature of genocide. Its *sui generis* features and characteristics could lead to the conclusion that it is more prone to be diligently prosecuted beyond the territorial state. To this

[2] See, for example, Mark Drumbl's preference for favouring a horizontal expansion of his own cosmopolitan pluralist vision of justice in Mark A Drumbl, 'Collective Responsibility and Post-Conflict Justice' in Tracy Isaacs and Richard Vernon (eds), *Accountability for Collective Wrongdoing* (CUP 2011) 25 (hereafter Drumbl, 'Collective Responsibility and Post-Conflict Justice').

[3] Sally Engle Merry, 'Beyond Compliance: Toward an Anthropological Understanding of International Justice' in Kamari Maxine Clarke and Mark Goodale (eds), *Mirrors of Justice: Law and Power in the Post-Cold War Era* (CUP 2010) 31.

[4] Bernard Victor Aloysius Röling, 'Aspects of the Criminal Responsibility for Violations of the Laws of War', cited by Elies van Sliedregt, 'System Criminality at the ICTY' in André Nollkaemper and Harmen van der Wilt (eds), *System Criminality in International Law* (CUP 2009), 183, footnote 1 (hereafter van Sliedregt, 'System Criminality at the ICTY').

[5] van Sliedregt, 'System Criminality at the ICTY' (n 4) 183.

[6] Kevin Jon Heller, 'The ICC Has Jurisdiction over One Form of Genocide in the Rohingya Situation' (*Opinio Juris*, 2018) <http://opiniojuris.org/2018/09/07/33644/> accessed 30 August 2019.

extent, after its consummation, that is, postgenocide, it may be more sensible to internationalize the investigation thereof.

Genocide is frequently considered as the crimes of crimes, or the ultimate crime.[7] Such characterization is meant to portray the gravity of the crime, as a result of which no scale of sanctions can ever match it.[8] Yet, what makes the crime exponentially serious to the extent that 'no punishment is severe enough'[9] is not merely its ingredients but the fact that it is, habitually, not investigated and not prosecuted.[10] The fact that it is generally territorially confined complicates matters substantially. Genocide is committed by members of a group against members of another group. Although, in theory, genocide can be committed by a lone *génocidaire* where such individual is capable of 'effecting the destruction' of one of the protected groups,[11] this is 'little more than a sophomoric *hypothèse d'école* and a distraction for judicial institutions'.[12] The collective dimension of genocide conveys that members of the group perpetrating genocide will seek the protection of fellow members who are, most frequently, persons enjoying power within the ruling political administration or government. These same other members possess the knowledge and, in most circumstances, share the same criminal intent of the physical perpetrators. To give a practical example of the Holocaust, there subsisted 'a plan and design, to which all Nazis were fanatically committed, to annihilate all Jewish people'.[13] Similarly, members of the group perpetrating genocide will target members of the group who they have specifically singled out. The crime is not habitually committed at one point in time, but it protrudes throughout a span of time in such way and manner as to displace any investigation of a single crime.

[7] For a contestation of this view, see Larry May, *Genocide: A Normative Account* (CUP 2010). May upholds that: 'Genocide is not morally unique ... it is not the crime of crimes', Larry May, *Genocide: A Normative Account* (CUP 2010) 20, 88.

[8] Pierre Hazan, 'How the ICTY Has Changed Our World' (*Justice Info*, 3 January 2018) <https://www.justiceinfo.net/en/tribunals/36013-how-the-icty-has-changed-our-world.html> accessed 3 August 2019.

[9] Hannah Arendt, 'Letter to Karl Jaspers', in Hannah Arendt and Karl Jaspers (eds), *Correspondence 1926-1969*, Lotte Kohler and Hans Sanner, translating Robert Kimber and Rita Kimber, Harcourt Brace Jovanovich (New York 1992) 51 and 54.

[10] Christopher Soler, *The Global Prosecution of Core Crimes under International Law* (T.M.C. Asser Press & Springer 2019) 46–55 (hereafter Soler, *The Global Prosecution of Core Crimes under International Law*).

[11] See Article 6 of the Rome Statute of the International Criminal Court (opened for signature 17 July 1998, entered into force 1 July 2002) (hereafter the Rome Statute of the ICC); *vide Prosecutor v Jelisić* (ICTY Judgment) [5 July 2001] IT-95-10-A, paras 16, 42, 45, 46, and 51; and see also Claus Kreβ, 'On the Outer Limits of Crimes Against Humanity: The Concept of Organization Within the Policy Requirement: Some Reflections on the March 2010 ICC Kenya Decision' (2010) 23 (4) Leiden Journal of International Law 855, 871.

[12] William Schabas, 'Darfur and the Odious Scourge: The Commission of Inquiry's Findings on Genocide' (2005) 18 (4) Leiden Journal of International Law 871, 877.

[13] Trial of the Major War Criminals Before the International Military Tribunal, Vol II (1947) 118, cited in Payam Akhavan, *Reducing Genocide to Law: Definition, Meaning, and the Ultimate Crime*, Cambridge Studies in International and Comparative Law (CUP 2012) 109 (hereafter Akhavan, *Reducing Genocide to Law: Definition, Meaning, and the Ultimate Crime*).

I contend that, in many circumstances, genocide, more than any other core crime, is perpetrated by virtue of an underlying holistic plot. The holistic plot includes, incorporates and subsumes the guarantee of impunity after the commission of the first crime and/or the first set of crimes. The impunity becomes structural when it becomes the rule rather than the exception. It is structural because it is ingrained and embedded within the system itself, in such manner and to such extent that nothing needs to be done and no further decision needs to be taken to have it duly implemented. It is 'a product of a structured system that by its very nature disposes people to behave violently' and conditions their moral choices.[14] This is because the organization, be it a state (by means of the 'cogs in the machine')[15] or a non-state actor, is assured that, no matter how long it takes to achieve its goal (for example the annihilation of a group), its members (being the physical perpetrators of the core crime) will remain untouched and will be held harmless, enjoying freedom from prosecution. This understanding need not take the form of a specific and written agreement or undertaking but can be inherent and implicit in the prevailing scenario. States are unwilling to investigate and prosecute genocide either when they perpetrate it under the direction of ruthless dictators or when they are unable to curb it because they have no control over some territories, or else they are unable because they are severely under-resourced and blatantly disorganized. Genocide will not be investigated and prosecuted by a state which is either unwilling or unable to do so. In turn, this could lead to a very dangerous state of affairs: 'if a structured system is generating violence nobody in particular is responsible for it'.[16]

This holistic plot, in and of itself, is a calculated agreement which, in the words of Andrew Ashworth, is commonplace in complicity cases.[17] It possesses the features of a charted strategy which is laid out *ab initio*, rather than a mere plan which endeavours to ensure that the perpetrators act in unison. Hence, whereas planning can be an act committed by one person or several persons who design the commission of a crime at both the preparatory and execution phases,[18] plotting presupposes a pre-ordained and sophisticated scheme which is not only intended

[14] Richard E Rubenstein, *Resolving Structural Conflicts: How Violent Systems Can Be Transformed* (Routledge, Taylor & Francis 2017) 9, 21 (hereafter Rubenstein, *Resolving Structural Conflicts: How Violent Systems Can Be Transformed*).

[15] Hannah Arendt, *Eichmann in Jerusalem: A Report on the Banality of Evil*, Postscript (Revised Edition, Penguin Books 1964) 289. For an analysis of this work, see, inter alia, David Luban, 'Hannah Arendt as a Theorist of International Criminal Law' (2011) 11 (3) International Criminal Law Review 621, 625, footnote 22, *et seq*.

[16] Rubenstein, *Resolving Structural Conflicts: How Violent Systems Can Be Transformed* (n 14) 12.

[17] Andrew Ashworth cited in Marina Aksenova, *Complicity in International Law: A Case for Clarification* (Mississippi College of law, New Perspectives in Comparative Law—Inaugural YCC Conference, 20 April 2012) 23 <law.mc.edu/index.php/download_file/view/697/> accessed 17 August 2019.

[18] *Prosecutor v Akayesu* (ICTR Judgment) [2 September 1998] ICTR-96-4-T (hereafter *Akayesu*) para 480; *Prosecutor v Blaškić* (ICTY Judgment) [3 March 2000] IT-95-14-T, para 279.

to ensure that the crime be duly committed but that it also goes unpunished. Since it goes unpunished it facilitates the commission of further crimes amidst the prevailing pattern of criminality. In other words, the plot exceeds the plan. Even if this were not so, one would still be able to argue that the plot may be deemed to be a foreseeable off-shoot of the initial plan. The former (the plot) is constituted by virtue of a collective scheme devised, or at least understood, by a plurality of persons, whereas the latter (the plan) can be a solitary task.[19] The main difference lies in the juridical distinction between complicity and conspiracy. Yet, 'for the purpose of completing the crime of genocide, it is irrelevant whether the conduct in question is capable of posing any concrete threat to the existence of targeted group, or a part thereof'.[20] The plot is holistic both because it does not stop at the preparation of the manner of commission and/or commencement of execution of the crime/s and also because the additional confidence it gives accompanies the physical perpetrator before, during, and after the consummation of genocide. If this were not so the plot would be tantamount to a common design which would have the hallmarks of conspiracy, rather than complicity. It partakes of complicity more than conspiracy not only because the core crimes, with the exception of the attempt, solicitation, inducement, and incitement (instigation) thereof,[21] are not inchoate (incomplete) crimes, but also since complicity presupposes some form of participation which entails 'all the other kinds of contributions to the offence by other persons than the principal'.[22] The plot is holistic also because its execution has the characteristics of a continuous nature. In other words, the moment a crime is committed, it serves to consolidate an attack which can only be consummated with the perpetration of a pattern of crimes. The first crime is perpetrated in pursuance of the second, and so on and so forth. In the meantime, those who perpetrate the first crime know they do so with the blessing of an organizational policy, or at the very least, feel safeguarded by the state's failure to investigate it. Committing the second, third, and fourth crime hence becomes less risky. The course of conduct, a pattern of wrongdoing, spreads like cancer, no matter how banal it may initially seem.

This is more plausible when one delves into the constitutive elements of genocide. Besides the criminal intent for the underlying offence,[23] genocide requires

[19] *Prosecutor v Kordić and Čerkez* (ICTY Judgment) [26 February 2001] IT-95-14/2-T, para 386, cited in Amenge Okoth, *The Crime of Conspiracy in International Criminal Law* (T.M.C. Asser Press & Springer 2014) 142–43, footnote 272.

[20] Situation in Darfur, Sudan, *Prosecutor v Omar Hassan Ahmad Al Bashir, Decision on the Prosecutor's Application for a Warrant of Arrest Against Omar Hassan Ahmad Al Bashir* (Decision on the Prosecution's Application for a Warrant of Arrest Against Omar Hassan Ahmad Al Bashir) ICC Pre-Trial Chamber I [4 March 2009] ICC-02/05-01/09, para 119.

[21] These modalities of conduct are reflected in Articles 25(3)(f), 25(3)(c) and 25(3)(e) of the Rome Statute of the ICC (n 11) respectively.

[22] André Klip, *European Criminal Law: An Integrative Approach* (2nd edn, Intersentia 2012) 205.

[23] For a comprehensive analysis of the five acts or omissions (*actus reus*) with accompanying jurisprudence, see Lars Berster, 'Article II' in Christian J Tams, Lars Berster, and Björn Schiffbauer (eds), *Convention on the Prevention and Punishment of the Crime of Genocide: A Commentary* (C.H. Beck

an aggravated *mens rea*, the so-called *dolus specialis*. This is the specific intent to destroy a group. Proving genocide would hence necessarily presuppose that the perpetrators thereof intended to destroy a protected group. The group on the receiving end, the victims, are largely curtailed by a multiple *realpolitik*. Firstly, any prosecution of genocide will look as a spiteful measure intended to wreck shame and misery on the members of the group who have allegedly perpetrated the genocide. Any investigation and prosecution which follows a change in the political administration can only be met with disdain and smells of vindication. It conjures perceived feelings of the 'paradigm of victor's justice attached to the Nuremberg and Tokyo Tribunals'.[24] Secondly, not only the actual consummation of the genocide but also the failure to prevent it, as was the case with Serbia, engenders states aggravated responsibility.[25] The prosecution of a genocide can constitute the admission of liability consisting, *inter alia*, in the breach of a multilateral treaty, the Convention for the Prevention and Punishment of the Crime of Genocide. One must here remember that the conventional prohibition of genocide is broad in so far as it encompasses various modes of liability which include inchoate crimes such as attempt, incitement, and conspiracy to commit genocide.[26] Thirdly, a new political regime would, in all probability, not undergo the risk of the investigation and prosecution of its own members if and when a genocide is investigated independently, impartially and diligently.

All this gives rise to a shocking predicament which may be said to belong to all core crimes, but most especially to genocide for the reasons outlined here above. Whereas the *forum conveniens* is the *locus delicti commissi*, such territorial state is most unlikely to investigate and prosecute. On the contrary, such domestic states frequently promulgate controversial amnesty laws. Yet, such amnesties only have a legal effect within the confines of the domestic state and do not preclude prosecution before an internationalized court or tribunal.[27] This is also why

oHG, Munich 2014) 79–156 (hereafter Tams, Berster and Schiffbauer, *Convention on the Prevention and Punishment of the Crime of Genocide: A Commentary*).

[24] Luc Côté, 'Independence and Impartiality' in Luc Reydams, Jan Wouters, and Cedric Ryngaert (eds), *International Prosecutors* (OUP 2012) 366.

[25] Soler, *The Global Prosecution of Core Crimes Under International Law* (n 10) 111–15.

[26] For a thorough analysis of these inchoate crimes, as penalized by the Convention on the Prevention and Punishment of the Crime of Genocide (opened for signature 9 December 1948, entered into force 12 January 1951) 78 UNTS 277 (hereafter the Genocide Convention), see Jens David Ohlin, 'Attempt to Commit Genocide' in Paola Gaeta (ed), *The UN Genocide Convention: A Commentary*, Oxford Commentaries on International Law (OUP 2009) 193–206; see also Jens David Ohlin, 'Incitement and Conspiracy to Commit Genocide' in Paola Gaeta (ed), *The UN Genocide Convention: A Commentary*, Oxford Commentaries on International Law (OUP 2009) 207–27. A jurisprudential compendium in connection with such inchoate crimes may be found in Willem-Jan van der Wolf (ed), *Genocide and International Criminal Law*, International Criminal Law Series (International Courts Association Press 2010) 94–101.

[27] Mark Freeman, *Necessary Evils: Amnesties and the Search for Justice* (CUP 2009) 181.

postgenocide justice has to rely on non-domestic, or rather internationalized, avenues.[28] Solutions deriving from supranationalism are needed even for their moral impact, although internationalized criminal justice 'can only aim for symbolic prosecutions of heads of State' and such 'prosecutions are the ones most fraught with political considerations, and thus are difficult to pursue'.[29]

It is these solutions which this chapter shall now scrutinize. Before doing so, a preliminary remark is warranted. I place internationalized courts and tribunals in one category since I shall analyse their impact on postgenocide justice. This should not be construed to convey that there is no legal significance which stems from the differences between each and every internationalized criminal court or tribunal.[30]

The Nuremberg Military Tribunals

So much has been said and written about these tribunals.[31] Consequently, I will limit myself to only one pertinent observation which shows how the Nuremberg trials have veritably sown the seeds for postgenocide justice, although the acts or omissions constituting genocide were merely tantamount, at the time, to 'a crime without a name', as Winston Churchill had described the distinctive horror perpetrated against European Jewry during a radio broadcast.[32] Although Churchill's broadcast was dated 1941, it must be recognized that subsequently thereto, both in the indictment (third count) and during the Prosecution's speech at Nuremberg, genocide was officially referred to and recognized as a crime.[33]

International criminal law and international criminal procedure were at their embryonic stages at Nuremberg. But since 'the longest journey begins with the first step'[34] my failure to make reference, albeit restrictively, to the conceptual milestones reached at Nuremberg would not make justice to international criminal law itself. Such failure would shroud the *point de départ* of international criminal law.

[28] For an analysis of the main reasons why we need to rely on internationalized courts and tribunals to try genocide, see Soler, *The Global Prosecution of Core Crimes Under International Law* (n 10) 156–60.

[29] Mohammed Cherif Bassiouni, *Introduction to International Criminal Law* (Second Revised Edition, Martinus Nijhoff Publishers 2014) 1042 (hereafter Bassiouni, *Introduction to International Criminal Law*).

[30] These differences are explained in Roger O'Keefe, *International Criminal Law*, The Oxford International Law Library (OUP 2015) 111–13.

[31] For instance, Kevin Jon Heller, *The Nuremberg Military Tribunals and the Origins of International Criminal Law* (OUP 2012); Eugene Davidson, *The Trial of the Germans: Account of the Twenty-two Defendants Before the International Military Tribunal at Nuremberg* (University of Missouri Press 1997); Joe J Heydecker, Johannes Leeb, and R A Downie, *The Nuremberg Trial: A History of Nazi Germany as Revealed through the Testimony at Nuremberg* (World Publishing 1962).

[32] Prime Minister Winston Churchill's Broadcast to the World about the Meeting with President Roosevelt, 24 August 1941 <https://www.ibiblio.org/pha/timeline/410824awp.html> accessed 14 August 2019.

[33] Philippe Sands, *East West Street: On the Origins of Genocide and Crimes Against Humanity* (Weidenfeld & Nicolson 2016) 280.

[34] Bassiouni, *Introduction to International Criminal Law* (n 29) 1045, citing an Arabic proverb.

This said, I do not intend to postulate a historical or chronological account of the development of international criminal law by means of the headings to this chapter.

The Nuremberg trials predated the Genocide Convention which was preceded, only by a day, by the adoption of the UN Universal Declaration of Human Rights. Their crucial nature predominantly lies in the execution of the Nuremberg Principles which find their contemporary counterpart in the fundamental doctrine of individual criminal responsibility,[35] and in post-Nuremberg proceedings. These include those under Control Council Law No 10 and the so-called subsequent proceedings (*Nachfolgeprozesse*).[36] The statutes and case-law of the International Military Tribunal at Nuremberg 'developed new legal norms and standards of responsibility which have advanced the international rule of law, for example the elimination of the defence of obedience to superior orders and the accountability of Heads of State'.[37] Robert Jackson emphasized the transcendent importance of punishing the major Nazi war criminals, responsible for the Holocaust, by remarking that 'what makes this inquest significant is that these prisoners represent sinister influences that will lurk in the world long after their bodies have returned to dust'.[38]

Nowadays the international community has matured enough to acknowledge that, notwithstanding criticisms which were levelled at alleged violations of the principle of legality,[39] 'the Nuremberg proceedings provided both a general architecture and the philosophical underpinning for a new international penal legal order that is still being built'.[40]

The *Ad Hoc* International Criminal Tribunals: The ICTY and the ICTR

In 1993, after a United Nations investigation on crimes committed in the wars of the dissolution of the former Yugoslavia, the United Nations Security Council ('UNSC') adopted resolutions 808 and 827 to create the ICTY.[41] Upon a finding

[35] For a thorough analysis of the doctrine, see Elies van Sliedregt, *Individual Criminal Responsibility in International Law*, Oxford Monographs in International Law (OUP 2012).

[36] Kai Ambos and Stefanie Bock, 'Procedural Regimes' in Luc Reydams, Jan Wouters, and Cedric Ryngaert (eds), *International Prosecutors* (OUP 2012) 499.

[37] Antonio Cassese, 'From Nuremberg to Rome: International Military Tribunals to the International Criminal Court' in Antonio Cassese, Paola Gaeta, and John RWD Jones (eds), *The Rome Statute of the International Criminal Court: A Commentary*, Volume I (OUP 2002) 8.

[38] Trial of the Major War Criminals Before the International Military Tribunal, Vol II (1947) 99, cited in Akhavan, *Reducing Genocide to Law* (n 13) 110.

[39] Mohammed Cherif Bassiouni, 'Revisiting the Architecture of Crimes Against Humanity: Almost a Century in the Making with Gaps and Ambiguities Remaining—the Need for a Specialized Convention' in Leila Nadya Sadat (ed), *Forging a Convention for Crimes Against Humanity* (CUP 2011) 50.

[40] Guénaël Mettraux, 'Trial at Nuremberg' in William A Schabas and Nadia Bernaz (eds), *Routledge Handbook of International Criminal Law* (Routledge, Taylor & Francis Group 2011) 13.

[41] David Luban, Julie R O'Sullivan, and David P Stewart, *International and Transnational Criminal Law* (Wolters Kluwer, Aspen Publishers 2010) 95 (hereafter Luban, O'Sullivan and Stewart, *International and Transnational Criminal Law*).

that the Rwandan genocide had created a threat to international peace and security, the ICTR was also created by the UNSC[42] by virtue of its resolution 955. These *ad hoc* international criminal tribunals are considered here under one heading not because they are very similar, but because the prevailing main differences between the ICTY and the ICTR do not relate to genocide but to other core crimes.[43]

The ICTY's Srebrenica-related genocide jurisprudence is the most developed to date.[44] Its contribution to international criminal law is unprecedented. Suffice to mention the development of the doctrine of joint criminal enterprise,[45] and its several expansions, as a mode of liability when group criminality is concerned.[46] The ICTY also clarified what constitutes a part of a group for the purposes of the definition of genocide.[47]

In view of the above, amongst other major developments which concerned the substantive law on war crimes and the international criminal law of procedure, it stands to reason that 'national courts set up in Kosovo, East Timor and Lebanon to deal with war crimes also borrowed heavily from the Yugoslav tribunal'.[48] Even ICC proceedings, namely in the filing of judicial acts and in the decisions of Chambers, make explicit reference to the jurisprudence of the *ad hoc* tribunals.[49] Alex Whiting is hence correct to refer to the ICTY as a laboratory of international criminal procedure.[50] However, I share the thoughts of prosecutor Serge

[42] Luban, O'Sullivan and Stewart, *International and Transnational Criminal Law* (n 41) 116.

[43] The ICTY has jurisdiction over crimes in both international armed conflicts and internal armed conflict whereas the ICTR has jurisdiction over crimes committed in internal armed conflict only. Moreover, the ICTY has jurisdiction over crimes against humanity only if they are 'committed in an armed conflict' whereas the ICTR has jurisdiction over crimes against humanity only if they are committed 'on national, political, ethnic, racial, or other religious grounds', Mohammed Rabiul Islam, 'The International Criminal Court: Its Success and Limitations for Pursuing International Justice' (2016) 5 (2) Journal of Civil and Legal Sciences 1, 4.

[44] Michelle Jarvis and Alan Tieger, 'Applying the Genocide Convention at the ICTY: The Influence of Paradigms Past' (2016) 14 (4) Journal of International Criminal Justice 857, 860; see also Christos Ravanides, 'Srebrenica at 20: The ICTY Issues Long-Due Final Convictions' (10 March 2016) 20 (6) *Newsletter of the American Society of International Law* <https://www.asil.org/insights/volume/20/issue/6/srebrenica-20-icty-issues-long-due-final-convictions> accessed 12 August 2019.

[45] For an understanding thereof see Harmen van der Wilt, 'Joint Criminal Enterprise and Functional Perpetration' in André Nollkaemper and Harmen van der Wilt (eds) *System Criminality in International Law* (CUP 2009), 158–82; see also Neha Jain, *Perpetrators and Accessories in International Criminal Law: Individual Modes of Responsibility for Collective Crimes* (Hart Publishing 2014) 197–208 (hereafter Jain, *Perpetrators and Accessories in International Criminal Law: Individual Modes of Responsibility for Collective Crimes*).

[46] Jain, *Perpetrators and Accessories in International Criminal Law: Individual Modes of Responsibility for Collective Crimes* (n 45) 171–73.

[47] *Prosecutor v Krstić* (ICTY Appeals Chamber Judgment) [19 April 2004] IT-98-33-A, paras 6–38.

[48] World Without Genocide, 'ICTY: Implications for Justice and Impunity' (2017) <https://worldwithoutgenocide.org/genocides-and-conflicts/bosnia/icty> accessed 11 August 2019.

[49] Volker Nerlich, 'The Status of ICTY and ICTR Precedent in Proceedings Before the ICC' in Carsten Stahn and Göran Sluiter (eds), *The Emerging Practice of the International Criminal Court* (Martinus Nijhoff Publishers 2009) 305–06.

[50] Alex Whiting, 'The ICTY as a Laboratory of International Criminal Procedure' in Bert Swart, Alexander Zahar, and Göran Sluiter (eds), *The Legacy of the International Criminal Tribunals for the Former Yugoslavia* (OUP 2011) 83–107.

Brammertz, who declared that the ICTY's legacy would not be measured by its own work 'but by whether the countries of the former Yugoslavia [will] build the rule of law'.[51] It might be still too early to determine the ICTY's impact on the Balkans given that the process of consolidation of the rule of law is long-term, just like it took Germans generations to come to terms with Germany's past.[52] It is reasonable to uphold that 'the debate is still open. It will be ultimately for historians to issue a verdict'.[53] Diane Orentlicher, who conducted field research in Bosnia and in Serbia to determine how local communities were experiencing Hague justice, traced an evolution of various distinct perceptions by citizens within their respective cognitive landscapes.[54] In a nutshell, she concludes that:

> beyond the satisfaction survivors may derive from local trials, the wider impact of Bosnia's and Serbia's war crimes institutions is unknowable. But an intriguing body of research has found a striking correlation between domestic prosecutions for past atrocities and heightened enjoyment of human rights over time, despite periodic and significant setbacks in many countries.[55]

Analysing the anthropological dimension of international criminal justice, Ilias Bantekas upholds that:

> a significant part of the Rwandan genocide was predicated on a myth or symbolism reiterated and spread by the Hutu that the Tutsi were cockroaches and inferior beings. Whereas no Hutu would typically act on this myth unilaterally, it was the seed for future events, when animosity was stirred through artificial means and channels; and an illiterate and highly polarised populace was unable to separate myth from reality.[56]

In point of fact, there is no surprise in the recent warning to the UNSC that 'there is a resurgence in genocide denial and revisionism in both the former Yugoslavia

[51] Owen Bowcott, Yugoslav Tribunal Closes, Leaving a Powerful Legacy of War Crimes Justice (The Guardian, 20 December 2017) <https://www.theguardian.com/law/2017/dec/20/former-yugoslavia-war-crimes-tribunal-leaves-powerful-legacy-milosevic-karadzic-mladic> accessed 1 August 2019.

[52] Marko Milanovic, 'Understanding the ICTY's Impact in the Former Yugoslavia' (*EJIL: Talk! Blog of the European Journal of International Law*, 11 April 2016) <http://www.ejiltalk.org/understanding-the-ictys-impact-in-the-former-yugoslavia/> accessed 1 August 2019.

[53] Ruth Mackenzie and Others, *The Manual on International Courts and Tribunals* (2nd edn, OUP 2010) 210 (hereafter Mackenzie and Others, *The Manual on International Courts and Tribunals*).

[54] Diane Orentlicher, *Some Kind of Justice: The ICTY's Impact in Bosnia and Serbia* (OUP 2018) 2, 4–6 (hereafter Orentlicher, *Some Kind of Justice: The ICTY's Impact in Bosnia and Serbia*). Such landscapes include everyday conditions, economic circumstances, dominant elite discourses, local community perspectives and local reverberations of citizens' initiatives [ibid 3–4].

[55] ibid 429–30.

[56] Ilias Bantekas, 'The Anthropological Dimension of International Crimes and International Criminal Justice' in Ilias Bantekas and Emmanouela Mylonaki (eds), *Criminological Approaches to International Criminal Law* (CUP 2014) 252.

and Rwanda'.[57] From a normative point of view,[58] the ICTR's contribution to postgenocide justice is praiseworthy. It set an important precedent in the development of international criminal law when for the first time ever it convicted a former *bourgmestre* (mayor) for genocidal rape.[59] In this ground-breaking *dictum*, considered as a significant innovation,[60] rape was defined as a form of genocide since it was tantamount to serious bodily or mental harm constituting a fully fledged genocidal act. Additionally, ICTR has also 'recognized the role of the media in inciting genocide',[61] and emphasized the importance of distinguishing between the discussion of ethnic consciousness and the promotion of ethnic hatred.[62]

As a result of 'pressure from the Rwandan government, combined with a reluctance to offend the government and jeopardize its cooperation with the ICTR', the ICTR focused 'exclusively on genocide-related crimes'.[63] Other core crimes were largely dealt with by Rwandan domestic courts and *gacaca* tribunals. Distinctive legal cultures have stood in the way of effective cooperation and evidence gathering between these three institutions.[64] The lack of a symbiotic relationship and of interaction between these institutions should not however be imputable to ICTR.

ICTY and ICTR cases which are still *sub iudice* have been transferred unto the International Residual Mechanism for Criminal Tribunals which was established by means of United Nations Resolution 1966 (2010). It is tasked with the 'enforcement of sentences, administrative review, assignment of cases, review proceedings, appeal proceedings, contempt, requests for revocation of the referral of cases to national jurisdictions, the variation of witness protection measures, access to materials, disclosure, changes in classification of documents and requests for compensation and assignment of counsel'.[65] It is currently dealing with various appeals,

[57] Carmel Agius, Address of the President of the International Residual Mechanism for Criminal Tribunals to the UN Security Council (17 July 2019) <https://www.irmct.org/en/news/19-09-04-president-agius-presents-his-first-progress-report-un-security-council> accessed 3 September 2019.

[58] Such a perspective is not intended to comprise the extent to which ICTR managed to address the rights of victims. As a matter of fact, surviving victims have consistently complained of the absence of ICTR compensation programmes Patrick Rowanda and Susanne Buckley-Zistel, 'Changing Patterns of Acceptance. International Criminal Justice After the Rwandan Genocide' (International Nuremberg Principles Academy, 2017) 8 <https://www.nurembergacademy.org/fileadmin/user_upload/Rwanda.pdf> (hereafter Rowanda and Buckley-Zistel, 'Changing Patterns of Acceptance. International Criminal Justice After the Rwandan Genocide').

[59] *Akayesu* (n 18).

[60] William A Schabas, *Genocide in International Law: The Crime of Crimes* (CUP 2000) 384.

[61] Rowanda and Buckley-Zistel, 'Changing Patterns of Acceptance. International Criminal Justice After the Rwandan Genocide' (n 58) 3.

[62] *Prosecutor v Nahimana, Barayagwiza and Ngeze* (ICTR Trial Chamber I Judgment and Sentence) [3 December 2003] ICTR-99-52-T, para 1020.

[63] Human Rights Watch, 'Rwanda: Justice After Genocide—20 Years On' (28 March 2014) <https://www.hrw.org/news/2014/03/28/rwanda-justice-after-genocide-20-years> accessed 3 August 2019.

[64] Leila Ulrich, Book Review of Nicola Palmer, *Courts in Conflict: Interpreting the Layers of Justice in Post-Genocide Rwanda* (OUP 2015), in (2018) 16(5) Journal of International Criminal Justice 1127, 1128.

[65] United Nations International Residual Mechanism for Criminal Tribunals <https://www.irmct.org/en/cases> accessed 21 May 2020.

inter alia, the one filed by Ratko Mladić[66] who, after a trial which exceeded five years, was found guilty of genocide, crimes against humanity, and violations of the laws and customs of war by the ICTY Trial Chamber which sentenced Mladić to life imprisonment.[67] Another high-profile case which the International Residual Mechanism for Criminal Tribunals shall be dealing with is the one relating to the infamous Hutu businessman Félicien Kabuga, who was recently arrested in the outskirts of Paris.[68] He is believed to have established the notorious Interahamwe militia and provided training, equipment, and other resources which were used in the 1994 genocide that led to the extermination of around 800,000 Tutsis.[69]

The most direct and tangible legacy of the *ad hoc* criminal tribunals has been the creation of the ICC. In the words of Cherie Booth, 'the Rwanda and Yugoslav tribunals provided the strongest support for the idea that a permanent international criminal court was desirable and practical'.[70] It is to the consideration of the ICC that the analysis now turns.

The International Criminal Court

By virtue of Article 25 of the Rome Statute of the ICC ('the Rome Statute'), the ICC executes individual criminal responsibility, strengthens the individualization of guilt and formalizes the personification of wrongdoing and blameworthiness. It can counter the attribution of collective responsibility for criminal acts perpetrated by human beings. This judicial institution, to which 122 states are parties, is currently conducting various preliminary examinations[71] and investigating many situations around the globe.[72]

In so far as the crime of genocide is concerned, the track record of the ICC—the only permanent institution designed to deliver international criminal justice—is bleak. Nonetheless, this does not mean that the ICC has somehow failed in

[66] United Nations International Residual Mechanism for Criminal Tribunals <https://www.irmct.org/en/cases/mict-13-56> accessed 21 May 2020.

[67] *Prosecutor v Mladić* (ICTY Trial Chamber I Judgment) [22 November 2017] IT-09-92-T.

[68] The Economist, 'A Genocide Suspect Faces Trial: Félicien Kabuga, Africa's Most Wanted Man is Arrested', 21 May 2020 <https://www.economist.com/middle-east-and-africa/2020/05/21/felicien-kabuga-africas-most-wanted-man-is-arrested> accessed 25 May 2020.

[69] For further details on this pending case see <https://www.irmct.org/en/cases/mict-13-38> accessed 25 May 2020. See also Andrew Wallis' Chapter 8 in this volume.

[70] Cherie Booth, 'Prospects and Issues for the International Criminal Court: Lesson from Yugoslavia and Rwanda' in Philippe Sands (ed), *From Nuremberg to The Hague: The Future of International Criminal Justice* (CUP 2003) 159 (hereafter Booth, 'Prospects and Issues for the International Criminal Court: Lesson from Yugoslavia and Rwanda').

[71] Such preliminary examinations are being conducted in Afghanistan, Colombia, Guinea, Iraq/UK, Nigeria, Palestine, The Philippines, Bangladesh/Myanmar, Ukraine, and Venezuela, <https://www.icc-cpi.int/#> accessed 1 September 2019.

[72] Situations currently under investigation include Uganda, The Democratic Republic of the Congo, Darfur (Sudan), Central African Republic, The Republic of Kenya, Libya, Côte d'Ivoire, Mali, Georgia, and Burundi, <https://www.icc-cpi.int/#> accessed 1 September 2019.

fulfilling its mandate. The principle of complementarity,[73] which constitutes and is conceptualized as a catalyst for compliance,[74] conveys that the ICC will exercise its jurisdiction only when a case is admissible in terms of Articles 17–20 of the Rome Statute. The ICC should not be judged on the number of convictions it secures but on its potential to leave an impact on national criminal justice systems. Veritably, the ICC's success should not be measured on the basis of the judgments it delivers in terms of their effectiveness. Paradoxically, the ICC would have reached its ultimate objective when there would no longer be any need for it. Its capacity-building dimension could be deemed to be more important than its direct deliverables especially when an unable state, as opposed to an unwilling state, is concerned.[75]

No fingers should be pointed at the ICC for its slow pace, the main culprit of which is the dynamic admissibility test dictated by the Rome Statute, to which the ICC is subject. Likewise, the ICC should not be blamed for the shortcomings of states and other institutions. In the only case dealing with genocide which has been brought before the ICC so far, the UNSC triggered the jurisdiction of the ICC by virtue of Article 13(b) of the Rome Statute. It is hence up to the UNSC to take the appropriate measures to secure the surrender of *Omar Hassan Ahmad Al Bashir* to the ICC. The former Sudanese President, a fugitive since 4 March 2009 who was charged with three counts of genocide on 12 July 2010,[76] has been detained since he was ousted from power on 11 April 2019.[77] The ICC has hardly engaged with genocide since *Al Bashir* remains at large,[78] though, as stated here above, this is not directly imputable to it. It has elucidated the constitutive elements of the crime of genocide, hence, at best, contributing to a progressive restatement of international law. The value of its decisions relate to genocide law more than to postgenocide justice. This is why I shall not deal with them here.

At this juncture, I should stress that the ICC's contribution to international criminal justice necessitates that it holds 'individuals responsible for their roles or

[73] The principle, in all its shapes and sizes, is scrutinized in detail in Carsten Stahn and Mohamed M El Zeidy, *The International Criminal Court and Complementarity: From Theory to Practice*, Volumes I & II (CUP 2011).

[74] Jann K Kleffner, *Complementarity in the Rome Statute and National Criminal Jurisdictions*, International Courts and Tribunals Series (OUP 2008) 338.

[75] Olympia Bekou, 'Building National Capacity for the ICC: Prospects and Challenges' in Triestino Mariniello (ed), *The International Criminal Court in Search of its Purpose and Identity*, Routledge Research in International law (Routledge, Taylor & Francis Group 2015) 141.

[76] A case information sheet containing all the relevant information on the situation in Darfur, Sudan, is available at <https://www.icc-cpi.int/CaseInformationSheets/AlBashirEng.pdf> accessed 1 September 2019.

[77] The Guardian, 'Sudan's Bashir Appears in Public for First Time Since Being Ousted' (16 June 2019) <https://www.theguardian.com/world/2019/jun/16/sudan-omar-al-bashir-in-public-since-ousted> accessed 2 August 2019.

[78] Its 4 March 2009 and 12 July 2010 Pre-Trial Chamber decisions, with the former having been reversed by the Appeals Chamber on 3 February 2010, are aptly examined in Claus Kreβ, 'The ICC's First Encounter with the Crime of Genocide: The Case Against Al Bashir' in Carsten Stahn (ed), *The Law and Practice of the International Criminal Court* (OUP 2015) 669–704.

parts in these larger organized efforts'.[79] By way of constructive criticism, it should be noted that the ICC has been a bit passive in so far as the important regime of state cooperation is concerned. Its recent failure to refer Jordan's non-compliance to the Assembly of State Parties of the ICC and the UNSC[80] does not augur well and does little to shed a light on this thorny matter. The current state of play shows that genocide has a sizeable underlying political background which can stultify the investigation and prosecution thereof. This is more so when attempts to undertake prosecutions for genocide collide with the pretension and/or the exercise of diplomatic privileges and immunities. In fact, at least thirty-three states have ignored warrants for arrest issued by the ICC.[81] The ICC, therefore, is seriously undermined by lack of state cooperation. Yet, postgenocide justice before the ICC hinges entirely on the surrender of individuals to the ICC which has no jurisdiction to try individuals *in absentia*.[82] Three juridical avenues can be conceived via which the failure to surrender an individual wanted by the ICC could be criminalized. These are:

i. a *sui generis* form of *ex post facto* criminal liability consisting in aiding and abetting by omission;
ii. a *sui generis* form of *ex post facto* criminal liability consisting in contribution to a group crime by omission; and
iii. the introduction of a new, distinct and separate crime of perverting the course of justice.

Although not dealt with here,[83] reference shall be made to some relevant arguments which convey the significance of the above mentioned holistic plot in connection herewith and in the hope that the ICC courageously adopts a teleological approach in its *dicta*. These arguments, which also have a penological magnitude, fit well in the context of this postgenocide analysis.

With this in mind, it is worth emphasizing that the plot to perpetrate genocide is executed by virtue of the lack of investigation and prosecution, and by the failure to surrender individuals wanted for the commission of genocide.[84] When

[79] Larry May, *Genocide: A Normative Account* (CUP 2005) 175.

[80] Situation in Darfur, Sudan, in the case of *Prosecutor v Omar Hassan Ahmad Al-Bashir* (ICC Appeals Chamber, Judgment in the Jordan Referral re Al-Bashir Appeal) [6 May 2019] Case No. ICC-02/05-01/09 OA2, paras 207 and 212.

[81] The Guardian, 'States "failing to Seize Sudan's Dictator Despite Genocide Charge"' (21 October 2018) <https://www.theguardian.com/global-development/2018/oct/21/omar-bashir-travels-world-despite-war-crime-arrest-warrant> accessed 4 September 2019.

[82] See Article 63 of the Rome Statute.

[83] I dealt with these juridical avenues in my doctoral thesis which I defended at *Agnientekapel, Universiteit van Amsterdam* on 22 December 2017 (see Christopher Soler, *The Global Prosecution of Core Crimes under International Law* (PhD Thesis, Amsterdam Centre for International Law, University of Amsterdam 2017) 107–54.

[84] It is also possible (though arduous) to infer the existence of the plot from the circumstances of the case without a need to identify its subsistence before the commission of genocide. In other words,

dealing with accessories after the fact (ie, accessorial criminal liability), admittedly, non-surrender does not come to mind first,[85] although the obstruction of punishment has been categorized as the 'most important kind of subsequent assistance'.[86] Instead, one may think of other modes of conduct, such as burying bodies,[87] cremating bodies,[88] conserving looted property,[89] and laundering blood diamonds.[90]

However, the effects of the plot can be demonstrated by using the non-punishment of genocide as a *casus classicus*. Such omission can constitute, in and of itself, a contribution in terms of Article 25(3)(d) of the Rome Statute. This may be argued especially because punishing genocide can also be tantamount to preventing genocide since deterrence is a principal objective of punishment. It is settled that punishment, which flows from international criminal trials, besides having a denunciatory and educational function,[91] can be deemed to have a primarily forensic purpose consisting in both retributive and deterrent purposes.[92] The fact that retribution and deterrence are the ICC's primary sentencing objectives[93] is largely undisputed, notwithstanding the absence of a provision within the Rome Statute which 'prescribes the goals to be considered in meting out penalties within the ICC system'.[94] Indeed, the failure to surrender can also *ipso facto*

circumstances arising after the commission of the genocide can infer the prior existence of a latent plot. These can be deduced from presumptions of fact and may include the manner of execution of the crimes, some of which are consummated blatantly and without any attempt to conceal such crimes. Ultimately, these considerations boil down to the availability and production of evidence.

[85] In the light of the drafting history of the Genocide Convention, one can however mention that Venezuela argued that complicity after the fact involved acts performed subsequently to the crime, specifically referring, by way of example, to 'acts assisting the culprits to escape the punishment they deserved' (UN Doc E/AC.25/SR.84, 209 (Mr Perez Perozo), cited in Tams, Berster and Schiffbauer, *Convention on the Prevention and Punishment of the Crime of Genocide: A Commentary* (n 23) 162, footnote 32).

[86] Tams, Berster, and Schiffbauer, *Convention on the Prevention and Punishment of the Crime of Genocide: A Commentary* (n 23) 178.

[87] *Prosecutor v Blagojević and Jokić* (ICTY Appeals Chamber Judgment) [9 May 2007] IT-02-60-A, para 298, footnote 814.

[88] *United States of America v Werne Rohde and eight other* (the *Rohde* case) (International (Nuremberg) Military Tribunal) [1 June 1946], cited in *Prosecutor v Taylor* (Special Court for Sierra Leone Appeals Chamber Judgment) [26 September 2013] SCSL-03-01-A, para 369, footnote 1151 (hereafter *Taylor*).

[89] *United States of America v Oswald Pohl et al* (the *Pohl* case) (International (Nuremberg) Military Tribunal) [3 November 1947], para 989, cited in *Taylor* (n 88) para 369, footnote 1151.

[90] Christoph Burchard, 'Ancillary and Neutral Business Contributions to "Corporate-Political Core Crime": Initial Enquiries Concerning the Rome Statute' (2010) 8 (3) Journal of International Criminal Justice 919, 926.

[91] Elies van Sliedregt, 'Perpetration and Participation in Article 25(3)' in Carsten Stahn (ed), *The Law and Practice of the International Criminal Court* (OUP 2015) 511.

[92] Gideon Boas, 'The Difficulty with Individual Criminal Responsibility' in Carsten Stahn and L van den Herik (eds), *Future Perspectives on International Criminal Justice* (T.M.C. Asser Press 2010) 503.

[93] Kevin Jon Heller, 'The Rome Statute of the International Criminal Court' in Kevin Jon Heller and Markus D Dubber (eds), *The Handbook of Comparative Criminal Law* (Stanford University Press 2011) 601.

[94] Silvia D'Ascoli, 'The First Decision on Sentence of the International Criminal Court in the Lubanga Case: Great (Unmet) Expectations' in Triestino Mariniello (ed), *The International Criminal Court in Search of its Purpose and Identity* (Routledge Research in International Law, Routledge 2015) 198.

constitute a violation of the duty to prevent genocide when the genocide is still ongoing and if the international arrest warrant has been issued whilst the genocide was still being consummated. This argument is more compelling when an arrest warrant is issued by the ICC Pre-Trial Chamber further to a UNSC referral since Article 13(b) of the Rome Statute specifically refers to Chapter VII powers, hence presupposing that the genocide itself endangers international peace and security. The duty to prevent the continuation thereof and the duty to punish its perpetrators become imperative and inter-dependent also because the duties to prevent and punish are allied obligations. More so, 'seen as a due diligence obligation, prevention is the mirror image of protection'.[95] In fact, 'punishment is an inherent part of prevention of future crimes'.[96] Though inter-related, the obligation to prevent and the obligation to punish remain autonomous legal obligations.[97] The ICC has already upheld that 'failure to arrest these individuals emboldens them and potential future perpetrators, and fuels the perception that they can remain beyond the reach of the Court and perpetrators can continue to commit crimes with impunity'.[98] The United Nations General Assembly has also recognized that 'impunity ... has provided a fertile ground for further violations and abuses'.[99] Guénaël Mettraux, with reference to the *Hadžihasanović* trial judgment[100] appropriately held that 'a proven failure to punish crimes may be relevant to establishing a failure to prevent subsequent criminal occurrences by the same group of subordinates'.[101] *The Velásquez Rodríguez* seminal decision[102] also shows how and why 'punishment is an aspect of prevention'.[103] Notwithstanding the above assertions, Mark Drumbl opines that 'there is limited cause to believe that retrospective

[95] Sheri Rosenberg, 'Responsibility to Protect: A Framework for Prevention' in Alex J Bellamy, Sara E Davies, and Luke Glanville (eds), *The Responsibility to Protect and International Law* (Martinus Nijhoff Publishers 2010) 169 (hereafter Rosenberg, 'Responsibility to Protect: A Framework for Prevention').

[96] *Prosecutor v Halilović* (ICTY Trial Chamber Judgment) [16 November 2005] IT-01-48-T, para 96.

[97] *Application of the Convention on the Prevention and Punishment of the Crime of Genocide (BiH v Serbia and Montenegro)* (International Court of Justice Judgment) [26 February 2007] ICJ Reports (2007) (hereafter *BiH v Serbia and Montenegro)* para 427, cited by Rosenberg, 'Responsibility to Protect: A Framework for Prevention' (n 95) 177, footnote 73.

[98] ICC Report on Cooperation for the 12th Assembly of State Parties [9 October 2013] I-ASP/12/35, para 64, cited by Beth Van Schaak, 'International Criminal Court Fugitives: The Need for Bespoke Solutions' (2014) *Santa Clara Law Digital Commons*, Santa Clara University School of Law, p 3, <http://digitalcommons.law.scu.edu/cgi/viewcontent.cgi?article=1856&context=facpubs> accessed 20 August 2019.

[99] United Nations General Assembly Resolution adopted, in its seventy-first session, the International, Impartial and Independent Mechanism to Assist in the Investigation and Prosecution of those Responsible for the Most Serious Crimes under International Law Committed in the Syrian Arab Republic Since March 2011 [19 December 2016] Doc A/71/L.48, seventh preambular paragraph.

[100] *Prosecutor v Hadžihasanović and Kubura* (ICTY Trial Chamber Judgment) [15 March 2006] IT-01-47-T.

[101] Guénaël Mettraux, *The Law of Command Responsibility* (OUP 2009) 234.

[102] *Velásquez Rodríguez v Honduras* (Inter-American Court of Human Rights, Merits, Judgment), 29 July 1988 (Series C, No 4).

[103] Rosenberg, 'Responsibility to Protect: A Framework for Prevention' (n 95) 174.

criminal punishment serves much of a preventive function',[104] whereas Miguel de Serpa Soares assertively submits that 'there is a direct connection between accountability and achieving sustainable peace'.[105]

The law on the state responsibility for complicity in genocide can shed a light on these thorny issues. This is particularly so because, on the basis of the *Genocide Case*:[106]

> the notion of providing 'aid or assistance' to another State for the commission of a wrongful act by that other State in the law of state responsibility was analogous to the notion of complicity (though not directly applicable as the former concerns a situation characterized by a relationship between two States).[107]

Out of all core crimes, the juridical avenue of aiding and abetting is more conspicuous in the core crime of genocide in so far as the repression thereof has both a pre-emptive and a sequential dimension, this being the *erga omnes* obligation both to prevent and to punish genocide respectively. This is a double-edged sword. Whereas not punishing genocide can be a form of aiding and abetting, punishing genocide can also be tantamount to preventing genocide if deterrence is deemed to be a principal objective of punishment. This is why the fifth preambular paragraph of the Rome Statute stipulates that putting an end to impunity contributes to the prevention of crimes. Gerhard Werle postulates that 'there is much to be said for the belief that the practice of impunity for human rights violations (a "culture of impunity") is an important reason for their persistent recurrence'.[108] He cites the UNSC in substantiation of his assertion. When the ICTY was established, the UNSC declared that the prosecution and punishment of the guilty would contribute to preventing future human rights violations.[109] Werle also acknowledges that retribution is essential but 'the preventive effect of international criminal law is even more important (deterrence; norm stabilization)'.[110] This can be deemed to be correct especially if rehabilitation and incapacitation are typically considered to fall under the special deterrence paradigm.[111] Deterrence can be

[104] Mark A Drumbl, 'The Crime of Genocide' in Bartram S Brown (ed), *Research Handbook on International Criminal Law*, Research Handbooks in International Law (Edward Elgar 2011) 59.

[105] Miguel de Serpa Soares, 'An Age of Accountability', Special Editorial (2015) 13 (4) Journal of International Criminal Justice 669, 673 (hereafter de Serpa Soares, 'An Age of Accountability').

[106] *BiH v Serbia and Montenegro* (n 97).

[107] Nina H B Jørgensen, 'Complicity in Genocide and the Duality of Responsibility' in Bert Swart, Alexander Zahar, and Göran Sluiter (ed), *The Legacy of the International Criminal Tribunal for the Former Yugoslavia* (OUP 2011) 251 (hereafter Jørgensen, 'Complicity in Genocide and the Duality of Responsibility').

[108] Gerhard Werle, *Principles of International Criminal Law* (2nd edn, T.M.C. Asser Press 2009) 35 (hereafter Werle, *Principles of International Criminal Law*).

[109] ibid.

[110] ibid 34–35.

[111] Akhavan, *Reducing Genocide to Law* (n 13) 14, footnote 10.

both general and special. The former consists in the assumption that punishing an individual dissuades others from committing the same crime, whereas the latter aims at preventing the same criminal from reoffending.[112] Irrespective of the criminological contours of punishment at the ICC, there seems to be consensus that 'international criminal law may have a specific preventive effect on individual (potential) perpetrators'.[113] Suffice to say that 'there may be no clear distinction between the mental element for complicity and failing to prevent'.[114] On these lines, Nina Jørgensen rightly upholds that:

> the essence of complicity in genocide has been seen not to differ significantly whether the subject is an individual or a State, either in terms of its legal elements (and difficulties in defining the *mens rea*) or its purpose in ensuring that all those associated in genocide who are not principal offenders may be held responsible. Aiding and abetting genocide has emerged as the main form of complicity to be considered in terms of both individual criminal responsibility and State responsibility.[115]

In this way, aiding and abetting may assume the indicia of complicity in genocide, committed by omission and *ex post facto*. This is where the pre-conceived plot assumes a pivotal role to the extent that Ines Peterson correctly argues that 'one should even demand evidence of a prior agreement between perpetrator and assistant because otherwise, aiding and abetting liability could extend to situations where the perpetrator erroneously assumes that someone is willing to assist him in the aftermath of his crime'.[116] She subsequently concedes that although a fully-fledged plan might not be necessary, at the very least 'an advance understanding' would be required.[117]

Hence, I contend that the guarantee (or at least the reasonable likelihood) of impunity has a real bearing on the perpetration of genocide which festers as a result thereof. This contention, reminiscent of the natural and probable consequences rule of criminal law may be said to mirror the doctrine of presumed effect[118] in its various manifestations, particularly in the light of *res ipsa loquitur*.[119] Senior

[112] ibid 14.

[113] Otto Triffterer, *Zeitschrift fur die gesamte Strafrechttswissenschaft* 114 [2002] 321 and 334 *et seq*, cited in Werle, *Principles of International Criminal Law* (n 108) 35.

[114] Jørgensen, 'Complicity in Genocide and the Duality of Responsibility' (n 107) 270.

[115] ibid 274.

[116] Ines Peterson, 'Open Questions Regarding Aiding and Abetting Liability in International Criminal Law: A Case Study of ICTY and ICTR Jurisprudence' (2016) 16 (4) International Criminal Law Review 565, 588–89.

[117] ibid 590.

[118] See a reference to this doctrine in Miles Jackson, *Complicity in International Law*, Oxford Monographs in International Law (OUP 2015) 44.

[119] Fred E Heckel and Fowler V Harper, 'Effect of Doctrine of *Res Ipsa Loquitur*' (1928) 22 Illinois Law Review 724, 724–47.

leaders possess a position of high authority which enables them to provide for the legal, political, and social framework that allows the direct perpetrators to commit genocide in a climate of total impunity.[120] The continued commission of genocide is a side effect of impunity.

Genocide, more than any other crime, has the potential to unmask the geopolitical rivalry between powerful states within the international community. Political discourse is also relevant when another enigma is analysed, this being selectivity or selective prosecutions, a phenomenon which is not associated with the ICC only; it plagued the *ad hoc* tribunals too.[121] Suffice to note how 'Serbia's war crimes institutions suffered the increasingly corrosive effects of political pressure'.[122] The ICC prosecutes only those bearing the greatest responsibility. Although this has left a positive impact in the human rights records both in Bosnia and Serbia,[123] it may seem unfair since it is the antithesis of the crucial concept of 'equality before the law'. Yet, not only international prosecutors but also national ones 'prefer cases against big fish to those versus small fry'.[124] There is general consensus that 'law with selective enforcement lacks legitimacy'.[125] However, the *realpolitik* dictates that the ICC cannot be flooded with so many cases against so many perpetrators and their accomplices. Selectivity happens at various layers. It occurs between accomplices when the same crime is investigated and/or prosecuted. It also subsists in so far as the choice of so-called 'situations' are concerned. In fact, African leaders have persistently lamented a harassment of Africa by the ICC,[126] and the prospect of a mass exodus by African countries therefrom looms on the horizon.[127] The best solution to minimizing the valid criticism levelled towards the ICC in this regard may be an effective press agency which conducts an ongoing comprehensive awareness campaign. It seems that the ICC may lack some depth in its outreach. Selectivity also arises as a result of the inherent nature of the ICC. Its jurisdiction *rationae temporis*, for example, 'may also be open to claims of selectivity'.[128] This is,

[120] Verena Haan, 'The Development of the Concept of Joint Criminal Enterprise at the International Criminal Tribunal for the Former Yugoslavia' (2005) 5 (2) International Criminal Law Review 167, 196.

[121] Peter Verovšek argues that 'in selectively focusing only on elite decision-makers, the international community risks sending the signal that whoever is not indicted by the ICTY is innocent', Peter J Verovšek, 'The Lessons of the ICTY for Transitional Justice' (Eurozine, 12 January 2018) <https://www.eurozine.com/the-lessons-of-the-icty-for-transitional-justice/> accessed 25 May 2020.

[122] Orentlicher, *Some Kind of Justice: The ICTY's Impact in Bosnia and Serbia* (n 54) 123.

[123] ibid 430.

[124] Mark Osiel, *Making Sense of Mass Atrocity* (CUP 2009) 160.

[125] Hans Köchler, *Global Justice or Global Revenge? International Criminal Justice at the Crossroads: Philosophical Reflections on the Principles of the International Legal Order Published on the Occasion of the Thirtieth Anniversary of the Foundation of the International Progress Organization* (Springer 2003) 45.

[126] Soler, *The Global Prosecution of Core Crimes under International Law* (n 10) 20–21.

[127] Christopher R Rossi, 'Hauntings, Hegemony, and the Threatened African Exodus from the International Criminal Court' (2018) 40 (2) Human Rights Quarterly 369, 381.

[128] Robert Cryer, *Prosecuting International Crimes: Selectivity and the International Criminal Law Regime*, Cambridge Studies in International and Comparative Law (CUP 2005) 223.

inter alia,[129] why other options for internationalized criminal justice must be explored. I shall now embark to consider some relevant aspects thereof.

The Hybrid Criminal Tribunals

After the setting up of the above mentioned judicial institutions, 'the international community has established an assortment of other *ad hoc* judicial processes, including hybrid domestic-international courts'.[130] Some have suggested that the shortcomings of the ICC have led to the resurgence of hybrid tribunals.[131] Yet, this conclusion seems to displace the advantages of such structures, particularly their flexibility and their customizability, consisting in the fact that they deliver justice *in situ* and incorporate locals in the court's structure, and waters down the limitations of the jurisdiction *rationae temporis* of the ICC.[132]

There is no standard definition or model for a hybrid tribunal, but common features such as criminal judicial functions and an *ad hoc* or temporary basis.[133] Hybrid (semi-internationalized) criminal courts and/or tribunals develop national capacity by blending international supervision with local ownership.[134] There are a handful of such courts and tribunals. Antonio Cassese, who also called them 'mixed tribunals', refers to the Special Court for Sierra Leone, the East Timor Special Panels, the Extraordinary Chambers in the Courts of Cambodia ('ECCC'), and the Special Tribunal for Lebanon as examples thereof.[135] Other legal experts adopt the same approach.[136] This is probably because some structures, such as the Serbian War Crimes Chamber, are not considered to be mixed tribunals,[137]

[129] Other obvious reasons why the international community has to resort to other internationalized courts and tribunals to ensure the prosecution and punishment of genocide are the lack of jurisdiction of the ICC, both *rationae temporis* and *rationae loci*.

[130] Ellen L Lutz and Caitlin Reiger, 'Introduction' in Ellen L Luz and Caitlin Reiger (eds), *Prosecuting Heads of State* (CUP 2009) 8.

[131] The London School of Economics and Political Science (Hybrid Justice Project, 2019) <http://www.lse.ac.uk/iga/research-and-publications/rockefeller-funding-calls/hybrid-justice> accessed 19 May 2020.

[132] Mackenzie and Others, *The Manual on International Courts and Tribunals* (n 53) 244–45.

[133] James Mehigan, Book Review of Sarah Williams, '*Hybrid and Internationalised Criminal Tribunals: Selected Jurisdictional Issues*' (Hart Publishing 2012), in (2012) 19 Australian International Law Journal 283, 284 (hereafter Mehigan, 'Book Review of Sarah Williams, *Hybrid and Internationalised Criminal Tribunals: Selected Jurisdictional Issues*').

[134] Roberto Bellelli, 'The Establishment of the System of International Criminal Justice' in Roberto Bellelli (ed), *International Criminal Justice: Law and Practice from the Rome Statute to its Review* (Ashgate 2010) 14.

[135] Antonio Cassese, 'The Rationale for International Criminal Justice' in Antonio Cassese (ed), *The Oxford Companion to International Criminal Justice* (OUP 2009) 127.

[136] Mackenzie, Romano, Shany, and Sands consider the Special Court for Sierra Leone, the ECCC and the Special Tribunal for Lebanon in the eighth chapter of their book (see Mackenzie and Others, *The Manual on International Courts and Tribunals* (n 53) 212–47).

[137] Mehigan, 'Book Review of Sarah Williams, *Hybrid and Internationalised Criminal Tribunals: Selected Jurisdictional Issues*' (n 133) 283.

whereas the Bosnian War Crimes Chamber lost its hybridity when it was transformed into a domestic court operating under national law.[138] The former, the Special Court for Sierra Leone, by way of example, had no *rationae materiae* jurisdiction over genocide.[139] Likewise, the latter, the Special Tribunal for Lebanon, prosecuted crimes in connection with the car bomb explosion of 14 February 2005 which killed former Lebanese Prime Minister Rafiq Hariri and others, and other relevant attacks provided that, in terms of nature and gravity, they resemble the 14 February 2005 attack. The UNSC failed to entrust the international prosecutors in East Timor with a specific mandate.[140]

Thus, I will focus on the ECCC because, to date, they are the only hybrid court which secured a conviction for genocide. For the purposes of considering postgenocide justice, it is the most relevant. This judicial institution, severely criticized for its slow place, high costs, and allegations of corruption,[141] had jurisdiction to prosecute only those most responsible for the crimes committed by the Khmer Rouge in Cambodia between 1975 and 1979. The Khmer Rouge, also known as the Party of Democratic Kampuchea, seized power in Cambodia from the American-backed Lon Nol government on 17 April 1975, and under the leadership of Pol Pot, 'dismantled Cambodian society and installed a brutally repressive State'[142] which claimed the lives of around 1.7 million people, earning 'the title of "the Killing Fields" in reference to the scale of execution'.[143] The ECCC delivered its first genocide convictions and the first ever convictions by a hybrid tribunal for genocide[144] by finding that the Khmer Rouge committed genocide against persons of Vietnamese ethnicity and against the Cham, a Muslim minority group in Cambodia. One may pose the question: what can be gained from a conviction of

[138] Bogdan Ivanišević, 'Prosecutions: Case Studies Series: The War Crimes Chamber in Bosnia and Herzegovina: From Hybrid to Domestic Court' (*International Centre for Transitional Justice*, 2008) 39–44 <file:///C:/Users/csol1/Downloads/ICTJ-FormerYugoslavia-Domestic-Court-2008-English.pdf> accessed 15 August 2019; see also International Crimes Database, Bosnian War Crimes Chamber (TMC Asser Institute, 2013) <http://www.internationalcrimesdatabase.org/Courts/Domestic> accessed 14 August 2019; see also Human Rights Watch, 'Looking for Justice: The War Crimes Chamber in Bosnia and Herzegovina' (7 February 2006) <https://www.hrw.org/report/2006/02/07/looking-justice/war-crimes-chamber-bosnia-and-herzegovina> accessed 16 August 2019.

[139] Charles Chernor Jalloh, 'Introduction: Assessing the Legacy of the Special Court for Sierra Leone' in Charles Chernor Jalloh (ed), *The Sierra Leone Special Court and Its Legacy: The Impact for African and International Criminal Law* (CUP 2014) 10.

[140] Luc Reydams and Jed Odermatt, 'Mandates' in Luc Reydams, Jan Wouters, and Cedric Ryngaert (eds), *International Prosecutors* (OUP 2012) 101.

[141] Eli Meixler, 'Why a Genocide in Cambodia Could Be the Last of its Kind' (*Time*, 30 November 2018) <https://time.com/5467567/cambodia-genocide-verdict-court-last-verdict/> accessed 23 May 2020.

[142] Beth Van Schaak and Ronald C Slye, *International Criminal Law and its Enforcement: Cases and Materials* (2nd edn, Foundation Press 2010) 162.

[143] Verity Bowman, 'Forty Years On, Khmer Rouge Verdict is First Ruling that Cambodian Regime Committed Genocide' (*The Telegraph*, 16 November 2018) <https://www.telegraph.co.uk/news/2018/11/16/forty-years-khmer-rouge-verdict-first-ruling-cambodian-regime/> accessed 23 May 2020.

[144] Andre Boyle, 'A Long Time Coming: Understanding the Landmark Ruling from the Khmer Rouge Trials' (*Just Security*, 19 November 2018) <https://www.justsecurity.org/61514/long-time-coming-understanding-landmark-ruling-khmer-rouge-trials/> accessed 23 May 2020.

two old individuals who were anyway sentenced to life imprisonment? This question gathers more momentum when one realizes that Noun Chea died at the age of 93, just some months after his conviction.[145] The answer lies in the 'pertinent precedent'[146] which has been created. More than merely creating a precedent, 'victims and survivors of the Pol Pot era may still benefit psychologically from the long-overdue official acknowledgement of their suffering and the opportunity for younger generations to learn the truth of what happened'.[147] Therefore, the prosecution and punishment of genocide has a deep expressive function. They are:

> an appropriate vehicle both for conveying to offenders that their conduct was wrong and for reinforcing that idea to a wider (in this case worldwide) audience. Where punishment is the conventional vehicle for conveying deep social condemnation, not to punish can be taken as condonation of wrongful behaviour.[148]

The Cambodian hybrid structure could constitute a meaningful frame of reference for similar courts which have been formed in the meantime. By way of example, both the UN Human Rights Commissioner and the Sri Lankan Panel of the Consultation Task Force on Reconciliation Mechanisms recommended the establishment of a hybrid court to investigate and prosecute core crimes committed in Sri Lanka with the involvement of international investigators and prosecutors.[149]

Concluding Observations

Another option to the national (local), internationalized, and hybrid systems seems to be gradually emerging. This is the quasi-prosecutorial model which can lead to a prospective prosecution by a state willing to prosecute. It is particularly plausible owing to the imprescriptibility of genocide and the non-applicability of statutory limitations thereto. The International, Impartial and Independent Mechanism to

[145] George Wright, 'Nuon Chea: Cambodia Former Khmer Rouge Deputy Leader Dies' (*BBC News*, 4 August 2019) <https://www.bbc.com/news/world-asia-49228123> accessed 23 May 2020.

[146] Sara L Ochs, 'Cambodia's Genocide Conviction: A Sense of Justice?' (*International Law Under Construction: Shaping Sustainable Societies, Blog of the Groningen Journal of International Law*, 19 December 2018) <https://grojil.org/2018/12/19/cambodias-genocide-conviction-a-sense-of-justice/> accessed 23 May 2020.

[147] Wendy Lambourne, 'Justice After Genocide: Impunity and the Extraordinary Chambers in the Courts of Cambodia' (2014) 8 (2) Genocide Studies and Prevention: An International Journal 29.

[148] Deirdre Golash, 'The Justification of Punishment in the International Context' in Larry May and Zachary Hoskins (eds), *International Criminal Law and Philosophy*, ASIL Studies in International Legal Theory (CUP 2010) 219.

[149] Isabelle Lassée, 'Preface' in Isabelle Lassée (ed), *Sri Lanka's Time to Try: Prosecuting Conflict-Related Abuses* (South Asian Centre for Legal Studies 2019) 3 <https://www.ecchr.eu/fileadmin/Publikationen/Schueller_Mehta_Sri_Lanka_s_Time_to_Try.pdf> accessed 19 May 2020; see also Jurist Twenty, Documenting Law Since 1996, Supported by University of Pittsburgh School of Law (*Jurist Twenty*, 2017) cited in <http://www.internationalcrimesdatabase.org/> accessed 9 August 2019.

Assist in the Investigation and Prosecution of Persons Responsible for the Most Serious Crimes under International Law Committed in the Syrian Arab Republic since March 2011 has been set up by means of a resolution adopted by the United Nations General Assembly.[150] By virtue of the tasks they are undertaking, prosecutors 'have assembled damning documentary evidence and eye-witnesses' testimony'.[151] Another example thereof is the United Nations Investigative Team for Accountability of *Daesh* established by the Secretary-General pursuant to UNSC Resolution 2379 (2017), which is mandated to support domestic efforts to hold *Daesh* accountable by collecting, preserving, and storing evidence of core crimes committed by *Daesh* in Iraq. More recently the Human Rights Council has voted to establish an independent mechanism to collect, consolidate, preserve, and analyse evidence of violations of international humanitarian law and of human rights in Myanmar.[152] The ultimate aim of these quasi-prosecutorial institutions is to bring the perpetrators of core crimes before the competent courts of a state willing to exercise jurisdiction. Since the ultimate decision-maker shall be a competent court in a domestic state, the United Nations connection gives an internationalized dimension to the venture.

The quasi-prosecutorial model points to an increasing trend towards accountability which substantiates the deterring dimension of the criminal sanction, this being incarceration. Sociologists tend to agree that 'perhaps the most important sociological interpretation of punishment is as a mechanism by which social order is maintained'.[153] Although, in domestic criminal justice systems, the trend is to move towards restorative justice mechanisms, retributive justice is a device which can trigger postconflict reconciliation.[154] Retribution may sound crude and cruel, but it is the very essence of proportionality in so far as it 'postulates equivalence between the seriousness of the crime and the punitive reaction' and it also 'requires that the reproach is commensurate with the (degree of) *mens rea*'.[155] It seems to be the most sensible argument when atrocities such as genocide are at stake. It is essential for a culture which embraces the concept of an international rule of law because such a culture requires accountability mechanisms.[156] In the context of

150 United Nations General Assembly (2016) Resolution 71/248 (2016), UN Doc A/RES/71/248 adopted in its seventy-first session (UN Doc A/71/L.48, para 4).

151 Thomas W Smith, '"O War, Thou Son of Hell!": Grasping the Carnage in Syria' (2019) 41 (3) Human Rights Quarterly 596, 619.

152 Polina Levina Mahnad, 'An Independent Mechanism for Myanmar: A Turning Point in the Pursuit of Accountability for International Crimes' (*EJIL: Talk! Blog of the European Journal of International Law*, 1 October 2018) <https://www.ejiltalk.org/a-turning-point-in-the-pursuit-of-accountability-for-international-crimes/> accessed 5 September 2019.

153 Lucia Zedner, *Criminal Justice,* Clarendon Law Series (OUP 2004) 76.

154 For a contrary view, see Geneviève Parent, 'Reconciliation and Justice After Genocide: A Theoretical Exploration' (2010) 5 (3) Genocide Studies and Prevention: An International Journal 277, 277–92 (hereafter Parent, 'Reconciliation and Justice After Genocide: A Theoretical Exploration').

155 Harmen van der Wilt, 'Why International Criminal Lawyers Should Read Mirjan Damaška' in Carsten Stahn and Larissa van den Herik (eds), *Future Perspectives on International Criminal Justice* (T.M.C. Asser Press 2010) 51.

156 André Nollkaemper, *National Courts and the International Rule of Law* (OUP 2011) 5.

upholding the rule of law, Cherie Booth rightly highlights that 'to respond to mass atrocity with legal prosecution is to exact retribution by embracing legal order'.[157] The overarching concept of the rule of law is an end in itself, a destination point, the quest for the arrival at which should override any other valid consideration. Its corollary is truth telling. To this extent, trials have a commemorative potential in so far as they construct an objective and impartial record of events.[158] In safeguarding the human right of access to justice, prosecutions significantly contribute to the constitutionalization of international law. Quintessentially, 'redress to victims is a core element of all transitional justice initiatives in their varying forms. However, beyond the prosecution of the perpetrators, this task is broad and largely undefined—both by mechanisms of transitional justice themselves and commentators of their processes'.[159]

Some legal analysts may be more susceptible to overstate the importance of the rule of law, just like political scientists (over)emphasize the state, and just like social psychologists focus on individuals and social groups. But even basic human logic dictates that crimes which lead to an irreversible state of affairs are best met with punishment rather than with a 'societal process where each party is supposed to acknowledge the other and the other's sufferings'.[160] Even leading sociologists, such as Émile Durkheim, had found that punishment plays an important role in the development and maintenance of social bonds.[161] What leads to such punishment, being the trial, also has a unique value *per se*. It is an event where social norms are either articulated, or where they already articulated, they are solemnly affirmed.[162] On the contrary, the above mentioned societal process is most likely to dehumanize victims since it divests them of their ultimate right, the right to have their day in Court. It also carries the risk of legitimizing genocidal acts or, at the very least, of purportedly legitimizing them by seeking 'to restore the humanity of the perpetrator and his/her relationship with the victim',[163] and, with more detriment to the quest for a faithful and veritable snapshot of the state of play, by promoting 'the separation between the perpetrator's actions and identity'.[164] Moreover, it can incentivize violence which would be committed by the victims against the alleged perpetrators since it lays the groundwork 'for a different perception of the other's behaviour than inherent "evilness"'.[165] Worse still, it encourages the victim

[157] Booth, 'Prospects and Issues for the International Criminal Court: Lesson from Yugoslavia and Rwanda' (n 70) 180.

[158] ibid 183.

[159] Claire Garbett, *The Concept of the Civilian: Legal Recognition, Adjudication and the Trials of International Criminal Justice* (Routledge, Taylor & Francis, a GlassHouse Book 2015) 161.

[160] Parent, 'Reconciliation and Justice After Genocide: A Theoretical Exploration' (n 154) 278.

[161] Émile Durkheim, *The Division of Labour in Society* (Macmillan 1984).

[162] Mirjan R Damaška, *The Faces of Justice and State Authority: A Comparative Approach to the Legal Process* (Yale University Press 1986) 62.

[163] Parent, 'Reconciliation and Justice After Genocide: A Theoretical Exploration' (n 154) 286.

[164] ibid 287.

[165] ibid.

to 'get an understanding of what happened from the perpetrator's perspective'.[166] Maybe, supporters of restorative justice could first ask themselves: how would a helpless mother of an innocent boy who was tortured, massacred, and killed in Srebrenica feel about apportioning blame to all sides of the conflict? The answer is self-evident. Apportioning blame to all sides of this atrocity would be an insult to the dignity of the victim, and to the boy's mother. It is evident that, in the aftermath of mass violence, ingrained, and innate resentments will impede reconciliation. This is also why international law prohibits blanket amnesties.[167] Impunity is the very antithesis of the rule of law and of accountability because it connotes 'the impossibility, *de jure* or *de facto*, of bringing the perpetrators of violations of human rights to account'.[168]

Some courts, such as the Inter-American Court of Human Rights, are already at the forefront of the development of a duty to prosecute serious human rights violations.[169] I opine that the international community should strive to prosecute and punish genocide as a matter of principle[170] irrespective of side effects the prosecution itself may trigger at national, regional, or international level. This should be considered as a corollary of the responsibility to protect principle. Elsewhere, I examine the conceptual genesis of the responsibility to protect and the requisite components which must subsist to ensure its transformation from a concept to a legal principle.[171]

The prosecution of genocide is not only a relevant fact-finding exercise which serves for purposes of establishing authoritative knowledge about the crimes committed and the planning by the perpetrators thereof, but also contributes towards advancement of the protection of group/identity rights by enhancing national reconciliation and breaking the cycle of violence, hatred, and extra-judicial retribution.[172] Even if this assertion may be challenged, I advocate '"justice for its own sake", a phrase used to distinguish the inherent value of prosecutions from their presumed social effects'.[173] In my view, the international community should seek

[166] ibid 286.

[167] Soler, *The Global Prosecution of Core Crimes under International Law* (n 10) 245.

[168] Louis Joinet, 'Question of the Impunity of Perpetrators of Human Rights Violations (Civil and Political)—Final Report Prepared by Mr. Joinet Pursuant to Sub-Commission Decision 1996/119' (26 June 1997) (UN Doc E/CN.4/Sub.2/1997/20), cited in de Serpa Soares, 'An Age of Accountability' (n 105) 670 and 673–74.

[169] Ward N Ferdinandusse, *Direct Application of International Criminal Law in National Courts* (T.M.C. Asser Press 2006) 187.

[170] Even the first Chicago Principle on Post-Conflict Justice dictates so, see Cherif Bassiouni, 'International Guidelines on Post-Conflict Justice: The Chicago Principles' in Mohammed Cherif Bassiouni (ed), *The Pursuit of International Criminal Justice: A World Study on Conflicts, Victimization, and Post-Conflict Justice* (Volume 1, Intersentia 2010) 44–50.

[171] Soler, *The Global Prosecution of Core Crimes under International Law* (n 10) 73–82.

[172] ICTY Press Release, Joint Statement by the President Antonio Cassese and the Prosecutor Richard Goldstone (24 November 1995), ICTY Doc CC/PIO/027-E, cited in Orentlicher, *Some Kind of Justice: The ICTY's Impact in Bosnia and Serbia* (n 54) 105, footnote 87.

[173] ibid 5 and 94–96.

criminal justice, no matter how elusive it may prove to be, simply because criminal justice is such a priceless value *per se* that laws, be they national, regional, or international, should be designed to serve justice and to fit its ultimate needs. In this way, laws serve as utensils which facilitate 'justice, even if the latter cannot be (fully) achieved'.[174] The promulgation of laws, their interpretation and application by means of case-law (jurisprudence) and the execution, implementation, and enforcement of such *dicta* are means to an end, this being criminal justice itself. In a nutshell, prosecutions in response to genocide which materialized in internationalized courts and tribunals are indispensable as a means to achieving (criminal) justice.

[174] Mulaj, 'Introduction: Postgenocide: Living with Permutations of Genocide Harm' (n 1) 20.

5

Responsibility to Protect in International Criminal Law

The Case of the Genocide against the Rohingya

Jobair Alam

The genocide against the Rohingya in Myanmar's Rakhine state has elevated the question about the authority and effectiveness of International Criminal Law ('ICL'), since as of today, the mechanisms under the ICL to ensure criminal justice through indictments and prosecutions of the perpetrators have not been extended to this egregious case. Considering the limited approach of ICL to curb the proliferation of atrocity crimes—including genocide—there has been a considerable exigency to engender a compelling and effective method of preventing atrocity crimes in their early stages, or at least ending them before a colossal loss of life has transpired, as well as rebuild societies subjected to such crimes. This unorthodox wave of thinking finds expression in the emergence of the Responsibility to Protect ('R2P') principle which accentuates that sovereignty entails not only state rights but also responsibilities to protect its people from severe violations of human rights.

The Rohingya have undergone decades of discrimination and disenfranchisement and human rights violations. The reasons are manifold, but the underlying one is that the concept of 'national race' as a key criterion for membership in Myanmar's political community—originated in the 1960s—has framed the Rohingya as the 'Other' and excluded them from the polity. The antagonistic marginalization of the Rohingya continued in the 1970s and 1990s when the military regime applied their exclusionary vision in practice through state laws and policies to restrict their rights.[1] For instance, the Protection of Race and Religion laws have placed harsh restrictions on fundamental religious freedoms, as well as reproductive and marital rights. MacLean has used the concept of 'lawfare' to analyse how the Rohingya have been treated under Myanmar laws.[2] The genocide against

[1] UNHRC 'Report of the Independent International Fact-Finding Mission on Myanmar' (24 August 2018) UN Doc A/HRC/39/64 (hereinafter *FFM Report*).

[2] Lawfare indicates 'the negative manipulation of international and national human rights laws to accomplish purposes other than, or contrary to, those for which they were originally enacted'. See Ken MacLean, 'The Rohingya Crisis and the Practices of Erasure' (2019) 21(1) Journal of Genocide Research 83.

Jobair Alam, *Responsibility to Protect in International Criminal Law* In: *Postgenocide*. Edited by: Klejda Mulaj, Oxford University Press (2021). © The Several Contributors. DOI: 10.1093/oso/9780192895189.003.0005

the Rohingya correlates with the politics of identity which manifests itself in the process of nation-state building and nationalism. The doctrine of nationalism in Myanmar, at its core, entails homogenizing tendency of constructing a single common identity known as the Burmese identity based on cultural (primarily religious and linguistic) and ideological characteristics. This ideal of unity encourages not only forced assimilation but violent extrusions (transfers, deportations, and even mass killings) of any Other who stand outside—such as the Rohingya—who are seen to pose a threat to the collective identity of the dominant group.

The systematic genocidal violence against the Rohingya has been clearly documented.[3] The atrocities became unconcealed in 2012 when a major violence left scores of people dead and displaced. On October 2016 a 'clearance operations' by the Myanmar Army (after an attack on Burmese border posts) resulted in arbitrary arrests, extrajudicial killings and gang rapes of the Rohingya. More recently violent attacks occurred in August 2017 when Tatmadaw (the Myanmar armed forces) and Rakhine men killed an estimated 10,000 Rohingya, burned the bodies and disposed of them in mass graves.[4] These abuses and apartheid-like conditions have been referred in several reports as 'genocide', not least the UN Human Rights Council Reports of 2018 and 2019.[5] Moreover respected academic research teams have reached the same conclusion. For example, a Yale Law School Paper[6] found that 'the acts committed against the Rohingya, individually and collectively, meet the criteria for finding acts enumerated in the "Genocide Convention" ['GC'])'.[7] Similarly, the International State Crime Initiative of the Queen Mary, University of London found that the state persecution of the Rohingya amounts to genocide.[8] The UN Human Rights Council in its 2018 report concluded that 'there is sufficient information to warrant the investigation and prosecution of senior officials in the Tatmadaw chain of command, so that a competent court can determine their liability for genocide in relation to the situation in Rakhine State'.[9] Amnesty International also divulges that the Rohingya atrocity amounts to genocide and the situation requires an urgent international response to bring the responsible for atrocity crimes to justice.[10]

[3] For instance, *FFM Report* (n 1); UNHRC, 'Detailed findings of the Independent International Fact-Finding Mission on Myanmar' (16 September 2019) UN Doc A/HRC/39/CRP.2; Penny Green, Thomas MacManus, and Alicia de la Cour Venning, *Countdown to Annihilation: Genocide in Myanmar* (International State Crime Initiative 2015) (hereinafter Green et al, *Countdown to Annihilation*).

[4] *FFM Report* (n 1).

[5] See n 3.

[6] Alina Lindblom et al, *Persecution of the Rohingya Muslims: Is Genocide Occurring in Myanmar's Rakhine State? A Legal Analysis* (Yale Law School 2015).

[7] Convention on the Prevention and Punishment of the Crime of Genocide (opened for signature 9 December 1948, entered into force 12 January 1951) 78 UNTS 277.

[8] Green et al, *Countdown to Annihilation* (n 3).

[9] *FFM Report* (n 1) 16.

[10] Amnesty International, '"No One Can Protect Us": War Crimes and Abuses in Myanmar's Rakhine State' (May 2019) < https://www.amnesty.org/download/Documents/ASA1604172019ENGLISH.PDF> accessed 16 June 2020.

Despite these predicaments, the response by the national and international law communities to protect the Rohingya is exiguous. When a state and its agencies perpetrate atrocity crimes for various reasons including race and ethnicity against any section of its own population (as happened to the Rohingya by the Tatmadaw), they violate many fundamental human rights including the right to life, the right not to be subjected to sexual violence, and the right not to be tortured. Over time, such practices erode the legitimacy of the basic principles of human rights law, encourage further violations and promote populations to find radical means of redressing injustice.[11] However, the inadequate protection of the Rohingya by the national and international communities under the national, international, and universal jurisdictions raises the question if the international institutions can and should invoke the R2P principle to protect the Rohingya against atrocities owing to the promise of R2P as a response mechanism to atrocity crimes.

As a principle, R2P demands that national governments essentially do not take sovereignty for granted. It is based on the notion that sovereignty requires a responsibility to protect all populations from atrocity crimes, a responsibility which has not been undertaken by Myanmar's civilian authorities, including State Counsellor Aung San Suu Kyi. This makes a strong case for an intervention by the international community on R2P grounds. In contrast, many contend that the R2P would not help the Rohingya owing to the intrinsic limits in the R2P's framework and its restricted ability to protect the stateless people in states undergoing a process of nation building with an idiosyncratic history of democracy, nationalism, and citizenship.[12] Moreover, uncertainty exists about the unanimous endorsement of the R2P in the Association of Southeast Asian Nations ('ASEAN') context, where states follow a consensual style of decision-making and non-interference in their intra-regional relations.

Based on the above background, this chapter applies pertinent ICL principles relating to the genocide against the Rohingya, in a postgenocide context, to evaluate the response of ICL on its treatment and standard of protections under the national, international, and universal jurisdictions, and if such protection incorporates the R2P. As set out in the Introduction to this volume, the term 'postgenocide' signifies not only the era 'after' genocide came to an 'end', but the entire period following the outset of genocide including the effects of it in shaping and aggravating realities of societies and the impacts and ramifications caused by such heinous crime to all the actors involved including the victims and the perpetrators.[13] In

[11] Alex J Bellamy, 'Ending Atrocity Crimes: The False Promise of Fatalism' (2018) 32(3) Ethics & International Affairs 329, 335–36.

[12] Yukiko Nishikawa, 'The Reality of Protecting the Rohingya: An Inherent Limitation of the Responsibility to Protect' (2018) 16(1) Asian Security 90, 91 (hereinafter Nishikawa, 'Reality of Protecting the Rohingya'). See also Alan Collins, *Security and Southeast Asia: Domestic, Regional, and Global Issues* (Institute of Southeast Asian Studies 2003); Yan Razali Kassim, *The Geopolitics of Intervention: Asia and the Responsibility to Protect* (Springer 2014).

[13] See the contribution by Klejda Mulaj in this volume, 'Postgenocide: Living with Permutations of Genocide Harm' 3–7.

contrast to the idea that R2P seems to have more to do with stopping genocide than its aftermath, this chapter does also consider about legal recourses associated with R2P after the commission of genocide considering that there is still danger in relapsing back into evil in Myanmar.

This chapter draws two major conclusions. First, that the Rohingya are entitled to protections under the national, international, and universal jurisdictions—as the commission of genocide constitutes a violation of *obligatio erga omnes* (obligations to the world) and the perpetrators are *hostis humani generis* (enemies of the humankind)—which has not yet been extended to the Rohingya. Second, their maltreatment brings to the surface the relevancy of the R2P, this principle at least for three reasons (namely, the flawed idea of sovereignty as responsibility in Myanmar, the statelessness of the Rohingya, and ASEAN's contextual application of the R2P) would not help protect the Rohingya. R2P therefore is insufficient to deliver on its promise to end suffering of genocide victims and help them rebuild their lives in postgenocide setting.

Application of Different Jurisdictions over the Rohingya Atrocity

The laws relating to atrocity crimes—including genocide—are applied primarily by International Criminal Tribunals (ICTs) including the International Criminal Court (ICC). Conversely, the principle of complementarity in the Rome Statute invites a potential exclusive role of national criminal law to achieve the permanent court's objectives and thereby authorizes ordinary courts in states to exercise jurisdiction over genocide and other atrocity crimes. The following considers the national, international, and universal jurisdictions that can legitimately be exercised on the crime of genocide and if they have been applied to the Rohingya situation.

National Jurisdiction

The obligation to prevent genocide contained in the GC Article 1 has become a norm of Customary International Law ('CIL') and is mandatory for all states,[14] including Myanmar (ratified on 14 March 1956). International human rights law also places similar obligations. For example, the Convention Against Torture ('CAT')[15] Article 2 specifies that state parties shall take necessary measures to prevent acts of

[14] Paola Gaeta, 'On What Conditions Can a State Be Held Responsible for Genocide?' (2007) 18(4) European Journal of International Law 631.

[15] Convention Against Torture and Other Cruel, Inhuman or Degrading Treatment or Punishment (opened for signature 10 December 1984, entered into force 26 June 1987) 1465 UNTS 85.

torture. Since the adoption of the CAT, the absolute and non-derogative character of this prohibition is accepted as a matter of CIL[16] and, thus, binding on Myanmar.

The above reaffirms that the primary responsibility to protect the Rohingya from genocide lies with the Myanmar government, either by bringing the perpetrators to ordinary courts or to an *ad hoc* tribunal.[17] Any such national prosecutions are more effective in terms of gathering of evidence and affecting deterrence and reconciliation than legal proceedings conducted elsewhere. Further, the restoration of human rights can be achieved mainly through the establishment of national rights in the national jurisdiction and the maintenance of the contract between the government and the governed as propounded by contrarian theorists such as Hobbes and Locke.[18] For many, this is the relationship embedded in constitutional law. The preamble of the 2008 Myanmar Constitution signals that the state is constituted for 'securing the justice, liberty, equality, peace and prosperity of its people and upholding racial equality'. Therefore, the idea that 'the protection of individuals from the systematic and widespread violation of their human rights is central to the social contract and the primary purpose of a constitutional government',[19] where the rights of individuals 'precede the state and the state is obligated to protect the rights and freedoms of its citizens'.[20]

Yet, to date, Myanmar has not undertaken any initiatives to bring the perpetrators to justice—an 'unwillingness or inability' to carry out the investigation and prosecution. This concerns 'both the inability to stop violence and the obligation to prosecute the individuals engaged in that violence'.[21] For instance, the ICC established that 'the Kenyan authorities failed to arrange criminal prosecution of those allegedly guilty for crimes against humanity during the post-electoral violence of 2008–2009, thus creating an environment of impunity for those *erga omnes* crimes'.[22] In Myanmar, such 'unwillingness or inability' lies in the political domain owing to the reason that the genocide was authorized and committed by the same bodies now tasked with the duty of prosecution.[23] It is in these cases that

[16] Committee Against Torture, General Comment 2, 39th sess, UN Doc CAT/C/GC/2/CRP.1/Rev.4 (23 November 2007).

[17] Hao Trien Phung, *Preventing Atrocity Crimes in Myanmar: A Case Study in the Responsibility to Protect* (University of Alberta 2013).

[18] Thomas Hobbes, *Leviathan* (Barnes & Noble Publishing 2004); John Locke, *Two Treatises of Government* (Whitmore and Fenn and C Brown 1821).

[19] Norman Weib and Jean-Marc Thouvenin (eds), *The Influence of Human Rights on International Law* (Springer 2015).

[20] Alex J Bellamy, 'Ending Atrocity Crimes: The False Promise of Fatalism' (2018) 32(3) Ethics & International Affairs 329, 336.

[21] Hovhannes Nikoghosyan, 'Government Failure, Atrocity Crimes and the Role of the International Criminal Court: Why Not Syria, but Libya' (2015) 19(8) The International Journal of Human Rights 1240, 1248–49.

[22] *Situation in the Republic of Kenya (Decision Pursuant to Article 15 of the Rome Statute on the Authorization of an Investigation into the Situation in the Republic of Kenya)* [31 March 2010] ICC-01/09, paras 183–184.

[23] Christiane Wilke, 'A Particular Universality: Universal Jurisdiction for Crimes Against Humanity in Domestic Courts' (2005) 12(1) Constellations 83.

international criminal courts and courts in other countries are called on to prosecute atrocity crimes on the grounds that they violate *jus cogens* norms and warrant *obligatio erga omnes*.

International Jurisdiction

This section examines whether the atrocity against the Rohingya constitutes *jus cogens* violations and infer *obligations erga omnes* to bring the perpetrators to justice under international jurisdiction. The Vienna Convention Article 53 articulated *jus cogens* as a norm accepted and recognized by the international community of which no derogation is permissible.[24] Article 53 did not identify any norm having peremptory status but left it to the 'international community' to identify.[25] Traditionally, to qualify as *jus cogens* a norm should be binding and accepted by the majority of states[26] without any derogation.[27] They are reiterated in international *opinio juris*, the preambles and provisions of treaties, states' ratifications of these treaties, and the international prosecutions of these crimes.[28]

Genocide is now universally deemed a *jus cogens* violation. In 1946, the UN General Assembly unanimously identified genocide as a crime that the civilized world condemns.[29] Even prior to this, the Nuremberg Tribunal prosecuted and punished perpetrators of genocidal acts.[30] Further, the GC—with 149 ratifying state parties, including Myanmar—explicitly regards genocide as an international crime that states must punish and prevent (Article 1). The GC also provides that 'immunities are no bar to prosecution and obliges states to enact legislation to punish offenders' (Articles 5–6).

The recent inclusion of the prohibition of genocide in the statutes of the ICTY, ICTR, and ICC shows the international community's revitalized determination to eradicate genocide. The International Court of Justice (ICJ) held that the crime of genocide is 'contrary to moral law and to the spirit and aims of the UN'.[31] Emphasizing the binding character of the prohibition of genocide, the ICJ also

24 Vienna Convention on the Law of Treaties (opened for signature 23 May 1969, entered into force 27 January 1980) 1155 UNTS 331.

25 Anthony Aust, *Modern Treaty Law in Practice* (CUP 2000) 258.

26 Lauri Hannikainen, *Peremptory Norms (Jus Cogens) in International Law* (Finnish Lawyers' Publishing 1988) 210–12.

27 A J J de Hoogh, 'The Relationship Between Jus Cogens, Obligations Erga Omnes and International Crimes: Peremptory Norms in Perspective' (1991) 42 Austrian Journal of Public and International Law 183.

28 M Cherif Bassiouni, 'From Versailles to Rwanda in Seventy-Five Years: The Need to Establish a Permanent International Criminal Court' (1997) 10 Harvard Human Rights Journal 11.

29 UNGA Res 96(I) (11 December 1946) UN Doc A/RES/96.

30 M Ragazzi, *The Concept of International Obligations Erga Omnes* (Clarendon 1997) 92–93.

31 Application of the Convention on the Prevention and Punishment of the Crime of Genocide *(Bosnia and Herzegovina v Yugoslavia)* (Order of 8 April 1993) [1993] ICJ Rep 3.

clarified that 'the prohibition against genocide is a *jus cogens* norm that cannot be reserved or derogated from'.[32] The Court referred explicitly to *jus cogens* in a majority opinion in *Congo v Rwanda* in 2006.[33] Similarly, the ICTY regarded 'the prohibition of genocide as a norm of *jus cogens*'.[34] Almost all legal authors from around the world confirm the *jus cogens* character of the prohibition of genocide.[35]

The above evidences that genocide being committed against the Rohingya constitute a violation of *jus cogens* prohibition from which no derogation is permissible. Before the establishment of the ICC, *ad hoc* ICTs were established on a temporary basis to exercise international jurisdiction over some or all of these crimes committed during or within a fixed period of time or event.[36] Once this one-off exercise of international jurisdiction is over, these *ad hoc* tribunals/courts cease to exist without any precedential effects of their decisions. Moreover, the UN Security Council has been inconsistent in forming such *ad hoc* ICTs.

To overcome these shortcomings, the ICC was established as a permanent international criminal court with international jurisdiction over *jus cogens* core crimes embodied in its Statute.[37] But the jurisdiction of the ICC is not universal as its Statute does not apply to non-state parties.[38] Myanmar is a classic case in this regard. The genocide committed against the Rohingya falls within the subject matter jurisdiction of the ICC (Article 5 of the Statute), but it lacks territorial jurisdiction as Myanmar is a non-party to the Rome Statute (Article 12). This deficiency thus demonstrates the necessity of *ad hoc* ICTs. If the UN Security Council desires it, an *ad hoc* ICT can be established, although the politics of such a decision is quite another question.

The limitation of the ICC's territorial jurisdiction regarding the Rohingya can be mitigated by the UN Security Council's referral to the Court (Article 13), or when the Court is satisfied that it has such jurisdiction. For instance, Myanmar's actions and inactions in its territory regarding the Rohingya have transborder effects and

[32] Reservations to the Convention on the Prevention and the Punishment of the Crime of Genocide (Advisory Opinion) [1951] ICJ Rep 15.

[33] Armed Activities on the Territory of the Congo (New Application: 2002) *(Democratic Republic of the Congo v Rwanda)* (Jurisdiction and Admissibility) [2006] ICJ Rep 32.

[34] *Prosecutor v Zoran Kupreškić et al* (Judgement) ICTY-95-16-T [14 January 2000], para 520.

[35] See P Malanczuck, *Akehurst's Modern Introduction to International Law* (Routledge 1997) 58; M N Shaw, *International Law* (CUP 2014).

[36] Roger O'Keefe, *International Criminal Law* (OUP 2015) 86.

[37] Silvia D'Ascoli, *Sentencing in International Criminal Law: The UN Ad Hoc Tribunals and Future Perspectives for the ICC* (Bloomsbury Publishing 2011).

[38] During the treaty negotiations, some states argued that the jurisdiction of the ICC should be extended over non-party since state party has universal jurisdiction over *jus cogens* crimes under CIL. Conversely, the United States argued that jurisdiction over non-party nationals were unlawful. Eventually, the UN negotiator agreed that the statute is applicable only for the state parties. See Kenneth Randall, 'Universal Jurisdiction Under International Law' (1998) 66 Texas Law Review 785, 798 (hereinafter Randall, 'Universal Jurisdiction'); Michael Scharf, 'The ICC's Jurisdiction Over the Nationals of Non-Party States' in Sarah B Sewall and Carl Kaysen (eds), *The United States and the International Criminal Court* (Rowman and Littlefield Publishers 2000) 220.

directly impacted Bangladesh[39] (an ICC member). Accordingly, the ICC's jurisdiction is not totally inoperative. The Pre-Trial Chamber I already ruled that the ICC has jurisdiction on the crimes of humanity of deportation—a crime commencing in Myanmar and ending in the territory of Bangladesh.[40]

However, allowing the ICC to prosecute serious crimes or the development of ICTs was never meant to dislodge the domestic prosecutions of the perpetrators in the places (countries) of commission of crimes; rather, they are complementary to national criminal jurisdictions (ICC Statute Preamble, Article 1) (with the exception of *ad hoc* tribunals that have primacy over national courts). When Myanmar orchestrates atrocity crime and allows perpetrators to act with impunity, the international jurisdiction, particularly of the ICC, is in order and indeed imperative to hold the perpetrators responsible. Yet, to-date, no actions have been undertaken for the prosecution of Rohingya atrocity crime perpetrators by the ICC and other forums developed by the ICL to prosecute criminal offenders.

Universal Jurisdiction

It is frequently stated that 'all states have an interest in exercising jurisdiction over atrocity crimes'.[41] To avoid any exceptions of its prosecutions in the wake of states' unwillingness or inability, absence of ICC jurisdiction or lack of *ad hoc* ICTs, the jurisdiction over these crimes, and their perpetrators have been thoroughly universalized to be prosecuted by national, regional, and international forums under universal jurisdiction regardless of the place of commission of crimes and perpetrators' national identity.

The emergence and consolidation of the notion of *obligatio erga omnes* provides a strong conceptual background to rationalize the exercise of universal jurisdiction by the state over individuals. This is also because, for many, 'the implications of *jus cogens* are those of duty and not of optional rights (otherwise, *jus cogens* would not constitute a peremptory norm of international law)'.[42] Bassiouni added that 'proponents of natural law advocate that *jus cogens* is based on a higher legal value to be observed by prosecuting offenders, while proponents of legal positivism argue

[39] Bangladesh is currently shouldering a heavy burden of hosting more than one million Rohingya refugees fled from Myanmar. See Jobair Alam, 'The Status and Rights of the Rohingya as Refugees under International Refugee Law: Challenges for a Durable Solution' (2020) Journal of Immigrant & Refugee Studies <https://www.tandfonline.com/doi/full/10.1080/15562948.2020.1746872> accessed 16 June 2020.

[40] *Decision on the Prosecution's Request for a Ruling on Jurisdiction Under Article 19(3) of the Statute* [6 September 2018] ICC-RoC46(3)-01/18-37, para 71.

[41] Bernhard Graefrath, 'Universal Criminal Jurisdiction and an International Criminal Court' (1990) 1 European Journal of International Law 67.

[42] M Cherif Bassiouni, 'States of Emergency and States of Exception: Human Rights Abuses and Impunity Under Color of Law' in Daniel Prémont (ed), *Non-Derogable Rights and States of Emergency* (Brussels 1996) 125.

that another principle whose values and goals are, at least in principle, of that same dignity, namely the "principle of legality"—*nullum crimen sine lege*—should prevail'.[43] Yet, the problem is that 'a value-neutral approach' is impossible and thus Bassiouni suggests to rely on the codification of ICL.[44] Based on this suggestion, it can be noted that the ICC Statute Article 17(1)(d) has introduced the 'sufficient gravity' threshold for the court's cognizance of cases in which sovereign governments are 'unwilling or unable' to prevent and prosecute.[45] It is based on the conviction that, *erga omnes* as 'compelling law'[46] engenders an obligation 'flowing to all' as distinct from 'flowing to some',[47] since the crime is committed with 'sufficient gravity' in which all states have a legal interest.[48] In this vein, the following explores if the Rohingya genocide satisfies the 'sufficient gravity' tests to be under universal jurisdiction.

In *Abu Garda*, the Pre-Trial Chamber agreed that 'in assessing the gravity of a case, the issues regarding the nature, manner, and impact of the alleged attack are critical'.[49] In the Rohingya crisis, the scale of the crimes in terms of geographical expansion and intensity; the nature of the crimes committed; and the impact of the crimes and harm caused to victims satisfy all these determinants. The ICTY has suggested that sufficient gravity entails a continuous repetition of similar crime over time against any targeted groups in a systematic pattern.[50] In the Rohingya crisis, tangible evidence exists to show the continuity of 'analogous breaches that are sufficiently numerous and interconnected to amount to a pattern or system'.[51]

Pursuant to Article 15 of the Draft articles on Responsibility of States for Internationally Wrongful Acts, the International Law Commission ('ILC') concluded that any repetitive breaches of the same laws in a specific time limit by the

[43] M Cherif Bassiouni, 'International Crimes: *Jus Cogens* and *Obligatio Erga Omnes*' (1996) 59 (4) Law and Contemporary Problems 63, 71–72. For details about the principle of legality see Gabriel Hallevy, *A Modern Treatise on the Principle of Legality in Criminal Law* (Springer 2010); Kenneth S Gallant, *The Principle of Legality in International and Comparative Criminal Law* (CUP 2010).

[44] M Cherif Bassiouni, 'The History of the Draft Code of Crimes Against the Peace and Security of Mankind' (1993) 27 Israel Law Review 1.

[45] Hovhannes Nikoghosyan, 'Government Failure, Atrocity Crimes and the Role of the International Criminal Court: Why Not Syria, but Libya' (2015) 19(8) The International Journal of Human Rights 1240.

[46] Luc Reydams, 'Universal Jurisdiction Over Atrocities in Rwanda: Theory and Practice' (1996) 1 European Journal of Crime, Criminal Law and Criminal Justice 18.

[47] Articles 42 and 48 of the Articles on Responsibility of States for Internationally Wrongful Acts drew a distinction between breaches of bilateral obligations and obligations of a collective (community) interest. Obligations stemming from regional or universal human rights treaties would have *erga omnes* parties effect towards other states parties as well as *erga omnes* effect to the extent that they have been recognized as CIL. See Responsibility of States for Internationally Wrongful Acts, UNGA Res 56/83 (12 December 2001) (corrected by document A/56/49(Vol. I)/Corr.4)).

[48] Barcelona Traction, Light and Power Company Ltd (*Belgium v Spain*) (Judgments, Advisory Opinions and Orders) [1970] ICJ Rep 4, para 32.

[49] *Prosecutor v Abu Garda*, (Decision on the Confirmation of Charges) [8 February 2010] ICC-02/05-02/09-243-Red, para 31.

[50] *Prosecutor v Ratko Mladic*, (Judgement) ICTY-09-92-T [22 November 2017].

[51] *FFM Report* (n 1).

commission of genocide constitute 'composite acts' which are sufficiently grave in nature. The Rohingya genocide satisfies this ILC formulated sufficient gravity scale as well to be under universal jurisdiction,[52] which authorizes any state to prosecute the perpetrators. For example, in Belgium, the *Act Concerning the Punishment of Grave Breaches of International Humanitarian Law* of 1999 (under Article 7) gives the national criminal courts necessary authority to prosecute international core crimes under which, in 2001, four Rwandan civilians (accused of genocide and crimes against humanity in Rwanda) were brought under its jurisdiction under the principle of universal jurisdiction.[53] In his opening statement, the Attorney-General stated that 'he represented the international community who has the right and the duty not to tolerate the commission of barbarous acts, giving Belgian courts the possibility to judge war crimes, crimes against humanity and genocide, regardless of the place where the acts were committed, the nationality of the offender or the nationality of the victim, but simply because of their very (serious) nature'.[54]

Similarly, the genocide of the Rohingya can be brought under the national court of any state. In 2007, the ICJ issued an important judgment[55] stating that 'to prevent', within the scope of the GC, imposed an obligation that was not territorially limited. It also confirmed that 'the rights and obligations enshrined by the Convention are rights and obligations erga omnes' and 'that the obligation each State thus has to prevent and to punish the crime of genocide is not territorially limited by the Convention',[56] lending support to the widely held view that universal jurisdiction for genocide is in conformity with modern international law and the Rohingya genocide can be prosecuted by any national court.

Historically, in numerous cases of prosecution of war criminals (for both violations of the international laws of war and genocide) after the Second World War, reliance was placed, *inter alia*, on the universality principle. A seminal example is the *Eichmann* case, where both the judgements of the Jerusalem District Court[57] and Supreme Court of Israel[58] contain specific statements on universal jurisdiction. The District Court emphatically stated that 'the crimes dealt with in this case

[52] Theodor Meron, 'International Criminalization of Internal Atrocities' (1995) 89(3) American Journal of International Law 554, 569; Randall, 'Universal Jurisdiction' (n 38) 835–37.

[53] Article 7 states that 'the Belgian courts shall be competent to deal with breaches provided for in the present Act, irrespective of where such breaches have been committed'.

[54] Taken from the transcript of the trial session of 22 May 2001. For discussions see Tom Ongena and Ignace Van Daele, 'Universal Jurisdiction for International Core Crimes: Recent Developments in Belgium' (2002) 15 (3) Leiden Journal of International Law 687.

[55] Case Concerning the Application of the Convention on the Prevention and Punishment of the Crime of Genocide (*Bosnia and Herzegovina v Yugoslavia*) (Preliminary Objections) [1996] ICJ Rep 595.

[56] ibid para 31.

[57] Case 40/61 *Attorney General v Adolf Eichmann* [11 December 1961] (hereinafter *Attorney General v Adolf Eichmann*).

[58] *Attorney-General of the Government of Israel v Eichmann* [1961] 36 ILR 5.

are not crimes under Israeli law alone but are in essence offences against the law of nations. Indeed, the crimes in question are not a free creation of the legislator who enacted the law for the punishment of Nazis and Nazi collaborators, but have been stated and defined in that law according to a precise pattern of international laws and conventions which define crimes under the law of nations'.[59] Thus, Eichmann was found 'guilty of crimes against the Jewish people, of crimes against humanity on a dual foundation: the universal character of the crimes and their specific character as intended to exterminate the Jewish people'.[60] Considering the magnitude of the crimes that affect the community of the humanity, Hannah Arendt added that 'only a universally framed charge could legitimize any capture abroad and teach the international community the right moral lessons'.[61]

Similarly, in *Pinochet*, the House of Lords rejected Augusto Pinochet's claim that 'he was entitled to immunity from arrest with respect to the acts of torture he allegedly committed during his presidency in Chile'.[62] This echoes that 'the denial of immunity is substantiated by the pre-eminence of the violated rule and its underlying values (the status of a non-derogable norm is recited to legitimize the submission of the state or its official to the jurisdiction of another state) and the normative implications of sovereignty are not immutable when the jurisdiction is one universal in nature'.[63] Lord Millett held that 'English courts have and always have had extraterritorial criminal jurisdiction in respect of crimes of universal jurisdiction under customary international law, including "the systematic use of torture on a large scale and as an instrument of state policy" which has already attained the status of an international crime of universal jurisdiction'.[64]

In the same scale, the genocide against the Rohingya with the necessary knowledge of widespread and systematic attacks including torture have the universal character of crimes that cannot be left to Myanmar alone, in particular, given the state's failure to bring the perpetrators to justice. The UN General Assembly Resolution 2840 affirms that a state's failure or refusal 'to cooperate in the arrest, extradition, trial, and punishment' of persons accused or convicted of genocide is 'contrary to the [UN Charter] and to generally recognised norms of international law'.[65] This is underpinned by Resolution 3074 on principles of international cooperation in the detention, arrest, extradition, and punishment of persons guilty of genocide.[66] Therefore, other states have a stake to the crimes of genocide committed against the Rohingya under universal jurisdiction.

[59] *Attorney General v Adolf Eichmann* (n 57), para 16.
[60] Gideon Hausner, *Justice in Jerusalem* (Schocken Books 1966).
[61] Hannah Arendt, *Eichmann in Jerusalem: A Report on the Banality of Evil* (Penguin 1994) 269.
[62] *Regina v Bow Street Metropolitan Stipendiary Magistrate, ex parte Pinochet Ugarte (Amnesty International Intervening) (No 3)* [2000] 1 AC 147.
[63] ibid.
[64] ibid.
[65] UNGA Res 2840 (1971) GAOR 26th Session Supp 29, 88.
[66] UNGA Res 3074 (1973) GAOR 28th Session Supp 30, 78.

Despite the above, to date, no action under the universal jurisdiction has been taken by any state including the ASEAN. A major reason is that the international politics has extensively distorted the original ideal of universal jurisdiction. The other reasons include the implications of universal jurisdiction on geopolitical and economic interests, state sovereignty, and ramifications on bilateral relations and regional cooperations. According to Amnesty International, as of 1 September 2012, a total of 163 states can exercise universal jurisdiction. Yet, since the end of the Second World War, only nineteen countries have exercised universal jurisdiction principles.[67] Leonard Lewis observes that 'States are now moving away from absolute universal jurisdiction towards a more limited version—conditional universal jurisdiction—that requires a stronger link between the alleged crime and the forum state'.[68] As a consequence of this move the response to genocide has ultimately become fragile, restricted, and event- or country-specific (as states are more willing to consider the nexus between the crime and the forum state and other interests involved before undertaking any actions) rather than general and universal, despite the fact that genocide is a crime that affects the international community wholly and is harmful to international interests. This deviation has the effect of not only tampering the very idea of the principle of universal jurisdiction but also undermining international justice.

The above demonstrates that although the Rohingya genocide comes within the purview of national, international, and universal jurisdictions, the perpetrators have not been brought to justice under any of them. In the postgenocide era, this has resulted in not only sabotage and dangerous distortion of criminal justice but also a risk of repetition of the crime by the same perpetrators through inscribing a belief that they can violate the ICL with impunity in Myanmar. Given the failure of these jurisdictional coverages, the following section—with a brief focus on the promise of R2P as a response mechanism to genocide—explores the possibility and challenges of protecting the Rohingya under the R2P principle.

Promise of R2P as a Response Mechanism to Genocide

The 2005 World Summit Outcomes Document asserted that 'governments have a responsibility to protect civilians from mass atrocity crimes of genocide, crimes against humanity, war crimes and ethnic cleansing'.[69] The essence of R2P was later

[67] Amnesty International, 'Universal Jurisdiction: Strengthening this Essential Tool of International Justice' (October 2012) < https://www.amnesty.org/download/Documents/24000/ior530202012en.pdf> accessed 17 June 2020.

[68] Leonard Lewis, 'The Politics of Universal Jurisdiction' (Human Security Centre, 15 October 2015) < http://www.hscentre.org/global-governance/politics-universal-jurisdiction/> accessed 18 June 2020.

[69] UNGA '2005 World Summit Outcome' (15 September 2005) UN Doc A/60/1, paras 138–40 (hereinafter UNGA, *World Summit Outcome*). Also see UNSC Res 1674 (28 April 2006) UN Doc S/RES/1674; UNSC Res 1894 (11 Nov 2009) UN Doc S/RES/1894.

captured in the 'three pillar structure': 1) the responsibility of individual states to protect their populations from atrocity crimes; 2) the responsibility of the international community, through the UN, to 'assist' states in effectively discharging the above duty; and 3) the responsibility of the international community to take, on a case-by-case basis, timely and decisive action if a state manifestly fails to protect its population.[70] The preventive and responsive aspects[71] as contained in these pillars are mutually reinforcing and do not necessarily require any particular order. The UN Secretary-General's report mentions that 'the three pillars of the R2P are of equal importance and without all three, the concept would be incomplete, and the pillars must be implemented in a manner fully consistent with the purposes, principles, and provisions of the Charter'.[72]

In the decade following the 2005 UN World Summit, the R2P has quickly moved from theory to practice at the UN and it makes 'sovereign rights conditional on the state protecting the rights of its people'.[73] In his first report on R2P, the UN Secretary-General Ban Ki-moon reaffirmed that 'action to prevent or halt atrocities requires the adoption of R2P as national policy by key state actors, and as international policy by the UN community collectively'.[74] Following this, not only several UN member states have acknowledged their responsibility to prevent atrocity crimes and protect populations under threat (both at home and internationally), but also the Security Council has explicitly referenced R2P in thirty-five resolutions that authorized robust measures to prevent atrocities in Libya, Côte d'Ivoire, the Central African Republic (CAR), Syria, and South Sudan, among others. To this date, the Human Rights Council has further adopted thirteen resolutions that feature the R2P, including three on the prevention of genocide. Apart from them, thematic resolutions on threats to international peace and security, on conflict prevention, on genocide prevention, policing in UN peacekeeping operations, and on small arms and light weapons have also made explicit reference to R2P.[75] The desire to institutionalize the concept further into the UN system and to challenge any pushback from member states on human rights norms is also

[70] Report of the Secretary General, 'Implementing the Responsibility to Protect' (12 January 2009) UN Doc A/63/677.

[71] Preventive aspect of the R2P addresses an early response to potential atrocities and the responsive one ensures no further deterioration of an ongoing atrocity. See Maley, 'Humanitarian Law, refugee protection, and the Responsibility to Protect' in Ramesh Thakur and William Maley (eds), *Theorising the Responsibility to Protect* (CUP 2015) 249.

[72] Report of the Secretary-General, 'Responsibility to Protect: Timely and Decisive Response' (25 July 2012) UN Doc A/66/874–S/2012/578 (hereinafter Report of the Secretary-General, *Responsibility to Protect*).

[73] Charles Sampford and Ramesh Thakur, 'From the Right to Persecute to the Responsibility to Protect: Feuerbachian inversions of rights and responsibilities in state–citizen relations' in Ramesh Thakur and William Maley (eds), *Theorising the Responsibility to Protect* (CUP 2015) 38.

[74] Report of the Secretary-General, *Responsibility to Protect* (n 72).

[75] Alexandra Buskie, *From Promise to Practice: Strengthening the UK's approach to atrocity prevention and R2P* (UNA-UK 2015) (hereinafter Buskie, *From Promise to Practice*).

heightening, which is very recently reflected in the Sustainable Development Goals framework, with Goal 16 on promoting peaceful and inclusive societies.[76]

A major reason for states' attention on the application of R2P lies in the reconceptualization of 'humanitarian intervention' as R2P and its (R2P) promise to respond quickly to atrocity crimes anywhere in the world. The idea of humanitarian intervention dates back to Hugo Grotius[77] and its practice could be found throughout nineteenth-century European politics.[78] Drawing on the ideas of Kant[79] and Hegel,[80] Bjorn Gomes argues that 'intervention on humanitarian grounds is not just permissible, but may indeed be obligatory', since ending the violations of human right is contingent upon such intervention.[81] Based on a comparison of the text of Articles 1(1–3) (purposes of the UN), 2(4) (prohibition of the use of force), and 55(c) (universal respect for, and observance of, human rights and fundamental freedoms) of the UN Charter, John Heieck concluded that humanitarian intervention can be construed as 'due diligence obligations' within the meaning of the R2P to prevent genocide.[82]

The promise of R2P is even more powerful and goes beyond the intervention as the International Commission on Intervention and State Sovereignty ('ICISS') ascertained that the issue is not the 'right to intervene' of any State, but the 'responsibility to protect the innocent' from atrocity crimes.[83] On the ICISS reading, Natalie Oman also opines that R2P is a crystallizing principle of international law mandating a range of forms of coercive intervention for human protection and human security purposes that underpins a proactive agenda for root cause prevention of the domestic conditions associated with atrocity crimes.[84]

R2P is linked to the human protection norm and addresses the issue from the perspective of the victims. Ramesh Thakur states that 'R2P was meant to compel an

[76] ibid.

[77] See Evan J Criddle, 'Three Grotian Theories of Humanitarian Intervention' (2015) 16(2) Theoretical Inquiries in Law 473.

[78] See Ellery C Stowell, *Intervention in international law* (John Byrne & Company 1921); Natalino Ronzitti, *Rescuing nationals abroad through military coercion and intervention on grounds of humanity* (Brill 1985).

[79] Immanuel Kant, translated by Ted Humphrey, *To Perpetual Peace: A Philosophical Sketch* (Hackett Pub Co. Inc. 2003) (hereinafter Kant, *Perpetual Peace*); A Franceschet, 'Kant, International Law, and the Problem of Humanitarian Intervention' (2010) 6(1) Journal of International Political Theory 3.

[80] See H G ten Bruggencate, 'Hegel's Views on War' (1950) 1 Philosophical Quarterly 58; C I Smith, 'Hegel and War' (1965) 26(2) Journal of the History of Ideas 282; S Avineri, *Hegel's Theory of the Modern State* (CUP 1972).

[81] Bjorn Gomes, 'The duty to oppose violence: humanitarian intervention as a question for political philosophy' (2011) 37 (3) Review of International Studies 1045.

[82] John Heieck, *A Duty to Prevent Genocide: Due Dilligence Obligations among the P5* (Edward Elgar 2018) 166–206.

[83] ICISS, 'The Responsibility to Protect: the Report of the International Commission on Intervention and State Sovereignty' (December 2001) <https://idl-bnc-idrc.dspacedirect.org/bitstream/handle/10625/18432/IDL-18432.pdf?sequence=6&isAllowed=y> accessed 17 June 2020 (hereinafter ICISS, 'Responsibility to Protect')

[84] Natalie Oman, *The Responsibility to Protect in International Law: Philosophical Investigations* (Routledge 2019) 3, 15.

analysis of—and policy response to—atrocities from the point of view of those in need of urgent protection, not the rights, privileges and interests of the intervening powers'.[85] Being victim-centric, the whole regime of R2P appears to be suitable to respond to atrocity crimes holistically in an integrated way. The preventive aspect of the R2P in this connection is also useful since it contains the characteristics of mobilizing the political will (of peoples and governments) to intervene to prevent atrocities when the other measures and mechanisms of international law do not function. Sharma and Welsh have argued that the operationalization of the R2P is possible 'through the conceptual lens of crimes prevention and using approaches like sanctions, mediation, international criminal justice, and military force'.[86]

R2P has a strong basis and in customary international law and in the UN Charter since it 'epitomises the humanitarian character and central purpose of international human rights, humanitarian law, refugee law and international criminal law'.[87] Under international law principles, there is also a responsibility to protect populations from genocide and other atrocities. Accordingly, R2P provides a solid impetus to states to meet their existing obligations and responsibilities under international law principles as a subject of international law and a member of the UN.[88] Although the shared understandings of R2P to date are not deep enough (but not shallow either) and its practice remains inconsistent,[89] some, like Peter Hilpold, argue that the R2P is slowly 'hardening' into a norm of customary international law,[90] which can also be argued to be a congealed basis and source of upholding the promise to respond to atrocity crimes.[91]

The role of R2P as a response mechanism to mass atrocity is often conflated with the limitations and past examples that according to many ultimately failed to keep the promise of R2P. Critiques in this connection cite the example of Resolution 1973[92] that according to them has been used as 'a means to carry out regime-change' in Libya, rather than protecting the civilians.[93] True that it has raised a number of questions (eg, the role of the UN Security Council in overseeing the interpretation and implementation of its mandate, as well as the responsibilities of the intervening parties). Yet, the majority member states did not feel that R2P

[85] Ramesh Thakur, 'The Responsibility to Protect at 15' (2016) 92(2) International Affairs 415, 433 (hereinafter Thakur, 'Responsibility to Protect').

[86] Serena K Sharma and Jennifer M Welsh (eds), *The Responsibility to Prevent* (OUP 2015).

[87] Gentian Zyberi, 'Sharing the Responsibility to Protect: Taking Stock and Moving Forward' in Zyberi (ed), *An Institutional Approach to the Responsibility to Protect* (CUP 2013) 511.

[88] Dieter Fleck, 'The Law Applicable to Peace Operations' in Andrew Clapham and Paola Gaeta (eds), *The Oxford Handbook of International law in Armed Conflict* (OUP 2014) 206.

[89] Jutta Brunnee and Stephen Toop, 'The Responsibility to Protect and the Use of Force: Building Legality?' (2010) 2(3) Global Responsibility to Protect 191.

[90] See Peter Hilpold, *The Responsibility to Protect (R2P): A New Paradigm of International Law?* (Brill 2014).

[91] For a detail discussion see Thakur, 'Responsibility to Protect' (n 85).

[92] UNSC Res 1973 (17 March 2011) UN Doc S/RES/1973.

[93] This point is elaborated further below in this chapter.

as a principle was to blame for the way Resolution 1973 was interpreted rather the problem lies in the operation of the R2P. It was also felt that the resolution needed more provisions balancing the use of force, such as mediation and the creation of a ceasefire.[94]

Another example relates to the genocidal violence in Darfur where no action has been undertaken by the international community under the R2P. According to some, the continued inaction in this crisis underscored the limitations of the R2P in delivering protection to civilians.[95] According to others, 'inaction on Darfur reflected heightened skepticism about interventionism after the 2003 Iraq War, western strategic interests in Sudan, and the complex linkages with Sudan's other wars'.[96] However, given the practical difficulties of using force against the Sudanese government, Gareth Evans argues that the failure lies not in the R2P framework but rather in the application of other measures including 'the functional convergence between Western actors, the Chinese Government, and the African Union around the practice of intervention'.[97] These examples show that despite optimism regarding the potential of R2P as a response to atrocity crimes, its operationalization and socialization in the international realm remains limited. The following discussion applies the promise of R2P over the Rohingya genocide to examine whether it can provide a basis for their protection from genocide.

Application of the R2P over the Rohingya Genocide

At the very centre of the R2P is the idea that the international community should help with preventing gross violations of human rights and abuses through diplomatic, humanitarian, and other peaceful means. It is reported that such means have been taken by the international community to prevent the Rohingya atrocity although they have become unsuccessful.[98] R2P as a principle permits the international community to take more coercive measures including economic sanctions, arms embargoes, referring the matter to the ICC and use of military force through the Security Council. Yet, to date, no coercive measures have been

[94] Buskie, *From Promise to Practice* (n 75) 13.

[95] For instance, Alex de Waal, 'Darfur and the failure of the Responsibility to Protect' (2007) 83(6) International Affairs 1039.

[96] Paul D Williams and Alex J Bellamy, 'The Responsibility to Protect and the crisis in Darfur' (2005) 36 (1) Security Dialogue 27.

[97] Gareth Evans, *The Responsibility to Protect: Ending Mass Atrocity Crimes Once and for All* (Brookings 2008). See also Ricardo Soares de Oliveira and Madhan Mohan Jaganathan, 'To Intervene in Darfur, or Not: Re-examining the R2P Debate and Its Impact' (2015) 30(1) Global Society 21; Robert I Rotberg, 'Deterring Atrocity Crimes: The Cause of Our Era' in Robert I Rotberg (ed), *Mass Atrocity Crimes: Preventing Future Outrages* (Brookings Institution Press, 2010) 1.

[98] For example, in 2007, the USA and the UK have taken several diplomatic measures including naming and shaming as a violator, diplomatic humiliation, pressure from allies and trade barrier to uphold human rights norms in Myanmar.

undertaken against Myanmar. In this vein, it is argued that the application of the R2P for the Rohingya would be difficult on at least three grounds: 1) that the idea of sovereignty as responsibility coined in the R2P is fundamentally flawed in Myanmar; 2) that the response of the states to the R2P paradoxically endeavours to remove stateless people from its protection; and 3) that the geopolitical and economic interests of the ASEAN work contradistinctively for the R2P's application for the protection of the Rohingya.

Sovereignty in Terms of R2P

The original idea of R2P suggested by the ICISS was to establish a possible way for intervention by the international community in state affairs 'by placing responsibility at the centre of the debate over the meaning of sovereignty'.[99] According to ICISS, 'sovereignty as responsibility' entails three things: 1) state authorities are responsible for protecting the lives and other fundamental rights of citizens; 2) national political authorities are responsible both to their citizens and to the international community; and 3) states are responsible for their actions.[100] In this interpretation, responsibility is considered as a constitutive element of sovereignty and if any state fails to fulfil its responsibility, it does not deserve the right to perpetuate sovereignty rather someone else must fulfil that responsibility.

The ICISS's illustration rests on the political theory of constitutionalism and its reliance on social-contract theory because 'state remains the fundamental guarantor of human rights locally, as well as the building block for collectively ensuring international order'.[101] Interference in such a case is justifiable, where 'the social contract of governance is annulled due to its violation by one of the parties'.[102] The contemporary constitutionalism rests on a series of normative values including the rule of law, separation of powers, and immutable human rights regimes. Sovereignty in such a situation is increasingly defined, not as an absolute and unconditional authority to rule and control those within one's territorial jurisdiction, but rather as a set of defined obligations towards citizens best defined under constitutional sovereignty—contradistinguished from parliamentary and popular sovereignty.[103]

However, Myanmar is a seminal example of a 'state as a sole possessor of national sovereignty'[104] that does not uphold some of the basic indicators of the

[99] ICISS, 'Responsibility to Protect' (n 83).
[100] ibid.
[101] Nishikawa, 'Reality of Protecting the Rohingya' (n 12).
[102] ibid.
[103] ibid.
[104] Hideaki Shinoda, *Re-examining Sovereignty: From Classical Theory to the Global Age* (Macmillan Press 2000) 152.

global constitutionalism including participatory democracy, rule of law, and minority rights' protection. Nishikawa states:

> Internal conflicts in Myanmar have not been resolved and moreover conflicts in Rakhine became more complex due to continuous violent incidences in Rakhine that regenerate distrust and identities among different groups. Nationalism in Myanmar is different from the civic nationalism that demands equal rights for all. Evidently, nationalism in Myanmar affects the country's understanding of citizenship, which is defensive and serves as a means of exclusion based on politically motivated groups, utilizing ethnoreligious lines. In fact, the contemporary wave of democratization in Myanmar tends to be primarily for the benefit of a particular dominant group, namely the Buddhist Bamar.[105]

Moreover, Nishikawa[106] opines that the varied discourses of sovereignty in Myanmar recall Turner's discussion of citizenship, who describes two types of citizenship as 'real and expansive' and 'formal'.[107] According to her analysis, 'the real and expansive citizenship emerges as a result of class struggles, war, migration, and egalitarian ideologies. In contrast, citizenship in Myanmar takes on a formal nature because of the primary focus on the question of who qualifies to be a citizen'.[108] Cheesman's elaboration of the term *taingyintha*, or 'sons of the soil', is relevant here. He shows that *taingyintha* has become the precondition of belonging in Myanmar and the recent Constitution of 2008 puts *taingyintha* over citizenship, making the political community of Myanmar an aggregation of 'national races' rather than 'citizens'.[109] Under the socio-political understanding and perception, the Rohingya are not considered as *taingyntha*. Moreover, owing to the impregnable connection between Buddhism and nationalism, the Rohingya remain unrecognized by the majority Burmans. These factors combine to cast the Rohingya as not part of the fabric of the Myanmar nation, but as a threat to that nation and unworthy of inclusion—non-compatible to the spirit of constitutional sovereignty.

The above in a nutshell depicts that the idea of sovereignty as responsibility or constitutional sovereignty coined in the R2P does not apply in Myanmar and thus R2P—in particular, the first pillar—does not come to protect the Rohingya. The following focuses on the applicability of the R2P to the Rohingya as stateless people.

105 Nishikawa, 'Reality of Protecting the Rohingya' (n 12) 97.

106 ibid.

107 S Brayan Turner, *Citizenship and Capitalism: The Debate over Reformism* (Allen & Unwin 1986) 67.

108 Nishikawa, 'Reality of Protecting the Rohingya' (n 12).

109 Nick Cheesman, 'How in Myanmar "National Races" Came to Surpass Citizenship and Exclude Rohingya' (2017) 47(3) Journal of Contemporary Asia 461, 470.

Protecting the Stateless under the R2P

The conception of R2P is strongly linked to the idea of state sovereignty since its first pillar emphasizes the responsibility of individual states to protect their populations, which is primarily fulfilled through protecting the citizen in a political community. Yet, one of the vexed issues regards those who lack very membership in any such community. This is so because the R2P cannot provide a suitable framework to help the stateless people whose membership in a political community is unacknowledged.[110] The Rohingya being stateless present a classic case in this connection. Their statelessness is commonly believed to be accrued from the 1982 Citizenship Law ('CL') that classifies three categories of citizens (eg, Full, Associated, and Naturalized) and stipulates the conditions necessary to qualify them.[111]

Full citizens are descendants of residents who lived in Myanmar prior to 1823 (s 3) or were born to parents who were citizens at the time of birth (s 5). Associate citizens are those who were qualified and applied for citizenship under the 1948 Union Citizenship Act (UCA) (s 23) but not finalized would come under the CL and, on fulfilling the conditions, one could gain associate citizenship.[112] Naturalized citizens are those who lived in Myanmar before 4 January 1948 and applied for citizenship after 1982 (s 42). These provisions, nonetheless, 'are of virtually no use to the Rohingya, for few Rohingya are in possession of the necessary documents that would provide "conclusive evidence" of entry and residence prior to the said timeline or could establish the necessary bloodlines as required by the law and thus are rendered stateless'.[113]

Nishikawa argues that the notion of the R2P addresses 'the constitutionalized relations between the state and its population in reference to the normative underpinnings of governance, justice, democracy, human rights, and legitimacy; and sovereignty tends to be used to enhance the power of governing elites in postcolonial states as seen in the idea of the right to rule'.[114] In such a context, in the independent Myanmar, the Rohingya's right to be citizens of the political community has been denied[115] and is placed outside the constitutional relations (between the state and its citizens). Parashar and Alam also made explicit the way Rohingya have been disempowered through legislation in Myanmar.[116]

110 Nishikawa, 'Reality of Protecting the Rohingya' (n 12).

111 Md Jobair Alam, 'The Rohingya Minority of Myanmar: Surveying Their Status and Protection in International Law' (2018) 25(2) International Journal of Minority and Group Rights 157.

112 The Rohingya were reportedly unaware of the UCA, nor was there any state-run programme to get them to apply for citizenship.

113 Archana Parashar and Jobair Alam, 'The National Laws of Myanmar: Making of Statelessness for the Rohingya' (2019) 57(1) International Migration 94 (hereinafter Parashar and Alam, 'National Laws of Myanmar').

114 Nishikawa, 'Reality of Protecting the Rohingya' (n 12) 99.

115 Jobair Alam, 'The Rohingya of Myanmar: Theoretical Significance of the Minority Status' (2018) 19(2) Asian Ethnicity 180.

116 Parashar and Alam, 'National Laws of Myanmar' (n 113).

In such a context, it is relevant to investigate whether the international community is able and willing to help the Rohingya—who are detached from the sovereign rule—on R2P grounds. The R2P concept affirmed in the 2005 World Summit addresses each country's 'responsibility to protect its population'.[117] Yet, stateless peoples can be brought under the human rights framework which provides protection for them as 'human beings' rather than as 'citizens'. An analogous point was elucidated by Arendt: statelessness symbolizes the dearth of place in the world, which is, in her terms, the 'rightless condition'.[118] Kant also introduced the idea of cosmopolitan law, which is concerned with 'the status of individuals vis-à-vis states of which they are not citizens and also concerned with the status of individuals as human beings, rather than as citizens of states'.[119]

Nevertheless, there is incongruity between sovereignty and universalized perception of human rights. Indeed, the orthodox perception of human rights protection without the support and recognition of states became fade in the post-Cold War world, and in the contemporaneous political thinking and practice it is undisputed that a connection to the state and its recognition is significant for not only ensuring human rights, but also defending any encroachment to the violations of human rights. Apparently, the emergence of R2P is part of such a new trend in the contemporary world. Nevertheless, question remains if the notion of R2P can help critically suffering people, including the Rohingya, who are outside the state-centred international order since, to date, R2P fails to decouple the citizenship with state responsibility.

R2P in the ASEAN

Even though the promise of the R2P appears to be upheld—rhetorically, at least—by some of the influential member states of the international community, in practice it is not unusual that the bloc politics plays a crucial role in R2P's application or non-application. The following examines if the geopolitical and economic interests of the ASEAN work contradistinctively for R2P's universal application and thus make its application a remote possibility for the Rohingya.

The members of ASEAN have shown a mixed reaction towards the Rohingya crisis. Their reaction is also mixed towards Myanmar (an ASEAN member since 1997) and the notions of R2P. Although initially some ASEAN states supported some aspects of the R2P, Myanmar entirely opposed this new principle. Nishikawa categorized ASEAN's response to the R2P into three: 1) accommodational—they accept the idea of the R2P in a flexible way, for instance during the natural

[117] UNGA, *World Summit Outcome* (n 69) para 138.
[118] Hannah Arendt, *The Origin of Totalitarianism* (Harcourt, Brase Company 1951) 281.
[119] Kant, *Perpetual Peace* (n 79). See also Nishikawa, 'Reality of Protecting the Rohingya' (n 12).

calamities; 2) sceptical—they recognize the usefulness of the R2P but consider it too early to be optimistic about its regional localization; and 3) incremental—they argue certain change in the existing systems and modalities before the application of the R2P in this region.[120]

Several reasons are involved in the insouciant standing of the ASEAN. But the major reason is the principle of non-intervention as enumerated in ASEAN Charter Article 2 that patrons a number of principles of diplomacy that ASEAN states maintain in their intra-regional relations, including dialogue and a consensus style of decision-making based on non-interference (Westphalian principles). This is inconsistent with the third pillar of the R2P and appears to have been controversial in ASEAN states that have colonial experience. Moreover, 'the governing patterns on which ASEAN structured their thoughts is "political realism" with power as the end of political actions in the municipal and international arenas. As an outcome of this pattern, ASEAN members are doubtful if there are legal and moral connotations in the intention to intervene or responsibility to protect, because in a State-centric international system, it is questionable if foreign policies are based on moral contents'.[121]

The UN General Assembly ('GA') has adopted several resolutions on the human rights situation in Myanmar.[122] The Security Council has also expressed 'alarm at the significantly and rapidly deteriorating humanitarian situation' in Rakhine State.[123] Yet to date, despite several calls from human rights groups and collective and bilateral leverage by many Asian states on the UN Security Council to adopt a resolution referring the situation to the ICC, the Council has not positively responded. The same response could be anticipated, if the R2P was invoked in the Security Council. Several factors are involved including geopolitical and strategic interests and the accompanying unwillingness of Myanmar's allies to subject the 'situation' to international discussion.

A case in context is Libya. On 19 March 2011, the Security Council approved Resolution 1973. This resolution reiterated the Libyan authorities' responsibility to protect the Libyan population.[124] Critics suggested that R2P-based intervention in Libya was used not for protecting the civilians, but rather as a means to carry out regime-change, undermining the core objective of the doctrine.[125] The

[120] Nishikawa, 'Reality of Protecting the Rohingya' (n 12).

[121] Dabiru Sridhar Patnaik, 'International Law and Responsibility to Protect: South Asian Perspective' (2003) 4 Journal of Global Studies 173, 183 (hereinafter Patnaik, 'International Law and Responsibility').

[122] UNGA Res 69/L.32 (31 October 2014) UN Doc A/C.3/69/L.32; UNGA Res 70/L.39 (16 November 2015) UN Doc A/C.3/70/L.39/Rev.1; UNGA Res 68/L.55 (12 November 2013) UN Doc A/C.3/68/L.55/Rev.1; UNGA Res 67/L.49 (16 November 2012) UN Doc A/C.3/67/L.49/Rev.1; UNGA Res 46/132 (17 December 1991) UN Doc A/RES/46/132.

[123] UNSC Presidential Statement 22 (2017) UN Doc S/PRST/2017/22, 2.

[124] UNSC Res 1973 (17 March 2011) UN Doc S/RES/1973.

[125] David Rieff, 'R2P, R.I.P.' (*The New York Times*, 7 November 2011) < https://www.nytimes.com/2011/11/08/opinion/r2p-rip.html> accessed 17 June 2020.

Libyan experience has further yielded global scepticism concerning proposed UN intervention in Syria, when the US government attempted to pass Security Council resolutions in the course of 2011–2013 to justify military intervention in the Civil War of Syria.[126] These were vetoed by Russia and China and they issued statements to the effect that, in their opinion, R2P had been abused by the US government.[127] This has a strong parallel to the Rohingya situation, as the political alignment of Myanmar with the West and China bears a significant impact on the R2P. Driven by economic gain through investment in Rakhine State and geopolitical and strategic interests, both India and China have been strong supporters to the Myanmar leadership, in contrast to the Western and Islamic countries, who have challenged the standing of the Aung San Suu Kyi government. Moreover, lack of common rules regarding the application of R2P in Libya complicated the debate of its application elsewhere hindering international consensus particularly between Western and non-Western states. Reflecting on the segmented viewpoints about the R2P, Patnaik rightly notes that 'the unprecedented debates about R2P such as those in Brazil and India certainly show not everybody's views are set in stone'.[128] Hence, it is not unrealistic to expect that any future chance of R2P's application in the ASEAN will be difficult, if not impossible.

Conclusion

The Myanmar Rohingya have suffered and continue to suffer serious and persistent human rights abuses by the Myanmar Government. These abuses are delineated in many reports as constituting genocide. This chapter investigated the Rohingya genocide using the ICL framework. In a postgenocide setting, this chapter considered a number of issues relating to the Rohingya genocide and its effects, including the treatment and standard of protection of the Rohingya under the ICL principles, the application of national, international, and universal jurisdictions to the said genocide in order to bring the perpetrators to justice, and the possibilities of the application of the R2P in Myanmar.

The analysis demonstrated that although the Rohingya genocide comes within the purview of national, international, and universal jurisdictions, the perpetrators have not been brought to justice under any of them. The mechanisms under national jurisdiction have not been exercised as the perpetrators are part of

[126] Justin Morris, 'Libya and Syria: R2P and the Spectre of the Swinging Pendulum' (2013) 89(5) International Affairs 1265.

[127] Paul D Williams and Alex J Bellamy, 'Principles, Politics, and Prudence: Libya, the Responsibility to Protect, and the Use of Military Force' (2012) 18(3) Global Governance 273.

[128] India upholds that 'internal affairs' are not subject to 'external intervention'. It is largely an outcome of the discussions India had with emerging likeminded powers like Brazil and South Africa. See Patnaik, 'International Law and Responsibility' (n 121) 179.

the current government. The apparatuses of international jurisdiction have also failed to protect the Rohingya as the UN Security Council has been inconsistent in creating *ad hoc* ICTs and the ICC lacks jurisdiction over crimes committed by Myanmar as a non-party to the Rome Statute. In addition, the principle of universal jurisdiction has not been applied to the Rohingya case as the original idea of this principle has been distorted by international politics. Under the contemporaneous international affairs, states are more willing to apply conditional universal jurisdiction—that requires a stronger link between the forum state and the alleged crime. Since no such links have been established, states are largely found to remain silent to take any action against the perpetrators under universal jurisdiction principle.

The geopolitical, economic, and strategic interests of some states, notably India and China, are also working as a catalyst on non-taking actions against the atrocities. India has reluctantly expressed concern about the Rohingya ordeals and always maintained a good relationship with the Myanmar Government. China, on the other hand, is seen as seeking to utilize the crisis to strengthen relations with Myanmar owing to its own geopolitical interests in Myanmar: China's ambitious Bet and Road Initiative is heavily contingent on the positive response of Myanmar.

The above failures are connected to the absence of political will to stop the genocide on the part of those who have the power to do so, including the state of Myanmar. The sweeping human suffering of the Rohingya caused by genocide is also connected to the failure to protect. Considering this, the chapter explored the possibility and challenges of protecting the Rohingya under the R2P that has recently gained international support and recognition as a deriving principle for collective global action. The analysis found that the application of the R2P for the Rohingya would be strenuous, owing to the flawed idea of sovereignty as responsibility in Myanmar, the statelessness of the Rohingya, and ASEAN's contextual application of the R2P. The application of the R2P for the Rohingya requires addressing not only the above issues but also, among others, the clarity over the reach and limits of this principle and 'localization' or 'reframing' of it in the ASEAN context to make it fit with regional norms. Failure to do so may result in a catastrophe with great socio-economic costs in Asia and beyond. The cost of further inaction would be high to the cause of international law; regional and international peace and security; and interstate neighbourly relationships.

PART II

GENOCIDE DENIAL AND REMEMBRANCE

6

Sovereignty, Subjectivity, Denial

The Armenian Genocide, Generative Denials, and Postgenocide Politics in Contemporary Turkey

Tatevik Mnatsakanyan

Introduction

Beyond specialized literature, the Armenian genocide is often perceived as 'distant in both time and place'.[1] While in Genocide Studies, it is one of the three 'canonical' or 'ideal type' genocides along with the Holocaust and the Rwandan genocide,[2] elsewhere a degree of privatization of the Armenian genocide is present: partly corollary to the denial/recognition politics between contemporary Turkish and Armenian states, scholarship has spent 'much energy proving that what happened to the Armenians *was* genocide';[3] thus overwhelming discussions beyond such matters.[4] In turn, the discipline of International Relations ('IR') has remained

[1] Stefan Ihrig, *Justifying Genocide: Germany and the Armenians from Bismarck to Hitler* (Harvard University Press 2016) 4 (hereafter Ihrig, *Justifying Genocide*).

[2] Adam Jones, *Genocide: A Comprehensive Introduction* (2nd edition, Routledge 2011) 149 (hereafter Jones, *Genocide*); Mark Levene, *Genocide in the Age of the Nation State*, Vol. I: *The Meaning of Genocide* (I.B. Tauris 2008) 65–67 (hereafter Levene, *The Meaning of Genocide*).

[3] Levene *The Meaning of Genocide* (n 2) 3.

[4] See ibid. cf Donald Bloxham, *The Great Game of Genocide. Imperialism, Nationalism, and the Destruction of the Ottoman Armenians* (OUP 2005) (hereafter Bloxham, *The Great Game of Genocide*). Therefore, I refrain from rehearsing the historical veracity of the genocide; debating the legal/political suitability of the term 'genocide'; or cataloguing and countering official Turkish denial. A veritable scholarship along those lines is well-established. eg Leo Kuper, *Genocide: Its Political Use in the Twentieth Century* (Yale University Press 1981) (hereafter Kuper, *Genocide*); Richard Hovannisian, 'The Armenian Genocide and Patterns of Denial' in Richard Hovannisian (ed) *The Armenian Genocide in Perspective* (Transaction 1986) (hereafter Hovannisian, 'The Armenian Genocide'); Vahakn Dadrian, *The History of the Armenian Genocide: Ethnic Conflict from the Balkans to Anatolia to the Caucasus* (6th edn, Berghahn Books 2003); Mark Levene, 'Creating a Modern "Zone of Genocide": The Impact of Nation—and State-Formation on Eastern Anatolia, 1878-1923' (1998) 3 Holocaust and Genocide Studies (hereafter Levene, 'Creating a Modern "Zone of Genocide"'); Tane Akçam, 'Anatomy of Genocide Denial: Academics, Politicians, and the "re-making" of History' (2005) 1 Occasional Paper, Center for Holocaust and Genocide Studies (University of Minnesota); Taner Akçam, 'Anatomy of a crime: The Turkish Historical Society's manipulation of archival documents' (2005) 2 Journal of Genocide Research; Taner Akçam, *A Shameful Act: The Armenian Genocide and the Question of Turkish Responsibility* (Constable 2006); Taner Akçam, 'Denial as a Security Concept' (2008-09) 10 Cardozo Journal of Conflict Resolution 10 (hereafter Akçam 'Denial as a Security Concept'); Taner Akçam, *Killing Orders: Talat Pasha's Telegrams and the Armenian Genocide* (Palgrave MacMillan 2018); Richard Hovannisian, *Denial of the Armenian Genocide in Comparison with Holocaust Denial* (National Academy of Sciences 2004); Fatma Müge Göçek, *Denial of Violence: Ottoman Past, Turkish Present,*

Tatevik Mnatsakanyan, *Sovereignty, Subjectivity, Denial* In: *Postgenocide*. Edited by: Klejda Mulaj, Oxford University Press (2021). © The Several Contributors. DOI: 10.1093/oso/9780192895189.003.0006

mostly disengaged from the study of genocide more broadly. For its Realist and Liberal versions, genocide is corollary to major wars, or else an aberration, the break-down of the rights- and law-based international order. Indeed, genocide 'becomes of international significance because it offends against international law'.[5] In turn, in the subdisciplines of Security and Peace and Conflict studies, genocides feature as 'cases' to debate 'humanitarian interventions', 'the responsibility to protect', or peace-building and postconflict reconciliation. There is far less study of genocide for the understanding of the very productions and transformations of the (inter)national and the violence these inhere through continued renegotiations of 'sovereignty' and political subjectivities.

This chapter hopes to generate insights towards this broader aim through the exploration of the Armenian genocide and its continued official Turkish denials. Integral to the aims and the central conceptual advancement of this volume, the chapter is ultimately concerned with 'postgenocide': distinct from 'post-genocide' that assumes a temporal before/after separation, 'postgenocide' draws attention to the continued and evolving effects of genocide on social and political processes long after the genocide.[6] The chapter's more specific contribution is a reconsideration of how we think about 'denial' in postgenocide—a revisiting of 'denial' through a productive interdisciplinary encounter and conversation: the chapter brings Critical IR theoretical explorations on 'sovereignty', 'subjectivity', and 'violence' to bear on Genocide Studies and on the conceptual, historical, and political issue of denial—something that has so far received little attention either in IR literature or in Genocide Studies. Thereby, it is claiming that we cannot ignore a very close interrelation between critical understandings of sovereignty and of postgenocide denial.

The chapter treats the Armenian genocide and its denials as a *via media* for exploring a wider theoretical and political concern: what can Critical IR theorizations of 'sovereignty', 'subjectivity', and 'violence' reveal about genocide and postgenocide denial; and conversely, what can a revisiting of genocide and denial reveal about 'sovereignty', 'subjectivity', and 'violence', and thereby, possibilities for resistance in postgenocide? In this treatment then, through the notion of postgenocide, the chapter responds to the volume's concern with 'the *effects* of genocide' in 're-imagining, re-understanding, reexperiencing political community

and Collective Violence against the Armenians, 1789-2009 (OUP 2015) (hereafter Göçek, *Denial of Violence*); Alan Whitehorn, 'Denial of the Armenian Genocide,' in Alan Whitehorn (ed) *The Armenian Genocide: The Essential Reference Guide* (ABC-CLIO 2015) (hereafter Whitehorn, 'Denial of the Armenian Genocide').

[5] Martin Shaw, 'From comparative to international genocide studies: The international production of genocide in 20th-century Europe' (2011) 4 European Journal of International Relations 645.

[6] Refer in this volume to Mulaj, Chapter 1, 'Introduction: Living with Permutations of Genocide Harm' (hereafter Mulaj, 'Introduction').

in the postgenocide setting',[7] by extending the analytical purchase of 'postgenocide' into explicating the very renegotiations of sovereignty and subjectivity.

The Armenian case is suitable for such exploration because: a) the genocide was one of the most violent episodes of the First World War, a war (trans)formative of the (inter)national, in turn implicated in transformative renegotiations of sovereignty and political subjectivity; b) it unfolded at the 'twilight of the Ottoman empire',[8] an empire most prominently formative of the idea and identity of Europe/ the 'West',[9] and thereby presenting an episode reflective of the fundamentally *relational* character of both the renegotiations of sovereignty and the genocidal violence they inhere;[10] and c) the denial of the Armenian genocide has been key to contemporary Turkish identity and politics and is integral to wider processes of foreclosure of the political and opportunities for resistance.[11] Being part of such transformative episode, the case allows teasing out the close relationship of genocide to continuous renegotiations of the myth of 'sovereignty' and forms of sovereign power and subjectivities.

The literature on the Armenian genocide has variously explained today's Turkish denial. Some centre on Turkey's transition from empire to nation-state at the start of the twentieth century, the accompanying founding of its national identity myth and the taboos this has produced including through what Ünlü calls the 'Turkishness Contract'.[12] Some conceive denial as a response to a perceived threat to post-First World War Turkey's national security.[13] Others, in a relational and postcolonial approach, have linked Turkish state denial to its 'ontological insecurity' and as part of its 'continuing struggl[es] with geopolitical belonging and relations with the "West" '.[14] While otherwise compelling, and sources upon which this study partly draws, these explorations reproduce the dominant frame of explicating denial in genocide literature more widely. Both in historical genocide scholarship and in reconciliation literature, denial is frequently conceived as a *post-factum* practice that ensues *after* a genocide, prominently dubbed as the 'final

[7] ibid 15. Page number to be checked

[8] Hilmar Kaiser 'Genocide at the Twilight of the Ottoman Empire' in Donald Bloxham and A Dirk Moses (eds), *The Oxford Handbook of Genocide Studies* (OUP 2010) 365 (hereafter Kaiser, 'Genocide at the Twilight of the Ottoman Empire').

[9] Iver Neumann and Jennifer Welsh 'The Other in European self-definition: an addendum to the literature on international society' (1991) Review of International Studies, 17 (hereafter Neumann and Welsh, 'The Other in European self-definition').

[10] Levene, *The Meaning of Genocide* (n 2); Mark Levene, *Genocide in the Age of the Nation State*, Vol. II: *The Rise of the West and the Coming of Genocide* (I.B. Tauris 2013) (hereafter Levene, *The Rise of the West*).

[11] Ayşe Zarakol, 'Ontological (In)security and State Denial of Historical Crimes: Turkey and Japan' (2010) 24(1) International Relations (hereafter Zarakol, 'Ontological (In)security').

[12] Boriş Ünlü, 'The Kurdish struggle and the crisis of the Turkishness Contract' (2016) 42(4-5) Philosophy and Social Criticism.

[13] Taner Akçam, *From Empire to Republic: Turkish Nationalism and the Armenian Genocide* (Zed Books 2004) (hereafter Akçam, *From Empire to Republic*); Akçam, 'Denial as a Security Concept' (n 4).

[14] Zarakol, 'Ontological (In)security' (n 11) 3; see also Pinar Bilgin, 'Thinking Past "Western" IR?' (2008) 29(1) Third World Quarterly (hereafter Bilgin, 'Thinking Past 'Western' IR?').

stage of genocide'.[15] Literature engaging with the Armenian genocide, too, conceives denial as something that *follows* the major genocidal events, arising after the establishment of the Turkish Republic in 1923.[16]

This chapter differs from the extant literature treating genocide as *post-factum*, by proposing two interrelated arguments. First, denials must be examined in close relationship with the unfolding of the genocidal violence itself.[17] A critical re-examination of the conditions of possibility for the Armenian genocide reveals that denials were not only part of the process of the genocide,[18] but were *generative* of the genocide itself. Without explicating what I call generative denials, the chapter argues that it would be futile to attempt an understanding of postgenocide denials or the wider postgenocide implications of such denials both for Turkish and international politics. To understand the present (ie, denial in postgenocide), we need to look at the past (denial as generative of genocide): this is because not only 'postgenocide … is shaped by genocide',[19] but also postgenocide denial is shaped by denials that were *generative* of the genocide itself.

The second argument is that the Armenian genocide and its generative denials were the culmination of a century of Ottoman *renegotiation of the meaning of 'sovereignty'* through encounters with Europe through two entwined processes. On the one hand, it was the renegotiation of 'sovereignty' as an organizing principle of inter-imperial relations in the long nineteenth century intimately linked with identity constructions and transformations of political idea(l)s *relationally* with Europe. On the other hand, the genocide was the radical re-articulation of 'sovereignty' as the mechanism of production of political subjectivities.[20] Developing this argument, the chapter traces how these renegotiations were implicated in generative denials. In turn, such violent renegotiations, and the grappling with contradictory encounters with Europe, were implicated in a deeper denial, that is, denial of the unfoundedness and contingency of sovereignty itself. Thereby, the chapter further argues that denial is a larger generative force: denial of violence is

15 Gregory H Stanton, 'The Ten Stages of Genocide' (2016) Genocide Watch < http://genocidewatch.net/genocide-2/8-stages-of-genocide >accessed 20 December 2020; Jones, Genocide (n 2).

16 Eg Akçam, *From Empire to Republic* (n 13); Akçam 'Denial as a Security Concept' (n 4); Zarakol, 'Ontological (In)security' (n 11). Where denial is shown to 'date back to the crime itself', it is about mechanisms of secrecy and deception (eg Whitehorn, 'Denial of the Armenian Genocide' (n 4) 13; Bloxham, *The Great Game of Genocide* (n 4) 208. A partial exception is Göçek, *Denial of Violence* (n 4), discussed later.

17 I opt for 'denials' (plural) as the amalgam of ideas, discourses, representations, practices, and affective elements that often present as contradictions, aporia, and justifications that are simultaneous acknowledgements.

18 See eg Göçek, *Denial of Violence* (n 4).

19 Refer in this volume to Mulaj, 'Introduction' (n 6).

20 These echo 'external' and 'internal' sovereignty in conventional understandings; eg Robert Jackson, 'Sovereignty in World Politics: A Glance at the Conceptual and Historical Landscape' (1999) XLVII Political Studies (hereafter Jackson, 'Sovereignty in World Politics'). However, I treat them as contingent; in continuous relational negotiations (see Jans Bartelson, *Genealogy of Sovereignty* (CUP 1995) (hereafter Bartelson, *Genealogy of Sovereignty*).

embedded in and is the condition of possibility for the very production of sovereign power more generally, marked by fear of the exposure of its arbitrariness, and therefore requiring subjectivization-through-denial, that is, *subjects of denial*.

The chapter proceeds as follows. Section one, via a conjunctural and relational approach,[21] explores the contradictions of the historical conjuncture, the diffusion of European political idea(l)s, and some of the conditions of possibility for the genocide and its denials. Section two traces the renegotiation of 'international sovereignty': conditioned by contradictions of the conjuncture, argues that the radicalization, at the start of the twentieth century, of the Turkish revolutionary elite (the Committee of Union and Progress ('CUP'), or the Young Turk regime) was the resolution to the decades-long renegotiation of the problem of 'international sovereignty'. Section three argues that intimately linked with this radical resolution was the re-articulation of sovereignty as the mechanism of production of political subjectivities. Drawing on Giorgio Agamben's thought on sovereign power, it argues that the genocide and its generative denials were intimately linked with the process of re-establishing what DeCaroli calls 'the field of sovereignty' as 'a space capable of being *obedient*',[22] thus allowing to explore a much deeper denial—conceptually, in close relationship to sovereignty. The concluding section ties in the different facets of generative denials and reflects on Turkish politics of denials today. Speaking to the wider concerns with postgenocide in this volume, the chapter calls for a different sort of intellectual and political-activist engagement with today's denial, than prevalent: if denials have been *generative* of the Armenian genocide, then countering today's denials and their postgenocide political implications should be a generative process too—generative of new imaginaries and subjectivities. Hence, it lends itself to re-examination of the volume's concern with 'postgenocide' by drawing out implications for possibilities for political engagement in postgenocidal context.

The Genocide Conjuncture and Generative Denials

Major genocides are often described as periods of 'acute convulsions', and in the Armenian Genocide case, one of collision of the 'tectonic plates' of empires.[23] The complex character of such processes calls for a *conjunctural* and *relational* approach to the study of genocide. Rather than a full conjunctural analysis, here the

[21] Stuart Hall and Doreen Massey, 'Interpreting the crisis' (2010) 44 Soundings: A Journal of Politics and Culture; Neumann and Welsh, 'The Other in European self-definition' (n 9); Iver B Neumann, *Uses of the Other: "The East" in European Identity Formation* (University of Minnesota Press 1999) (hereafter Neumann, *Uses of the Other*).

[22] Steven DeCaroli, 'Boundary Stones: Giorgio Agamben and the Field of Sovereignty', in Matthew Calarco and Steven DeCaroli (eds), *Giorgio Agamben: Sovereignty and Life* (Stanford University Press 2007) 46–47; 50–51 (hereafter DeCaroli, 'Boundary Stones').

[23] Levene, *The Meaning of Genocide* (n 2) 171; Levene, *The Rise of the West* (n 10) 222.

conjunctural approach is taken as broad analytical orientation inviting attention to 'multiple, heterogeneous and contradictory forces, tendencies, and trajectories', and thus to the complexity of a historical moment, guarding against reductionism.[24] A conjuncture results from the dissolution of previous economic, social, political, and cultural/ideological settlements and is marked by 'new alignments of political forces and the promise of new settlements'.[25]

We may conceive of the Armenian genocide conjuncture as roughly from the Congress of Berlin in 1878 leading up to the Hamidian massacres of 1894–1896 down to the period of the genocide itself (1914–1917) with the annihilation of estimated 1–1.5 million Armenians;[26] and the immediate aftermath of the genocide when the demographic engineering through ethnic cleansing and massacres of the remaining Armenians and other groups continued into the early years of the Turkish Republic in 1920s.[27]

Violence against the Armenians of the Ottoman Empire increased in the nineteenth century, with the intensifying administrative, military, and financial pressures, the national revival of several subject populations, and the subsequent losses of Ottoman territories.[28] Armenian demands for implementation of promised reforms came to be seen as instigated by European powers to tear apart the empire, and culminated in systematic massacres of up to 200,000 Armenians (the Hamidian massacres, 1894–1896), forced conversions to Islam, looting, and mass exile.[29] With the Young Turk revolution, the ultra-nationalistic faction of the CUP seized power in 1913, and led by the triumvirate of Talat, Enver, and Djemal, entered the First World War as a German ally, with the hope of creating a pan-Turkic empire stretching from Europe to Central Asia, based on the ideal of a homogeneous Turkish nation-state.[30] In February 1915, under the pretext of collusion with Russia, the Armenian soldiers in the Ottoman Army were unarmed, taken to labour camps, left to die of exertion or summarily executed.[31] Civilians suspected of concealing arms—an accusation *de facto* extended to the entire Armenian population—were next: searches were accompanied by mass killings,

[24] John Clarke, 'Doing the Dirty Work: The Challenges of Conjunctural Analysis,' in Julian Heriques and David Morley (eds) *Stuart Hall: Conversations, Projects, Legacies* (Goldsmiths Press 2017) 81 (hereafter Clarke, 'Doing the Dirty Work').

[25] John Clarke, 'Conjunctures, Crises, and Cultures: Valuing Stuart Hall' (2014) 70 Focaal—Journal of Global and Historical Anthropology 115.

[26] A general consensus on the estimate of 1–1.5 million is present in genocide scholarship (see Jones, *Genocide* (n 2); Kaiser, 'Genocide at the Twilight of the Ottoman Empire' (n 8), 382; Levene, *The Meaning of Genocide* (n 2) 73; Kuper, *Genocide* (n 4)). For recently revealed further Ottoman sources, see Ara Sarafian (ed) *Talaat Pasha's Report on the Armenian Genocide* (Gomidas Institute 2011).

[27] This periodization coincides with seminal treatments of the Armenian genocide (eg Bloxham, *The Great Game of Genocide* (n 4)).

[28] Hovannisian, 'The Armenian Genocide' (n 4); Kuper, *Genocide* (n 4).

[29] Levene, 'Creating a Modern "Zone of Genocide"' (n 4); Kuper, *Genocide* (n 4).

[30] Levene, 'Creating a Modern "Zone of Genocide"' (n 4); Hovannisian, 'The Armenian Genocide' (n 4).

[31] Kuper, *Genocide* (n 4).

rape, conversion, and plunder, while the Armenian political, intellectual, and cultural elite were culled in Constantinople on 24 April 1915. Orders of mass deportations followed, proclaimed as 'relocations from war zones', but in effect uprooting Armenians from across the empire.[32] Those surviving the immediate massacres would soon turn into 'convoys of exiles ... death caravans', the main destination being the desolate waste of the Syrian deserts.[33]

Building on historiographical and sociological literature on the genocide, it is possible to outline broad dynamics explicating the conjuncture and what I argue to be generative denials inherent to it. *Generative denials* here are conceptualized as a set of discourses and practices of erasure of past history, myth-making, and rationalizations that were borne out of the contradictions of the historical conjuncture and integral to the conditions of possibility for the genocide. To make this intelligible, the wider conjuncture and its contradictions need to be laid out.

A conjunctural orientation allows conceiving this historical period not in terms of a clear shift from empire to nation-state; nor merely as Western semi-colonial domination of Turkey: the latter risks depriving Turkish leaders of agency and thus off-loading the blame of violence and genocide on the European 'great power game'.[34] Instead, conceived *relationally*, a conjunctural approach allows inquiring how and to what effect, through Ottoman Turkey's often contradictory encounters, European political idea(l)s, economic, political, and military pressures *fused* with older Ottoman institutions. This invites attention to how 'long histories and the slow rhythms of change ... [were] given a new significance or urgency by their encounter with more immediate pressures, shorter rhythms, or faster, more urgent political demands'.[35] To explicate the present postgenocide context, it is imperative to scrutinize the past and extract the very conditions of possibility for the genocide and its generative denials. The conjunctural exploration offered here becomes a necessary part of such task.

The faster demands of the genocide conjuncture included the intensifying pressures of the Western-led globalizing economy,[36] and the ensuing 'informal' European empire as 'institutionalized relationship of control by one state over another'.[37] This manifested through unequal trade agreements imposed by European powers; control over parts of the Ottoman government including finances, and intensification of the much older capitulatory system whereby European merchants

[32] Hovannisian, 'The Armenian Genocide' (n 4) 29. The Turkish thesis of 'resettlement' for sake of protection of civilians has been countered by multiple studies. See eg Nora Vosbigian, 'Report: Missing Ottoman Archival Records on the Armenian Genocide, 1915' (7 March 2007) Gomidas Institute <http://www.gomidas.org/projects-and-studies/show/11> accessed 5 December 2018; Kuper, *Genocide* (n 4)

[33] Kuper, *Genocide* (n 4) 111.

[34] See Bloxham, *The Great Game of Genocide* (n 4) 17.

[35] Clarke, 'Doing the Dirty Work' (n 24) 83.

[36] Levene, *The Rise of the West* (n 10).

[37] Jesse Savage, 'The stability and breakdown of empire: European informal empire in China, the Ottoman Empire and Egypt' (2010) 2 European Journal of International Relations 162.

operated outside Ottoman laws including on taxes and customs. For the Turks, the capitulatory system was to become 'a prime symbol of external interference'.[38] Concomitant were the need for keeping up with technological and military advancements in Europe,[39] the resultant financial pressures, and the demands for bureaucratic routinization.[40] In turn, some of the long histories and the slow rhythms of the genocide conjuncture were in the peculiar Ottoman coloniality in relation to its non-Muslim subjects, institutionalized in hierarchies of rights and obligations. Part of such 'imperial structure of difference' was *dhimmi*, a 'protected'/'tolerated' status for the Armenians, Greeks, and the Jews, whereby religious and community autonomy was allowed *conditional* on submission to Islamic rule, paying of special taxes, and committing no resistance.[41]

The genocide conjuncture was marked by a denial of the violent foundations of the empire and the institutionalization of these relations of coloniality. Göçek has traced a consistent forgetting of the physical and structural violence of the empire in Turkish discourses of late nineteenth and early twentieth centuries.[42] Going beyond such tracing of denial of the 'domestic origins' of violence,[43] the relational and conjunctural approach requires examining how such denials enfolded into justificatory tropes through at least a century-long encounter and reckoning with political idea(l)s from Europe, particularly on 'empire', 'nation', 'national interest', 'security', changing conceptions on 'war', and 'military necessity', as well as new—Social Darwinist—conceptions on race.

The strong influence, and, later the extensive embeddedness, of German political, military, and knowledge production institutions into Ottoman state and army apparatuses is especially significant.[44] From the 1830s, directed by von Moltke, the Prussian architect of the doctrine of total offensive warfare, which came to dominate imperial competitions from 1870 to 1918, the Ottoman army departed from Middle-Eastern military traditions, and built a 'total war army … intended as a tool of aggression'.[45] The *Vernichtungsschlacht* (Battle of Annihilation) legitimized collective punishment of 'enemy civilians' for military necessity. Reid has argued

[38] Levene, *The Rise of the West* (n 10) 12.

[39] James J Reid, 'Total War, the Annihilation Ethic, and the Armenian Genocide, 1870-1918,' in Richard G Hovannisian (ed) *The Armenian Genocide: History, Politics, Ethics* (MacMillan 1992) (hereafter Reid, 'Total War').

[40] Göçek, *Denial of Violence* (n 4).

[41] Göçek, *Denial of Violence* (n 4) 72; Reid, 'Total War' (n 39). In different periods these groups were excluded from the military and politics and thus confined to trade, artisanship, medicine, and farming. Over time, this produced advantages for some Armenians in major municipalities (Göçek, *Denial of Violence* (n 4) 73). However, the vast majority were subsistence farmers in rural Anatolia (Ihrig, *Justifying Genocide* (n 3); Levene, *The Rise of the West* (n 10).

[42] Göçek, *Denial of Violence* (n 4).

[43] ibid 145

[44] On the scale and depth of the German military embeddedness and influence, and hypotheses for more direct involvement in the genocide, see Ihrig, *Justifying Genocide* (n 1) 94–95; 114; 136–37.

[45] The reformed army was mobilized for suppression of revolts in Kurdistan, Bosnia, Montenegro, Thessaly, Crete. Ihrig, *Justifying Genocide* (n 1) 93; Reid, 'Total War' (n 39).

that the Young Turk revolutionary elite internalized this ethic, which 'allowed free reign ... [for] the destruction of Armenia'.[46] Indeed, in justificatory/denialist discourses leading up to, during and after the genocide, a prevalent theme was that the Armenians were 'rightfully' punished—during the Hamidian massacres, described by German officials as justified 'administrative measures ... [towards] a tribe ... in open rebellion against its sovereign';[47] and during the First World War, as part of 'military necessity' for the alleged siding with the enemy.

On the other hand, a Turkish sense of injustice at the hands of Europe was often narrated through a defined claim of entitlement to empire, and thus to military necessity and the right-to-punish.[48] The writing-off of the Armenians as not the rightful or 'real population' of Turkey[49] was an erasure of Armenian history long pre-dating the Turks on those lands, and thus *denial-as-forgetting*. This was accompanied by the propagation of a contradictory myth that resonates in today's postgenocide denials—about a smooth and harmonious past of 'perfect peace ... from time immemorial' between Muslims and non-Muslims disturbed only by external interference.[50] This construction variously appears with another temporal image, again both then and today—the Armenian as 'treacherous from time immemorial', revealing how denials, rather than neat and coherent narratives, often present as contradictions. The trope of smooth and peaceful past inheres *denial-as-forgetting*, including of conquests and subjugations, and thus violence at the very foundations of the empire; entangled with *denial-as-justification*, that is, justifications of contemporaneous violence while denying 'wrongdoing'.

The relational production of this conjuncture includes wider processes of identity (trans)formation. From 1880s, German nationalists began identifying with the Turks as their 'atavistic self'; like Germans decades earlier 'oppressed by foreign powers and held back in their national development'.[51] As Ihrig has argued, widespread discussions of Ottoman Armenians were shaping debates on Germany's relations with the Ottoman Empire, own identity and place in Europe. Extending German anti-Semitism re-articulated in new—Social Darwinist—racialist terms, German nationalist and imperialist publications were constructing the Armenians as the 'Jews of the Orient' or 'uber-Jews'—who have 'sucked the life out of ['noble and tolerant' Turks] ... for centuries'.[52] This discourse, often directly excusing and morally and politically justifying the massacres of the Armenians on racial grounds, became mainstream for the following decades.[53] As I explore in the next

46 Reid, 'Total War' (n 39) 34.
47 Ihrig, Justifying Genocide (n 1) 51, 55.
48 See eg the memoir of a Young Turk official key to the deportations and massacres, and interior minister Talat Pasha's insistence on taking '*necessary measures*' against the Armenians to protect '*the real [Turkish] population of the country*' (quoted in Göçek, *Denial of Violence* (n 4) 248, 252).
49 Talat Pasha quoted Göçek, *Denial of Violence* (n 4) 252.
50 Göçek, *Denial of Violence* (n 4) 249.
51 Ihrig, *Justifying Genocide* (n 1) 60–61.
52 Quoted in ibid 78.
53 Ihrig, *Justifying Genocide* (n 1) 64–66; 77–79.

section, such German constructions were in direct contrast with the dominant Orientalist constructions in Europe, of the 'terrible Turk'.

However, the diffusion of these idea(l)s is not reducible to direct importation or imposition. A conjunctural approach 'explore[s] the dominant in its entangled relationships with the residual and the emergent'.[54] These transformative political idea(l)s gained currency in resonance with the much older cultural framings and institutions, that is, the slower rhythms of the empire. Thus, the German-influenced military ethic was adopted through a merger with elements of the Ottoman military tradition—with the periodic use of irregular bands raiding potentially 'disobedient' settlements; the practice of *sur gun* (forced mass migration); and elements of Islamic laws including laws on *dhimmi* conditional upon non-resistance, and Muslim supremacy. Morphed and merged with new ideas on 'nation-state' and 'military necessity', these old practices were mobilized 'in a far more destructive manner than ever before': after the 1914 Jihad declaration designating Armenians as enemies of the state, in breach of the no-resistance condition of *dhimmi*, the Armenians were now subject to annihilation.[55] In addition, the anti-Armenianism, under the German influence cast in new racialist terms, fused with existing logics on the inferiority of non-Muslims and folded into CUP ideology of nationalist Turkification. The Young Turk mystical theory of race 'connected the Turks with the heroic Mongols, and contrasted them to inferior and untrustworthy ... Armenians' in a pan-Turanic dream of unifying all Turkic-speaking peoples 'as the transmitter of civilization from China and Persia to Europe', while the entitlement to empire was re-narrated through the idea of 'one nation', and thus already through *nationalist*-imperialism.[56] It is in such context that the CUP resolved 'to cleanse the country of treacherous elements';[57] and the medicalized vocabulary on 'nation' became normalized: 'the weaknesses of the Ottoman Empire were equated with the presence of "cancers" of non-Turkish peoples in strategic areas, which then '[as] "internal tumours" had to be removed, once and for all'.[58]

Thus, through this exploration, we encounter the genocide conjuncture as intersections of rhythms and temporalities. The semi-colonial relationship with Europe, the faster demands and rhythms of modernization, reform militarism, the rising to prominence of the total war doctrine, nationalist revival and independence struggles of several subject peoples; and the diffusion and fusion of political idea(l)s

[54] Clarke, 'Doing the Dirty Work' (n 24) 82.

[55] Reid, 'Total War' (n 39) 40; Levene, *The Rise of the West* (n 10) 307.

[56] Jones, Genocide (n 2) 151–52; Levene, *The Rise of the West* (n 10) 283. 'Nation-state' and 'empire' are not antithetical; but have evolved co-dependently (see Krishna Kumar, 'Nation-States as Empires, Empires as Nation-States: Two Principles, One Practice?' (2003) 39 Theory and Society; Klejda Mulaj, 'War and State Making at the End of Empire: Ottoman Collapse and the Formation of the Balkan States' (2016) 4 Peace and Change: A Journal of Peace Research.

[57] Uğur Ümit Üngör, 'Seeing like a nation-state: Young Turk social engineering in Eastern Turkey, 1913–50' (2008) 1 Journal of Genocide Research 21 (hereafter Üngör, 'Seeing like a nation-state').

[58] ibid 21–22, quoting primary sources.

from Europe entangled with the older trajectories and slow rhythms of imperial Turkey, to produce a new resolution to perceived crises through the radicalized Young Turk ideology. The next two sections argue that integral to this perceived resolution was the process of renegotiating the meaning and practice of 'sovereignty' along two interrelated trajectories (external and internal sovereignty, in conventional parlance). On the one hand, it was the renegotiation of 'sovereignty' as a mechanism of inter-imperial interactions, as a way of renegotiating the semi-colonial relationship with Europe. On the one hand, it was the renegotiation of 'sovereignty' as a mechanism of production of political subjectivities within the empire under radically new terms. I take each of these in the two ensuing sections, while showing how generative denials were integral to each.

Sovereign Encounters and Denials

Critical IR engagements have argued, that rather than a fixed 'juridical idea and institution',[59] the meaning of sovereignty is 'open, contingent and unstable ... [in] multiple relations with other concepts'.[60] This section proceeds with the contention that renegotiations of sovereignty have not only been historically implicated in power and violence; but have been contingent upon relational encounters, closely entwined with identity constructions beyond Europe/the West. While Turkey as Europe's 'most important ... Other', and Orientalism as one of the discursive bases for European powers' interference into Ottoman affairs is established in critical and postcolonial literature,[61] the relationship of this to genocide in the context of negotiating the meaning of 'sovereignty' has received little attention.

The myth of 'Westphalian sovereignty' itself—the ideal of territory-based political systems entitled to non-interference—has evolved closely dependent on its opposite, the naturalized right of interference and governing of non-Europeans. As Hayman and Williams note, '[t]he sovereignty of the European states required the contrast to the subordination of the colonies to acquire meaning'.[62] With 'Westphalia', the old medieval distinction between Christendom and the rest of the world had transformed into a borderline between 'civilized Europe' and 'the not yet fully or properly civilized rest of the world' where political entities were taken lacking the 'standard of civilization' to make legitimate claims to sovereignty.[63] By

59 Jackson, 'Sovereignty in World Politics' (n 20) 432.

60 Bartelson, *Genealogy of Sovereignty* (n 20) 2.

61 Neumann and Welsh, 'The Other in European self-definition' (n 9) 333; Neumann, *Uses of the Other* (n 21); Viatcheslav Morozov and Bahar Rumelili, 'The external constitution of European identity: Russia and Turkey as Europe-makers' (2012) 1 Cooperation and Conflict; Bilgin, 'Thinking Past 'Western' IR?' (n 14).

62 PA Hayman and John Williams, 'Westphalian Sovereignty: Rights, Intervention, Meaning and Context' (2006) 4 Global Society 525.

63 Jackson, 'Sovereignty in World Politics' (n 20) 443.

the beginning of twentieth century, in the revised European articulation of sovereignty, 'there existed several different classes of sovereign States: those part of the family of nations and those outside; those fully sovereign, those partly so', now justified via the by-then dominant positive law: 'sovereignty was to . . . embrace the reality of power politics . . . to accommodate the very real and palpable differences between States'.[64]

It is in this context, that the 1856 Treaty of Paris often seen as having accepted the Ottoman empire into the Concert of Europe and thus into the European 'family of nations' should be considered: the declared principles of 'equal sovereignty' and 'non-interference' were in reality overwritten by the reaffirmation of the capitulatory regime, and by demands for reforms for the protection of Christians—through non-differential system of courts and public laws.[65] Meanwhile, Ottoman military defeats and economic decline 'had necessitated a grudging self-examination', leading to emulation of Europe 'to give the Porte some semblance of a secular, European-style state'.[66]

Linked with such renegotiation of sovereignty was the emergence of 'humanitarianism'—'mobilization of empathy' across borders reserved for Christians;[67] and justifications for interventions through a mix of racialized and religious stereotypes about the Christian peoples in contrast to 'the "barbarous" Muslim other'.[68] Along with the European demands for improvement of Christians' conditions, such humanitarianism was perceived in Turkish discourses as cover for intervention; while Armenian demands for the delivery of reform promises as direct foreign meddling. Kuper goes so far as to describe the Hamidian massacres of 1894–1896 as 'a sort of ambassadorial note to the European powers to refrain from intervention in the domestic affairs of Turkey'.[69]

The interpretation of the Armenian demands as foreign meddling was also a key narrative in the evolving German–Ottoman alliance.[70] Characteristic was the claim that the Ottomans were entitled to punishing their 'rogue elements' without outside interventions, consistent with the old German state law of '*cuius regio eius religio*: or the ruler determines the faith'.[71] The latter was symbolic reference to a key

[64] Matthew Craven, 'What Happened to Unequal Treaties? The Continuities of Informal Empire' [2005] 74 Nordic Journal of International Law 345, 358–60.

[65] Göçek, *Denial of Violence* (n 4). Also see Nicholas Onuf 'Humanitarian Intervention: The Early Years' (2004) 4 Florida Journal of International Law 760.

[66] Neumann and Welsh, 'The Other in European self-definition' (n 9) 344.

[67] Abigail Green, 'Humanitarianism in Nineteenth-Century Context: Religious, Gendered, National' (2014) 4 The Historical Journal 1174; Martha Finnemore, 'Constructing Norms of Humanitarian', in Peter J Katzenstein (ed) *The Culture of National Security: Norms and Identity in World Politics* (Columbia University Press 1996).

[68] Michelle Tusan, *Smyrna's Ashes: Humanitarianism, Genocide and the Birth of the Middle East* (University of California Press 2012) 43, 8.

[69] Kuper, Genocide (n 4) 116.

[70] Ihrig, Justifying Genocide (n 1).

[71] Quoted in ibid 65–66.

principle of the ideal of 'sovereignty', that of non-interference the Europeans had reserved for Europe. Thereby, the German discourse, in a break from the meaning of 'sovereignty' in Europe, was not only recognizing Ottomans' equal rights to non-interference, but also crucially that the massacres were within the sovereign right of the state. Such right-to-punish through killing was being constructed as necessary stage in nation- and empire-building at a time when *machtpolitical* ideals justifying the separation of morality from power politics were becoming dominant in Germany.

Widespread discussions in German press and elite circles were not only heightening a Turkish sense of victimhood—of being meddled by the Europeans—but were thereby casting the ideas of both unconditional non-intervention (externally) and of absolute and supreme rule over its subject (internally) as the natural right of the Ottoman Turks. Drawing parallels between the German and wider European traditions of empire-building, such Ottoman Turkish 'right' was simultaneously casting the Turks as both 'civilized' and 'European', in opposition to the European constructions of the Turk as the 'barbarian short of standards of civilization'. This in turn was feeding into the Turkish desire to become Western/modern enough to deserve an empire in 'Europe'.[72]

Set against the humiliating encounters with the other major European powers, these constructions were formative in the Turkish grappling of questions of identity, and the problem of sovereignty. The Turkish encounters with Germany produced an emerging identity that was simultaneously *of entitlement* and *of victimhood*: on the one hand, entitlement to naturalized right to non-interference and to unconditional right-to-punish; and on the other hand, victim of the violation of these very entitlements. More broadly, during this conjuncture, Turkey was being spatially and temporally doubly constructed through encounters with Europe: on the one hand, relationally with Germany as the must-be/would be European empire with the right to exist; on the other hand, through other European great powers as the barbarian onto which immoral violence could be displaced, and humanitarianism could be produced and tried out.[73] Through such contradictory encounters with Europe, and in such uneasy negotiation of sovereignty, a growing chasm emerged between conflicting constructions of the Turk: the 'terrible Turk' and the 'noble superior Turk'; the inferior Turk who could not fully be part of international (European) society of nations, versus the 'meddled and victimized empire' that was being unjustly torn apart.

Thus, the historical conjuncture was producing a *double-colonial complex*: on the one hand, marked by a semi-colonial relationship with European powers which was itself contradictory; on the other hand, marked by Ottoman denial of past

[72] Ayşe Zarakol, *After Defeat: How the East Learned to Live with the West* (CUP 2011) (hereafter Zarakol, *After Defeat*).
[73] See eg Jay Winter (ed), *America and the Armenian Genocide* (CUP 2003).

physical and structural violence towards Armenian and other subjects in the past, and justification of present violence. Hence, denials were already present in the double-colonial complex. In turn, the negotiations of sovereignty inhered a much deeper denial—through the mobilizations of the idea(l)s of, and demands for entitlement to, 'empire', 'nation', 'sovereignty', 'civilization', and 'superiority': Turkish appropriations of these ideas and entitlements as *ahistorical abstractions* required denying both their violent foundations in European history and beyond, and their intimate participation in Europe's semi-colonial rule over Turkey, and thus paradoxically denial of the implication of these idea(l)s in the very traumas and perceived humiliation associated with the Turks' encounter with Europe.

It is these denials that generated the radicalized revolutionary movement and genocidal violence as a *resolution* to the conjunctural contradictions. Through new, already nation-focused imperial project, the CUP simultaneously 'rediscovered the ingredients with which to transform the empire into an entity which could truly compete with the West on military, political, and technological terms';[74] as well as be 'like' European—a nation- and empire-building race, entitled to non-interference and equal terms in inter-imperial relations. Thereby, the CUP ideology and the Armenian genocide were a resolution to Ottoman grappling with the international problem of sovereignty.

Entwined with this resolution to the international problem of sovereignty was the re-articulation of the other facet of 'sovereignty'—traditionally, internal sovereignty, and below, drawing on Agamben, explored as the production of political subjectivities.

Sovereignty and Subjects-of-Denial

'Sovereignty' formulated 'as a question [rather than a forgone fact] … in need of a theory' in the context of Europe is often traced back to 16th century political thought.[75] This is when particularly modern political mythologies on the 'legitimacy to both the *right to rule* and the *duty to obey*' emerge; while a seventeenth-century answer to this problem notably becomes the Hobbesian passage from the state of nature to the state.[76] Demystifying this very tradition of social contract, Giorgio Agamben points instead at the production of subjectivities as the 'originary structure' of the state: sovereign power is the 'capacity… to produce (and reproduce) forms of subjectivity that… make sovereignty, and the subordination it entails, possible'.[77] Such production relies on a 'ban'—inclusion/exclusion in/from

[74] Levene, 'Creating a Modern "Zone of Genocide"' (n 4) 404.
[75] DeCaroli, 'Boundary Stones' (n 22) 43–44.
[76] ibid.
[77] Giorgio Agamben, *Homo Sacer: Sovereign Power and Bare Life* (Stanford University Press 1998) (hereafter Agamben, *Homo Sacer*); DeCaroli, 'Boundary Stones' (n 22) 45.

political community—that *captures life into its sphere.*[78] Here, sovereignty is the power to decide upon life, similar to the Ancient Roman logic of *homo sacer* (sacred life) that can be killed but not sacrificed: 'sovereign sphere is the sphere in which it is permitted to kill without committing homicide'.[79] Theorizing this in relation to the Nazi concentration camp as a zone of the state of exception, Agamben contends that in the camp power is exercised over 'bare life', that is, politically unqualified life, placed outside law's protections, while thereby over life that is included in the exercise of sovereign power.

Drawing on these theorizations, we could initially conceive genocide as the ultimate expression of sovereign power over an aggregate population—*homines sacri*—that could be killed without constituting homicide (genocide), both through direct killing and by 'exposing to unconditioned threat of death' rendering them the 'referent of the sovereign decision':[80] life was variously banished while captured—excluded and thereby included—into the sovereign sphere. However, through the relational and conjunctural approach pursued above, and through Connolly's corrective to Agamben emphasizing the 'complexity of sovereignty', we gain a more nuanced insight. Connolly calls attention to the 'ethos of sovereignty': rather than in a formal locale, sovereignty '*circulates uncertainly* between the multitude, the traditions it embodies ... [and] sanctioned authorities', and 'infuses with cultural habits, dispositions, sentiments and norms'.[81] This determines the 'thinkable' and the 'unthinkable', always operating 'within a global as well as internal context'.[82] An emphasis on circulations and the contingent ethos of sovereignty coheres with the conjunctural and relational approach pursued above. In case of the Armenian genocide conjuncture, sovereignty becomes further complexified given the monumental reconfiguration of the cultural habits, dispositions, sentiments, norms, and the formal institutions of sovereign power.

Such reconfiguration had fundamental effects on the re-establishment of what DeCaroli calls the 'sovereign field'. Sovereignty's constituting power—power to constitute the very zone over which the idea of law can apply—'precedes the law', creating a 'field of order' over a territory which is not merely a physical space; neither the space of a social contract, but 'a space capable of being *obedient*'.[83] Explicating historical renegotiations of sovereignty requires examining this very process of carving the field of sovereignty. This also draws attention to subjectivities and forms of life 'sovereignty ... fears most': 'when *the edges of the sovereign field*

[78] Agamben, *Homo Sacer* (n 77) 28.
[79] ibid 83.
[80] ibid, 183–84.
[81] William Connolly, 'The Complexity of Sovereignty,' in Matthew Calarco and Steven DeCaroli (eds), *Giorgio Agamben: Sovereignty and Life* (Stanford University Press 2007) 30–31 (hereafter Connolly, 'The Complexity of Sovereignty).
[82] ibid 33, 35–36.
[83] DeCaroli, 'Boundary Stones' (n 22) 46–47; 50–51.

are made to appear arbitrary, the challenge is directed at the heart of sovereignty itself'.[84]

The Armenian genocide and its generative denials can be intelligible in such understanding, that is, as *carving* of the very sovereign field: soon after the Young Turk revolution, the radicalized elements of the CUP became preoccupied with revitalizing an empire seen as weakening its grip.[85] When CUP seized power in January 1913 through a coup d'état, they were lacking control over vast territory populated by multitude of religious, linguistic, and ethnic groups.[86] The right-to-rule and duty-to-obey had been challenged by multiple sides, including by perceived and real interference by European powers, and loss of territories, 'underscore[ing] questions about the bonds that held the Empire together'.[87] The extermination of the Armenians was part of the creation of 'a material basis for a restructuring of the Ottoman demographic map': vast areas in Eastern Anatolia were designated as 'Turkification regions' resettling Muslim migrants and Kurds.[88] It was simultaneously production of sovereign subjectivities under radically new terms: the nation-building project based on pan-Turanism was the newly articulated solution to an age-old question of sovereignty as production of subjectivities.

Thus, perceived external and internal threats were challenges not to a fully formed entity, but more fundamental challenge revealing the *arbitrariness* of 'the edges of the sovereign field'[89] and its right-to-govern. That the unleashed violence was more about the fundamental constitution of grounds for the sovereign field itself is evidenced by contextual factors. First was the absence of significant uprising by Armenians, established by several studies: the deportations and killings were successful due to Armenians being largely unarmed and unprepared.[90] The second was the 'organic links and interdependencies between' the Armenian genocide and near-genocidal violence against other groups including Assyrians, Greeks, Jews, and Muslim groups such as Alevi Kurds who had refused to becomes tools for killing and plundering.[91] Viewing these episodes not in isolation but as a continuum prompts Levene to call Eastern Anatolia of the time a 'zone of genocide'.[92]

Closely interrelated was the third factor—the oft-overlooked symbiotic link between such exterminatory violence and violence aimed at 'capture' of life (in Agambean terms) and thus subjectification of hundreds of thousands of Muslim

[84] Ibid, 51 (emphasis added).
[85] Levene, 'Creating a Modern "Zone of Genocide"' (n 4).
[86] Üngör, 'Seeing like a nation-state' (n 57).
[87] Levene, 'Creating a Modern "Zone of Genocide"' (n 4).
[88] Kaiser, 'Genocide at the Twilight of the Ottoman Empire' (n 8); Levene, *The Rise of the West* (n 10) 311–12.
[89] DeCaroli, 'Boundary Stones' (n 22) 51.
[90] Levene, 'Creating a Modern "Zone of Genocide"' (n 4) 408; Kaiser, 'Genocide at the Twilight of the Ottoman Empire' (n 8) 366.
[91] See Üngör, 'Seeing like a nation-state' (n 57) 17; Levene, 'Creating a Modern "Zone of Genocide"' (n 4) 394; Kaiser, 'Genocide at the Twilight of the Ottoman Empire' (n 8).
[92] Levene, 'Creating a Modern "Zone of Genocide"' (n 4) 394–96.

refugees. The exterminatory violence was inflicted not only through the better-known Kurdish irregular forces;[93] but also through the mobilization of 'social forces' hostile to Armenians: Muslim refugees who had fled from the Balkans and the Russian Caucasus.[94] Re-settled in Armenian-populated regions 'to strengthen control over areas feared to be threatened by foreign occupation or national movements', without basic sustenance, they were encouraged to occupy non-Muslim property, inflamed by religious passion through the declaration of holy war.[95] Bloxham views this as 'internal colonization,' attempt to consolidate Ottoman control through 'instal[ling] "ethnically reliable" subjects'.[96] Both the use of Kurdish irregulars and these traumatized and dispossessed refugees indicates how *homo sacer* is exposed to sovereign violence often indirectly: banishment could be carried out by anyone—through de facto authorizing of killing 'with impunity', as well as by 'withholding necessities of life ... [as] a de facto sentence of death'.[97] By simultaneously casting these Muslim groups as having localized 'right-to-punish/kill', they were simultaneously being produced as sovereign subjectivities.

The Armenians, the last major group feared escaping the sovereign field, became the target of exterminatory violence also as 'proxy' for other minorities already broken away in past decades.[98] Thus, they were target of punishment symbolically and retrospectively for much wider perceived *questioning* of the very grounds for sovereignty. The conjunctural contradictions over several decades had conjoined to expose 'the edges of the sovereign field ... [as] arbitrary ... a broad-reaching conceptual threat'[99] to the very foundation for Ottoman sovereign power.

These processes constituted establishing anew, via a new resolution, the field of sovereign authority, involving capture of life while radically transforming the terms of such subjectification—from earlier hierarchized gradational exclusions to a homogenizing pan-Turanic imaginary that must subsume difference and exterminate any threat—a *new imaginary of obedience*. This led to mass killing of life, that is, life that could be killed without constituting homicide, and to production of other forms of bare life—the Muslim refugee forced to kill and repossess; the Kurd that must kill to assert 'loyal subject' status; Armenian women and girls assimilated into Muslim families; and the Muslim subjects of the Pan-Turanic identity as subjectivities who could not challenge the newly solidifying boundaries of inclusion/exclusion without risking subjection to sovereign violence.

93 Bloxham, *The Great Game of Genocide* (n 4); Reid, 'Total War' (n 39); Kaiser, 'Genocide at the Twilight of the Ottoman Empire' (n 8).

94 Kuper, *Genocide* (n 4) 118.

95 Kaiser, 'Genocide at the Twilight of the Ottoman Empire' (n 8) 367.

96 Donald Bloxham, 'Internal Colonization, Inter-Imperial Conflict and the Armenian Genocide' in A Dirk Moses (ed), *Empire, Colony, Genocide: Conquest, Occupation and Subaltern Resistance in World History* (Berghahn Books 2010) 326, 328.

97 DeCaroli, 'Boundary Stones' (n 22) 63–64.

98 See eg Levene, *The Rise of the West* (n 10) 304, 308.

99 DeCaroli, 'Boundary Stones' (n 22) 51, 67.

That the production of sovereign subjectivities was simultaneously the carving of the sovereign field of obedience is also manifest through the physical topography of the genocide as itself an expanding and territorializing process: when mass deportations of the Armenians started, the whole of Asia Minor was in motion.[100] Killing, and death by exposure took place at various points of these movements: indeed, 'the "Ottoman Auschwitz" … was mobile'.[101] Thus, Agamben's metaphorical camp was in this case a mobile and a radically generative process—unfolding and sweeping over a territory while radically casting anew the sovereign field.

However, to recall, sovereign power manifests through circulations producing 'the thinkable and the unthinkable'.[102] These circulations were cast in flux during the Young Turk revolution: political idea(l)s diffused through a long encounter with Europe, and the shorter and more immediate encounter with ally Germany made the annihilation of the 'enemy within' thinkable. This ethos of sovereignty became the wider condition of possibility for producing the Armenians as *homines sacri* that could be killed. On the other hand, the nineteenth-century European ethos of imperialism and the German-led augmentation of the Ottoman sense of entitlement to empire, eventually renegotiated through a modern 'nation-state' imaginary and fused with racialized imaginaries of a homogeneous nation-empire, made letting go of the imperial lands and subjects as unthinkable, in turn producing justifications—denial-as-justifications—for mass violence to a scale and coherence previously unthinkable in the older Ottoman imperial ethos of sovereignty.

Such re-establishment of the grounds for sovereignty was, in turn, a convulsive attempt to reverse the exposure of its arbitrary and contingent grounds. Any ethos of sovereignty is produced by and is caught up in a deep denial—*denial of the unfoundedness and contingency of sovereignty itself*: indeed, 'the element of arbitrariness in [sovereignty's] formation and maintenance [has] to be *obscure* to those who [are] its objects'.[103] However, while latent in other circumstances, it is denial that may, as the case here revealed, in certain conjunctures become *generative* of annihilatory violence.

Thus, I argue, that today's Turkish denial of the genocide is intimately linked with this originary denial—denial of sovereignty's contingency and arbitrariness during a monumental historical conjuncture, then; and denial of its contingency and the violence it takes to *conceal* such contingency, now. To recall, the analytical category of postgenocide 'suggests that the era following the genocidal killing is shaped by genocide': indeed, Mulaj notes the transferability of the dynamics of the genocide 'to (contests over) memory … and, crucially, re-imagining, re-understanding, reexperiencing political community'.[104] The next section explores

[100] Hovannisian, 'The Armenian Genocide' (n 4) 29.
[101] Ihrig, *Justifying Genocide* (n 1) 107.
[102] Connolly, 'The Complexity of Sovereignty' (n 81) 33, 35.
[103] ibid 25 (emphasis added).
[104] Refer in this volume to Mulaj, 'Introduction' (n 6).

how 'denial' itself must be reconsidered in postgenocide and explicated as the continuation of the renegotiations of sovereignty. If denial was shown to be *generative* of the Armenian genocide rather than a post-factum matter, and in turn was integral to the renegotiations of sovereignty (both internal and external) in the genocide conjuncture, then to explicate today's denials, we must consider their close relationality with continuous renegotiations of sovereignty and the (re)production of sovereign subjectivities today. Thus, postgenocide as a concern with the *effects* of genocide in this analysis and approach extends into the very renegotiations of sovereignty and subjectivity.

The Politics of Denial in Postgenocide

Rather than conceived *post-factum*, this chapter argued that denial can be *generative of* genocide itself. *Generative denials* were conceived as an amalgam of discourses and practices providing the conditions of possibility for the genocide. Through a conjunctural and relational approach, the chapter explored the Armenian genocide conjuncture as intersection of rhythms and temporalities that culminated in producing a violent resolution to perceived crises through the radicalized Young Turk ideology. It argued that integral to this process was nearly a century of Ottoman renegotiation of 'sovereignty' as an organizing principle of inter-imperial relations, intimately linked with identity constructions and transformations relationally with Europe. On the other hand, the genocidal process itself was the radical re-articulation of 'sovereignty' as the mechanism of the production of political subjectivities. Particularly formative in the Turkish grappling of questions of identity, state, and nation and their relation to the problem of sovereignty were the Turkish encounters with Germany, which produced an identity simultaneously *of victimhood* and *of entitlement*, while the conjuncture was producing a *double-colonial complex* marked by denials of past violence foundational of the empire (denial-as-forgetting); and justifications of contemporaneous violence (denial-as-justification). In turn, the genocide conjuncture inhered a deeper denial: mobilizations of the idea(l)s of, and demands for entitlement to, 'empire', 'nation', 'sovereignty', 'civilization' and 'superiority' as ahistorical abstractions were, ironically, denials of their intimate participation in Europe's semi-colonial rule over Turkey.

Today's genocide denials resonate with such generative denials, still caught up in the double-colonial complex. This manifests as fear of stigma, 'continuously liv[ing] with the fear of being discredited', seen as the 'uncivilized', the 'barbarian',[105]

[105] Zarakol, *After Defeat* (n 72) 3.

as well as in perceptions of any demands for recognition of the genocide as the continuation of 'Armenian conspiracy' and European imperialist meddling.[106]

The chapter further argued that denial is a larger generative force: denial of violence is embedded in and is the condition of possibility for the very production of sovereign power, marked by fear of the exposure of its arbitrariness, and therefore requiring subjectivization-through-denial, that is, *subjects of denial*. This, in turn, radically forecloses the political, that is, the possibility of keeping alternative imaginaries for a society open.[107] This lens sheds new light on today's Turkey's violence against the Kurds, and political opposition and academic activism—a dynamic that can only be explicated through 'postgenocide' as involving continuing renegotiations of sovereignty. If then, the genocide was carving anew a sovereign field, marked by its conjunctural denials; today's state denial is the continuous reproduction of the sovereign field, through violently suppressing any exposure of its contingency 'revealing the concealed (naturalized) bond uniting authority with territory'.[108] Thus, denial reconstitutes postgenocide Turkey in a ritual that is performed not only through articulated denials but through violence-as-denial.

If denials have been generative rather than *post-factum*, countering today's denials merely through demands for official recognition only reproduces the contradictions of the double-colonial complex, resonating with narratives of both victimhood and entitlement; both interference/meddling and supremacy. In turn, 'third party' countries, particularly heirs to nineteenth-century 'great power politics', even when officially 'recognizing' the genocide (eg, Russia, France), engage in much wider denial—denial-as-forgetting of connected histories, of relationality and complex complicities.[109]

Recognizing connected histories and complex complicities should not be taken to warrant off-loading responsibilities from Turkey. Neither should the conjunctural analysis sensitive to relationality and to the diffusion of European political idea(l)s be misinterpreted as 'blaming everything on the West', and/or as pre-determined.[110] A historical conjuncture inheres alternatives—scope for agency, resistance, and alternative imaginaries.[111] Indeed, there were moderate and conciliatory programmes even within the Young Turk movement; the genocidal violence was *not* the inevitable conclusion of the long nineteenth century.[112] Today, too, there *are alternatives* to postgenocide state-narrated denial and related

[106] See eg Turkish Ministry of Foreign Affairs website, section Foreign Policy: 'The Armenian Allegation of Genocide' (no date) <http://www.mfa.gov.tr/the-armenian-allegation-of-genocide-the-issue-and-the-facts.en.mfa> accessed 5 December 2018.

[107] Jenny Edkins and Veronique Pin-Fat, 'The Subject of the Political,' in Jenny Edkins, Nalini Persram, and Veronique Pin-Fat (eds) *Sovereignty and Subjectivity* (Lynne Rienner 1999).

[108] Agamben, *Homo Sacer* (n 77) 6; DeCaroli, 'Boundary Stones' (n 22) 54.

[109] Germany's recent acknowledgement is partial exception.

[110] See Bloxham, *The Great Game of Genocide* (n 4) for a critique.

[111] Clarke, 'Conjunctures, crises, and cultures' (n 25).

[112] Levene, *The Rise of the West* (n 10) 208.

closures of the political, and to orthodox demands for recognition. Indeed, resistance to the subjectification-by-denial constitutes resistance to the wider foreclosing of the political—from Turkish intellectuals' campaigns to the micropolitics of locals' remembering what the state denies.[113]

To start opening space to imagine alternatives, the main implication of the argument must be reckoned with: if denials have been *generative* of the genocide, and such generative denials have been produced *relationally*, then countering today's denials should be a generative process too, subverting denials generative of genocide and becoming *generative of mediation*. Rather than being theoretically prescriptive, this should be a political process. Nonetheless, this may be imagined as a 'mediation of estrangement' in multiple ways including through micro-practices mediating otherness[114]—between Armenians and Turks; among Turks; and among Armenians. This would require the refusal and resistance of the *subject of denial*, while generating new, mediative discourses and subjectivities.

In this respect, unfortunate are Turkish President Erdoğan's and the ruling AKP party's recent promises to build a 'New Turkey' with a 'new subjectivity' based on anti-hegemonic dissent claiming to depart from what is seen as Western-imposed Kemalism. As Çapan and Zarakol have exposed, Erdoğan's AKP party and government, since 2014, have actively distorted and appropriated the language of postcolonial critique, often through state-sponsored research centres 'generating intellectual capital for the regime … to legitimize and justify various hegemonic and essentialising projects'.[115] In light of this chapter's argument, this only continues generative denials and subjectification-via-denial. *Contra* the declared promise of new 'postcolonial Turkey', this keeps Turkey *precisely* in a semi-colonial relationship and thus trapped in the nineteenth century. So do the regular threats to withdraw 'useful ally' cooperation with the 'West' in response to genocide recognition debates externally (eg, in Germany and the US).

While a hundred calendric years have passed since the Armenian genocide, the 'social time'[116] in Turkish postgenocide politics, that is, time required for social processes to produce change, has followed a slower trajectory. The generative denials—denials generative of the new resolution to sovereignty in Turkey a hundred years ago—continue to generate today's sovereign imaginary via denial and subjectivities that deny. The way Turkey can create 'new subjectivity' is through

113 See Uğur Ümit Üngör, 'Lost in commemoration: the Armenian genocide in memory and identity' (2014) 2 Patterns of Prejudice.

114 James Der Derian, James, *On Diplomacy: A Genealogy of Western Estrangement* (Basil Blackwell 1987); C M Constantinou and James Der Derian, 'Sustaining Global Hope: Sovereignty, Power and the Transformation of Diplomacy' in C M Constantinou and James Der Derian (eds) *Sustainable Diplomacies: Studies in Diplomacy and International Relations* (Palgrave Macmillan 2010).

115 Zeynep Gülşah Çapan and Ayşe Zarakol 'Postcolonial colonialism? The case of Turkey' in Charlotte Epstein (ed) *Against International Relations Norms: Postcolonial Perspectives* (Routledge 2017) 198.

116 Refer in this volume to Mulaj, 'Introduction' (n 6).

radically subverting this process—overcoming of still affording a generative force to denials that anchor the sovereign myth. What we have instead is the recently revitalized centrality (albeit denied) of such past denials in today's negotiations of Turkish sovereign myth and identity.

Overall, the contribution of the chapter was two-fold. First, it brought Critical IR and postcolonial insights to bear on the explication of denial that goes beyond conventional treatments of denial as post-factum; and demonstrated how critical IR advancements on sovereignty and subjectivity help tease out some of the conditions of possibility for the genocide in new light—that of generative denials. Conversely, the case helped pay closer attention to what genocide and genocide denial reveal about 'state', 'sovereignty', and 'subjectivity': there is a close relationship of genocide to the historical negotiations of the myth of 'sovereignty' itself, and the (re)production of forms of sovereign power and subjectivities. Indeed, sovereign circulations are always caught up in conjunctural contradictions and when condensed and ruptured, may produce particularly violent—genocidal—ethos of sovereignty. It thus drew attention to the negotiation of sovereignty as implicated in a deeper denial, that is, denial of the unfoundedness and contingency of sovereignty itself, an unfoundedness that needs to be often violently concealed. Relatedly, second, it argued that genocide denial can be explicated only in such understanding; while resistance to exclusionary politics must involve reckoning with sovereign denial. This also invites considering the implications of generative denials for postgenocide in other cases and in their contextual specificities.

7

Constructions of Genocide Denial and Remembrance

Fractured National Identity in Postgenocide Bosnia

Klejda Mulaj

Introduction

The preceding chapters in this volume have elucidated various ways via which genocide impacts affected societies after termination of genocidal killing. This chapter expands on these themes by assessing effects of the genocide perpetrated in the course of the Bosnian War (1992–1995) with particular reference to the Srebrenica massacre (11–19 July 1995). It demonstrates how the genocide discourse and war narratives remain active in the efforts to construct, or contest, the Bosnian polity and its political community.[1] In the intervening years following the conclusion of the war, Bosnia's people have lived with the impact of the genocide. Their rather common sentiment of 'unsettled scores' reflects discontent with the postwar setting—discontent which is mediated, amongst other factors, by (divergent) explications or denial of genocide. This chapter presents a reasoned interpretation of the relationship between genocide and the fragile peace in genocide's aftermath. It shows how interpretations of genocide affect and sometimes undermine the

[1] The worst episode in the European history since the Second World War, the Bosnian War led to nearly one hundred thousand people dead and over two million displaced. A database compiled by Patrick Ball, Ewa Tabeau, and Philip Verwimp records 96,895 casualties—this figure being not the overall total number of victims but rather 'an approximation of a minimum ... total'. Patrick Ball, Ewa Tabeau, and Philip Verwimp, 'The Bosnian Book of Dead: Assessment of the Database (Full Report)' (*Households in Conflict Network*, 7 June 2007) <http://www.hicn.org/wordpress/wp-content/uploads/2012/07/rdn5.pdf> accessed 18 June 2020. A total of 24,826 of Bosnian War casualties were Serbs, of whom 20,000 soldiers and 661 were police. This leaves 4,165 Serb civilian casualties in the course of the four-year Bosnian War, which is roughly half of the number of Bosnian Muslims killed by Serb forces in Srebrenica (over 8,000) in just one week in July 1995. Some 62,069 Bosnian Muslims were killed in the course of the Bosnian War, 82 per cent of whom were civilians. These figures are approximations; they do not include numbers of missing victims unearthed from mass graves since 2007 (the year when the Ball et al report was published). For an authoritative study of the Bosnian War see David Campbell, *National Deconstruction: Violence, Identity, and Justice in Bosnia* (University of Minnesota Press 2008). For a detailed account of the 1995 Srebrenica genocide see United Nations, 'The Fall of Srebrenica, Report of the Secretary-General pursuant to General Assembly resolution 53/35' (United Nations, 15 November 1999) <http://www.refworld.org/docid/3ae6afb34.html> accessed 18 June 2020.

Klejda Mulaj, *Constructions of Genocide Denial and Remembrance* In: *Postgenocide*. Edited by: Klejda Mulaj, Oxford University Press (2021). © The Several Contributors. DOI: 10.1093/oso/9780192895189.003.0007

constitution of peace and the unity of the political community. The chapter can be read also as an interpretation of how violence of war permutates in times of peace.[2]

A peace deal does not mean that effects of genocide on affected societies come to an end. Indeed, there are long-term repercussions of genocide—social, political, and legal. Suffering of survivors continues after killings end. The harm of genocide and the status of victims and survivors are oftentimes denied, in turn undermining victims'/survivors' transition to a peaceful, postconflict community. Furthermore, frequently state officials resort to a purposeful use of genocide in the postgenocide era as a fragile peace takes hold. Such uses of genocide are oftentimes coupled with new manifestations of identity politics and (new) expressions of nationalist ideology. In the course of war, genocide violence—frequently used to advance war aims—benefits the perpetrators.[3] The illegality of such violence, nonetheless, is not lost on the side of organizers and perpetrators. In the entire course of the Bosnian War—including the Srebrenica genocide—there were extraordinary, coordinated efforts on the side of the Serb forces to conceal, and therefore deny, crimes they committed, efforts that ranged from coded language as the crimes unfolded to reburial of bodies in secret locations where they were expected to remain unfound.[4] Whilst genocide denial continues to-date, it bears emphasizing that denial is not merely an afterthought of genocide. Denial is an intrinsic part of genocide.

Denial accompanies the unfolding of genocide—*contra* to a section of the existing genocide literature that conceives denial as the 'final stage of genocide', as a *post-factum* practice that ensues after genocide.[5] Indeed, as the tragedy at Srebrenica was taking place in those fateful days of July 1995, the war indicted criminal—then army General overseeing Serb operations—Ratko Mladić told the

[2] As argued elsewhere, 'violence of war' is a broad term that includes 'asymmetrical violence against civilians—such as genocide, ethnic cleansing, rape and other dehumanizing acts of war, and their ensuing effects'. Klejda Mulaj, 'Violence of War, Ontopology, and the Instrumental and Performative Constitution of the Political Community' (2018) 44(1) Review of International Studies 67. 'Peace' may be conceived as a dynamic process of resolving disputes without violent conflict and transforming conditions that cause war so that war is no longer feasible. See David Cortright, *Peace: The History of Movements and Ideas* (CUP 2008) 8.

[3] But genocide does not benefit perpetrators in times of war only. As shown in the ensuing analysis, genocide can benefit them also in times of peace as is the case, for instance, of the Serb entity—Republika Srpska—in Bosnia.

[4] Marija Tausan and Denis Dzidic, 'Srebrenica Convictions are Triumph of Justice says Karadzic Prosecutor' (*BalkanInsight*, 11 July 2019) <https://balkaninsight.com/2019/07/11/srebrenica-convictions-are-triumph-of-justice-says-karadzic-prosecutor/> accessed 18 June 2020. Cover-up operations to conceal the crimes have included use of mechanical diggers, tearing bodies apart, and dispersal of mass graves' contents as a result of which partial remains of victims are found in several sites, many miles apart. In one instance remains of one individual were found in five separate graves. Shaun Walker, 'Genocide Denial Gains Ground 25 Years After Srebrenica Massacre', *The Guardian*, 10 July 2020, <https://www.theguardian.com/world/2020/jul/10/genocide-denial-gains-ground-25-years-after-srebrenica-massacre> accessed 10 July 2020 (hereafter Walker, 'Genocide Denial'); Annie Hylton, '"You Simply Die All Over Again:" The Agony of Srebrenica, 25 Years On', *The Guardian*, 14 July 2020, <https://www.theguardian.com/global-development/2020/jul/14/you-simply-die-all-over-again-the-agony-of-srebrenica-25-years-on> accessed 14 July 2020, (hereafter Hylton, 'You Simply Die').

[5] For a representation of this literature see Gregory H Stanton, 'The Ten Stages of Genocide' (*Genocide Watch*, 1996) <https://www.genocidewatch.com/ten-stages-of-genocide> accessed 15 June 2020.

press that the Serb takeover of the UN safe area was done to neutralize Muslim terrorists, fictitious operations of the Army of Bosnia and Herzegovina ('ARBiH') against Serb civilians. He used the notion of 'necessity' to justify atrocities. Then in the immediate aftermath of the tragedy, from September to November 1995, a massive cover-up operation was undertaken by forces of the Army of Republika Srpska and Ministry of Interior who moved dead bodies from original mass graves to secondary, secret locations. For years following the fall of the enclave, Serb leaders in Bosnia and Serbia even promoted the lie that killings in Srebrenica had been committed by ARBiH. As evidence of the truth emerged from court proceedings at the International Criminal Tribunal for the former Yugoslavia ('ICTY'), the Serb elite in Republika Srpska ('RS')—the Serb-ruled entity in Bosnia—and the Republic of Serbia gradually moved to a form of interpretative denial, arguing that what happened in Srebrenica was justified and contesting the gravity of crimes established via due process at the ICTY.[6]

In the course of war, genocide benefited perpetrators—although the latter seek to maintain their benefits in postgenocide by resorting to denial. In the aftermath of fighting, however, loss and suffering lend credibility to survivors' demands for accountability, recognition, and redress. Yet, the persistent denial of crimes by the perpetrators' and their supporters enables the community of perpetrators to avoid responsibility and reparations. According to a 2018 poll, 66 per cent of Serbs in RS deny genocide, whereas 74 per cent of Serbs consider genocide convicted criminal Radovan Karadžić to be a hero.[7] In Srebrenica—which before the war was a Muslim-majority town but where now Bosnian Muslims, known as Bosniaks, are in minority—genocide denial is mainstream. Its Serb mayor, Mladen Grujičić, denies the genocide without hesitation. Courts of law which have determined beyond reasonable doubt that genocide occurred in Srebrenica, according to him, are 'biased against the Serbs'.[8] Genocide denial has become mainstream in the political circles of Serbia proper too, as it will be explored below. These conflicting utilizations of genocide on the side of the community of victims and that of perpetrators—as the chapter shows—undermine societal cohesion and victims' aspirations for justice.

In Bosnia, recognition of genocide and its denial are part of a broader struggle over salient issues of national identity, authority, legitimacy, and security mediated by competing frameworks on the use of force in the course of war. This broader struggle—expressed by diverse viewpoints on the above mentioned issues on the side of the Bosnian Muslims and the Serbs—constitute an intense contest over the re-imagination of the Bosnian political community, or contestation of it, that have

[6] Refer to Lara J Nettelfield and Sara E Wagner, *Srebrenica in the Aftermath of Genocide* (CUP 2014), Chapter 8, particularly 255, 258–60, 267 (hereafter Nettelfield and Wagner, *Srebrenica*).

[7] Figures from Mersiha Gadzo, 'Canadians launch petition to ban Srebrenica genocide denial' (*Al Jazeera*, 28 December 2018) <https://www.aljazeera.com/indepth/features/canadians-launch-petition-ban-srebrenica-genocide-denial-181227115025333.html> accessed 18 June 2020.

[8] Walker, 'Genocide Denial' (n 4).

produced serious fractures in the national unity. The Bosnian political community suffers from fractures both from without—mainly due to Serb denial of genocide, and from within—not only owing to ethno-national divisions but also owing to denial of rights of surviving victims, including women and men violated in the course of genocide and war, and children born of rape.

Before unpacking some legal, political, and social effects of genocide in the post/war setting, it is worth noting that there is a contested terminological debate on genocide in Bosnia. The Bosniak survivors of war violence—who have been subjected to a systematic, organized attempt at annihilation due to their national identity, and religion—conceive themselves as victims of genocide. However, the ICTY has ruled that, out of all mass atrocities perpetrated in the duration of the Bosnian War, only that of Srebrenica (11–19 July 1995)—when Serb forces killed more than 8,000 Bosnian Muslim men and boys and expelled tens of thousands of women and children—qualifies as genocide. This legal determination—of crucial importance as it is—overlooks the fact that Bosnian Muslims were subjected to genocidal violence right from the onset of the war. Their systematic killing has been part of the same conflict and executed under the terms of the same Serb-designed war plan and strategy.[9]

That the Srebrenica massacre is the only atrocity in the entire Bosnian War to have been designated as genocide has disappointed victims' community and also many analysts. Critics argue that Srebrenica has been decontextualized from the rest of the Bosnian War. Their discontent stems from the fact that only one mass atrocity in the course of the four year Bosnian War has been classified as genocide, whereas too many similar such occurrences have not. Lara Nettelfield and Sara Wagner have argued that Srebrenica 'was neither isolated nor aberrant'.[10] Similarly, Ed Vulliamy writes: 'Srebrenica was not an isolated incident.... It "ticks the box" of appearing to reckon with Bosnia, without doing so. Who ever [*sic*] hears these days about Vlasenica, Bjeljina, Doboj, Brcko, Prijedor, Foca, Visegrad, Caplinja, East Mostar ... the list is endless, beyond those bereaved, shattered and scattered by the slaughter there?'[11] This decontextualization of genocide has created

[9] The latter theme has been expanded upon in Klejda Mulaj, *Politics of Ethnic Cleansing: Nation-State Building and Provision of In/Security in Twentieth Century Balkans* (Lexington Books/Rowman & Littlefield 2008) Chapter 3.

[10] Nettelfield and Wagner, *Srebrenica* (n 6) 8; Gregory Kent, 'Justice and Genocide in Bosnia' (2013) 3(2) Law, Crime and History 141–42 (hereafter Kent, 'Justice and Genocide').

[11] Ed Vulliamy, 'Srebrenica: The World fails, but never one's own government' (*Open Democracy*, 12 July 2014) <https://www.opendemocracy.net/can-europe-make-it/ed-vulliamy/srebrenica-world-fails-but-never-one%E2%80%99s-own-government> accessed 18 June 2020 (hereafter Vulliamy, *Srebrenica*). See also, Daniel Toljaga, 'Prelude to the Srebrenica Genocide: Mass Murder and Ethnic Cleansing of Bosniaks in the Srebrenica Region During the First Three Months of the Bosnian War (April—June 1992)' (*Congress of North American Bosniaks*, 23 November 2010) <https://bosniak.org/2010/11/23/prelude-to-the-srebrenica-genocide-mass-murder-and-ethnic-cleansing-of-bosniaks-in-the-srebrenica-region-during-the-first-three-months-of-the-bosnian-war-april-june-1992/> accessed 18 June 2020 (hereafter Toljaga, 'Prelude to the Srebrenica Genocide').

resentment in towns and cities across Bosnia where genocide memorials do not exist and demands for reparations remain unheeded. As Jelena Subotic observes, affixing different labels onto the same conflict matters greatly for the everyday politics in genocidal spaces. That Srebrenica only has been designated as genocide has created a particular type of postgenocide identity of the city that renders difficult rebounding in the aftermath of atrocity. Furthermore, deprivation of such designation for the rest of Bosnia allows Serbia to deny genocide and eschew responsibility for Serbian assistance during the war.[12] Genocide denial has attained more approval also outside the region. The award of the 2019 Noble Prize for Literature to the Austrian writer Peter Handke—a genocide apologist and an admirer of the genocide indictee Slobodan Milošević (having delivered a eulogy at the latter's funeral in Požarevac, Serbia, in 2006)—engenders truth and enrages survivors.[13] For victims of the Bosnian War and their community to be denied recognition of genocide harms is an injury to their identity—an injury to who they are.[14] As it will be argued in the penultimate section of this chapter, such denial undermines—too—victims' full integration in postgenocide Bosnia in so far as their suffering remains inadequately acknowledged and insufficiently addressed. But, before delving on the political and social effects of genocide in Bosnia, it is worth considering briefly the legal discourse related to the determination of genocide in courts of law and the construction of genocide knowledge therein.

Legal Effects: Construing Genocide Knowledge in the Courts of Law

Faced with the international community's hesitation to intervene and end the war, in March 1993, the newly recognized government of the Republic of Bosnia and Herzegovina filed in the International Court of Justice ('ICJ') a case against the Federal Republic of Yugoslavia (then comprising Serbia and Montenegro). This action marks the inception of the genocide debate in the setting of the Bosnian War. In this unparalleled case, the Bosnian government argued that the Federal Republic of Yugoslavia was responsible for violating the Convention on the Prevention and

[12] Jelena Subotic, 'The Meaning of Genocide and the Political Stakes of Naming' (*The Disorder of Things*, 4 July 2019) <https://thedisorderofthings.com/2019/07/04/the-meaning-of-genocide-and-the-political-stakes-of-naming/#more-17381> accessed 18 June 2020.

[13] Peter Maass, 'Congratulations, Nobel Committee, You Just Gave the Literature Prize to a Genocide Apologist', *The Intercept*, 10 October 2019, <https://theintercept.com/2019/10/10/congratulations-nobel-committee-you-just-gave-the-literature-prize-to-a-genocide-apologist/> accessed 18 June 2020 (hereafter Maass, 'Congratulations'); Ed Vulliamy, 'Peter Handke's Nobel Prize Dishonours the Victims of Genocide', *The Guardian*, 12 October 2019 <https://www.theguardian.com/commentisfree/2019/oct/12/a-nobel-prize-that-dishonours-the-victims-of-genocide-peter-handke> accessed 18 June 2020.

[14] For victims' views refer to Diane Orentlicher, *Some Kind of Justice: The ICTY's Impact in Bosnia and Serbia* (OUP 2018) especially 167–70 (hereafter Orentlicher, *Kind of Justice*).

Punishment of the Crime of Genocide (hereinafter the 'Genocide Convention').[15] This was not merely a legal case; it was also a political and social one. By way of it, the Sarajevo government aimed to bring the suffering of its people to the attention of the international community and convince world leaders to act and stop atrocities against civilians and make the Serb military end their aggression in Bosnia. Long delays were encountered in this case's proceedings mainly attributed to scarce resources by the Bosnian government and Serbia's hostile aversion to the court case. This notwithstanding the ICJ—following thirteen years of proceedings—concluded it and the relative judgment pronounced by the world court is discussed below.[16]

Legal contemplations related to atrocities perpetrated during the Bosnian War—including genocide—continued in numerous prosecutions considered by the ICTY in The Hague. A number of the charges related directly to Srebrenica including the proceedings against Radovan Karadžić and Radko Mladić, and the cases of Radislav Krstić, Vujadin Popović *et al*, and Zdravko Tolimir.[17] Of these cases, the 2001 *Krstić* judgment[18] is of seminal preponderance principally as it confirms without a shred of a doubt that genocide did actually take place at Srebrenica. Guided by the legal definition provided in the UN Genocide Convention that considers intent of the perpetrators and scale of the crimes as key, distinguishing elements of genocide, the *Krstić* judgment determined that the destruction of such a large number of Srebrenica men and boys would 'inevitably result in the physical disappearance of the Bosnian Muslim population at Srebrenica'.[19] Up to this point in time, this was the first and only case wherein the ICTY confirmed that genocide was perpetrated by Serb troops against Muslims of Srebrenica. The ICTY

[15] Francis Anthony Boyle, *The Bosnian People Charge Genocide: Proceedings of the International Court of Justice Concerning Bosnia vs. Serbia on the Prevention and Punishment of the Crime of Genocide* (Aletheia Press 1994).

[16] ICJ, *Case Concerning the Application of the Convention on the Prevention and Punishment of the Crime of Genocide (Bosnia and Herzegovina v Serbia and Montenegro)*, Judgment, *I.C.J. Reports* 2007, 43 (hereafter ICJ, *Bosina v Serbia*).

[17] ICTY, *Prosecutor v Radovan Karadžić and Ratko Mladić*, IT-95-18-I (Indictment, 14 November 1995) <http://www.icty.org/x/cases/karadzic/ind/en/kar-ii951116e.pdf> accessed 18 June 2020; ICTY, *Prosecutor v Radovan Karadžić*, IT-95-5/18-T (Judgment, 24 March 2016) <http://www.icty.org/x/cases/karadzic/tjug/en/160324_judgement.pdf> accessed 18 June 2020; ICTY, *Prosecutor v Radislav Krstić*, IT-98-33-T (Judgment, 2 August 2001) <http://www.icty.org/x/cases/krstic/tjug/en/krs-tj010802e.pdf> accessed 18 June 2020 (hereafter ICTY, *Prosecutor v Krstić* (n 17)); ICTY, *Prosecutor v Vujadin Popović et al*, IT-05-88-T (Judgment, 10 June 2010) <http://www.icty.org/x/cases/popovic/tjug/en/100610judgement.pdf> accessed 18 June 2020; ICTY, *Prosecutor v Zdravko Tolimir*, IT-05-88/2-T (Judgment, 12 December 2012) <http://www.icty.org/x/cases/tolimir/tjug/en/121212.pdf> accessed 18 June 2020.

[18] ICTY, *Prosecutor v Radislav Krstić* (n 17).

[19] Refer to ICTY, *The Prosecutor v Radislav Krstić*, (Appeals Judgment), IT-98-33-A. (19 April 2004) paras 28–33 <http://www.icty.org/x/cases/krstic/acjug/en/krs-aj040419e.pdf> accessed 18 June 2020. For in depth analysis of the Krstić decision see Mark Drumbl, 'Prosecutor v. Radislav Krstić: ICTY Authenticates Genocide at Srebrenica and Convicts for Aiding and Abetting' (2004) 5(2) Melbourne Journal of International Law 434–50; and Patricia M Wald, 'General Radislav Krstić: A War Crimes Case Study' (2003) 16 Georgetown Journal of Legal Ethics 445–72.

contemplated for another fourteen years before delivering—in 2015—the first full genocide judgment.[20] Only five indictees have been sentenced on genocide charges so far.[21] Moreover, only 161 individuals have been accused of war crimes and crimes against humanity—including genocide—perpetrated in the course of the wars of the dissolution of the former Socialist Federal Republic of Yugoslavia (referred to as Yugoslavia), of which 145 cases have been concluded.[22]

It was the 2007 ICJ Bosnia v Serbia ICJ judgment that brought about a breakthrough in categorizing as genocide the atrocious misdeeds that took place at Srebrenica. The ICJ proceedings dealt with 'the Application of the Convention on the Prevention and Punishment of the Crime of Genocide' and were filed by Bosnia against Serbia in 1993. Grounding its deliberations on ICTY material, the ICJ arrived at the view that the July 1995 killings taking place at Srebrenica fell squarely under the heading of the crime of genocide in terms of International Criminal Law. Noteworthy about the ICJ 2007 decision are two facts: first, the forcible clout exercised by Belgrade over Bosnian Serb leaders; and second the enormous amount of backing that Serbia provided to Bosnian Serb forces through military, financial, and political assistance. Both these factors contributed overwhelmingly to confirm Serbia's involvement as an accomplice in the monstrosities committed in Bosnia.[23]

Serbia was found by the world court's 2007 judgment guilty on three counts, these being: for failing to prevent genocide; for abstaining from taking the necessary measures to punish genocide; and for erecting obstacles to assist the ICTY in the latter's court proceedings.[24] Nevertheless, the judgment did not go as far as to declare Serbia guilty of genocide as the court concluded that Serbia did not have the *dolus specialis* to perpetrate genocide in Bosnia.[25] Understandably, this restriction of Serbia's culpability has caused upset to survivors' community. It has also exposed legal inconsistency regarding the ICJ interpretations. The ICTY, on

[20] ICTY, *Prosecutor v Vujadin Popović, Ljubiša Beara, Drago Nikolić, Radivoje Miletić*, and *Vinko Pandurević* (Appeals Judgment), IT-05-08-A. (30 January 2015) <http://www.icty.org/x/cases/popovic/acjug/en/150130_judgement.pdf> accessed 18 June 2020.

[21] As of December 2020 the indictees sentenced on genocide charges were: Radislav Krstić, Vujadin Popović, Ljubiša Beara, Zdravko Tolimir, and Radovan Karadžić. Ratko Mladić was also found guilty of genocide by the Trial Chamber but his case is still pending appeal. See United Nations International Residual Mechanism for Criminal Tribunals, 'MLADIĆ, Ratko (MICT-13-56)' <https://www.irmct.org/en/cases/mict-13-56> accessed on 28 December 2020; United Nations International Residual Mechanism for Criminal Tribunals, 'ICTY Remembers: The Srebrenica Genocide 1995–2015' <https://www.irmct.org/specials/srebrenica20/index.html> accessed on 28 December 2020; and United Nations International Residual Mechanism for Criminal Tribunals, 'Judgment List' <http://www.icty.org/en/cases/judgement-list> accessed 28 December 2020.

[22] Figures from the ICTY. See United Nations International Residual Mechanism for Criminal Tribunals, 'Key Figures of the Cases' <http://www.icty.org/en/cases/key-figures-cases> accessed 18 June 2020.

[23] Refer to ICJ, *Bosnia v Serbia* (n 16) paras 236–241. Paragraph 386 of this decision citing UN Security Council resolutions 752 (1992), 757 (1992), 762 (1992), 819 (1993), 838 (1993) demanded that Former Republic of Yugoslavia put an end to its support to Bosnian Serbs.

[24] ICJ, *Bosnia v Serbia* (n 16) paras 425–438 and 439–450.

[25] ibid paras 386–415, especially 413.

whose work the ICJ relied, inferred genocidal intent from factual, circumstantial evidence. Yet, the world court did not imply in its judgment that Serbia acted as an accomplice in the Srebrenica genocide, or had the intention to commit genocide, thereby demonstrating that the ICJ took a strict and conservative construction of the term notwithstanding the fact that the said court established that the Belgrade government exerted huge influence on its ethnic kin in Bosnia and offered massive support to Bosnia's Serbs.[26]

The space is limited here to engage more elaborately with relevant ICTY judgments.[27] The disappointment that only the Srebrenica massacre has been designated as genocide by the ICTY was noted in the introduction to this chapter. Moreover, 161 indictments may present an achievement of the legal process but is far from attaining justice for the victims especially in relation to those criminal architects and/or perpetrators who were not indicted or who, though indicted, died during the proceedings before judgment was delivered. Such distinct drawbacks notwithstanding, overall, the ICTY judgments have contributed to establish an all-encompassing accurate record of the genocidal happenings at Srebrenica, and also other atrocities perpetrated in the course of the Bosnian War. The ICTY's characterization of the Srebrenica massacre as genocide indelibly memorializes violence.[28] The ICTY and ICJ 2007 judgments narrate the evil which befell the people of Bosnia in the course of war: criminals involved, crimes committed, extent of planning, and details of such plans. One significant hallmark of the ICTY jurisprudence pertains to the recognition of mass rape as a war crime and a crime against humanity when perpetrated as part of a pre-planned war strategy.[29] Judgments pertaining to genocide and war crimes in Bosnia influence the understanding and interpretation of events as well as their implications for the postconflict era (regarding crimes perpetrated, suffering incurred, and the redress). It bears emphasizing that the gamut of court judgments brought about by penal proceedings have contributed to construction of social knowledge about the Srebrenica genocide as well as other serious human rights violations conducted during the Bosnian War.[30] The massive amount of evidence presented in the international criminal courts and

[26] An analysis of the ICJ 2007 judgment can be found in Kevin Aquilina and Klejda Mulaj, 'Limitations in Attributing State Responsibility under the Genocide Convention' (2018) 17(1) Journal of Human Rights (hereafter Aquilina and Mulaj, 'State Responsibility').

[27] The record of the ICTY is discussed by Orentlicher, *Some Kind of Justice* (n 14); Richard Ashby Wilson, 'Judging History: The Historical Record of the International Criminal Tribunal for the Former Yugoslavia' (2005) 27(3) Human Rights Quarterly; James Gow, Rachel Kerr, and Zoran Pajić (eds), *Prosecuting War Crimes: Lessons and Legacies of the International Criminal Tribunal for the Former Yugoslavia* (Routledge 2013).

[28] Mark A Drumbl, *Atrocity, Punishment, and International Law* (CUP 2007) 175.

[29] See Geoffrey Robertson, *Crimes Against Humanity: The Struggle for Global Justice* (Penguin Press 1999) 285.

[30] Refer to Nettelfield and Wagner, *Srebrenica* (n 6) Chapter 7.

tribunals shrink the space for denial.[31] Furthermore, these fora are key sites where the process of recognition of harms incurred unfolds—including gendered forms of harm. As feminist transitional justice scholars suggest naming and officially recognizing such harm is essential to the postconflict transitional constitution of social and political order.[32] Such recognition is the first crucial step in the process of addressing harms done to innocent civilians, even if the process of implementing the related law may be flawed.

Genocide Remembrance and Denial

It is not that the effects of genocide manifest themselves only in courts of law. Indeed, for Bosnia's people the significance of genocide is not constrained merely to legalistic criteria and court cases pertaining to the Srebrenica massacre of July 1995 and other massacres perpetrated during the war. In point of fact, genocide has become an intrinsic part of who Bosnians are.[33] Their thinking about the present and the past, and how they relate to the international community and their former opponents—Serbia and the Serbs—are informed by the genocide. The limited convictions notwithstanding, the designation of Srebrenica massacre as genocide has great importance for victims' families and their wider community because it recognizes their suffering and legitimizes victims' claims for redress. Victims' communities have persistently demanded recognition of their calamity. They have engaged in acts of commemorations—most remarkably those at the Memorial and Cemetery Centre at Potočari, the Peace March (Marš Mira), and acts of mass burials—which reinforce collective memory and exert public recognition of victims' ordeals.[34]

[31] Dianne F Orentlicher, 'Shrinking the Space for Denial: The Impact of the ICTY in Serbia' (Open Society Justice Initiative May 2008) <https://www.justiceinitiative.org/uploads/a0be82c5-aa8a-4bcd-9d23-bcef4d94f93c/serbia_20080501.pdf> accessed 18 June 2020.

[32] Doris Buss, 'Making Sense of Genocide, Making Sense of Law: International Criminal Prosecutions of Large-Scale Sexual Violence' in Amy E Randall (ed), *Genocide and Gender in the Twentieth Century: A Comparative Survey* (Bloomsbury 2015) 278 (hereafter Buss, 'Making Sense'); Fionnuala Ni Aoláin, 'Emerging Paradigms of Rationality: Exploring a Feminist Theory of Harm in the Context of Conflicted and Post-Conflicted Societies' (2009) 35(1) Queen's Law Journal 219–44.

[33] 'Bosnians' here refer to the inhabitants of the Bosnian republic who adhere to the idea of Bosnian statehood. Bosnia's population is estimated at 3.3 million people of whom 48 per cent are Bosniak, 37 per cent Serbs, 14 per cent Croats, and 0.6 per cent Other. World Population Review, 'Bosnia and Herzegovina Population 2020 Live' (World Population Review, 18 June 2020) <http://worldpopulationreview.com/countries/bosnia-and-herzegovina-population/> accessed 18 June 2020.

[34] The Potočari Memorial and Cemetery and the Peace March are important symbols of Bosnian identity, and part of a movement committed to remember the Srebrenica genocide. The Potočari Memorial and Cemetery—opened on 20 September 2003—honours victims of the Srebrenica genocide, supports efforts to identify and return to this cemetery remains of the missing, and encourages internally displaced people to return to Srebrenica. The Peace March—Marš Mira—is a commemorative walk in respect of about 15,000 men who sought to escape the genocide by undertaking a hazardous sixty-three-mile journey on foot through heavily mined woods from Srebrenica to Tuzla. The Peace March follows the same route taken by approximately one-fifth of the initial groups of men who managed to survive the genocide in 1995.

Commemorations and collective memoralization serve not solely a psychological need—expressing morning for death and suffering on a massive scale. Commemorations and collective memoralization are also profoundly *political*. They are a key element in the symbolic repertoire available to leaders for binding citizens into a collective national identity.[35] Sociological research has stressed the power of commemorations to draw upon the loss and sacrifice occasioned by war and genocide as a means of shaping national identity, and also as a means of reinforcing, or undermining, dominant ideologies in a given state.[36] Suffering incurred in the course of war and genocide becomes central to the identity as well as symbolic continuity of a nation. Benedict Anderson was right to observe that a nation 'ensures its symbolic continuity by construing its members as forming an imagined community that surpasses death', therefore securing the nation's imagined continuity and transcendence of time.[37] In the same vein, memory of loss, suffering and persecution has become a crucial marker of the Bosnian identity and heritage.[38]

The legacy of suffering and loss has become a core component of national identity, and claims for entitlements and redress. For instance, Srebrenica's Bosniak population, generally quite poor,[39] has developed its own criteria of suffering and entitlement which in turn have been tied up to humanitarian aid and social welfare. There are implicit criteria regarding who is most deserving of aid. These criteria are based on the view who has lost and suffered most. There is a distinction, for example, between those who fled in the spring of 1992—before the violence engulfed the city—and the 365 residents who remained in the enclave and suffered throughout the war including the Srebrenica massacre in July 1995.[40] The most

[35] T G Ashplant, Graham Dawson, and Michael Roper, 'The Politics of War Memory and Commemoration: Contexts, Structures and Dynamics' in T G Ashplant, Graham Dawson, and Michael Roper (eds), *The Politics of War Memory and Commemoration* (Routledge 2000) 7.

[36] Eric Hobsbawm, 'Inventing traditions' in Eric Hobsbawm and Terrence Ranger (eds), *The Invention of Tradition* (CUP 1983); Benedict Anderson, *Imagined Communities: Reflections on the Origins and Spread of Nationalism* (Verso 1983) (hereafter Anderson, *Imagined Communities*); Jay Winter and Emmanuel Sivan (eds), *War and Remembrance in the Twentieth Century* (CUP 1999).

[37] Anderson, *Imagined Communities* (n 36) 6–7, 9–10.

[38] Srebrenica is symbolic to genocide commemorations not only in Bosnia but also abroad. For example, the High Representative for the implementation of the Peace Agreement on Bosnia and Herzegovina—Mr Christian Schwartz-Schilling—urged the United Nations in May 2007 to establish the UN Day of Srebrenica to pay respect to genocide victims and families. United Nations Security Council, 'Press Release. Bosnia and Herzegovina has historic window of opportunity to move closer to Europe, Leaders must '"Seize the Moment" Security Council Told' (*United Nations*, 16 May 2017) <https://www.un.org/press/en/2007/sc9018.doc.htm> accessed 18 June 2020. In January 2009, the European Parliament declared July 11 Srebrenica Genocide Commemoration Day. Other parliaments of European countries have followed suit. Isabelle Delpla, Xavier Bougarel, and Jean-Louis Fournel, 'The Judge, the Historian, the Legislator' in Isabelle Delpla, Xavier Bougarel, and Jean-Louis Fournel (eds), *Investigating Srebrenica: Institutions, Facts, Responsibilities* (Bergham Books 2012) 15.

[39] Lorenzo Tondo, '"They've Abandoned Us": Srebrenica Survivors Still Living in Camps' (*The Guardian*, 17 February 2020) <https://www.theguardian.com/world/2020/feb/17/theyve-abandoned-us-srebenica-survivors-still-living-in-camps> accessed 18 June 2020.

[40] Sarah Wagner, *To Know Where He Lies: DNA Technology and the Search for Srebrenica's Missing* (University of California Press 2008) 66.

implicit measure of entitlement and suffering relates to loss of family members. As Sarah Wagner observes, although survivors do not compare their losses openly, 'there is an unspoken "hierarchy of sufferers" in which special status is reserved for those who suffered most'.[41] Therefore, the memory of Srebrenica genocide has infiltrated Bosnia's social structures; it permeates social practices of status and entitlement. This memory is also politically framed: it is mediated by Bosnian elites and their interests. In other words, the framing of Srebrenica genocide is conditioned not solely by the tragedy and suffering incurred in the past but also by present political circumstances and power relations.

It is not only Bosnian Muslim politicians who use genocide to ground their claims for entitlements and redress. Serbian nationalists—both in Bosnia and Serbia—have been keen to capitalize on the utility of genocide's denial. As observed in the introduction of this chapter, genocide denial is still common among the Serbs both in Republika Srpska and Republic of Serbia.[42] An expression of such denial is the memorial that Serbs have erected near Potočari—a symbol of antagonistic struggle over competitive memory and victimhood. Moreover, Serb leaders refuse to categorize the Srebrenica massacre as genocide. Promptly after assuming office in May 2012, the Serb President Mr Tomislav Nikolić (2012–2017) declared that no genocide took place in Srebrenica, openly contradicting the findings of the ICTY and ICJ.[43] The April 2013 President Nikolić's apology in relation to Srebrenica, whilst avoiding referring to the massacre as genocide, casts into doubt the value of his apology.[44] In a similar fashion, the current Serbian Prime Minister Ana Brnabic stated in an interview with broadcaster Deutsche Welle on 15 November 2018 that the massacre of Srebrenica was not a genocide—a denial that drew harsh criticism by legal experts and liberal circles.[45]

41 ibid.

42 See generally, Nettelfield and Wagner, *Srebrenica* (n 6) especially Chapter 8; Orentlicher, *Some Kind of Justice* (n 14) especially Chapters 7 and 8; Jelena Obradovic-Wochnik, *Ethnic Conflict and War Crimes in the Balkans: The Narratives of Denial in Post-Conflict Serbia* (I.B. Tauris 2013).

43 CBC News, 'Serbian President denies Srebrenica genocide' (Canadian Broadcasting Corporation, 2 June 2012 <https://www.cbc.ca/news/world/serbia-president-denies-srebrenica-genocide-1.1135489> accessed 18 June 2020.

44 Damien McElroy, 'Serbian President in historic Srebrenica massacre apology' (*The Telegraph*, 25 April 2013) <http://www.telegraph.co.uk/news/worldnews/europe/serbia/10017552/Serbian-preseident-in-historic-Srebrenica-massacre-apology.html> accessed 18 June 2020. Moreover, on 8 July 2015, President Nikolić praised the Russian veto of a United Nations Security Council Resolution that, twenty years after, would have condemned the Srebrenica massacre as genocide. Dan Bilefsky and Somini Sengupta, 'Srebrenica massacre, After 20 years, Still casts a long shadow in Bosnia' (*New York Times* 8 July 2015) <http://www.nytimes.com/2015/07/09/world/europe/srebrenica-genocide-massacre.html?_r=0> accessed on 18 June 2020.

45 Deutsche Welle, 'Serbian PM Ana Brnabic: "Srebrenica a Terrible Crime", not Genocide' (Deutsch Welle, 15 November 2018) <https://www.dw.com/en/serbian-pm-ana-brnabic-srebrenica-a-terrible-crime-not-genocide/a-46307925-0> accessed on 18 June 2020. Filip Rudic, 'Hague Court Chief Criticizes Serbian PM's Genocide Denial' (*Balkan Insight*, 20 November 2018) <https://balkaninsight.com/2018/11/20/hague-tribunal-chief-criticises-serbian-pm-s-genocide-denial-11-20-2018/> accessed 18 June 2020. Mersiha Gadzo, 'Canadians launch petition to ban Srebrenica genocide denial' (*Al Jazeera*, 28 December 2018) <https://www.aljazeera.com/indepth/features/canadians-launch-petition-ban-srebrenica-genocide-denial-181227115025333.html> accessed 18 June 2020).

Serb genocide denial can be conceived to be posited in relation to both the past and the present. On the one hand, the Serbian denial is predicated on a relation with the past, that is, a determined refusal to acknowledge the severity of Srebrenica crimes for what they were and for what they represent in international law. Serbs' denial of genocide denigrates claims to truth championed by survivors, in addition to eroding social knowledge about the past which emanates from the findings of the legal judgments. On the other hand, genocide denial is intertwined with the present. The Serbian elite in Belgrade are aware that admitting that the Srebrenica massacre classifies as genocide renders them liable for reparations. Furthermore, admitting Serbia's involvement in Srebrenica genocide—and in the Bosnian War, in general—unsettles the Belgrade sponsored narrative which claims that the war was a civil one, a narrative grounded on a false reciprocity of victimhood according to which all parties were portrayed as equally victims.[46] It is baffling that this rhetoric (of false reciprocity of victimhood) persists despite the fact that no less than 80 per cent of civilian casualties in the course of the Bosnian War were Bosnian Muslims, and that the overall number of Serb civilian casualties in this war is about half of the number of Bosniaks killed by Serb military in Srebrenica in one week alone.[47] Moreover, domestic stakeholders in Serbia have utilized the Srebrenica discourse for the purposes of defining their own political profile to take advantage in domestic political competition and also tarnish their competitors. Progressivist parties argue that Serbia should improve her international standing and work toward establishing its credibility in Europe, whereas nationalists accuse progressivists of 'selling the country out to Europe'.[48]

In a similar vein, for Serb politicians in Bosnia contestation of the war and Srebrenica's bloodshed offers not merely a response to the past, but also a distinct position towards the present. Mr Milorad Dodik—former President of Republika Srpska (2010–2018) and currently the Serb member of Bosnia's tripartite presidency—has reiterated that no genocide occurred at Srebrenica.[49]

[46] Refer to Nettelfield and Wagner, *Srebrenica* (n 6) 269–273; Maass, 'Congratulations' (n 13).

[47] Refer to figures cited in n 1 above.

[48] These themes were manifested in the Serbian parliamentary debate on Srebrenica in March 2010 initiated by then Serbian President Boris Tadić in response to the European Parliament's resolution of January 2009 which declared 11 July a Europe-wide day of remembrance for the Srebrenica genocide. The Serbian Parliament's declaration on Srebrenica omitted the term 'genocide'. See Daniela Mehler, 'Understanding narrative gaps in transitional justice: The Serbian discourse on the Srebrenica Declaration of 2010' (2013) 11(4) Journal on Ethnopolitics and Minority Issues in Europe, particularly 142–47.

[49] Dodik explicitly denied that the Srebrenica massacre amounted to genocide on 12 July 2010, the fifteenth anniversary of the Genocide. 'If a genocide happened', he said, 'then it was committed against Serb people of this region where women, children and the elderly were killed *en masse*'. *The Sydney Morning Herald*, 'Srebrenica Massacre not "genocide"' (*The Sydney Morning Herald*, 13 July 2010) <http://news.smh.com.au/breaking-news-world/srebrenica-massacre-not-genocide-20100713-1083q.html> accessed 18 June 2020; Walker, 'Genocide Denial' (n 4).

For Serb nationalists, genocide denial is self-serving: it challenges the construction of Bosnia's political community in postgenocide, because it undermines—even denies—survivors' return to their former homes, and the rebuilding of their lives. The announcement of the United Nations High Commissioner for Refugees ('UNHCR') in September 2004 that one million people had returned back home in Bosnia sounded encouraging. However, the reality of those returns is a largely sobering one. Indeed, the peak years for returns had passed by 2004. Furthermore, the 'one million' figure included only 40 per cent of the refugees who were forced out of the country during the war. Fifty-six per cent of returns were majority returns. In most places the number of minority returns is below 20 per cent; 720,000 Bosnians remained outside the country.[50] Specifically, genocide denial for the Serb elite of the Republika Srpska (within the jurisdiction of which Srebrenica has been assigned by the Dayton Agreement that ended the Bosnian War) is conducive to a new political reality where Bosnian Muslims have been uprooted permanently.

Divisive ethno-nationalist rhetoric is a striking element of the political discourse on Srebrenica in particular, and Bosnia in general. Noticeably, the conflict over the genocide terminology and genocide denial is part of a broader struggle pertaining to national identity mediated by irreconcilable interpretations of the use of armed force during the war. For the Serbs, genocide denial serves to render their meaning of violence dominant in order to secure acceptance for their own use of force in Srebrenica, and in the course of the Bosnian War in general, as well as to secure legitimacy for a new socio-political reality in Republika Srpska where Bosniaks have been ethnically cleansed. For the Bosniaks, on the other hand, the genocide debate and the recognition of loss and suffering present avenues for delegitimizing Serb violence in Srebrenica and in the entire course of the war, because genocidal violence can never be justified neither on legal nor on moral grounds. Therefore, naming the Srebrenica massacre as genocide or otherwise is grounded on attempts to use alternative frames of meaning, which in turn provide the basis for the contestation of (i) the use of armed force in the course of the Bosnian War, (ii) memories of genocide and other mass atrocities, and (iii) the postwar constitution of the political community.

[50] Gerard Toal and Carl T Dahlman, *Bosnia Remade: Ethnic Cleansing and Its Reversal* (OUP 2011) 285–87. Minority returns refer to returns of the people uprooted in the course of the war to areas where they form a minority. Most of the refugees and internally displaced Bosnians would be in the minority if they returned to the homes they occupied before the war. Refer to International Crisis Group (ICG), 'Minority Returns or Mass Relocations', Report 33 (*International Crisis Group*, 4 May 1998) <https://www.crisisgroup.org/europe-central-asia/balkans/bosnia-and-herzegovina/minority-return-or-mass-relocation> accessed 18 June 2020.

Letting Genocide Survivals Down: Denial of Victims' Rights and Fractures of National Unity

The fracturing of Bosnia's national community does not stem only from denial of genocide by the Serbs and their contestation of war narratives that underpin dominant interpretations of genocide. The national community is also split from within. There are multiple reasons for such inner split, including the constitutional organization of Bosnia that shapes the new federation along ethnic lines (not entirely detached from rationales that justified the war in the first place) which have led to persistent political crises.[51] As a result the rights of minorities are subordinate to those of majorities both at entity and municipality levels. In addition, there is ethnic grounding of citizenship, separate media sources for Bosnian Muslims, Serbs, and Croats, as well as segregation of education and politically driven text books.[52] Unlike the example of Germany, where Holocaust education has been incorporated in school curriculum since the 1960s, and open public debates on the Nazi crimes in the 1970s and 1980s provided a space for acknowledging and critically examining past crimes[53], there are no such undertakings either in Bosnia or in Serbia. It is not unreasonable therefore to suggest that a meaningful process of reconciliation between Serbia and Bosnia has not yet begun.

The remaining part of this chapter will emphasize a less mentioned reason for the inner fracturing of the national community in Bosnia, namely the failure to fully recognize and address the needs of victims of genocide and war—epitomized by the neglect of victims of sexual violence, referred to also as gender-based violence. Intensity of genocidal rape in the course of the Bosnian War brought visibility to rape in war and has been a key factor in the explicit recognition of this crime as a weapon of war. Scholars have analysed how gender-based violence has been used as a genocide weapon—and as a weapon of war more generally—developing frameworks that challenge older narratives which depict sexual violence, including rape, as incidental, merely a by-product of war. Their investigations of martial rape and genocidal violence has shown how construction of national identity is gendered—mediated by certain beliefs about gender and gender roles in society.[54] The popular

[51] See Sofia Sebastian-Aparicio, *Post-War Statebuilding and Constitutional Reform: Beyond Dayton in Bosnia* (Palgrave Macmillan 2014) Chapter 6.

[52] *Flávia Saldanha Kroetz*, 'Post-genocide Identity Politics in Rwanda and Bosnia and Herzegovina and their Compatibility with International Human Rights Law' (2016) 23 International Journal of Minority and Group Rights 328–54; Marianne Hanson, 'Warnings from Bosnia: The Dayton Agreement and the Implementation of Human Rights' (2001) 4(3-4) International Journal of Human Rights 86–104.

[53] Armen T Marssobian, 'Epilogue: Reconciliation in the Aftermath of Genocide' in Claudia Card and Armen T Marsoobian (eds), *Genocide's Aftermath: Responsibility and Repair* (Blackwell 2007) 264–65.

[54] Claudia Card, 'Rape as a Weapon of War' (1996) 11(4) Hypatia: A Journal of Feminist Philosophy 5–18 (hereafter Card, 'Weapon of War'); Amy E Randall, 'Introduction: Gendering Genocide Studies' in Amy E Randall, (ed), *Genocide and Gender in the Twentieth Century: A Comparative Survey* (Bloomsbury 2015) 2.

believe that a child's social identity is determined by his or her biological father, that women are vessels for paternal identity, and that their maternal biology and contribution to a child's upbringing does not determine a child's identity informed campaigns of rape and forced impregnation initiated by planners and perpetrators of the genocide. The Serb leaders and militias believed that impregnating Bosnian women would lead these women to bear Serb children through forced 'occupation of the womb'[55]—in the process fracturing Bosnian identity. As Claudia Card opines:

> there is more than one way to commit genocide. One way is mass murder, killing individual members of a national, political, or cultural group. Another is to destroy a group's identity by decimating cultural and social bonds. Martial rape does both. Many women and girls are killed when rapists are finished with them. If survivors become pregnant or are known to be rape survivors, cultural, political, and national unity may be thrown into chaos.... Martial rape can undermine national, political, and cultural solidarity, changing the next generation's identity, confusing the loyalties of all victimized survivors.[56]

Effects of martial rape therefore go beyond the immediate infliction of pain and suffering on directly affected individuals to destroy social bonds of solidarity and trust needed to sustain a healthy group life.[57] Sexual violence as a weapon of genocide attacks women's and men's physical and emotional sense of security while simultaneously launching an assault, through their bodies, upon the genealogy of security as constructed by the body politic.[58] Laura Sjoberg has argued that the gendered strategy of intentional victimization that targets women as a centre of gravity for states is a key war tactic due to the symbolic function it serves. Violence against women is intended not only as an injury to the women subjected to rape and men responsible for their protection. More importantly, genocidal rape is intended to disrupt the national or ethnic community by planting alien seeds, or worse destroying reproductive viability. Forced impregnation is a 'material attack on the sustainability of an ethnic group, state, or nation looking to corrupt its ability to reproduce, biologically and socially'.[59]

[55] Patricia A Weitsman, 'Constructions of Identity and Sexual Violence in Wartime: The Case of Bosnia' in Amy Randall (ed), *Genocide and Gender in the Twentieth Century* (Bloomsbury 2015) 123 (hereafter Weitsman, *Constructions of Identity*); Siobhan K Fischer, 'Occupation of the Womb: Forced Impregnation as Genocide' (1996) 46(1) Duke Law Review 91–133.

[56] Card, 'Weapon of War' (n 54) 8.

[57] Douglas Irvin-Erickson, *Raphael Lemkin and the Concept of Genocide* (University of Pennsylvania Press 2017) 236.

[58] Katrina Lee Koo, 'Confronting a Disciplinary Blindness: Women, War and Rape in the International Politics of Security' (2002) 37(3) Australian Journal of Political Science 528.

[59] Laura Sjoberg, *Gendering Global Conflict: Toward a Feminist Theory of War* (Columbia University Press 2013) 222 (hereafter Sjoberg, *Gendering Global Conflict*).

The final report of the United Nations Commission of Experts established pursuant to Security Council Resolution 789 (1992), has documented that there were 162 detention sites in Bosnia, Croatia, and Serbia, where civilians were routinely sexually and mentally violated.[60] Muslim, Croatian, and Serbian women have been subjected to rape, but the majority of cases pertain to Bosnian Muslim women raped by Serb men—solders, paramilitaries, policemen, and some civilians.[61] The Bosnian Government reported in October 1992 that as many as 50,000 Muslim women had been raped.[62] Forced impregnations camps in Bosnia gave rise to thousands of children born of rape, whose fate is by and large unspoken of and stigmatized to an identity of shame.[63] In the course of the Bosnian War, men, too, were subjected to sexual violence, as well as mental abuse. Around 3,000 male victims are estimated to have suffered rape during the Bosnian War.[64] Both female and male victims have been reluctant to speak out about their ordeal but more so the men. Generally there is silence regarding their suffering. Men's reluctance to speak out is conditioned by gender norms and stereotypes that render difficult to portray men as victims of sexual violence. There is greater social stigma regarding sexual violence against men which hinders reporting of their experiences.[65] As a result, male victims are paid little or no attention by local, national, and international communities. Male victims have neither received meaningful assistance to overcome their traumas, nor have their violators been prosecuted for crimes committed.[66]

[60] Final report of the United Nations Commission of Experts established pursuant to Security Council Resolution 789, under the direction of M Cherif Bassiouni, chairman and rapporteur on the gathering and analysis of the facts, S/1994/674 (*United Nations Commission of Experts*, 27 May 1994) particularly 55–57 <http://www.icty.org/x/file/About/OTP/un_commission_of_experts_report1994_en.pdf> accessed 18 June 2020.

[61] ibid 57–60.

[62] Aryeh Neier, 'Watching Rights: Rapes in Bosnia-Herzegovina', *The Nation*, 1 March 1993 259; see also Alexandra Stiglmayer, 'The Rapes in Bosnia-Herzegovina' in Alexandra Stiglmayer (ed), *Mass Rape: The War Against Women in Bosnia-Herzegovina* (University of Nebraska Press 1993) (hereafter Stiglmayer, *Mass Rape*).

[63] Patricia Weitsman, 'Children Born of War and the Politics of Identity' in Charli Carpenter (ed), *Born of War: Protecting Children of Sexual Violence Survivors in Conflict Zones* (Kumarian Press 2007) 110–27 (hereafter Weitsman, *Children Born of War*).

[64] All Survivors Project, 'Legacies and Lessons: Sexual Violence against Men and Boys in Sri Lanka and Bosnia & Herzegovina' (*UCLA School of Law*, May 2017) <https://allsurvivorsproject.org/wp-content/uploads/2017/05/Sexual-violence-against-men-and-boys-in-Sri-Lanka-and-BiH.pdf> accessed 18 June 2020.

[65] Douglas Page and Samuel Whitt, 'Confronting Wartime Sexual Violence: Public Support for Survivors in Bosnia' (2020) 64(4) Journal of Conflict Resolution 679 (hereafter Page and Whitt, 'Confronting Wartime Sexual Violence').

[66] Refer to Olivera Simić, 'Wartime Rape and its Shunned Victims' in Amy Randall (ed), *Genocide and Gender in the Twentieth Century* (Bloomsbury 2015). Research on male victimization in the course of war is emerging slowly. For an account of sexual violence against men and boys in the ongoing Syrian War, see Sarah Chynoweth, 'We Keep it in our Heart: Sexual Violence Against Men and Boys in the Syrian Crisis' (*United Nations High Commissioner for Refugees*, October 2017) <https://data2.unhcr.org/es/documents/download/60864#_ga=2.237354944.1734073480.1559823107-245140757.1552824982> accessed 18 June 2020. An Al Jazeera documentary has publicized sexual violence against men in the ongoing civil war in Libya. Refer to Al Jazeera, 'Unspeakable Crime: Rape as a Weapon of War in Libya', broadcast on 7 September 2019.

The rapes have had devastating effects on female victims, too. Women subjected to rape have suffered severe emotional and psychological trauma in addition to physical injuries.[67]

Feminist scholars contend that gendered experiences of genocide and war have sex-differential impacts which tend to be felt more severely by women.[68] Women constitute the largest group subjected to sexual maltreatment.[69] Not only do women suffer disproportionate levels of sexual violence in the course of conflict, but violence against them does not end in the postconflict era. They are subjected to additional violence, including sexual exploitation and verbal abuse. Martial/genocidal rapes customarily result in shame and abandonment of women subjected to sexual assaults. Many of the violated women, abandoned by their families, live in destitution unable to provide a decent standard of living and decent education to their children.[70] Gender perceptions that informed perpetrators' sexual assaults during genocide continue in postgenocide setting to enable victimization of women survivors and also their relatives.

Moreover, children born of rape have often been shunned and abandoned. They have been frequently rejected by both the community of the rapist father and the biological mother.[71] As Patricia Weistman has persuasively argued, the assumptions inherent in the policies of forced impregnation and maternity witnessed in the course of the Bosnian War continue to have a grave effect on the human rights of children born of violence. This can be seen in a number of ways, not least in the derogatory language used to describe these children which links them to the rapist

[67] Vera Folnegovic-Smalc, 'Psychiatric Aspects of the Rapes in the War Against the Republic of Croatia and Bosnia-Herzegovina' in Stiglmayer, *Mass Rapes* (n 62) 203.

[68] Sjoberg, *Gendering Global Conflict* (n 59) 286; Jeanne Vickers, *Women and War* (Zed 1993).

[69] Use of rape as a war tactic has been a recurring feature of many armed conflicts, including the Japanese invasion of China (1937–1944), the Second World War (particularly the operations in the Eastern front), East Pakistan (now Bangladesh) secessionist war (1971), and more recent armed conflicts in the Democratic Republic of Congo (DRC), Rwanda, Libya, Côte d'Ivoire, etc. Refer, for instance, to Takahasi Yoshida, *The Making of the 'Rape of Nanking': History and Memory in Japan, China, and the United States* (OUP 2006); Atina Grossman, 'A Question of Silence: The Rape of German Women by Occupation Soldiers' (1995) 72 *October* 42–63. See also Human Rights Watch, 'Shattered Lives: Sexual Violence during the Rwandan Genocide and its Aftermath' (*Human Rights Watch*, 24 September 1996) <https://www.hrw.org/reports/1996/Rwanda.htm> accessed 18 June 2020; Human Rights Watch, 'Côte d'Ivoire: Ouattara Forces Kill, Rape Civilians During Offensive' (*Human Rights Watch*, 9 April 2011) <https://www.hrw.org/news/2011/04/09/cote-divoire-ouattara-forces-kill-rape-civilians-during-offensive> accessed 18 June 2020. At least 200,000 Bengali women were reportedly raped by West Pakistani soldiers in the 1971 war. Susan Brownmiller, *Against Our Will: Men, Women and Rape* (Open Road Media 2103) 167.

[70] Card, 'Weapon of War' (n 54) 8. The rejection of women subjected to sexual violence is not an exclusive feature of Bosnia. It is also a feature of other societies which have suffered from genocide and war violence. See, for example, a study by Jeannie Annan and Moriah Brier on women experience in Northern Uganda, 'The Risk of Return: Intimate Partner Violence in Northern Uganda's Armed Conflict' (2010) 70(1) Social Science and Medicine.

[71] R Charli Carpenter, *Forgetting Children Born of War: Setting the Human Rights Agenda in Bosnia and Beyond* (Columbia University Press 2010) 29–30 (hereafter Carpenter, *Born of War*); Patricia A Weitsman, 'The Politics of Identity and Sexual Violence: A Review of Bosnia and Rwanda' (2008) 30(3) Human Rights Quarterly.

fathers. Shame hangs over the offspring of genocidal rape due to circumstances beyond their control. Moreover, they live in destitute conditions and have suffered a large incidence of infanticide. The Bosnian Government declined to allow them to be adopted overseas due to official preoccupation with repopulating the country.[72] Given that due to financial constraints few Bosnian families could adopt children, the chances of a normal family life for children born of rape have been slim.

It is saddening that the acute challenges that children born of violence face are by and large unaddressed. In a forceful critique of the human rights record of the offspring of wartime rape in Bosnia, Charli Carpenter has argued that lack of protection for these children is contingent to the fact that human rights advocates, when construing specific categories of rights claims, are conditioned by myriad political, organizational, cultural, structural, coalitional, and economic factors; which sometimes may draw attention away from the merits of their case. Children born of rape have been treated as marginal participants in transitional justice processes. This may be due to the fact that the crime of forced maternity is viewed as a crime against the victim of the rape; that is, the mother, whereas the children are viewed merely as evidence of the atrocity.[73] No provisions are made to award reparations to offspring of genocidal rape.

The marginalization of victims hurts and harms them beyond their agony incurred in the genocide. Yet, recognition of victims' suffering is an important aspect of redress. Victims cannot be reconnected with a society and a government that does not fully recognize their suffering. Echoing Hegel, Nancy Frazer has argued that mutual recognition is important for the dialogical construction of identity.

> [R]ecognition designates an ideal reciprocal relation between subjects ... (a) relation (that) is constitutive for subjectivity: one becomes an individual subject only by virtue of recognizing, and being recognized by, another subject. Recognition from others is thus essential to the development of a sense of self. To be denied recognition—or to be 'misrecognized'—is to suffer both a distortion of one's relation to one's self and an injury to one's identity.[74]

Misrecognizing victims—failing to recognize their suffering and providing redress—produces for victims a form of social subordination which is directly responsible for their disconnect with the community of the nation which ought to embrace them.[75] Doris Bus rightly suggests that the lawful acceptance of harms

[72] Weitsman, *Constructions of Identity* (n 55) 131–32; Weistman, *Children Born of War* (n 63) 110–27.

[73] Carpenter, *Born of War* (n 71) 100–08. See also Cécile Aptel and Patrick Nagler, 'Children and Transitional Justice' (2019) 13 International Journal of Transitional Justice 185–86.

[74] Nancy Fraser, 'Rethinking Recognition' (2000) 3 New Left Review 109.

[75] Although public programmes exist in Bosnia to provide legal aid and stipends for survivors, the implementation of such programmes has been hampered by disagreement on the side of Serb/Bosnian/Croat politicians as well as ethnocentric views and social stigma. Page and Whitt, 'Confronting Wartime Sexual Violence' (n 65). See also Eleanor Rose, 'Bosnia Accused of Failing Wartime Rape Victims' (*Balkan Insight*, 13 March 2017) <https://balkaninsight.com/2017/03/13/

experienced by genocide victims is a means of overcoming their status of subordination. Bus contends that the legal and social recognition of gendered forms of harm and in particular categories of victims and perpetrators afford a solid foundation for claims to full inclusion, both in relation to the reckoning with the widespread barbarity caused by atrocity and the societal reconstruction that ensues.[76] For so long as suffering of genocide victims is not recognized and meaningfully redressed their integration in the postgenocide political community will remain incomplete, with detrimental effect for the national unity.

Concluding Remarks

This chapter advances an understanding of correlations between genocide in Bosnia and the ensuing fragile peace. It has offered an appreciation of the long shadow genocide continues to cast twenty five years after the ending of the Bosnian War. Relations of power as well as social and gender mores have been pivotal to the happening of genocide as much as they remain central to ways of dealing with the devastation in the postgenocide setting. The tragedy of the Bosnian War, and genocide in its midst, has produced a legal discourse—in the form of extensive judgments and academic studies—that have deepened genocide scholarship and constructed social knowledge about the Srebrenica genocide and other atrocious crimes perpetrated during the war, extent of planning, and criminals involved. The extensive legal work produced by the ICTY has provided the ground for informed debates on the meaning of genocide and interpretations of its constitutive elements. Yet, this legal discourse is not entirely complete. The ICTY case law has not offered an unambiguous explication of intent, state responsibility for genocide, and the (size of the) group subjected to destruction.[77] In addition, critics are discontent that Srebrenica has been decontextualized from the rest of the Bosnian War since only this mass atrocity has been designated as genocide—amongst other similar cases in the midst of this war.[78] Such decontextualization of genocide is disappointing for the community of victims and also a source of contention amongst analysts.

A key feature of the genocide discourse has been a divisive ethno-nationalist rhetoric predicated on the political agendas of Bosnian and Serb elites as they vie to

amnesty-international-slams-bosnia-for-failing-victims-of-wartime-rape-03-13-2017/> accessed 18 June 2020.

[76] Buss, 'Making Sense' (n 32) 290.

[77] Aquilina and Mulaj, 'State Responsibility' (n 26). Gregory Kent, 'Genocidal Intent and Transitional Justice in Bosnia: Jelisic, Foot Soldiers of Genocide, and the ICTY' (2013) 27(3) East European Politics and Society.

[78] Nettelfield and Wagner, *Srebrenica* (n 6) 8; Vulliamy, 'Srebrenica' (n 11); Kent, 'Justice and Genocide' (n 10); Toljaga, 'Prelude to the Srebrenica Genocide' (n 11).

achieve legitimacy for their postwar policies. Not only can genocide provide elites with a symbolic repertoire for binding citizens into the national community but it can also underline social practices of status and entitlements, and claims to authority and political control. Central to recognizing or denying categorization of mass violence in Srebrenica (and elsewhere in Bosnia) as genocide are attempts to utilize competing frames of meaning that dispute narratives of war, memories of genocide, and postwar constitution of the political community. Therefore, the genocide discourse is profoundly divisive and political.

The Serb establishment continues to deny that genocide occurred at Srebrenica whilst the Bosnian Muslims memorialize this tragedy more so that novel tidings about brutal killings have come to the fore in court proceedings and the dissemination by the media of information about the unearthing of mass graves in Bosnian grounds.[79] These competing and divisive narratives have contributed to persistent misgivings and acrimony among Bosnian Muslim and Serb populations as well as their elites. Such suspicion and uneasiness diminishes the likelihood that the country moves forward to establish a shared historical chronicle of the past and develop a healthy dialogue between and within ethnic communities. The divisive legacy of genocide impedes the consolidation of peace, undermines Bosnia's socio-political cohesion, and hinders victims' search for justice.

At the present, Bosnia's political community is fractured both from without due to the denial of genocide by the Serbs and the latter's contestation of war narratives that underpin dominant interpretations of genocide, and from within due to failures to fully recognize and address the needs of victims—including victims of gender-based violence. In particular, misrecognizing victims—failing to recognize their suffering and providing redress—produces for them a form of social subordination which is responsible for their disconnect with the community of the nation which ought to embrace them. The legal and social recognition of harms experienced by genocide victims affords a sound foundation for victims' claims to full inclusion in the postgenocide polity. For so long as the suffering of genocide victims is not fully recognized and meaningfully redressed their integration in the postgenocide political community will remain incomplete, with detrimental repercussions for Bosnia's national cohesion.

[79] A mass grave was unearthed on Mount Igman near Sarajevo as recent as June 2019. Haris Rovcanin, 'Bosnia Finds Suspected Wartime Mass Grave on Mount Igman' (*Balkan Insight*, 5 June 5 2019) <https://balkaninsight.com/2019/06/05/bosnia-finds-suspected-wartime-mass-grave-on-mount-igman/> accessed 18 June 2020. Nine more newly identified genocide victims were buried in July 2020. Hylton, 'You Simply Die' (n 4). The remains of more than 1,000 victims killed at Srebrenica are still missing.

8

Politics of Inter/National Denial of the Genocide against the Tutsi in Rwanda

Andrew Wallis

Rwanda has become synonymous with the failure of the international community to respond to a genocide enacted before its eyes during thirteen fateful weeks in 1994. Between 6 April and 17 July that year, the country imploded as the Hutu extremist interim regime put into action a pre-planned and well-organized genocide targeting the Tutsi minority and moderate Hutu who threatened their hold on power, in the process killing around one million people.[1] This chapter outlines the unique postgenocide challenges faced by the country, internally and internationally, in fighting a rising tide of denial and revisionism which has in recent years moved insidiously into mainstream political and media coverage of the country and its current government. Such denial and revisionism are projected via a range of mediums by former perpetrators and supporters. They have surreptitiously and seamlessly impressed themselves into mainstream civil society organizations, within international broadcasting media, political and legal institutions (for example in France, the United Kingdom, and United States) and in the higher echelons of the Vatican. Despite being a 'failing state' and languishing at the bottom of global tables for lack of security, corruption, poverty, education, health, and child mortality in the 1990s, Rwanda has managed an impressive economic, administrative, and infrastructure turn around to become a continent leader in many areas in 2021. However, despite this, the post-1994 Rwandan government has struggled to counter the ongoing and increasingly successful campaign of genocide denial and revisionism, especially internationally. With their highly politicized intent, deniers seek not just to recast the truth of the past and responsibility for the genocide then but by doing so cause maximum reputational damage in the present to the leadership of President Paul Kagame and to undermine international financial, diplomatic, and political support for his government. Deniers of the genocide against

[1] See Andrew Wallis, *Stepp'd in Blood: Akazu and the Architects of the Rwandan Genocide Against the Tutsi* (Zero Books 2019); André Guichaoua, *From War to Genocide: Criminal Politics in Rwanda 1990-1994* (University of Wisconsin Press 2015); Des Forges, Alison/Human Rights Watch, *Leave None tell the Story: Genocide in Rwanda* (Human Rights Watch 1999).

Andrew Wallis, *Politics of Inter/National Denial of the Genocide against the Tutsi in Rwanda*
In: *Postgenocide*. Edited by: Klejda Mulaj, Oxford University Press (2021). © The Several Contributors.
DOI: 10.1093/oso/9780192895189.003.0008

the Tutsi and Hutu moderates—referred to also as the Rwandan genocide[2]—come from a wide range of backgrounds, including genocide perpetrators, political opportunists, church leaders, media, dissidents of the ruling Rwandan Patriotic Front ('RPF'), and conspiracy theorists. The negative effect of this denial impacts survivors who feel that they have again become the hidden victims of political conflict. The Rwandan government too, in its attempts to protect the validity of its response to the genocide, has become more entrenched in its position regarding the opening up of government, media, and civil society.

For the sake of the suffering and loss incurred by the victims, the political stability and recovery achieved in postgenocide Rwanda, and the factual evidence (established in ICTR jurisprudence and other respected sources that show beyond reasonable doubt that genocide against the Tutsi occurred in Rwanda in 1994) genocide denial must be resisted. Knowing the rationales of such denial facilitates confronting and challenging it. This chapter explores key issues related to the historical background of the genocide, and current debates pertaining to rationales of genocide denial and its resistance. The next section offers a brief prelude to the 1994 genocide and its denial. *Contra* to the view that genocide denial occurs after genocide,[3] it suggests that denial precedes genocide. The occurrence of the 1994 Rwandan genocide is grounded on a culture of denial and deception regarding intentional killing of the Tutsi minority even prior to 1994. The 'rebranding' of the perpetrators in the immediate aftermath of genocide, as a method to deny guilt and retain international and Rwandan Hutu support for their 'cause' is explored. This leads to an analysis of particular international politico-juridical re/actions to genocide/denial with especial reference to the case of France—a country which hosts a large Rwandan diaspora split between, on the one hand, genocide survivors and postgenocide Rwandan government supporters, and on the other, current Rwandan government opponents, including genocide deniers. Although it is generally argued that the ICTR has offered an immense contribution in establishing genocide knowledge, it is ironic that the ICTR has served, too, as one particular medium via which genocide denial has been projected—some aspects of which will be highlighted in the ensuing analysis. The closing two sections of the chapter refer to the role of the media and the churches as participants in the ongoing dynamics of genocide revisionism and denial. These reveal troubling trends for societies in Rwanda and the West where Western media productions prioritize profit at the expense of: (i) truth; (ii) acknowledgement and respect for victims; (iii) the norm that genocide is the most heinous crime known to mankind which must not be condoned; and (iv) a failure of due diligence in research, cases of causal

[2] On 26 January 2018 the UN General Assembly designated 7 April as the International Day of Reflection on the 1994 Genocide against the Tutsi in Rwanda, recalling that Hutu and others who opposed it were also killed.

[3] For instance, Adam Jones, *Genocide: A Comprehensive Introduction* (2nd edn, Routledge 2011).

racism in reporting, and a worrying trend to allow ideological editorial opinion to overrule objective comment.

Prelude to the 1994 Genocide and Its Denial

Genocidal massacres and pogroms against the Tutsi minority, that makes up around 13 per cent of the Rwandan population, began even before independence from Belgian colonial rule in 1962. From 1959 killings targeting the Tutsi, according to regime propaganda, were a reflection of popular, spontaneous Hutu anger at the preceding years when Belgium had used Tutsi kings (*Mwami*) and chiefs to administer the country. When, post-independence, groups of Tutsi rebels (‘*inyenzi*’) attempted to take back power in small-scale attacks, the result was increased pogroms, driving tens of thousands of Tutsis from their homes and into foreign and internal exile. In late 1963, after one such Tutsi raid was thwarted after Belgian military support for new Hutu President Gregoire Kayibanda, approximately 10,000 Tutsi civilians were slaughtered. An estimated 250,000 fled to neighbouring countries.[4] Kayibanda used the pogroms as a political tactic aimed at cementing the diverse Hutu majority support behind him and his fledgling one-party (MDR-Parmehutu) state. No official was ever sanctioned for the killings, mass rapes, or property/land seizures. The reaction of the international community was telling. While there was widespread disgust expressed by individuals, no action was taken by the United Nations (‘UN’) and only token assistance sent to help Tutsi refugees. Belgium dispatched new arms shipments and military advisers to the genocidal regime. The Catholic Church, notably Archbishop Andre Perraudin,[5] a close friend of Kayibanda, remained silent. These genocidal pogroms from 1959–1964, and again from 1972–1973, are vital to understanding the background to what occurred three decades later—both in the denial/justification of the perpetrators and their postgenocide actions.[6]

General Juvenal Habyarimana, who seized power in July 1973, established his own one-party state, with every individual from a newborn baby to a dying person automatically becoming a member of the *Mouvement Révolutionaire National pour le Développement* (‘MRND’). Tutsis and Hutu from the centre and south of the country were disenfranchised. Inside Habyarimana’s regime a small ‘mafia-like’ group around the president’s wife, Agathe, and her powerful family, notably her

[4] Aaron Segal, ‘Massacre in Rwanda’ (1964) Fabian Research Series No. 240, Fabian Society, 19.

[5] Perraudin, a Swiss national, was appointed by Kayibanda as his personal secretary and later editor of church paper *Kinyamateka*.

[6] Antoine Mugesera, *The Persecution of the Rwandan Tutsi before the 1990-1994 Genocide* (Dialogue Editions 2014); Catherine Newbury, *Cohesion of Oppression* (Columbia University Press 1993); Jason W Clay, ‘The Eviction of Banyaruanda: The Story Behind the Refugee Crisis in Southwest Uganda’ [1984] *Cultural Survival*, Cambridge, Mass (8).

bother Protais Zigiranyirazo (known as 'Monsieur Z'), and cousins Elie Sagatwa and Seraphin Rwabukumba, set up an unofficial parallel power structure that reached down into every part of society—military, business, churches, and administration. This '*Akazu*'—or 'little house'—ran the country as a self-serving business.[7] Habyarimana carefully projected an image of a benevolent, future-looking autocrat, and his Western backers were happy to buy into this 'coffee-table' image.[8] When, in 1990, he faced an invasion from the mainly Tutsi military force, the Rwandan Patriotic Army ('RPA'),[9] led by Paul Kagame and an increasingly popular internal political opposition, Habyarimana and *Akazu* faced losing power. Their chosen method to unify the 'country'—that is the majority Hutu population—replicated that used by Kayibanda. All Tutsi were denigrated as 'the enemy', as potential RPA infiltrators/supporters, and individual bourgmeisters (mayors) and prefects were encouraged and centrally enabled with finance, transport, and propaganda to undertake savage genocidal pogroms. An international commission and a UN report in 1993 both noted the regime's complicity at the highest levels. Denial by Habyarimana was equally forthright and replicated Kayibanda's: these massacres were 'spontaneous', 'local' attacks, and were caused by societal breakdown due to the ongoing civil war.[10]

The shooting down of Habyarimana's plane on 6 April 1994, killing the Rwandan president, marked the start of a genocide of such magnitude that it finally drew the world's attention. As with earlier genocides, the killing was accompanied by contemporaneous denial by political and military leaders. Ministers from the interim regime, selected after a *de facto* army coup led by Colonel Theoneste Bagosora, were sent on a 'charm offensive' to regional (e.g. Kenya, Tanzania and Ethiopia) and Western countries to secure arms and aid deals and deny any genocide was taking place.[11] Two senior regime representatives,[12] having been refused a diplomatic audience in the US and Brussels, were officially received by foreign minister Alain Juppé in Paris. France, which had provided vital military, financial, diplomatic and

[7] Wallis, *Stepp'd in Blood* (n 1).

[8] See, for example, the glossy, coffee-table pictorial book by Omer Marchal, *Au Rwanda* (Didier Hatier 1987), which was specially commissioned by Habyarimana to portray Rwanda as a peaceful, 'Switzerland of Africa' where the people lived simple, happy lives in 'the land of a thousand hills'.

[9] The Rwandan Patriotic Army ('RPA') was the military wing of the Rwandan Patriotic Front ('RPF'). It was initially led by Fred Rwigyema, who was killed within days of the invasion. He was replaced by Paul Kagame.

[10] Fédération internationale des droits de l'homme, Africa Watch, Union interafricaine des droits de l'homme et des peuples, Centre international des droits de la personne et du développement démocratique, *Rapport de la Commission internationale d'enquête sur les violations des droits de l'homme au Rwanda depuis le 1er octobre 1990*, March 1993; *Report by Mr. B.W. Ndiaye. Special Rapporteur, on his mission to Rwanda from 8 to 17 April 1993*, E/CN.4/1994/7/Add.1, 11 August 1993.

[11] For example, Justin Mugenzi, the interim regime's minister of commerce, told a press conference in Nairobi that the slaughter of Tutsis in Rwanda was merely the result of spontaneous anger at the death of Habyarimana and could not be stopped by the regime due to the ongoing civil war. See Human Rights Watch, 'Press Release' (New York 29 April 1994).

[12] Foreign Minister Jerome Bicamumpaka and CDR party founder and RTLM co-director Jean-Bosco Barayagwiza.

political support that had kept Habyarimana/*Akazu* in power since 1990, was content for geo-strategic reasons to continue a full diplomatic (and behind the scenes, military) backing for the interim regime.[13] On 30 April 1994 at the UN Security Council in New York, the Hutu representative Jean-Damascene Bizimana peddled disinformation, denial and persuaded other non-aligned countries to block the word 'genocide' from being used in the wording to a statement on the ongoing tragedy. In June, the Anglican archbishop used a press conferences in Nairobi to deny the genocide, shift blame onto the RPF for any 'massacres' that were taking place and, according to Human Rights Watch, acted as spokesmen for the genocidal government.[14]

Rebranding the Guilty in the Aftermath of Genocide

For a defeated regime and individuals that have participated in or supported genocidal policies, the political rationale is transformed once they lose power. Denial is predominant—and takes three major forms: 'the denial of the facts of the genocide, the denial of the responsibility for it, and the denial of the applicability of the term "genocide"'.[15] The aim of such denial is personal protection from any judicial proceedings and political rehabilitation with the objective to regain power and position, or at the very least to retain the spoils accumulated in previous years, in order to start a new and secure life. The comparison with Germany is insightful here. Former Nazis who took part in the Holocaust, almost to a person, denied both the crime and any part in it.[16] For them, with total defeat ruling out any return of the Third Reich, the best outcome was to avoid prosecution and rehabilitation through 'reinvention' of themselves in societal terms. Within five years of the end of the Second World War, numerous senior Nazis had returned to, or taken up key positions in, the new West German government of Konrad Adenauer. The UK and USA had, from late 1947, already begun to dismantle judicial proceedings against suspected war criminals as the political climate changed and the perceived enemy became Stalin's Soviet Union. For Rwandan genocide perpetrators immediately postgenocide, unlike in 1945 Germany, the priority was not hiding from justice. There was no imminent threat against them, military or judicial. The interim

[13] For the rationale behind French actions see Andrew Wallis, *Silent Accomplice: The Untold Story of the Role of France in the Rwandan Genocide* (I.B. Tauris/Bloomsbury 2014); Jacques Morel, *La France au coeur du génocide des Tutsis* (L'Esprit Frappeur 2010).

[14] See Hugh McCullum, 'Role of the Church in the Rwanda Genocide: Expert report prepared at the request of the ICTR' (ICTR 2001).

[15] Roger W Smith, 'Legislating against Genocide Denial: Criminalizing Denial or Preventing Free Speech?' [2010] University of St Thomas Journal of Law and Public Policy 4 (2).

[16] See the work of Katherina von Kellenbach, in particular, *The Mark of Cain* (OUP 2013); Donald Bloxham, *Genocide on Trial: War Crimes Trials and the Formation of History and Memory: War Crimes Trials and the Formation of Holocaust History and Memory* (OUP 2001).

regime's political, military, and administrative personnel were allowed to flee *en masse* into neighbouring countries, notably the border region of Zaire (renamed as the Democratic Republic of Congo (DRC) in 1996), Tanzania, and Burundi.[17]

The postgenocide focus and soul-searching by the UN/international community has been how it so spectacularly failed to prevent a tragedy that its own peacekeeping operation (United Nations Assistance Mission for Rwanda ('UNAMIR')) had forewarned, together with its failures to react once the genocide began. However, as disastrous for the short- and long-term peace and security of the region was its postgenocide response. The hundreds of thousands of desperate refugees housed in vast unsanitary camps became the overriding concern. There was negligible effort to apprehend those known or suspected to be the political and military leaders behind the genocide. This purely short-term humanitarian response to a political/military situation encouraged perpetrators within the camps to seek a renewal of the conflict and genocide. It also allowed significant time for their ideological and political cadres to create a carefully constructed and planned denial and disinformation campaign that was then diffused to the diaspora, media, and non-governmental organizations ('NGOs').[18]

The camps, funded by hundreds of NGOs and the UN High Commission for Refugees ('UNHCR'), were controlled by the interim regime and its appointed prefects and bourgmeisters who had carried out the genocide only weeks earlier. From July to October 1994, an effective disinformation campaign was undertaken by the *génocidaires*, claiming the interim regime of Prime Minister Jean Kambanda were the real victims in the narrative of events. The aim was to achieve continued arms deliveries, as well as financial and diplomatic support. In the aftermath of genocide, while no country, even supportive ones like Mitterrand's France, could be seen to deal with the interim regime leaders, friendly regional heads of state—notably Bongo (Gabon), Eyadema (Togo), Biya (Cameroon), Gaddafi (Libya), Moi (Kenya), and Mobutu (Zaire)—sanctioned illegal arms deals and deliveries, and accommodated the killers in exile.[19]

[17] The French military intervention, Operation Turquoise allowed, and in some cases actively assisted, the refugees to flee across the border, including fully armed Rwandan Armed Forces ('FAR'), militiamen and the interim regime. See Wallis, *Stepp'd in Blood* (n 1) 433–84.

[18] An MSF-USA press release of December 1994 noted: 'Is it acceptable for the international community to not only ignore the reality existing in the camps, but to directly contribute to the coercion and manipulation of a population by giving legitimacy and means to a leadership accused of perpetrating genocide? Is it acceptable to continue to support a "sanctuary" from which a military force can launch an attack on Rwanda, and perhaps finish the genocide that they commenced in April?' The UNHCR justified their actions noting they had no mandate to judge who was a killer or not, and that they had a duty to provide humanitarian relief to everyone. 'MSF withdraws teams from Rwandan Refugee Camps in Tanzania', press release, MSF USA (20 December 1994).

[19] Human Rights Watch, 'Rearming with impunity: International Support for the Perpetrators of the Rwandan Genocide' [1995], 7(4); UN Security Council, S/RES/1013 (7 September 1995); UN Security Council, S/1996/67 (January 1996) and UN Security Council S/1996/195 (March 1996).

International media groups broadcast a number of interviews with leading *génocidaires* such as Joseph Nzirorera, Theoneste Bagosora, and Ferdinand Nahimana, all of whom used the platform to deny the crime and any involvement in 'massacres' that had taken place.[20] In Nairobi, where many of the more affluent *Akazu* fled and from where the invasion of Rwanda was planned and funded,[21] Hassan Ngeze's extremist Hutu newspaper *Kangura* continued to be published, now as an 'international' edition with articles in English and French. Its target audience was less the Hutu refugee population, but influential interested Western parties in Washington, Paris, Brussels, London, and the Vatican. While there was still every chance of a successful invasion by the Hutu extremist regime and its military, which continued for two years after their defeat, postgenocide atrocities continued with incursions by *Interahamwe* based in the international refugee camps back into Rwanda targeting border villages in the north west. Such attacks, though mainly contained, have carried on sporadically to the present.[22]

The decision to establish the ICTR in Arusha, Tanzania, four months after the genocide, in November 1994, was significant. Now confronted with the possibility they could face justice the perpetrators focused on the need for a defence strategy. Former first lady, Agathe Habyarimana, hired Jacques Verges, a colourful French lawyer who had previously defended Claus Barbie, head of the Gestapo in Lyon and Holocaust denier Roger Garaudy. She promoted a 'victim' image—that she was an impoverished widow, living in Paris/Nairobi, who was the real wronged party in the Rwandan 'tragedy'. The former military commander, Theoneste Bagosora, engaged Belgian lawyer Luc de Temmerman, who put together a strategy that would be used not just by the accused at the ITCR but in other judicial jurisdictions too. Temmerman explained to a journalist: 'It is going to come out clearly that it is not Hutus who are guilty of this so-called genocide ... there was no genocide. It was a situation of mass killings in a state of war where everyone was killing their enemies.'[23] Michael Karnavas, an American defence lawyer who was part of this group, was told by de Temmerman that he was not representing an individual but 'the Hutu nation' and 'the cause'. 'I was instructed that the genocide had not occurred, that it was simply Tutsi propaganda; but that if a genocide had taken place, the Tutsis were responsible for exterminating the Hutus.'[24] This '*tu quoque*' defence has a long history. Its essence is that both sides in a conflict are guilty, therefore

[20] For example, the interview Colonel Theoneste Bagosora gave to journalists in Goma, Zaire, August 1994, produced by Theopresse, Paris.
[21] Wallis, *Stepp'd in Blood* (n 1) 485–521.
[22] See African Rights 'A Welcome expression of Intent: the Nairobi Communication and the ex-FAR/Interahamwe' (African Rights 2007); African Rights *Rwanda: the insurgency in the Northwest* (African Rights 1999). On the FDLR threat see 'UN Group of Experts final report on the Democratic Republic of Congo', S/2009/603 (23 November 2009).
[23] 'Rwandan International Tribunal: first trial "on hold"' *The Guardian* (London 28 September 1996).
[24] Thierry Cruvellier, *Court of Remorse: Inside the International Criminal Tribunal for Rwanda* (University of Wisconsin Press 2010).

neither side is guilty. Any 'justice' is just that of the victors and so is not justice at all, only a form of punishment of the defeated. Holocaust deniers, and Serbs seeking to obfuscate around the genocidal attack at Srebrenica have used the same tactic in an effort to destabilize the dominant genocide narrative.

The Nuremberg trials began within months of the end of the Second World War and the capture of leading suspects. Military defeat was accompanied simultaneously with political defeat and legal proceedings. Denial was given little space to be dissimulated. The International Military Tribunal (IMT) had been in discussion about judicial proceedings postwar for several months before the end of the conflict. The contrary was true regarding postgenocide Rwanda. Despite the ICTR having been set up in November 1994, its chaotic and confused initial years of operating allowed significant time for perpetrators to begin the task of changing the genocide narrative. Prime Minister Jean Kambanda and his interim regime were forcibly discarded by the ex-FAR military leadership in April 1995. Their replacement, the Rally for the Return of Refugees and Democracy to Rwanda (RDR), was created with a view to presenting to the international community a credible political organization untarnished by the recent genocide.[25] The RDR set up cells in France, Belgium, the Netherlands and Canada all pushing to persuade the international community and the refugees in the camps that it was the true 'democratic' representative of Rwanda and should be in power in Kigali; that past horrors should be forgotten (and forgiven); that the UN and the West should press the new Rwandan government to allow them to return; and that the real villains of the piece were the RPF.[26]

One year after the genocide, the journal *Liberation* noted:

> The RDR is an ingenious initiative, the fruit of miniscule and laborious research that has been put together by political and military forces of the Rwandan community in exile with their sponsors and foreign tutors. But what is it really? The RDR is a politico-military movement instigated by and for the *Akazu* or the authors of the genocide and massacres in Rwanda. Its real vision is to protect the criminals and paradoxically reclaim for them political posts that the famous Arusha Accords [of August 1993] had anticipated.[27]

[25] The RDR was founded after a meeting in Goma from 29 March–3 April 1995 that included the head of the military, General Augustin Bizimungu, and a sizeable number of prominent MRND, and Hutu extremist political parties, the Coalition pour la Défense de la République ('CDR') and the Mouvement Démocratique Republicain ('MDR') 'power' faction. See UNICTR, *Prosecutor v Theoneste Bagosoara et al*, [2003] 'Aloys Ntabakuze account of meeting of 29 March–3 April 1995', Prosecution Exhibit P.415B, ICTR-98-41-T.

[26] See RDR 'United Nations Security Council misled about the presumed "Tutsi genocide" in Rwanda' (Cameroon June 1996); *Kangura*, [69] (May 1995), 13–15; For an analysis of the RDR membership and rationale see Tom Ndahiro, *Friends of Evil* (online publication) part I <https://friendsofevil.wordpress.com/2013/08/29/the-friends-of-evil-when-ngos-support-genocidaires-2/> accessed 23 June 2002.

[27] 'Le RDR ou le MRND Rénové' *Libération* (1995) 9.

In its 1996 strategy report, the RDR urged a common stance to questions by the international media about the genocide, the role of militia and death-squads, the involvement of the former Rwandan army, and issues around 'impunity'. It noted that continued press releases should present a saleable image of the organization to the international community with the objective of providing an alternative view to what it termed the 'Rwandan tragedy'. Sympathetic or unsuspecting Western media, NGOs, and the UN aid agencies were targeted to employ RDR personnel or use them as expert assistants. The Hutu extremist leadership set up a '*Société Civile*' group inside the refugee camps, aiming to become the sole representatives of the latter to the international community. As Médecins Sans Frontières ('MSF') documented, within one year from the ending of the genocide, the group's work was already extensive:

> Ninety-two affiliated non-profit-making organizations such as: *l'Association des Journalistes Rwandais en Exil, le Cercle des Intellectuels, l'Association pour la Promotion Féminine et la Réhabilitation de la Famille Rwandaise*, and *l'Association des Juristes pour les Droits de l'Homme* ... Most were founded by members of Rwanda's well-educated elite, the MRND, and the extremist media that functioned in Rwanda before the genocide. Some receive substantial funding from abroad ... Another one of these NGOs, the *Association Justice et Paix pour la Réconciliation au Rwanda* in collaboration with the *Société Civile*, states that no evidence incriminating the self-proclaimed government-in-exile has come to light and that it was the RPF who committed the genocide of the Hutu.[28]

Ideological revisionist 'histories' were penned and distributed to local journalists, sent to the UN and ICTR, lawyer groups and NGOs within which many extremist sympathizers were already working. In Cameroon, a report by leading interim regime/RDR figures[29] flatly denied the genocide against the Tutsi stating that 'the UN Security Council is misled about the alleged 'Tutsi genocide' in Rwanda as there had been no genocide of the Tutsi'. According to this report, the term genocide 'was just part of an 'expertly orchestrated' media campaign by the RPF and its allies to gain the sympathy of the international community'.[30] This RDR report targeted its attack on the UN special rapporteur, René Degni-Segui and his

[28] See Médecins Sans Frontières 'Breaking the Circle: Activities in and Around Rwanda' (December 1994); Médecins Sans Frontières 'Deadlock in the Rwandan Refugee crisis: Virtual Standstill on Repatriation' (July 1995). This latter report noted 'While some believe that these recent political developments herald the dawning of a new era, the host of new leaders appears to have emerged from the same Hutu extremist ideological position. The expansion of the camp leadership, the creation of the *Société Civile* and a new 'independent' political party have not broadened the political spectrum. Indeed, they have served further the monopoly of extremism'.

[29] These included Ferdinand Nahimana, Théoneste Bagosora, Anatole Nsengiyumva, and Bagosora's brother, the banker Pasteur Musabe. See RDR, 'United Nations' (n 27).

[30] RDR, 'United Nations' (n 27). This report/open letter was produced by Theoneste Bagosora, Ferdinand Nahimana and Anatole Nsengiyumva, among others.

recently published findings that specified a 'genocide' against the Tutsi had indeed occurred.[31] According to the RDR rebuttal, 'utilization of the term "genocide" to designate inter-ethnic massacres was adopted by the RPF in order to get sympathy and enlist the assistance of the international community'.[32]

Arrests of suspected perpetrators in Kenya and across West Africa from 1996 led to a flight to the West where many had already sent their families to begin new lives. A variety of strategies were used to protect them from possible legal action: changing names and identities with the use of forged documents; the use of illicit funds already accumulated and/or political/church ties to outwit tracking teams from the ICTR; the use of human rights legislation in the West to claim the right to family reunion and that any extradition would threaten their right to life or a fair trial. Finally, and perhaps most useful in terms of avoiding prosecution was the apathy and lack of judicial will by Western states to take very expensive legal action against citizens of a foreign country for crimes committed abroad which in no way affected their own domestic concerns or citizens. In the case of those accused genocidaire who began new lives in France, a natural choice given historic cultural and linguistic links, they could also depend on the acute political animosity between Paris and Kigali to shield them from possible action being taken to put them on trial. In the coming decades, political considerations would far outweigh judicial ones.

Politico-Juridical Re/Actions to Genocide/Denial: The French Factor

François Mitterrand viewed Rwanda as a bulwark between the creeping spread of Anglophone influence into Francophone East Africa. Military cooperation pacts, aid support as well as a strong personal (and business) bond between the Mitterrand-Habyarimana families cemented the close relationship. After the RPA invasion of Rwanda in October 1990, the French government, unlike Belgium, chose to intervene militarily,[33] fearing damage to its geostrategic interests. During the following three years, despite ongoing genocidal massacres by the regime, Mitterrand continued to give substantial military, political, and financial backing to keep Habyarimana's failing regime in power.[34] Within days of the start of the

[31] United Nations, 'Report on the Situation of Human Rights in Rwanda submitted by Mr René Degni-Segui, Special Rapporteur of the Commission on Human Rights, under paragraph 20 of the resolution S-3/1 of 25 May 1994', E/CN.4/1996/68 (29 January 1996).

[32] RDR, 'United Nations' (n 27).

[33] Operation Noroit ('North Wind') was a French military intervention in Rwanda, begun within days of the RPA invasion in early October 1990 with the objective of shoring up Habyarimana's regime. The mission continued until December 1993, when the troops were withdrawn under the terms of the Arusha Accords.

[34] This was particularly decisive in February 1993 when an RPA offensive came with 25 kilometres of Kigali, and was only stopped after elite French military reinforcements were sent to the front line.

genocide, Agathe Habyarimana was evacuated to Paris, along with other key members of *Akazu* who took advantage of French government antipathy to Kagame. Operation Turquoise, a military operation with the public agenda of saving Tutsi lives, was launched in late June as the RPA closed in on victory. Essentially a product of domestic political infighting with upcoming domestic elections, Turquoise became mired in controversy. Its rationale has continued to haunt both those politicians who ordered it and those military who took part on the ground in Rwanda.[35]

During the following years, the French government used an opaque policy towards Rwanda and the region. It initially blocked EU emergency funding for the new 'anglophone' unity government in Kigali, in which Kagame was named as minister of defence. At the same time French military continued to train ex-FAR and *Interahamwe* units inside Zaire, and arranged arms shipments to them with support from Gaddafi (Libya) and Omar Bongo (Gabon).[36] In 1998, under intense domestic political and media pressure to explain its role before and during the genocide, the French National Assembly undertook a limited investigation which came to the underwhelming—and evidentiary lacking—conclusion that France had been 'duped' into assisting a regime whose motivations and objectives it had not fully appreciated.[37]

While the outcome of the National Assembly inquiry amounted to little more than a token critical analysis of Mitterrand's policies, it was a watershed moment. Unlike the numerous previous military French interventions in Africa, such as its highly controversial role in Algeria during the late 1950s or even in regard to the Vichy regime, the fact some form of inquiry took place showed a level of limited transparency and awareness that allegations about Rwanda had caused considerable public disquiet. The inquiry coincided with renewed public interest and awareness of 'La Francafrique',[38] in the main due to the contemporary, ongoing,

[35] For critics, this operation provided a safe zone not so much to the remaining Tutsi still alive in the south in the Cyangugu/Gikongoro region but to *génocidaires* who welcomed the French troops with displays of genuine affection having been led to believe they would once again 'save' them from the RPA advance as they had previously under Operation Noroit. French military whistle-blowers have condemned aspects of the operation, not least that the FAR/militia were able to cross the border without being arrested or disarmed. Senior officers have closed ranks, writing books, and blogs defending their individual actions and that of the intervention. See Guillaume Ancel, *Rwanda, La Fin Du Silence: Témoignage d'un officier français* (Les Belles Lettres 2018); Jean-Claude Lafourcade, *Operation Turquoise, 1994* (Perrin 2010), Jacques Morel, *La France au coeur du génocide des Tutsis* (L'Esprit Frappeur 2010).

[36] I explore these dynamics in Wallis, *Stepp'd in Blood* (n 1) 507–514. See also UN Security Council, S/RES/1013 [1995] (7 September 1995); United Nations Disarmament Commission (UNDC) Report S/1996/67 (January 1996); UNDC Report S/1996/195 (March 1996).

[37] This was known as the Quilès report after the president of the inquiry, Paul Quilès, a former defence minister under Mitterrand. It heard evidence from eighty-eight people—twenty politicians, twenty-one diplomats, thirty-four army personnel, and thirteen African experts but not under oath. Important documents were not declassified and some witnesses refused to have testimonies published. Assemblée Nationale, 'Enquête sur la Tragédie Rwandaise (1990–1994), Mission d'Information commune, [Report No 1271] (Paris 1998). For a critical response see *Billets d'Afrique*, 'Special Rapport Rwanda' no. 66B (21 December 1998).

[38] A term used by a critic of French policy in Africa, François-Xavier Verschave, who founded the pressure group 'Survie', it was a play on the phrase 'France-Afrique'. 'Fric' is slang for cash.

and lengthy Elf corruption scandal.[39] NGOs and civil actors began to seek greater government transparency and an opening up of official archives regarding past action on the 'black' continent.

The past two decades have seen a number of highly damaging controversies by individual parties who contest the truth of the French intervention in Rwanda. For some French political and military actors, accused of complicity with a genocidal regime, 'revising' the genocide against the Tutsi has been used as a means to shield themselves and/or their country from accountability. For example, the journalist Patrick de Saint Exupéry was sued by political and military figures following the publication of his book *Complices de l'inavouable* ('Accomplice of the shameful'), which accused them of complicity in war crimes during the genocide.[40] Prime Minister Dominique de Villepin sought to distance himself from allegations about his own role by use of the double genocide theory—telling a radio interviewer when questioned about what had happened whether they should be talking about 'genocides rather than genocide'.[41] Mitterrand shrugged off criticism by noting 'in countries like that, genocide is not so important'.[42] Other political/military figures involved in 1994 have sought to move the debate away from their own actions and onto those of Kagame/RPF by fuelling accusations they were responsible for the April plane crash or war crimes against the Hutu population—making common cause with RDR and denial groups in doing so.[43]

Judge Jean-Louis Bruguière's lengthy eight-year inquiry into the crash, launched in the same year as the National Assembly's effort, was a political tool primarily aimed at spreading disinformation, speculation and denial. Bruguière did not visit the crash site—or indeed Rwanda—and relied on evidence from a French mercenary, Paul Barril, who was in the pay books of Agathe Habyarimana, and RPF defectors who had been promised French visas in return for evidence that the RPF

[39] An eight-year investigation led to thirty-seven managers of the oil firm Elf Aquitaine being prosecuted in 2003 in one of the biggest financial scandals to hit France. The trial uncovered the vast, opaque network of illegal payments, begun under Charles de Gaulle and expanded under Mitterrand's presidency during the 1980s and early 1990s, with more than $350 million syphoned off from the private company and used to buy favourable trading terms from African heads of state and support from domestic politicians and political parties. See David Ignatius, 'True Crime: the scent of French scandal' Legal Affairs Magazine (May–June 2002) <https://www.legalaffairs.org/issues/May-June-2002/story_ignatius_mayjun2002.html> accessed 23 June 2020.

[40] Patrick de Saint Exupéry, *Complices de l'inavouable* (Arenes 2009).

[41] Patrick de Saint Exupéry, *L'inavouable: La France au Rwanda* (Saint-Amand-Montrond: Arenès 2004) 14

[42] Patrick de Saint-Exupéry, 'France-Rwanda: un genocide sans importance' *Le Figaro* (12 January 1998).

[43] The military leaders of Turquoise formed their own organization specifically to counter charges against them. They have been particularly vocal in support of accusations against Kagame/RPF and while not denying the genocide against the Tutsi have consistently repeated claims of a 'Hutu genocide'. See, for example, Association France–Turquoise aims to 'defend and promote, by all appropriate means, the moral, legal and social interests of these soldiers.' <https://www.france-turquoise.com/association-france-turquoise/> accessed 23 June 2020.

were responsible for shooting down the plane.[44] The Bruguière report and the arrest warrants issued by the judge against nine senior aides of Kagame resulted in Rwanda breaking off all political and diplomatic relations.[45] In response, two Rwandan reports, in 2008 and 2009, sought to prove French complicity in the genocide and to disprove Bruguière's theory on the crash by using technical analysis to pin responsibility for the missile attack on extremist FAR units based in Kanombe military camp adjacent to Kigali airport.[46]

The presidency of Nicolas Sarkozy initiated a slow thawing in relations. The visit by the French president to the Rwandan capital in February 2010 where he admitted French 'mistakes' but stopped short of an apology came one year after Rwanda became only the second Francophone country to join the Commonwealth. It was notable on the reciprocal state visit to Paris by Kagame that senior French politicians such as Alain Juppé, the foreign minister during 1994, chose to shun any meeting with the Rwandan head of state. The political rapprochement temporarily loosened the judicial blockage; Agathe Habyarimana, who had lived freely in Paris since the late 1990s, was arrested, though she was released later the same day.[47] In the nineteen years from 1995 to 2014, dozens of alleged perpetrators—senior

[44] Diplomatic cables released by Wikileaks indicate the Bruguière inquiry had been used as a political tool aimed at undermining the Rwandan government. According to a French diplomat based in West Africa, Chirac's government had not expected the very strong reaction by Kigali—entirely breaking off diplomatic relations—when it gave the green light to the report being finally published in late 2006. See cable 07PARIS186_a, from: amEmbassy Paris (Stapleton), to: RUEHC/SECSTATE WASHDC 4245 (18 January 2007); In another cable sent on 26 January 2007 Bruguière confirmed he has consulted with Chirac as to the exact timing to issue arrest warrants against nine of Kagame's top aides. He did not hide his personal desire to see Kigali isolated and warned against closer US ties with the country while pressing for the US to take action against Kigali. Cable 07PARIS322_a, from: amEmbassy Paris (Stapleton) to: RUEHC/SECSTATE WASHDC (26 January 2007).

[45] Andrew Wallis, 'Rwandan Rifts in La Francafrique' (*opendemocracy.net*, 14 December 2006) <https://www.opendemocracy.net/en/rwanda_france_4183jsp/> accessed 23 June 2020.

[46] In 2008 the Rwandan government published a report of its own inquiry into French complicity in the genocide, known after its principal author, Jean de Mucyo: <http://mucyoreport.rw/index.php/report/> accessed 23 June 2020. In 2009 it published, in collaboration with the UK's National Defence Academy at Cranfield University, a Committee of Experts Investigation into the plane crash; this Mutsinzi report (<http://mutsinzireport.com> accessed 23 June 2020) blamed Hutu extremists for shooting down the plane. A later French report by Marc Trevidic, made with the cooperation of Rwandan authorities who allowed access to the crash site, documentary evidence, and witnesses, reached the same conclusion in 2012. See BBC, 'Rwanda genocide: Kagame 'cleared of Habyarimana crash', 10 January 2012 <https://www.bbc.co.uk/news/world-africa-16472013> accessed 23 June 2020.

[47] Having been welcomed to the French capital by Mitterrand, she returned to live there in the late 1990s after the arrests began of suspect *génocidaires* in Nairobi where she had been living under the protection of President Arap Moi. Her application to the French Office of Protection for Refugees and Stateless Individuals ('OFPRA') in December 2005 for refugee status was denied after its inquiry found she was 'at the heart of the genocidal regime responsible for the preparation and execution of the genocide'. This decision was later upheld by the appeal court and the Conseil d'État, which noted there was serious reason to think that she committed a crime under the Geneva Convention 'because of her central role within the regime in power before April 6th, 1994, which had prepared and planned the genocide, as well as with her personal actions for the decisive period at the start of the genocide between 6 and 9 April 1994, and links which she then continued to maintain with the authors of the genocide: Decision Droit d'asile, Mme Agathe Habyarimana', Conseil d'État, 10ème et 9ème sous-sections réunies, No. 311793 (16 October 2009). Despite such damning verdicts, she continues to live in an affluent suburb in southern Paris and has faced no further judicial inquiry.

politicians, administrators, professionals, clergy, and military who fled to France after the genocide—have remained free. This judicial outcome reflected the complex political and diplomatic impasse between Paris and Kigali. Despite moves by civil society groups and the media, French justices have consistently refused requests that suspected *génocidaires* be extradited to stand trial in Rwanda. The legal pretext was that as Rwanda did not have the crime of genocide on its statue book in 1994, the accused could not face trial retrogressively.

One positive outcome of the Sarkozy-Kagame diplomatic thaw and resumption of diplomatic ties in November 2009 was the setting up during 2010 of a special war crimes unit to investigate alleged *génocidaires* living in France. In 2014, on the occasion of the twentieth commemoration of the genocide against the Tutsi, France initiated, and in a matter of weeks completed, the trial and conviction of Pascal Simbikangwa, a former intelligence operative in Habyarimana's regime. The timing was, to critics in civil society and the media, entirely cynical. They noted the sudden trial on the eve of a significant anniversary seemed to be a political stunt in judicial guise to silence those who had been campaigning against French 'impunity'.

In the past six years to 2020, two other individuals[48] have been successfully convicted. The arrest of businessman Felicien Kabuga in Paris in May 2020, with indications he had been living in the capital for several years with the support of his family, has put French judicial and political authorities under renewed pressure. More than twenty-six high-profile alleged *génocidaires* continue to live in France and though subject to civil party actions, have yet to face formal investigation.[49] This judicial impasse continues to have a detrimental effect on political/diplomatic relations, though under President Macron there has been attempts to move on from the postgenocide narrative of accusation and counter-accusation to a normalization of affairs.[50] However, the arrest of Kabuga in Paris, coming soon after the hosting at the French senate of an event in March 2020 in which known deniers and revisionists presented papers, despite strong protests by the Rwandan

[48] Tito Barahira and Octavien Ngenzi, two former bourgmeisters, were sentenced to life imprisonment for genocide on 6 July 2016; the verdict was upheld on appeal.

[49] The civil parties, notably International Federation for Human Rights ('FIDH'), Survie, and the Collectif des Parties Civiles pour le Rwanda ('CPCR') have brought the legal complaints. All three successful prosecutions have happened due to civil party pressure and investigations rather than from state judicial initiatives. The suspects include *Akazu*, military, clergy, and administrators accused by survivors and human rights groups of participation in the genocide, These include Agathe Habyarimana, Col Laurent Serubuga, Dr Sosthene Munyemana, Lt Col Marcel Bivugabagabo, Eugene Rwamucyo, Felicien Barigira, Claver Kamana, Pierre Tegera, Alphonse Ntilivamunda, Enoch Kanyondo (alias Pheneas Gakumba), Callixte Mbarushimana, Stanislas Mbonampeka, Isaac Kamali, Eugene Rwamucyo, and Hyacinthe Rafiki.

[50] In April 2019 Macron ordered the setting up of a panel of eight experts to study and analyse the role and involvement of France in Rwanda, looking at previously unseen archives and documentary sources. He turned down an invitation to attend the twenty-fifth commemoration of the genocide in Kigali but welcomed Kagame on a visit to Paris and announced an annual official national day of remembrance of the genocide in France on 7 April.

government and survivor groups, has magnified doubts that relations between the two countries can move forward without real, open and frank bilateral talks on past actions. While several senior French political and military figures from the 1990s retain influence and power, vested interest may mean the presidency can only normalize political ties to a nominal degree and will be unable to prevent continued strong kick-backs against any real and substantive change. François Hollande, as president, while refusing to issue an apology for the French role in the Algerian war of Independence that cost more than one million lives, noted on a visit to the country in December 2012 that 'nothing is built in secretiveness, forgetting, denial'.[51] However, it took fifty years for a French President, Jacques Chirac, to issue a public recognition that the French state was culpable in the voluntary deportation of 70,000 French Jews to Nazi death camps 'in an action that would forever sully our history and are an insult to our past and our traditions'. Now it was time 'to recognize the errors of the past and the errors committed by the state and not to hide the dark hours of our history'.[52] Both President François Hollande and Jacques Chirac were heavily criticized by reactionary political and military groups for their comments.

Economic and geo-strategic rationale may lead to some normalization of Franco-Rwandan political ties in the foreseeable future, however personal and institutional denial by actors involved during 1990–1994 remains the major block to substantive change. Judicial action against alleged *génocidaires* will remain subject to political currents, and the resultant denial and revisionism looks likely to get unofficial backing both by the accused and high-profile political/military individuals who feel under legal or reputational threat. France has become home to a large Rwandan diaspora, and this community, as in Belgium, is deeply split between genocide survivors/pro-government supporters of Kagame and his political opponents, who include within their ranks known genocide proponents and linked denier networks who have had no judicial proceedings taken against them. Some political opponents, who are unable to take part in debate and electioneering inside Rwanda due to the highly regulated political space there, have been drawn into revisionist groups. A number of erstwhile diaspora political parties based in France, Belgium, and Germany are linked with the RDR and its ideology, as well as with militia such as the Forces Démocratiques pour la Libération du Rwanda (FDLR) and the P.5 amalgamation of armed groups also located in eastern DRC's Kivu provinces that aim to destabilize Rwanda with terror attacks across the border.[53]

[51] Associated Press (AP), 'François Hollande acknowledges Algerian suffering under French rule' *The Guardian* (London, 20 December 2012).

[52] Marlise Simons, 'Chirac affirms France's guilt in the fate of Jews' *New York Times* (New York, 17 July 1995).

[53] Two FDLR leaders based in Germany were found guilty in 2015 for massacres the group planned in the DRC. The Stuttgart trial judge noted it was a criminal not political case; the FDLR spokesman dismissed this, calling it an 'injustice with the aim of snuffing out the armed opposition against the Rwandan dictator (Kagame)'. AFP, 'Rwandan rebel leaders jailed in Germany for war crimes', *The Guardian* (London, 28 September 2015). See 'Universal jurisdiction for Germany'? *European Centre for*

Western critics of the Kagame government—in the media, NGOs and some politicians—have urged a freeing up of civil society, the media, and political space within Rwanda. However, the issue is not a binary one, given Rwanda's complex history going back into three decades of authoritarian rule since independence, and the intense regional, ethnic, and structural divisions brought about by five decades of Belgian colonial 'divide and rule' strategies. There remains an appreciable underlying fear/anxiety at the heart of Rwandan rural society and the government. Polls have consistently put more than 20 per cent of the population as still harbouring genocidal ideology, though this figure is slowly diminishing. Rwanda is in no way a 'simple' post-independence African country undergoing a slow, erratic growth to what, by Western liberal standards, would be deemed an 'acceptable' democracy.

There has become a slow, creeping movement by some Western critics that Kagame's perceived anti-democratic rule, and alleged human rights abuses of opponents inside and outside the country, now brings into doubt the previously accepted orthodoxy that his RPF forces 'saved' the country in 1994 by defeating the genocidal interim regime. Such critics accuse Kagame of being the original transgressor by invading Rwanda in 1990 and so starting the conflict that 'led to the genocide'; of being behind the plane crash that was the 'trigger' for the hundred day tragedy that followed; that he was complicit in a planned and organized genocide against the Hutu or delayed his conquest of the country in May/June 1994 in order to allow the genocide to be completed.[54] While such views, as seen, were directly disseminated by the Habyairmana regime/RTLM [Rwandan radio station Radio Télévision Libre des Mille Collines] in 1990–1993 and the interim regime/RDR as a denial strategy from 1994, Western media and NGOs are increasingly 'buying into' such accusations/ideology as a means to underscore their own intrinsic political/editorial position on Kagame. While the Rwandan government strongly refutes all such accusations and seeks to minimize reputational damage or loss of aid and development funding, the victims of the genocide continue to have their pain questioned and delegitimized.

Constitutional and Human Rights (Berlin, 8 June 2016). See also UNSC, 'Midterm report of the Group of Experts submitted in accordance with paragraph 4 of resolution 2424', S/2018/1133 (2018).

[54] These views have attracted recent 'mainstream' media coverage/publicity as part of the marketing drive by former Radio-France Internationale ('RFI') journalist Judi Rever in her book 'In Praise of Blood' (Random House 2019). The decision by four Flemish universities to allow her to a platform to speak in late 2019 attracted a storm of controversy, with fifty-nice academics, authors, and journalists, as well as survivor groups, protesting she was merely reiterating the denial theories that had been used for the previous twenty-five years and should not be allowed to promote her views. See 'Genocide des Tutsis: letter internationale a des recteurs des universite Flamandes' *La Libre Afrique* (9 October 2019) <https://afrique.lalibre.be/41976/opinion-genocide-des-tutsis-lettre-internationale-a-des-recteurs-duniversite-flamands/> accessed 23 June 2020.

ICTR and Genocide Denial

The international community sought to deal with the issue of postgenocide justice in Rwanda by the setting up of a standalone tribunal, the International Criminal Tribunal for Rwanda ('ICTR') 1,000 kilometres away from the site of the crime in Arusha, Tanzania.[55] Significantly, the new, postgenocide Rwandan unity government voted against it: it argued that justice which could not be seen by the people who were most affected—the survivors and present and future generations of Rwandans—would not be justice at all. In terms of the ongoing battle against denial, especially within Rwanda, the fact its population could not see and hear the witnesses, documents, exhibits, and arguments allowed the accused an anonymity for both themselves and their alleged crimes. In words that continue to resonate within Rwanda and its understanding of how justice should be served—and denial countered—the Rwandan ambassador to the UN told the Security Council that Resolution 955 which established the ICTR would 'serve only to appease the conscience of the international community, as it will not meet the expectation of the Rwandan people'.[56] Despite such significant misgivings over its location, during its twenty-one years of existence[57] the ICTR produced ground-breaking judgments and established a vast archive of witness testimonies, documentary evidence, police reports, and audiovisual proofs. Such an archive is critical in the ongoing and future fight against denial and revisionism.

In June 2006 ICTR appeal bench judges made the judicial finding that in 1994 'there were throughout Rwanda widespread or systematic attacks against a civilian population based on Tutsi ethnic identification . . . Between 6 April 1994 and 17 July 1994 there was genocide in Rwanda against [the] Tutsi ethnic group'.[58] Until this point, in each trial the prosecutor had to spend significant time challenging the defence case that there was no genocide, only massacres, which affected both Hutu and Tutsi. In March 2014 the Assize Court in Paris reached a similar judicial notice.[59] However, as with the initial setting up of the courts and bringing the accused

55 UNSCR, 'Establishment of an International Tribunal and adoption of the Statute of the Tribunal' S/RES/955 (8 November 1994).

56 Zachery Kaufman, 'The United States Role in the Establishment of the United Nations International Criminal Tribunal for Rwanda', in Clark P and Zachery Kaufman (ed), *Transitional Justice, Post-conflict Reconstruction and Reconciliation in Rwanda and Beyond* (C Hurst 2009); Bakuramutsa, Manzi, *Le Monde* (Paris, 10 November 1994).

57 The ICTR officially closed at the end of 2015, handing over its remaining work to the Residual International Mechanism for Criminal Tribunals ('IRMCT') to include preservation of archives, the arrest of remaining fugitives and outstanding judicial cases. The work of IRMCT can be found at <https://unictr.irmct.org/en/cases> accessed 23 June 2020.

58 ICTR, *Prosecutor v Karemera, Ngirumpatse and Nzirorera*, 'Appeals Chamber on Prosecutor's Appeal on Judicial Notice', ICTR-98-44-AR73 (C) (16 June 2006). It meant that 'the ruling should now silence the "rejectionist" camp which has been disputing the occurrence of genocide'. 'ICTR Appeals Chamber takes Judicial Notice of Genocide in Rwanda' ICTR press release (Arusha, 20 June 2006) <https://unictr.irmct.org/en/news/ictr-appeals-chamber-takes-judicial-notice-genocide-rwanda> accessed 23 June 2020.

59 *Prosecutor v Pascal Simbikangwa* (Judgement) [2014] Assize Court of Paris.

before them, the time lag in making such an important judicial finding allowed denial and conspiracy theories to grow.

Another significant drawback was the lack of publicity and transparency regarding the tribunal's operation, work, and judgments. Unlike the International Criminal Tribunal for the former Yugoslavia ('ICTY') in the Hague, which streamed court sessions via a live weblink, the ICTR was handicapped from the start by exceptionally poor, indeed often non-existent coverage of the cases. Survivors in Rwanda had no understanding of who was on trial or eventual judgments, which in many instances were made more than ten years after the case began. The failure to encourage interest in its work outside Arusha left a void which has been filled by deniers. Few in the West know the names of Bagosora, Nsengiyumva, Nahimana, Ngeze, and Kambanda. By contrast, their defence teams have been proactive in protecting their clients from publicity while pushing forward conspiracy theories about the RPF. The controversy surrounding the arrest of American defence lawyer Peter Erlinder summarized this attitude.[60]

Furthermore, the ICTR, as with the ICTY, ran into a storm of controversy over sentencing and the early release of convicted *génocidaires*. Theodor Meron, the President of the ICTY from 2011 to 2015, and its successor the International Residual Mechanism for Criminal Tribunals ('IRMCT') from 2012, presided over all eight acquittals at the ICTR Appeals chamber, in addition to lengthy sentences given by original trial judges in a number of high-profile cases. The two men seen as most culpable for the instigation of the slaughter, Theoneste Bagosora and co-accused Anatole Nsengiyumva, were both beneficiaries—the latter walking free after his life sentence was downgraded by Meron to fifteen years. Meron promoted a change to the legal understanding of 'superior command'. Even if a commander knew his troops were committing genocide and made no effort to stop the crime, they were, for Meron, not guilty. Proof was needed that they had given 'specific command' for genocide to occur.[61] On 6 June 2013 Frederik Harhoff, a Danish Judge working at the ICTY, questioned Meron's motivation for his interpretive changes in an email sent to fifty-three fellow judges, friends, and family. It was leaked to the media.[62] It came after the controversial acquittal by Meron's appeal bench of two Croatian and Serbian generals at the ICTY. The intimation in Harhoff's email was that the leading force behind Meron's change was the military establishment in America and Israel fearing prosecutions of their own commanders. A former legal

[60] Arrested in Rwanda in 2010 and charged with offences under the Rwandan 2003 Constitution [Article 13] against 'revisionism, negationism and trivialisation of genocide', Erlinder was freed after protests, especially from many in the USA, who argued for his freedom of speech and that he had immunity from prosecution due to working as a defence lawyer at the ICTR. The arrest brought into focus the controversial use of genocide denial laws, which in some European countries have been used against Holocaust deniers such as David Irving, and countries such as the USA and UK in which freedom of speech allows such views to be legally promulgated.

[61] See David Rohde, 'How International Justice Is Being Gutted' *The Atlantic* (Boston, 14 July 2013).

[62] <http://a.bimg.dk/node-files/511/6/6511917-letter-english.pdf> accessed 23 June 2020.

adviser to the ICTY, speaking anonymously, noted that 'the perception among my colleagues is that Meron takes instructions from the US government and that this reining in of the legal standards—as we have seen with the acquittals—would have implications for the US and probably Israel'.[63] The acquittals led to acrimonious debate as to whether costly tribunals were purely political pawns rather than implementers of justice. Were they contributing to denial and revisionism rather than promoting transparent justice and postgenocide reconciliation?[64]

Meron, as president of the tribunals, unilaterally decided on the early release of prisoners from their sentences. Rwanda complained at the UN in 2018 that:

> early releases have been granted in non-transparent circumstances and inconsistent procedure ... We wonder the criteria considered given the gravity of the crimes committed by the convicts and their lack of remorse. A number of convicts released before the end of their sentences have since regrouped and organized themselves in an association denying the 1994 Genocide against the Tutsi and propagating genocide ideology. They are free to undertake such criminal activities without fear of consequences because they were released without conditionalities. This is an inescapable part of the legacy of the current President of the IRMCT [Theodor Meron].[65]

A comparison was made with the impressive and thorough handling of the issues around early release achieved by the least well-known or funded of the special international tribunals, the Special Court for Sierra Leone ('SCSL'). Several years before the ICTR/ICTY gave detailed thought and action to the issue, in 2013 the SCSL issued its 'Practice Direction' that stipulated early release of a prisoner convicted of such heinous crimes was conditional upon a convict making a 'public acknowledgement of guilt, public support for peace projects, public apology to victims, or victim restitution'.[66] The Sierra Leone court made 'stringent requirements

[63] Cited in Martin Burcharth, 'Did a supporter of International criminal law turn into a stooge of the US?' *Information.dk* (18 June 2013) <https://www.information.dk/indland/2013/06/did-a-supporter-of-international-criminal-law-turn-into-a-stooge-of-the-us> accessed 23 June 2020.

[64] See Daniel M Greenfield 'The Crime of Complicity in Genocide: How the International Criminal Tribunals for Rwanda and Yugoslavia Got It Wrong, and Why It Matters' The Journal of Criminal Law and Criminology (2008) 98, 3; Christine Bishai, 'Superior Responsibility, Inferior Sentencing: Sentencing Practice at the International Criminal Tribunals', Northwestern Journal International Human Rights (2103), 11, 3, p.84; Marko Milanovic, 'The self-fragmentation of the ICTY Appeals chamber', Blog of the European Journal of International Law (23 January 2014), <http://www.ejiltalk.org/the-self-fragmentation-of-the-icty-appeals-chamber> accessed 23 June 2020; Marlise Simons, 'Hague Judge Faults Acquittals of Serb and Croat Commanders' *New York Times* (New York, 14 June 2013).

[65] Statement by the Rwandese ambassador Valentine Rugwabiza to the United Nations at the UNSC (6 June 2018) <http://rwandaun.org/site/wp-content/uploads/2018/11/Final-MICT-JUNE-6-Statement-UNSC-FINAL-1.pdf> accessed 23 June 2020.

[66] Special Court for Sierra Leone, 'Practice Direction on the Conditional Early Release of Persons Convicted by the Special Court for Sierra Leone', Article 2(C)(iii), Special Court for Sierra Leone (Freetown: 1 October 2013).

for supervision, restitution to victims, and renunciation of ideologies contrary to peace and reconciliation, and proposed areas of resettlement'.[67] The Practice Direction noted the President of the SCSL should consult with those judges who imposed the original sentence or, if they were unavailable, at least two other judges who were on its panel.[68] By contrast, under Meron, who acted unilaterally in determining release, the MICT process had no such 'probationary' clause to allow the close supervision of the released individuals.

National courts in Europe and North America have seen a steady rise in the politicization of genocide denial and revision in their own proceedings against the few accused *génocidaires* where action has been taken. Extradition and criminal courts in London, Paris, Frankfurt, Netherlands, Belgium, Canada, and the US have had defence lawyers consistently use the tactic that charges are politically motivated and aimed at silencing critics in the diaspora. In essence, they seek to claim 'victimhood' for the accused and instead to place Kagame in the dock. The long-running UK extradition case against five alleged *génocidaires*[69] accused of responsibility for the slaughter of thousands of Tutsis, was notable for this tactic. Defence witnesses, most of whom did not know the accused, spoke at length about the current government in Rwanda, using the dock to make political points and promoting the accused as 'victims' and political dissidents.

The failure by many Western countries to extradite or try in national courts those charged with the most serious of crimes has serious ramifications. First, it significantly diminishes the crime. Genocide and crimes against humanity, the most serious charges that could be brought against a person, are shown to be relevant and notable only if there is political and financial will by the state to prosecute them. Universal jurisdiction is seemingly only enacted when states deem it to be in their political—not necessarily judicial—interest. However, without evidence being produced in a legal setting, such as a courtroom, the accused are free to reframe events to deny they occurred or that they played any role in them. Rwandan genocide suspects in the UK have used frequent media interviews to deny any personal involvement in 'massacres', to insist they are innocent, peace-loving 'family' men, and have reframed legal action against them [ie, the accused] as purely politically motivated by the Kigali government.

[67] Rugwabiza (n 65).

[68] Practice Direction (n 66), 8(A).

[69] Vincent Bajinya [aka Brown], Célestin Ugirashebuja, Emmanuel Nteziryayo, and Charles Munyaneza were arrested in 2006 and legal proceedings to extradite them to Rwanda took place at Westminster Magistrates Court in London between 2007–2009. The extradition was refused, on appeal. The accused were subsequently arrested in 2013, together with Celestin Mutabaruka, but the extradition was again refused in 2017. In 2019 it was announced that the Metropolitan police were investigating the accused with regard to prosecuting them in the UK, but justice minister Ben Wallace estimated it would take five to ten years for this process to be completed, by which time the alleged *genocidaire* would have lived in the country for three decades.

The Role of the Media

In a groundbreaking ruling in 2003, ICTR judges determined that in using the extremist radio station RTLM 'without a firearm, machete or any physical weapon, [Ferdinand Nahimana *et al*] caused the deaths of thousands of innocent civilians'.[70] It was the first time since the Nuremberg trials journalists had been found guilty in an international court for what they had written or caused to be said on the radio. While this trial led to renewed interest in the role of radio and journals to incite, instruct, and assist genocide, since 1994 the international media has arguably played its own role in disseminating genocide denial and revisionism in a way unparalleled by any other such tragedy.

During the genocide itself the media was, for the most part, notable by its absence as it chose to cover other world and domestic stories,[71] and it was not until the postgenocide refugee crisis that journalists and editors arrived at the refugee camps in Zaire/Tanzania to cover unfolding events. Notably few chose to cover the devastated state of postgenocide Rwanda. Later depictions and analysis have been commissioned with historical accuracy often compromised by the filmmakers need to generate increased viewing figures or income streams. This inevitably has led viewers or readers into historical ambivalence with regards to the truth of what occurred. At times this has been unwitting—at other times it is clear the producers or journalists have an overarching political agenda which can include deliberate disinformation and revisionism.

For the twentieth commemoration of the genocide in 2014, the BBC commissioned a one-hour documentary, 'Rwanda: The Untold Story'. It was written by, and featured, the journalist Jane Corbin. In 1988 she had made the highly controversial BBC documentary 'The Shadow of the Swastika' that was accused by Holocaust survivors and the Simon Wiesenthal Center of seeking to undermine the aims and methods of war crimes investigations.[72] 'The Untold Story's' underlying narrative was a political attack on Kagame made possible by questioning the historical veracity of the genocide against the Tutsi and his role in it. Corbin ignored tens of thousands of hours of witness statements and video evidence at the ICTR, reports from the UN, NGOs, and journalists on the ground in Rwanda and focused her response on two discredited American academics, whose book had been ridiculed by scholars when it appeared in 2010.[73] Corbin, as with Bruguière, chose to include interviews with former RPF defectors who had fallen out with Kagame rather than

70 *Prosecutor v Ferdinand Nahimana, Jean-Bosco Barayagwiza, Hassan Ngeze* (Judgement) [2003] ICTR-99-52-T.

71 These included the death of singer Kurt Cobain (April), the inauguration of Nelson Mandela as president of South Africa (May) and OJ Simpson's arrest in the USA (June).

72 BBC 'Panorama' Producer: Charles Furneaux, Editor: Tim Gardam (12 December 1988).

73 Gerald Caplan, 'The politics of denialism: the strange case of Rwanda' *Pambazuka News* (17 June 2010) <https://www.pambazuka.org/governance/politics-denialism-strange-case-rwanda> accessed 23 June 2020.

survivors or witnesses.[74] While questions about BBC's impartiality, accuracy, and political bias have been made before, notably in its coverage of Israel–Palestine, it seems inconceivable that such a film could be made today about the Holocaust or genocide in Bosnia.

The later BBC/Netflix drama 'Black Earth Rising',[75] 'based on true events', was an entertainment vehicle based on the genocide in Rwanda and the after effects on the region. While using no Rwandan locations or actors, it pulled together over eight episodes several narrative themes and storylines, effectively blurring the responsibilities of all involved. The difficulty in attempting to portray highly complex political, social, and historical events in a 'factional' manner, with the overriding aim of selling the feature as entertainment inevitably meant compromising truth and accuracy. For the BBC/Netflix, success would be measured in revenue generated. The same logic has been true of docu-dramas based on the Holocaust. The current growth of Auschwitz 'based on a true story' literature has been dismissed by one critic for being 'a feelgood Holocaust [that] exploits the dead and demeans the living'.[76] For audiences who may know little of the historical reality of the events portrayed, these entertainment vehicles can be more destructive than outright genocide denial and revisionism in their ability to shape conceptions and judgments based on emotionally charged 'factional' stories which are not designed to inform but to entertain.

In the same vein, Hollywood released the film 'Hotel Rwanda' in 2004 which became an unlikely box office success. It remains perhaps the reason most people have heard about the genocide in Rwanda. However, the actions and ideology of the controversial hotel manager Paul Rusesabagina, the 'hero' of the film to Western audiences, has highlighted how a highly creative public image, made in Holliwood, can distort truth and reality. The 'Hotel Rwanda Rusesabagina Foundation', which has raised millions of dollars from international donors since its creation, has been criticized for a lack of accountability and whether funds have been used for stated humanitarian projects; or to support Rusesabagina's political party, the Rwandan Movement for Democratic Change (MCRD) and its militia wing the National Forces of Liberation (Forces Nationales de Libération—'FNL') based in eastern DRC that was formed with the explicit public aim of overthrowing the Kagame

[74] The programme was widely condemned by survivor groups. A letter of complaint to the BBC director general Peter Hall on 12 October 2012 and signed by forty-five academics, senators, journalists, lawyers, and survivors, noted: 'in broadcasting this documentary the BBC has been recklessly irresponsible. The program has fuelled genocide denial. It has further emboldened the *génocidaires*, all their supporters and those who collaborate with them. It has provided them the legitimacy of the BBC. Denial of genocide causes the gravest offence to survivors. For them, the genocide is not a distant event from 20 years ago but the reality with which they live every day'. See Andrew Wallis, 'Rwanda, the Untold Story: Questions for the BBC' *opendemocracy.net* (6 October 2014) https://www.opendemocracy.net/en/rwanda-untold-story-questions-for-bbc/ accessed 23 June 2020.

[75] BBC/Netfix, directed by Hugo Blick (2018).

[76] Howard Jacobson: 'A feelgood Holocaust exploits the dead and demeans the living' *The Guardian* (London, 23 January 2020).

'dictatorship' by any means necessary. Previously, Rusesabagina had been questioned by Belgian investigators in 2011 about his active support for the FDLR which he named a 'Rwandan Liberation Movement', despite its widespread, murderous campaign in the Kivu and into Rwanda which has left thousands dead in the past two decades. On 31 August 2020 Rusesabagina was arrested, in still unclear circumstances, on arrival at Kigali airport and faces trial in January 2021 on nine charges resulting from attacks launched by the FNL in 2018 on villages inside Rwanda that left many dead, wounded, and property destroyed.[77] The charges include financing terror, murder, abduction, robbery, and arson. The arrest of a man feted by supporters such as US Congressmen, international human rights groups and global Western media has brought into sharp focus the debate over how Rwanda's past and present are treated. The 'Holliwood' vision of Rusesabagina as hero and democratic peace envoy has been widely touted since his arrest, with media opinion rehashing his 1994 'heroics' as portrayed in the film, and fund-raising launched to support his legal costs in Kigali and his family in the USA. There was little, if any reporting outside Rwandan news outlets of counter-factual evidence that strongly questioned this narrative. An open letter, sent by 23 US-based scholars on 18 November 2020, to the US Senate Committee on Foreign Relations,[78] urged them to 'move beyond the fictional movie' version of Rusesabagina that has been sole reference point for 'a number of news outlets, social media, human rights organizations, and commentators' so the real reasons for his arrest and trial are discussed. In effect, that the narrative of the present is fully informed not by a fictional account of the past, but by precise and objective understanding of Rusesabagina's background in 1994, his ideology, close relationship to the Interahamwe militia and FAR leaders and his activities with genocide deniers and revisionists to the present. Since the release of the film in 2004, survivors, including those at Hotel Milles Collines,[79] attacked Rusesabagina as a fraud, a Hutu extremist, and a genocide denier, though their voice has largely been lost as the personality-led Hollywood version of events has

[77] The MRCD-FLN (Rwandan Movement for Democratic Change-National Liberation Forces) formation has been documented by Claver Ndushabandi, 'New rebel group declares war on Rwanda's Paul Kagame' *Chimp reports* (Kampala, 16 July 2018) <https://chimpreports.com/exclusive-new-rebel-group-declares-war-on-rwandas-paul-kagame/> accessed 23 June 2020; FDLR leader and former FAR Presidential Guard commander Sylvestre Mudacumura, indicted by the International Criminal Court for war crimes, was killed in September 2019, but the remnants of his forces have continued to terrorize and kill local Congolese villagers and mount raids into Rwanda. In April 2020, seventeen civilians, including twelve park rangers, were massacred. 'DRC: Rangers, civilians killed in attack in Virunga National Park' *Al Jazeera* (Doha, 25 April 2020) <https://www.aljazeera.com/news/2020,/04/drc-rangers-civilians-killed-attack-virunga-national-park-200424161459752.html> accessed 23 June 2020.

[78] 'US scholars on arrest and trial of Paul Rusesabagina', https://rwanda-news.com/2020/11/30/us-scholars-on-arrest-and-trial-of-paul-rusesabagina-in-rwanda accessed 23 December 2020.

[79] Survivors of the Mille Collines Hotel have testified about their experiences during the genocide, countering Rusesabagina's narrative and alleging he was 'a profiteering and politically ambitious Hutu power sympathiser who extorted money from those who sought refuge' and that his falsely created 'hero' status was dangerously misplaced. See Edouard Kayihura and Kerry Zukus, *Inside the Hotel Rwanda* (Benbella Books 2014).

continued to dominate the narrative. In 2008 Rusesabagina acted as an 'expert' defence witness at the extradition case in London of four suspected *génocidaires*. Judge Anthony Evans noted his 'evidence was not that of an independent expert but rather that of a man with a background strongly allied to the extremist Hutu faction, and as such cannot be considered independent or reasoned'.[80] While Jane Corbin has not personally defended accused genocide suspects in court, her revisionist BBC documentary has been used by defence lawyers within Europe as a means to promote the RDR version of the genocide and diminish responsibility for those on trial or facing extradition.

While these examples come from postgenocide mainstream 'Anglophone' media, a steady stream of revisionist programmes and newspaper articles/cartoons have appeared in French broadcast and print outlets. On 20 December 2013, the Canal+ television channel aired a programme that was widely interpreted as ridiculing the genocide and its victims. Actors in a comedy sketch parodying Rwanda sang a song to the tune of a French nursery rhyme. The lyrics noted, 'mum is upstairs, cut into pieces; daddy is downstairs, he lacks an arm', to the evident amusement of the studio audience. In 2015, Charlie Hebdo reproduced a cartoon captioned *Tutsi Crush: Le Genocide Rwandais enfin adapté en jeu sur smartphone* ('The Rwandan genocide is finally adapted as a smartphone game'). The candy 'crush' were Tutsi skulls being smashed. In 2019, another cartoon depicted two headless Rwandans fighting each other. In the foreground, the heads of the two figures talk to each other, with one noting '*et si on se reconcilait . . .*' ('how about we make up . . . '). Such work reflects the continued colonial-era mindset of Africans continually involved in ethnic and tribal warfare, with both as guilty (and ignorant) as each other.

In July 2015 UK Independent Television News ('ITN') broadcast an 'exclusive' interview with its senior Africa correspondent John Ray travelling to Mali to speak to former interim regime prime minister Jean Kambanda, serving a life sentence for genocide at the UN detention facility in Bamiko. Kambanda used this prime-time media appearance to tell the millions watching, 'I can't express any regrets for something I have not done. Someone else did it'.[81] He went on to launch further denials about the crime and castigate Kagame's government. After strong criticism from survivors and academics at this breach of UN protocol in giving such a high-profile *génocidaires* a platform to espouse denial, ITN issued a justification, noting 'fundamentally it is our duty to inform the public. This can include

[80] There have been some documentaries exploring certain aspects of the genocide, notably 'Tuez-les tous! Rwanda: histoire d'un génocide "sans importance" ', directed by Raphaël Glucksmann, Dum Dum Films (2004); 'Shake Hands with the Devil', directed by Peter Raymont, CBC (2004); 'Ghosts of Rwanda', Directed by Greg Barker, PBS (2004).

[81] On 1 May 1998 Kambanda pleaded guilty to six charges including genocide and Crimes against Humanity and was sentenced to life imprisonment. This was upheld on appeal on 19 October 2000. *Jean Kambanda v the Prosecutor* (Judgment) [October 2000] ICTR-97-23-A.

interviews with controversial individuals'.[82] The ITN justification sought to defend its 'public interest story' by pointing to postgenocide human rights violations and revenge killings by RPA troops during 1994. The narrative is deliberately blurred, with both sides accused of atrocities. However, as seen, conflating the genocide against the Tutsi with reprisal/revenge attacks or with later human rights abuses as a way to diminish and undermine the Kagame government may make sense in terms of media sensationalism and ratings. Survivors point out double standards. When filming programmes about the First or Second World War, or even the Iraq and Afghanistan wars, it is rare for Allied/UK revenge/reprisal attacks to be mentioned at length. There is some irony that while some Western academics and media have accused Kagame of politicizing his role in stopping the genocide to gain greater leverage in judicial, business, and aid matters, they have themselves sought to diminish and at times deny the role of the RPF in 1994 in order to politically undermine him and his government.

The Church: A Failure of Forgiveness?

The Catholic Church was deeply embedded in Rwandan state and politics from the start of the colonial period. Archbishops Andre Perraudin (appointed by President Gregoire Kayibanda) and Augustin Nsengiyumva (appointed by President Juvenal Habyarimana) fully endorsed the one-party state and the status quo regarding regionalist and ethnic discrimination. Neither challenged the corruption, genocidal massacres, or inequalities that beset the country from independence in 1962 until the 1994 genocide. Nsengiyumva, who served on the MRND central committee, was a close personal friend of the former first lady Agathe Habyarimana, along with Anglican archbishop Augustin Nshamihigo and Presbyterian leader Michel Twagirayesu. During 1994 Rwandan clergy were divided between perpetrators, victims, and those who tried to save their congregations. Dozens of clergy and religious implicated in the killing were spirited out of the region, often under assumed names, and into parishes in Europe where they were not known.

During the trial in Brussels in 2001 of two Benedictine nuns, Sister Gertrude and Sister Kizito, accused of assisting *Interahamwe* to burn to death hundreds of Tutsis sheltering in their convent, the Belgian judge complained of undue pressure by the Catholic hierarchy to get prosecution witnesses to change their stories. In France, the longstanding, highly politicized case against Fr Wenceslas Munyeshyaka has come to embody not just the denial of specific crimes by the individual concerned

[82] '"My conscience is clear" Former Rwanda PM Jean Kambanda tells ITV News he was tricked into genocide confession', ITN (London, 21 July 2015) <https://www.itv.com/news/2015-07-21/my-conscience-is-clean-former-rwandan-pm-jean-kambanda-tells-itv-news-he-was-tricked-into-genocide-confession/> accessed 23 June 2020.

and his high-profile clerical backers, but of the role of the Church in the genocide and its apparent attempt to frustrate justice in order to deny its own wider involvement in the crime.[83] No priest or religious who has been found guilty of genocide—at the ICTR, national courts, or in Rwanda—has been disciplined or defrocked by the Vatican. Convicted killers have continued to be able to say mass while in prison. Fr Emmanuel Rukundo, found guilty of genocide by the ICTR, was included in a list of religious honoured by the Catholic Church for twenty-five years of service in holy orders. Senior figures within the Vatican have continued to oppose any apology for the actions of the Church in Rwanda. One year after the genocide, Papal Nuncio Monsignor Nguyen Van Tot dismissed the crime as 'certain unfortunate events' in a six-page letter to the Rwandan justice minister. Van Tot added that the moral authorities in society should not be questioned, and there should be rigorous control of the press and radio in the country to keep it from defaming the church.[84]

In an open letter to Pope John Paul II, the NGO African Rights noted that:

> members of the Church, both in Rwanda and abroad, continue to exert intense pressure on priests and nuns to whitewash the crimes of those accused of genocide. Those who refuse to comply have been intimidated ... The Catholic Church cannot play a constructive role in Rwanda as long as it continues to provide sanctuary to genocide suspects ... The failure of the Catholic Church to investigate its role in the genocide has not only driven away many of the faithful; it is destroying the Church from within. Increasingly, priests and nuns who survived the genocide question whether they have a place in an institution that refuses to recognise the enormity of the genocide, its consequences, and its own contribution.[85]

While the Anglican Church has taken some strides towards fully accepting its responsibility for failures before and during the genocide, the Catholic Church, in both individual cases of wrongdoing and on an institutional level, has continued to seek to downplay, obfuscate, and disguise the critically important role it played not just in 1994, but in the years 1959–1993 in supporting successive genocidal

[83] See Timothy Longman, 'Church Politics and the Genocide in Rwanda' [2001] *Journal of Religion in Africa* 31; Tharcisse Gatwa, *The Churches and Ethnic Ideology in the Rwandan Crises 1900-1994* (Wipf and Stock 2008); Chris McGreal, *Chaplains of the Militia: The tangled story of the Catholic church during Rwanda's genocide* (2014) Guardian Shorts Book 12; Carol Rittner, *Genocide in Rwanda: Complicity of the Churches* (Paragon House 2004); 'Rwanda: The Protestant Churches and the Genocide' *African Rights* (London 1998); McCullum, *The Angels Have Left Us: The Rwanda Tragedy and the Churches*, World Council of Churches (1998).

[84] Letter from Monsignor Van Tot to Alphonse Nkubito, Kigali, 9 January 1995, cited in: Christian Scherrer, Genocide and Crisis in Central Africa (Praeger 2002) 114, 135n; see also 'Vatican newspaper defends jailed Rwandan bishop', *Associated Press* (18 May 1999) <https://www.theguardian.com/world/1999/apr/17/chrismcgreal> accessed 23 June 2020.

[85] <https://www.pambazuka.org/human-security/letter-pope-african-rights> accessed 23 June 2020.

regimes. While Pope Francis travelled to the US to issue an apology for the role of the Church in the child abuse scandal, no pontiff has visited Rwanda since 1994, and no apology has yet been proffered.[86]

As with state actors, senior individuals within the Vatican continue to put the danger of institutional reputational damage—and possible financial claims for compensation—before encouraging an open, transparent discussion regarding its role in Rwanda between 1959 and 1994. On a global level, the Vatican has strategized downplaying the controversy, which has received little media coverage. However, inside Rwanda, the failure of the Church to accept fully its past has stymied its efforts to recover pre-1994 levels of trust and popularity. Continued attempts in the present time to 'gag' Rwandan clerical whistle-blowers[87] does not bode well for an institution trying to renew and find a place in a much changed, more critically responsive, society. The perceived protection of clerical killers by the Vatican has led survivor groups to question if the Church can have a meaningful role in the ongoing societal attempts since 1994 at reconciliation, forgiveness, and restitution.

Closing Thoughts

President Konrad Adenauer's post-war West German government dealt with Nazi crimes and criminals involved in the Holocaust by simply ignoring them. Most were seamlessly reintegrated into society, often at senior level. Jewish survivors had fled to Palestine and those remaining in Europe were now poorly represented. Countries such as East Germany and Poland continued an anti-Semitic culture where Jews were as unwelcome as the mention of the crimes against them during the war. By contrast, in Rwanda, survivors had no option but to continue to live in villages where perpetrators and their families returned after Gacaca. No other country has had to deal with a genocide that fragmented its society in such a disturbing manner, and continues to leave strong elements of fear, anxiety, and distress less than one generation after the event: children born from some of the 500,000 rapes; perpetrators and survivors suffering long-term mental and emotional PTSD as a result of the horror; survivor poverty as a result of the loss of their home or family to support them in old age; fears of future pogroms should security inside or outside the country collapse. The highly complex and nuanced configuration

[86] On 20 March 2017 Kagame visited the Vatican where Pope Francis asked forgiveness for the 'sins and failings of the Church' but stopped short of an apology, noting only individual—not institutional—failings of priests and religious who had 'succumbed to hatred and violence'. Chrispian Balmer, 'Pope asks forgiveness for Church role in Rwanda genocide' *Reuters* (20 March 2017) <https://www.theguardian.com/world/2017/mar/20/pope-francis-asks-for-forgiveness-for-churchs-role-in-rwanda-genocide> accessed 23 June 2020.

[87] See the work of Fr Jean Ndorimana; Bartov, Omer and Phyllis Mack (ed) *In God's Name: Genocide and Religion in the Twentieth Century* (Berghahn Books 2010).

of Rwandan society today can be understood only through a complete empathetic understanding of the genocide but also the decades that led up to it.

As with the cases of the Holocaust, genocides in Bosnia, Cambodia, Darfur, and at the present that of the Rohingya—where genocide has been enacted with the full knowledge of world leaders—the international failure to prevent and punish this heinous crime in Rwanda, too, continues to place a question mark over the effectiveness of the 1948 Genocide Convention. The egregious crimes perpetrated in Rwanda by Bagosora, Nsengiyumva, Nzirorera, Kambanda *et al*, were planned and enacted for political reasons, yet the response by the international community was—merely—a humanitarian one. A lukewarm judicial response followed in later years with the ICTR and (very) occasional prosecutions in national courts under the legal framework of universal jurisdiction. Having failed to prevent genocide, this 'second' failure to arrest and bring to justice perpetrators had, and continues to have, a devastating effect on the region.

Moreover, the continuing, insidious, growth of denial and revisionist ideology, most notable in some of the recent media coverage seen earlier in the chapter, presents another factor with a devastating potential for the region and beyond. The RDR strategy to focus attention away from the crime and onto the person of Kagame, onto RPF reprisals or later human rights abuses has entered the mainstream Western media's approach to Rwanda. Deflecting blame, excusing the 'violence'—apparent in some state postgenocide responses (France, USA, Switzerland, UK) or by the Catholic Church, international media and some academics[88]—has been prioritized before searching for an authentic historical truth and understanding of institutional and individual political failure. However, conflating the genocide against the Tutsi with current debates over governance and democracy in the country is simplistic and dangerous. Survivors complain that there is more than a hint of hypocrisy and racism in the postgenocide treatment of the country by the West, which continues to harbour wanted *génocidaires* while lecturing Rwanda and its leadership about democracy and human rights.[89]

[88] An example can be seen in the recent work of American academic Helen C Epstein. In her critique of US policy and its support for Ugandan leader Yoweri Museveni, she wrote of the Rwandan genocide against the Tutsi that: 'the violence was not spontaneous. It emerged from a century or more of injustice and brutality on both sides, and although the génocidaires struck back against innocents, they were provoked by heavily armed rebels supplied by Uganda, while the US looked on'. In excusing the genocide on the basis that the RPA had invaded the country four years earlier in 1990 with Ugandan military support, Epstein rehashed the well-used rhetoric of Bagosora/RDR—justifying the unjustifiable. Her rationale for using this denial thesis was seemingly simply to make her central critique about perceived US foreign policy errors. Helen C Epstein, 'America's secret role in the Rwandan genocide' *The Guardian* (London, 12 September 2017).

[89] Rwandan researcher Tom Ndahiro noted, 'The problem is indifference to what happens here. Because of racism, they don't care about the truth and facts. They can't entertain a known Holocaust denier or someone who openly supports terrorist activities.' James Karuhanga, 'Uproar as Rusesabagina is given platform to negate Genocide against Tutsi' *New Times* (Kigali, 5 January 2020) <https://www.newtimes.co.rw/news/uproar-rusesabagina-given-platform-negate-genocide-against-tutsi> accessed 23 June 2020.

During his recent presidency of the African Union, Kagame pushed for a more positive and confident attitude by the continent's leaders and people to what he regarded as continuing lazy and derogatory international stereotyping. His autocratic manner and style of leadership has riled many liberal Western commentators while attracting admiration from others. In the aftermath of genocide, all aspects of Rwanda—business, economy, society, justice, security—are too often viewed through the prism of this one individual. However, to see the genocide of 1994 through this single lens, as has become increasingly common, is a fallacy. That it suits the perpetrators to move attention elsewhere and remain out of sight and mind is obvious. Concomitantly they use genocide denial to construct dubious narratives as a route to rehabilitation and power. This notwithstanding, for the sake of the suffering and loss incurred by the victims, the political stability and recovery achieved in Rwanda since 1994, and the aspiration that no genocide must be condoned, it is imperative that genocide denial be resisted. The continuing need in the present to confront and resist its spread will allow energies and resources to focus on Rwanda's continued physical and emotional regeneration and the opening up of governance and civil society.

PART III

POSTGENOCIDE IDENTITIES, MEMORY, AND IR/RECONCILIATION

9

Memory, Identity, and Possession

Personal Objects from Genocide in Galleries, Museums, and Archives

Martine Louise Hawkes[*]

Introduction

The personal objects of people murdered through genocide, which are subsequently displayed in galleries, archives, and museums (hence 'GAMs'), are objects of identity, memory, and forgetting. These are those objects collected either *from* genocide or *through* genocide. Personal objects are on display either as what Laurie Beth Clark calls the 'mnemonic objects'[1] of genocide, or as objects whose connection to genocide is disconnected. Objects collected from the genocides of the twentieth century are on display in museums or galleries or are held by archives, largely as Clark's mnemonic objects. Meanwhile, objects collected as part of a genocide are those personal belongings stolen through colonial genocide, in which European settler-colonial actions have included the murder, cultural destruction, and separation of first nations peoples.[2] These actions facilitated the taking of objects, including cultural belongings and human remains, which are now stored and displayed in GAMs throughout the world. These objects are most often not mobilized in memory of that genocide or even with this provenance recorded. All of these personal objects are objects which remain, which are still here, and which, in the institution, are stilled.

In looking at personal objects from genocide on display in museums and galleries and available through archives, this chapter asks what it means to remember, in the present, genocide through objects and what it means to encounter these

[*] I acknowledge the Kaurna people as the custodians of the lands and waters on which I work and live. Aboriginal sovereignty has never been ceded. Thank you to Deanne Hanchant-Nichols for her generosity in spending time with me discussing her deep knowledge of the repatriation of Aboriginal ancestral remains. Though not the direct focus of this chapter, her reflections on repatriation have greatly informed my thinking on what it means to hold personal objects.

[1] Laurie Beth Clark, 'Mnemonic Objects: Forensic and Rhetorical Practices in Memorial Culture' in Marc Silberman and Florence Vatan (eds), *Memory and Postwar Memorials: Confronting the Past as Violence* (Palgrave 2013) 155.

[2] Ann Curthoys and John Docker, 'Introduction—Genocide: Definitions, Questions, Settler-Colonies' (2001) 25 Aboriginal History 13.

Martine Louise Hawkes, *Memory, Identity, and Possession* In: *Postgenocide*. Edited by: Klejda Mulaj, Oxford University Press (2021). © The Several Contributors. DOI: 10.1093/oso/9780192895189.003.0009

objects in GAMs. These personal items, retained or recovered from attempts to mark-out and erase a people, are not inert objects but important markers and maintainers of identity. These objects of both belonging and of evidence, together with their display or availability in GAMs, may form, reconstruct, or bolster collective or national identities that are simultaneously difficult to bear, because of what has been destroyed, and deeply important. As will be explored in this chapter, these objects may be used in restoring identities and seeking redress for past trauma,[3] in acknowledging the past or attempting to atone through the construction of spaces for these objects or through their return to original custodians, while also, in the case of objects taken through colonial genocide, they may be used to form the civic identity of the colonizers.[4] In performing these functions personal objects from genocide on display in GAMs—through their materiality and their physical persistence—offer an unbroken connection from the time before the genocide, through the event, to postgenocide; a connection that has the potential to affect the construction of the narrative of genocide and our understanding of such events.

In exploring how narratives of genocide and postgenocide are constructed, this chapter focuses on both the objects salvaged after the genocides of the twentieth century, which have gone on to form institutional collections of genocide memory around the world, and the objects taken through the genocide of Aboriginal people in Australia. These latter objects are retained through an assumption of the right to retention that is not so different from the colonial logic of value that informed the original 'collection' of these objects, as well as of the land of Australia itself. All of these objects can tell us much about the power that institutions hold over both the retention of the objects and of the narrative that an object will (or will not) be used to tell.

This chapter begins with a short overview of the types of objects that might be encountered in GAMs, followed by a description of these institutions as collectors and curators of personal objects. While this chapter performs a conflation-of-sorts when discussing these three institutions, it is hoped that by so doing we might effectively capture the characteristics of and difficulties within institutions charged with constructing the social memory of genocide through personal objects. These objects do not simply mirror the world, but also produce what we know about particular histories and people. The role GAMs play in producing public knowledge of genocide is particularly apparent in the power they hold over what an institution will collect or keep, what it will not collect or keep, and which story it will tell through the arrangement and description of these objects. I am concerned not to characterize these institutions as being inflexible in their display or retention of

[3] Sue McKemmish, Shannon Faulkhead, and Lynette Russell, 'Distrust in the Archive: Reconciling Records' (2011) 11 Archival Science 211–39 (hereafter McKemmish *et al* 'Distrust in the Archive').

[4] Paul Turnbull, *Science, Museums and Collecting the Indigenous Dead in Colonial Australia* (Palgrave Macmillan 2017) (hereafter Turnbull, *Science, Museums and Collecting*) 139.

personal objects any more than I represent the personal objects they hold as being fixed in their meanings. I, therefore, note at the outset that this chapter is written at a time of significant shifts in how memory institutions think about (or are encouraged to think about) their collections of objects gathered from genocide in particular. At a broad level, there are shifts in terms of how these institutions describe themselves. At the time of writing, the International Council of Museums was seeking a new definition for museums.[5] More pertinent to this chapter, these shifts also include a global proliferation in the representation of genocide in memory institutions, the growing mobilization of collections to redress past trauma and reinforce or restore the identity of descendants of genocide victims and their communities, and how memory institutions might be decolonized.

Personal Objects and Genocide

The focus of this chapter is how personal objects from genocide can transmit meaning and continue to make new meaning in the postgenocide era. A personal object could be any material item that belongs to an individual, such as an item of clothing or a tool. It is any physical, created thing that is given meaning and significance through our interaction and relationship with it. For Jean Baudrillard, each object has two functions: 'to be put to use and to be possessed'.[6] The uses to which an object is put shift once its owner has died. It may lose its original function altogether and become an object of mourning. For example, a pipe belonging to a grandfather may never be smoked again once he dies, but a grandchild may keep it as an object that recalls her grandfather. An object may also break or be discarded altogether. There emerges a difference between the object that is still in practical use and the object that has become abstracted from its original function and which is either retained as the physical evidence of a broader narrative or relationship (possessed) or is discarded (not possessed).

When possessed after the death of their original owner, why is it that personal objects can perform mourning and memory work? Once they are no longer in everyday use or fulfilling their original function, objects can be the link between the past and present and also to a particular person or a group's history. We tell stories around these objects, which also shift with time and space. Storytelling of this sort is possible because objects are things which have multiple connections to people (as well as their identities), time, and place. Objects are linked to their maker, their original owner, the place and period in which they circulated and the uses to which they were put and, finally, to the people or institutions which may

[5] International Council of Museums, 'Museum Definition' (ICOM 2019) <icom.museum/en/activities/standards-guidelines/museum-definition> accessed 20 February 2019.
[6] Jean Baudrillard, *The System of Objects* (Verso 1996) 92.

hold an object once its original owners die or the object becomes functionally obsolete. All of this becomes part of the history of an object[7]—and its given meaning.

Vamık D Volkan proposes that there is a deep relationship between personal objects and mourning. He understands the personal objects that connect us to grief and memory of the dead as a set of linking objects.[8] For Volkan, linking objects include:

1. Personal possession of the deceased (eg, an item of clothing)
2. Gift or symbolic farewell note (eg, a letter)
3. Something the deceased used to extend senses/body (eg, a camera)
4. Realistic/symbolic representation of the deceased (eg, a photograph)
5. 'Last-minute' object (eg, an object at hand when the news of death arrived or an object present during a funeral)
6. Created linking object (eg, a painting created in memory by the mourner).[9]

While it is perhaps easy to understand how an object connected to a loved one might be used in mourning (eg, the grandfather's pipe), my interest in this chapter is in how museums, galleries, or archives might also use personal objects as objects of public mourning for genocide. While Volkan, writing from a psychiatric perspective, has variously focused on the pathological aspects of the linking objects,[10] he also considers these objects as items that facilitate a 'future' mourning.[11] This is also the role that they might play in GAMs.

Additionally, though when Volkan first proposed the classification of linking objects, they were as private mourning objects used by individuals,[12] he also turned his attention to societal mourning,[13] framing public memorials as a type of shared linking object.[14] It is in this spirit that I tentatively read Volkan's six linking objects as also being readable as the personal objects that we find today in GAMs that are

[7] Samuel Alberti, 'Objects and the Museum' (2005) 96 *Isis* 559.

[8] Vamık D Volkan, 'The Linking Objects of Pathological Mourners' (1972) 27 Archives of General Psychiatry 215 (hereafter Volkan, 'The Linking Objects'); Vamık D Volkan, *Linking Objects and Linking Phenomena: A Study of the Forms, Symptoms, Metapsychology, and Therapy of Complicated Mourning* (International Universities Press 1981) (hereafter Volkan, *Linking Objects and Linking Phenomena*); Vamık D Volkan, 'After the Violence: The Internal World and Linking Objects of a Refugee Family' (2018) Freud Conference <www.freudconference.com.au/online_papers/After_The_Voilence.pdf> accessed 3 January 2019 (hereafter Volkan, 'After the Violence').

[9] Volkan, 'After the Violence' (n 8).

[10] Volkan, 'The Linking Objects' (n 8).

[11] Volkan, 'After the Violence' (n 8).

[12] Volkan, 'The Linking Objects' (n 8); Volkan, *Linking Objects and Linking Phenomena* (n 8).

[13] Vamık D Volkan, *Bloodlines: From Ethnic Pride to Ethnic Terrorism* (Farrar, Straus and Giroux 1997); Vamık D Volkan, *Blind Trust: Large Groups and their Leaders in Times of Crisis and Terror* (Pitchstone 2004); Vamık D Volkan, Gabriele Ast, and William F Greer, *The Third Reich in the Unconscious: Transgenerational Transmission and its Consequences* (Brunner-Routledge 2002).

[14] Vamık D Volkan, 'Individuals and Societies as "Perennial Mourners": Their Linking Objects and Public Memorials' in by Brent Willock, Lori C Bohm, and Rebecca C Curtis (eds), *On Death and Dying: Psychoanalysts' Reflections on Finality, Transformations and New Beginnings* (Routledge 2007) 42.

either positioned as places of public memory of genocide or as places which have in their collection personal objects gathered during genocide.

The potential for the objects from genocide found in a museum, gallery, or archive to be linking objects for a wider public is only possible through the materiality of those objects. As already touched upon, personal objects are the link between the past and present and also to a particular person or a history. However, they can only perform this link because of their materiality. The materiality—the very plasticity—of an object on display in the museum allows the object to become the physical carrier for the past for anybody who comes to see it on display. Due to its physical persistence, the object was present before the genocide, at the time of the genocide, and here, after the genocide. Here, the object shapes the visitor's experience in a way that is only possible through its materiality. Alison Landsberg describes the tangibility of this experience at the United States Holocaust Memorial Museum ('USHMM') on the museum floor entitled 'The Final Solution':

> On this floor your freedom of movement is much more restricted. You find yourself on a boardwalk-like walkway. The ground under your feet is uneven. You are walking on cobblestones—cobblestones, you learn, which came from the Warsaw ghetto.... There is no longer a clear distinction between your space and the exhibit, your body and the history of the objects all around you ... [T]o your left are objects from these places—tools from the ghetto workshops, stained-glass windows from the Cracow synagogue, the Lodz hospital door. Even though you are not invited to touch these objects, their very materiality, I would argue, their seductive tangibility, draws you into a lived relationship with them.[15]

However, its materiality alone is not enough for an object to be a linking object for grief in a museum, gallery or archive. The context in which we encounter these objects is also of great importance. In describing the contexts in which personal objects from genocide might be publicly encountered after genocide, GAM institutions have been selected to facilitate our discussion of those objects made publicly available after genocide. In these institutions, the context in which a visitor encounters an object is both highly mediated and at times unpredictable. The object's relationship to genocide might be immediately and contextually clear to the visitor, as with the objects encountered by Landsberg at the USHMM, or the visitor may not know that the object they are viewing is an artefact from genocide.

To better understand how we might experience personal objects from genocide in the context of a public institution, we must first understand the relationship between a museum, gallery, or archive and the objects which they hold.

[15] Alison Landsberg, *Prosthetic Memory: The Transformation of American Remembrance in the Age of Mass Culture* (Columbia University Press 2004) (hereafter Landsberg, *Prosthetic Memory*) 132.

Galleries, Museums, and Archives

While their access rules, collection focus, and usages might vary, GAMs can be broadly understood as institutions which place objects within a particular and fixed context. This may be an institutional, taxonomic, historical, or personal context. Such a context is arguably crucial to giving meaning to items within an institution, telling a particular narrative, and to supporting access.[16] In an archive, though also applicable to galleries and museums, context is assigned to objects through the principles of appraisal, arrangement, and description.[17]

In deciding whether to accession an object into a collection, it must first be appraised. Appraisal is a process that allows a museum, gallery, or archive to determine the evidential, historical, or administrative value of an object and to establish its provenance and context.[18] Provenance is a fundamental principle concerned with the context of and relationship between the creation, origins, custody, and ownership of an object.[19]

The principle of arrangement is the decision to place objects in either their original order or with their context protected.[20] Objects might be arranged in a strict, systematic order with, for example, all the pinned butterflies grouped together, all the Cubism in the same room, and all the letters in chronological order. Increasingly, museums and galleries, in particular, might choose to arrange their objects in terms of their impact on a visitor's affect or experience. Description, meanwhile, attaches critical information to objects. In a museum or gallery, this will usually be via a label next to the object. In an archive, the description of items is provided via finding aids to help users locate records. Descriptions of objects might include information about the provenance, relationships, and historical context of an object.

The decisions made during the assignation of context to an object are further dependent on a series of curatorial decisions guiding all aspects of their access and display. This includes decisions about how to preserve and prepare an object for display, how to display and light an object, how to protect it from visitors and the

[16] International Council on Archives, 'ISAD(G): General International Standard Archival Description' (ICA 2000) <www.ica.org/sites/default/files/CBPS_2000_Guidelines_ISAD%28G%29_Second-edition_EN.pdf> accessed 1 June 2018.

[17] Australian Society of Archivists Committee on Descriptive Standards, *Describing Archives in Context: A Guide to Australasian Practice* (Australian Society of Archivists 2008); Lyn Milton, 'Arrangement and Description' in Jackie Bettington and Others (eds), *Keeping Archives* (3rd edn, Australian Society of Archivists 2008) 252

[18] Jackie Bettington and Others (eds), *Keeping Archives* (3rd edn, Australian Society of Archivists 2008) 633; Carol Couture, 'Archival Appraisal: A Status Report' (2005) 79 Archivaria 84; Richard Pearce-Moses, *A Glossary of Archival and Records Terminology* (Society of American Archivists 2005) (hereafter Pearce-Moses, *A Glossary*) 22–23.

[19] Rowena Loo, Kim Eberhard, and Jackie Bettington, 'What are Archives & Archival Programs?' in Jackie Bettington and Others (eds), *Keeping Archives* (3rd edn, Australian Society of Archivists 2008) 16.

[20] Pearce-Moses, *A Glossary* (n 18) 35.

environment, and how to make an object historically, scientifically, culturally, or socially coherent. The preservation of objects and their stories is, in many ways, the primary function of a museum, gallery, or archive. At a different level, there is also the preservation of the role of museum, gallery, and archive as the 'keeper' of a history. The role of the museum (in particular) as the self-appointed best place for the preservation and protection of objects has been brought into question, most prominently through the ongoing retention of the Parthenon Sculptures—removed from Greece in the early 1800s by Lord Elgin—by the British Museum. The voices calling for the return of cultural objects and remains stolen via colonial plunder are increasing, underpinned by what Nathan Sentance has termed the 'paternalistic nature of collecting'.[21] This theme will be discussed in more detail later in this chapter.

In the multiple meaning of preservation presented here, once an object is placed in a memory institution, we see its meaning and context shift from being personal to becoming a representative or explanatory tool for a particular history available to people who may bear no relation to the original owner or creator. In this, a museum, gallery, or archive plays a role in forming the social memory of objects. Museums and galleries have, for several centuries, been charged with forming the social memory of most modern societies. For archives, this role dates back much further, for as long as humans have needed to understand and order their societies.[22] The social memory formed by GAMs comes in many forms. For Maurice Halbwachs, 'no memory is possible outside frameworks used by people living in society to determine and retrieve their recollections. When there is no living memory of an event, we are left with its archives'.[23] After an event, the objects which it has left behind and which, crucially, are thought worthwhile to be accessioned into a collection, become the support or substrate for a particular historical narrative. GAMs, therefore, also play a crucial role in legitimating a particular view of history through the objects they choose to display and the information they provide that informs the legibility of these objects. As Sarah Williamson and Darlene Clover point out, GAMs are reflexive, as they 'not only mirror but actually produce and mobilize our knowledge about culture, the world and even, ourselves'.[24] This is

[21] Nathan Sentance, 'The Paternalistic Nature of Collecting' Archival Decolonist (12 June 2017) <archivaldecolonist.com/2017/06/12/the-paternalistic-nature-of-collecting/ 2017> accessed 20 October 2018.

[22] Martine L Hawkes, *Archiving Loss: Holding Places for Difficult Memories* (Routledge 2018) 34–35; Adrian Cunningham, 'Archival Institutions' in Sue McKemmish (ed), *Archives: Recordkeeping in Society* (Charles Sturt University 2005) 26–30; Terry Cook, 'What is Past is Prologue: A History of Archival Ideas Since 1898, and the Future Paradigm Shift' (1997) 43 Archivaria 17.

[23] Maurice Halbwachs, *On Collective Memory* (trans Lewis. A Coser, University of Chicago Press 1992) 43.

[24] Sarah Williamson and Darlene Clover, '"Deeper, Quicker": "Hacking" a Critical Consciousness in the Art Gallery' in Robert McGray and Vera Woloshyn (eds), *CASAE 2018 Conference Proceedings* (Canadian Association for Studies in Adult Education 2018) 259.

particularly so in the power they hold over what is to be included and what is excluded and how a story will be told.

In considering the social memory and historical narratives formed by GAMs through their objects, we are lead to the primary question we want to consider, this being, what happens when we encounter personal objects from genocide in GAMs, and what role do institutions play in shaping and mediating memory through these objects?

Encountering Personal Objects from Genocide in GAMs

Since the end of the Second World War, a number of memorial museums dedicated specifically to genocide have been established. One of the first museums with this remit was opened in November 1944, when the Nazi concentration camp Majdanek was turned a museum of the Holocaust following its liberation in July of the same year.[25] Since then, memorial museums dedicated to the Holocaust, Armenian, Cambodian, Rwandan, and Srebrenica genocides and more have emerged. However, one may encounter a personal object from genocide during a visit to Belgium's Africa Museum, the Louvre, or the National Archives of Australia.

To understand how objects from genocide are likely to be encountered in GAMs, we return to Volkan's set of six linking objects, which are all present in these institutions. They might include clothing recovered from Srebrenica at the Srebrenica-Potočari Memorial Room; glasses from those murdered in European concentration camps at the former Auschwitz I concentration camp; letters from Aboriginal people in Australia dispossessed from land, culture, family, and language at the Public Records Office Victoria. Linking objects from genocide might also include object at hand when the news of death arrived, such as the objects from war childhoods held onto and donated to the War Childhood Museum in Sarajevo and created linking objects. Created linking objects might be artworks created in response to genocide or the built spaces of genocide memorial museums themselves.

What primarily differentiates the linking objects from genocide found in GAMs from linking objects from a personal grief is the public and institutional space in which they are encountered. Objects obtained by a museum, gallery, or archive assume new links to the genocide and its memory and grief once they are 'institutionalized'. In the museum, gallery, and archive, objects might serve multiple, intersectional purposes. For example, the photographs taken of victims of the Cambodian genocide immediately as their blindfolds were removed at the Tuol Sleng Museum of Genocide, then the S-21 Prison, are objects of evidence when

[25] Amy Sodaro, *Exhibiting Atrocity: Memorial Museums and the Politics of Past Violence* (Rutgers University Press 2018) (hereafter Sodaro, *Exhibiting Atrocity*) 32.

displayed at Tuol Sleng and, controversially, objects of art when they were part of an exhibition at Museum of Modern Art.[26]

Dependent, then, on the institution which comes to hold the object, the narrative that it will inform may vary widely. The multiple purposes that the one same object will serve in its relationship to genocide and the linking object categories that it will occupy are highly dependent on the narrative that a museum, gallery, or archive wishes to transmit. Memory institutions mobilize the objects deemed to represent the historical or political narrative of a genocide in order to give a physical shape to this narrative. The selected objects, removed from their original contexts, now stand not only in the context of a museum collection but also in the broader political context of the construction of the narrative of the genocide and the 'present' more generally.[27] For example, objects held by the British Museum stolen as part of the genocide of Aboriginal people in Australia are *not* mobilized in memory of genocide or even with this particular provenance recorded, because this is not yet the historical narrative that Britain wishes to tell. Conversely, the construction of history in memorial museums often takes place in political or national environments—as in Rwanda—where denying the genocide is a punishable crime,[28] or in Germany, where remembering the Holocaust has become deeply tied with German national identity.[29] In this way, GAMs are not only offering a mediated historical account decided within the confines of the museum itself, but are also telling a story about the national, civic, and political identity and direction of the nation in which the institution stands.

When encountered in a public institution, the links between the objects on display to the genocide from which they were collected may be either strengthened or severed. Add to this the connection between the object and its maker, original owner, and, indeed, the story of how it came to be in a museum, gallery, or archive. As James E Young, who was appointed to Findungskommission for Germany's national 'Memorial to Europe's Murdered Jews', points out, '[i]mplied in any museum's collection is that what you see is all there is to see, all that there ever was'.[30] The objects, how they are positioned, and the labels or descriptions attached to them, all influence how we understand (or not) a genocide from looking at the objects that once belonged to somebody who was murdered or suffered through that genocide.

[26] Williams Paul, 'Witnessing Genocide: Vigilance and Remembering at Tuol Sleng and Choeung Ek' (2004) 18 Holocaust and Genocide Studies 223.
[27] Sodaro, *Exhibiting Atrocity* (n 25) 183.
[28] Sodaro, *Exhibiting Atrocity* (n 25) 166–67.
[29] Lars Rensmann, 'Collective Guilt, National Identity, and Political Processes in Contemporary Germany' in R Nyla, R Branscombe, and Bertjan Doosje (eds), *Collective Guilt, International Perspectives* (CUP 2004)
[30] James E Young, *At Memory's Edge: After Images of the Holocaust in Contemporary Art and Architecture* (Yale University Press 2000) 179.

In encountering an object within the narrative shaped by the institution, I propose that there are two comprehensive categories which objects might occupy when encountered:

1. Affective objects
2. Stolen/disconnected objects.

An affective object is a personal item obtained by GAMs after genocide to remember the genocide and narrate a history. This might be an item of clothing or the diary of someone murdered through genocide. Meanwhile, a stolen/disconnected object is an object stolen through genocide and subsequently stored or displayed by museums primarily as an anthropological, cultural, archival, or scientific object, with little context given to its links to genocide. This object might be the artwork or woven basket produced by an artist and then stole by those who murdered her. It is to these two categories of institutional encountering that we now turn our attention.

Ways We Encounter Objects 1: Affective Objects

Affective objects are usually everyday objects recovered after genocide and used in collections to describe a particular aspect of the genocide. As with all the objects discussed in this chapter, affective objects were once the personal belongings of a person killed through genocide. These objects tend to be on display in memorial museums, and are usually on display because of their ability to resonate with visitors due to the familiarity or poignancy that they might hold for the visitor and the traces of the individual that they hold. Such objects are usually not primarily displayed for the anthropological, scientific, archival, or cultural interest they might hold, but specifically to illustrate and aid interpretation of the history of a genocide.

Affective objects might include the slightly faded family photos of victims of the genocide in Rwanda on display in the Kigali Genocide Memorial or the battered suitcases on display in the museum rooms of the former Auschwitz I concentration camp. The most well-known examples of affective objects are, like the suitcases, personal items seized at the moment of their owners' entrance into a concentration camp on display at Holocaust museums throughout the world.

The items that perhaps best describe the affective possibilities of personal objects once put on display, as well as forming what Landsberg calls 'the "aesthetic" of the Holocaust',[31] are the 4,000 shoes from Majdanek at the USHMM. These were pieces of leather made into shoes and then put to ordinary use by their owners. In

[31] Landsberg, *Prosthetic Memory* (n 15) 133

their use, the shoes have creased and show signs of wear. The shoes were removed from those to be killed, retained by the murderers, and then found by those who liberated the camps. As Landsberg, reflecting on her visit to the USHMM, writes:

> Standing in the room of shoes at the Holocaust Museum, I was struck not by the commodity-like seriality of these shoes but by their worn, lived individuality: a sandal, a cracked leather work shoe, a boot. Each shoe bears the trace of the absent body that lived and marked it.[32]

The meaning of these shoes radically shifted when they were kept, while their owners were murdered. Here, in the USHMM their meaning is modified again as they become both the objects that survived and stand-ins for the magnitude of genocide and the murdered individuals. They hold the traces of an event while still being physical, plastic, objects.

Affective objects, such as the 4,000 shoes, are displayed in genocide memory institutions for two key reasons:

1. The object can be understood universally and across time and place
2. The object has the potential to inspire historical imagination and feeling in a visitor.

I will briefly describe each of these possibilities, together with the interventions which allow these objects to become more than only 'things'. In its potential to be affective, an object must also hold the potential to be understood universally, with its original uses or purpose understood by the majority of visitors. This is important in ensuring that the history told by a museum, and described by the object, resonates with as many of its visitors as possible. For Michael Birenbaum, then project director of the USHMM, for example, this meant telling the history of the Holocaust 'in such a way that it would resonate not only with the survivor in New York and his children in Houston or San Francisco, but with a black leader from Atlanta, with a midwestern farmer, or a northeastern industrialist'.[33] The need for affective objects to resonate with all visitors means that this category of objects most usually includes objects that bear a functional similarity to those which visitors might be wearing or might use or encounter regularly. However, it might also include objects such as typewriters or a letter written in a language unknown to the visitor, which, though obsolete or unfamiliar, are broadly recognizable and also demonstrate a particular period (and the passage of time), place, or group of people.

[32] ibid 134.
[33] Michael Berenbaum, *After Tragedy and Triumph: Modern Jewish Thought and the American Experience* (CUP 1990) 20.

In the potential for an affective object to inspire historical imagination and feeling in a visitor, the visitor, as well as the institution in which the object is encountered, changes the original meaning of an object. When encountered in the context provided by the museum, the object is imbued with meanings that it did not hold when it acted as a functional object. Klaus Wehner describes this experience in his 2006 encounter with a tin dish from Ravensbrück at the Museum für Angewandte Kunst Frankfurt:

> The label informed me that the object was an important 'tool of survival' for Aenne Saekow, a Ravensbrück concentration camp inmate in 1945. I was disturbed by the thought that this very dish, which shows 'traces of use' that came into being through the handling of, thus direct contact with, the body of this tortured concentration camp inmate, who must have been at any moment an inch away from sudden violent death; that it was held, by her hands and touched her lips as she consumed life-preserving drink and food out of it, fighting to survive, surrounded by grime, blood and utterly depersonalising violence. Although no biological traces of food or lip imprints have survived on the dish itself, I know that such traces-have-been-there.[34]

Here, the object is no longer a tin dish. It is no longer simply a functional object or an aesthetic object. It is transformed into an affective object belonging to Aenne Saekow, whose suffering is imagined in this object. In encounters with objects such as this one, a feeling for the life (and the anguish) of the original owner of the object intervenes with the conceptual historical understanding of genocide provided by an object taken out of its original context, labelled, and placed on display. In this, an affective connection to an event that we ourselves did not experience is simulated.

However, the curatorial decision to describe genocide through these types of objects belonging to individuals killed in that genocide—together with the tendency to display them as a mass collection—has been the subject of criticism. In the tin dish, we meet Aenne Saekow only in the time that she was in Ravensbrück and only this period of her life and her suffering are imagined. The dish tells us nothing of who she was. After all, objects such as the dish and also the pile of shoes are also often those objects that were thought by those who carried out the genocide to hold more value than the person who used them in life. While such items allow an understanding of the magnitude of genocide and allow visitors to imagine the individuals murdered, they only allow the suffering and death of the former owner of the object to be remembered. Young writes of the display of such objects

[34] Klaus Wehner, 'Photography—Museum: On Posing, Imageness and the Punctum' in Sandra Dudley and Others (eds), *The Thing About Museums Objects and Experience, Representation and Contestation* (Routledge 2012) 87.

as the problem of using the objects retained by the murderers (the shoes, the hair, the glasses) to stand in for the entirety of what was lost in genocide:

> That a murdered people remains known in Holocaust museums anywhere by their scattered belongings and not by their spiritual works, that their lives should be recalled primarily through the images of their death, may be the ultimate travesty. These lives and the relationships between them are lost to the memory of ruins alone—and will be lost to subsequent generations who seek memory only in the rubble of the past. Indeed, by adopting such artifacts for their own memorial presentations, even the new museums in America and Europe risk perpetuating the very figures by which the killers themselves would have memorialized their Jewish victims.[35]

In the use of objects that elicit an affective response through an emphasis on the destruction and the magnitude, we must ask which narrative is privileged in the selection and arrangement of objects from genocide. In genocide memorial museums, though the former owners of these objects are too often remembered 'by the moment of their destruction',[36] it is the context given by a museum, gallery, or archive to affective objects that might serve to make possible memory of the life, and not only the death, of the owners of these objects.

At the Srebrenica-Potočari Memorial Room in Bosnia-Herzegovina, there are twenty showcases containing objects belonging to twenty men (twenty of more than 8,000) murdered in the Srebrenica genocide. Accompanying each showcase is a short text describing the man whose objects these are. As Olivera Simić, visiting the Memorial Room, writes, 'these personal affects provide a narrative to their lives, and rebuild the memory of what happened to Srebrenica and its people'.[37] The texts that accompany these objects are written by Emir Suljagić, himself a survivor and the author of a firsthand account of the Srebrenica genocide.[38] Suljagić spoke to Ed Vulliamy about the importance of telling the stories of the owners of these objects and their connections to others, instead of presenting them as an anonymous mass:

> When you tell someone that 10,000 people died, they cannot understand or imagine it. What I want to say is that these people were peasants, car mechanics or

[35] James E Young, *The Texture of Memory: Holocaust Memorials and Meaning* (Yale University Press 1993) (hereafter Young, *The Texture of Memory*) 133.

[36] ibid 133.

[37] Olivera Simić, 'Remembering, Visiting and Placing the Dead: Law, Authority and Genocide in Srebrenica' (2009) 13 Law Text Culture 278.

[38] Emir Suljagić, *Postcards From the Grave* (trans Lejla Haveric, Saqi Books 2005).

> masons. That they had daughters, mothers, that they leave someone behind; that a lot of people are hurt by this person's death.[39]

In this collection, the objects elicit affect, not for their connection to death, but to life. We can approach an understanding of the loss of the lives of these brothers, fathers and sons, rather than only the violence and magnitude of deaths. The objects in the Srebrenica-Potočari Memorial Room are recognizable as belonging to these individuals because of Suljagić's labels, which allow us to know something of who they were when they were alive. In this Room, people who were transformed into a mass by their killers are, for a moment, here restored. These objects take us to the time before death, the time of death, and this time now without them. The person is remembered through these items rather than repeating the effect of genocide, which treats people as a mass.

However, why is an affective response desirable from objects left behind at the end. Young, again, asks what response the display of such objects is hoping to elicit:

> What precisely does the sight of concentration-camp artifacts awaken in viewers? Historical knowledge? A sense of evidence? Revulsion, grief, pity, fear? That visitors respond more directly to objects than to verbalized concepts is clear. But beyond affect, what does our knowledge of these objects—a bent spoon, children's shoes, crusty old striped uniforms—have to do with our knowledge of historical events?[40]

When accompanied, as in the Srebrenica-Potočari Memorial Room, with thought-out explanatory or contextual text, perhaps the display of these objects can inform our knowledge of what was lost in genocide. However, in wondering what an object taken through genocide that does not inform our knowledge of that genocide might be, I turn now to those objects that Young, as cited earlier, might call their 'spiritual works'. These are not the 'scattered belongings' found and recovered at the end of a genocide, but are those precious objects whose presence in a museum or gallery is often part of the ongoing colonial-genocide and dispossession of a people. These objects include Aboriginal cultural materials stolen by force or plunder as part of the Australian colonial genocide and held in GAMs the world over. However, due to the context of their collection and subsequent display, these cultural works are rarely accompanied with the type of information or context that accompanies the everyday personal objects in the Srebrenica-Potočari Memorial Room, the tin dish from Ravensbrück, or the pile of shoes at the USHMM. It is to these stolen and disconnected objects that we now turn.

[39] In Ed Vulliamy, 'After the Massacre, a Homecoming' *The Guardian* (30 April 2005) <www.guardian.co.uk/weekend/story/0,,1472153,00.html> accessed 18 February 2019.

[40] Young, *The Texture of Memory* (n 35) 132.

Ways We Encounter Objects 2: Stolen and Disconnected Objects

The second category of objects from genocide found in GAMs are objects stolen and disconnected through colonial genocide. The personal and cultural belongings of people who were murdered, who were removed from family, or whose culture was destroyed by colonial genocide are in GAMs throughout the world. These personal objects include, for example, the shields, photographs, artworks, and letters taken[41] by colonial settlers (whether by exchange, barter, gift, or theft) and acquired by GAMs as part of the cultural genocide enacted by the British against First Nations peoples in Australia. It also includes their bodily remains. The storage, arrangement and display of these objects often make little or no reference to the genocide which facilitated their collection, disconnecting them from this history.

Cultural institutions in the west are linked to colonial genocide through the collections they hold and the way they decide to retain or exhibit these collections. National museums and galleries around Europe were primarily established during the enlightenment era; a time of building collections and colonies. The collections gathered largely supported colonial ideologies and were public displays of colonial expansion, supporting the empire's views of themselves as great exploring nations. The collection of these objects was facilitated by the genocide that accompanied colonization.

The genocide of Aboriginal peoples in Australia has included massacres, punitive killings, the forced removal of children, and dispossession from land, family, culture, and language. This genocide continues to have deep and pervasive impacts for Aboriginal people today with a generationally accumulated social and economic impact, a lack of political or community will to make reparations, an overrepresentation in the prison system, and a suicide rate that is at crisis level, far exceeding that of non-Aboriginal people, and on and on.[42] There are some 6,000 Aboriginal

[41] The ways in which objects were acquired from Aboriginal people by British colonists in this period may have been by gift, barter, exchange or other means. It is the context of the colonial genocide which facilitated this acquisition, by whichever means, with which I am interested here. For more information on this topic see: Isabel McBryde, '... To Establish a Commerce of this Sort': Cross Cultural Exchange at the Port Jackson Settlement' in John Hardy and Alan Frost (eds) *Studies from Terra Australis to Australia* (Australian Academy of the Humanities 1989) 169.

[42] For more information see: Judy Atkinson, *Trauma Trails, Recreating Song Lines: The Transgenerational Effects of Trauma in Indigenous Australia* (Spinifex Press 2002); Megan Davis and Marcia Langton (eds), *It's Our Country: Indigenous Arguments for Meaningful Constitutional Recognition and Reform* (Melbourne University Press 2016); Andrew Gunstone, 'Reconciliation, Reparations and Rights: Indigenous Australians and the Stolen Generations' in Corinne Lennox and Damien Short (eds), *Handbook of Indigenous Peoples' Rights* (Routledge 2016) 301 (hereafter Gunstone, 'Reconciliation, Reparations and Rights'; Human Rights and Equal Opportunity Commission, *Bringing Them Home: Report of the National Inquiry into the Separation of Aboriginal and Torres Strait Islander Children from their Families* (HREOC 1997); A Dirk Moses, *Genocide and Settler Society: Frontier Violence and Stolen Indigenous Children in Australian History* (Berghahn Books 2004); Bruce Pascoe, *Convincing Ground: Learning to Fall in Love with your Country* (Aboriginal Studies Press 2006); Irene Watson, 'Aboriginality and the Violence of Colonialism' (2009) 8 *Borderlands e-journal* <www.borderlands.net.au/vol8no1_2009/iwatson_aboriginality.pdf> accessed 1 June 2020.

and Torres Strait Islander artefacts held by the British Museum alone. In 2015, part of this collection returned to Australia as part of the *Encounters: Revealing stories of Aboriginal and Torres Strait Islander objects from the British Museum* exhibition at the National Museum Australia in Canberra. Twenty of the objects on display were collected by Robert Christison on his Lammermoor station property and donated to the British Museum in 1901.[43] Even if acquired as gifts or as exchange and even if Christison had good relations with the people who lived on what he had taken as his land, it is unavoidable that these objects could only be 'collected' through the context of colonial genocide, enacted against Aboriginal Australians since the arrival of the First Fleet in 1788 and the subsequent colonial settlement of Australia. As Young, writing of objects in Holocaust museums though deeply relevant here, summarizes, 'it was destruction itself that caused the collection in this museum to come into being. Otherwise, these objects would all belong to living, breathing families; they would be installed in private homes, not the exhibition spaces of a museum'.[44]

How objects taken from the Australian genocide are encountered through the (polysemic) *Encounters* exhibition is, as with affective objects, largely dependent on the context provided by the museum. As noted above, one of the ways that a museum, gallery or archive provides context is through the provenancing of objects. One of the items that returned to Australia during *Encounters* was the Gweagal Shield (hereafter 'the Shield'), an object which, through its provenancing, tells us how objects stolen from genocide can inform our knowledge of genocide when we encounter them in an institution.

The entry in the British Museum catalogue for the Shield, which is also called 'the Bark Shield of Botany Bay', describes it as follows:

> Shield, undecorated, made of bark and wood. Elongated, oval form, with pointed ends, and slightly convex. Bark has rough surface and appears blackened in places with traces of white kaolin on outer surface. Thin handle attached vertically to the reverse of the shield at centre. Both shield and handle are made of red mangrove (Rhizophora stylosa). Pierced hole near centre, with ragged edges, and smaller hole near one end.[45]

The catalogue entry also offers the place in which the Shield was likely found or acquired (Botany Bay) and where it was produced ('New South Wales East coast,

[43] National Museum Australia, 'The Objects Being Borrowed by the National Museum of Australia for *Encounters: Revealing Stories of Aboriginal and Torres Strait Islander Objects* from the British Museum' (National Museum Australia, 20 September 2015) <https://www.nma.gov.au/__data/assets/pdf_file/0008/466127/Encounters-exhibition-international-loans-web.pdf> accessed 2 June 2020.

[44] James E Young, *The Stages of Memory: Reflections on Memorial Art, Loss, and the Spaces Between* (University of Massachusetts Press 2016) 88.

[45] British Museum, 'Shield' (British Museum, nd) <www.britishmuseum.org/research/collection_online/collection_object_details.aspx?objectId=490919&partId=1> accessed 2 December 2018.

likely in an area where red mangrove grows'). We are also told who took the Shield from the people who made and used the Shield ('found/acquired' in Botany Bay, thought to be during Captain Cook's first voyage to Australia on 29 April 1770) and the exhibitions in which the Shield has been displayed (five since 1987). The catalogue entry also notes that the Shield was found unregistered in the museum's collection in 1978, at which point it was assigned a Q number (Q.839), which is given to objects for which the method of acquisition is unknown. From this information, we have a material description of the Shield and a history of the object since it was taken from Australia and acquired by the Museum. However, this object is decontextualized from its original context in the lack of information collected about the creation and origins of the object. Also disconnected from these objects was cultural knowledge on how an object was (and was not) to be used. As Sentance writes:

> [G]alleries, libraries, archives and museums did not capture contextual information about collections. This could be because a lot of cultural heritage ends in collections because it was recorded by a white European or was stolen or taken without further enquiry about the knowledge that surrounds the cultural heritage.[46]

The British Museum, in its possession of the Shield, has assumed the final say on decisions made about the object and how claims will be acted upon. Decisions made by the British Museum about the fate of this object, together with the protection of the object from seizure when it is on loan, are informed by the British Museum Act 1962 and the Australian Protection of Cultural Objects on Loan Act 2013.[47] Some of the provenance information available on the Shield described above is the result of recent work undertaken following a plea for repatriation from a Gweagal man, Rodney Kelly.[48] The British Museum acted to re-establish the provenance of the Shield through a process including X-ray fluorescence testing (to search for the lead from bullets) and wood identification. Following this, the museum claimed that this particular shield could no longer be definitively said to have been collected at Botany Bay.[49] We might add a rejoinder to this, that nor was the Shield collected in Britain.

[46] Nathan Sentance, 'The Paternalistic Nature of Collecting' Archival Decolonist (12 June 2017) <archivaldecolonist.com/2017/06/12/the-paternalistic-nature-of-collecting/ 2017> accessed 20 October 2018.

[47] The British Museum Act 1963, in section 5c on the disposal of objects, states that the Trustees of the museum can sell, exchange, give away or otherwise dispose of an object if it is deemed unfit to be retained, as long as this will not be detrimental to the interest of students. The Australian 2013 Protection of Cultural Objects on Loan Act grants an object immunity from suit and seizure.

[48] Maria Nugent and Gaye Sculthorpe, 'A Shield Loaded with History: Encounters, Objects and Exhibitions' (2018) 49 Australian Historical Studies 28 (hereafter Nugent and Sculthorpe, 'A Shield Loaded with History'); Sarah Keenan, 'How the British Museum Changed its Story About the Gweagal Shield' ACRAWSA (18 May 2018) <acrawsa.org.au/2018/05/18/how-the-british-museum-changed-its-story-about-the-gweagal-shield/> accessed 1 June 2020.

[49] ibid.

What it means to encounter objects like the Shield in the context of the museum's ongoing assumed ownership is summarized by Yidindji woman and direct descendent of Ye-i-nie, Henrietta Fourmile Marrie, who describes her encounter with objects that belonged to Ye-i-nie during the *Encounters* exhibition:

> when I walk through that corridor and have a look at the many items which have been brought here, and particularly when I stand in front of the section of the Yidindji people and see my grandfather's emblems right there in front of me and the strong spiritual connection which I have with that ... and knowing that in a few weeks' time they will be gone. It came this far, his spirit ... the sweat that he made ... [is] within those items, that spirit had returned home ... for short while and in two weeks['] time that spirit will be gone again. And I feel that when I walk past him – it is so heavy ... we will miss him, again.[50]

The provenance information provided about the Shield, alongside the objects described by Fourmile Marrie, and the legal context of the British Museum's ongoing possession of such objects does not tell us anything about the context of colonial genocide which facilitated the taking of these objects or about their value to Aboriginal Australians. Instead what we learn continues to be deeply subjective in its privileging of a particular type of knowledge and assumption of the right to retention that is not so different to the colonial logic of value that informed the taking of this object, thousands of others like it, as well as the land of Australia itself.[51] Hans Booms, writing of archives specifically, though also applicable to museums, proposed a means of countering this problem of subjectivity in provenancing. He maintained that the value of objects be determined by consultation with the society in which they circulated and were created, for:

> only the society from which the material originated and for whose sake it is to be preserved can provide archivists with the necessary tools to assess the conceptions by which they bring the past into the present.[52]

Indeed, as Maria Nugent and Gaye Sculthorpe, in their presentation of the reappraisal of this object, point out '(m)aterial analysis only takes us so far'.[53] What

[50] In Paul Daley, 'Indigenous Treasures, Briefly on Loan to Australia, are About to be Taken Away—Again' *The Guardian* (22 March 2016) <www.theguardian.com/australia-news/postcolonial-blog/2016/mar/22/indigenous-treasures-briefly-on-loan-to-australia-are-about-to-be-taken-away-again> accessed 1 June 2020.

[51] See Henrietta Fourmile, 'Who Owns the Past? Aborigines as Captives of the Archives' (1989) 13 Aboriginal History 1; Aileen Moreton-Robinson, 'The Possessive Logic of Patriarchal White Sovereignty: The High Court and the Yorta Yorta Decision' (2004) 3 Borderlands e-journal <www.borderlands.net.au/vol3no2_2004/moreton_possessive.htm> accessed 1 June 2020.

[52] Hans Booms, 'Society and the Formation of a Documentary Heritage: Issues in the Appraisal of Archival Sources' (1987) 24 Archivaria 104.

[53] Nugent and Sculthorpe, 'A Shield Loaded with History' (n 47) 40.

we know about the material facts of the object do not allow us to know its connection to culture or its history. However, its materiality—the physical presence of the Shield—presents the opportunity for a different way of encountering this object. Schlunke, writing of the Shield, notes that objects such as this—active objects of defence—were often missing from depictions of Cook's arrival in Australia.[54] However, here it is in the museum. Inerasable in its material presence:

> The Bark Shield of Botany Bay, when materially remembered, can be seen as productive of the assemblage that connects the tree from which it was made (red mangrove), the Indigenous hands that shaped and then used it, the rock, marsh and air it moved along at Botany Bay, to the hands that picked it up, stored it, sold it and finally displayed it. This shield therefore gathers to it both the colonial and those times and activities that continue beyond and alongside the colonial – that is the actions, existence and ongoing vitality of Indigenous Australia. Material remembering gets us to reorganize what it is to remember, and so experience, the way in which we make ourselves up as people and as nations with things that become through their effects forces of becoming and belonging.[55]

These 'forces of becoming and belonging' present an opportunity to reorganize how objects stolen through genocide are encountered in GAMs. In remembering with these objects, we have the opportunity, through their materiality, to understand not just their physical description or history since acquisition, but questions of *before*. In its materiality, we must wonder who made this Shield and how an object of defence from 'an area where red mangrove grows' came to be 'found/acquired' and placed in a British museum. Further, in the plea for repatriation of the Shield by Kelly, we can encounter this Shield and meet something of its unbroken connection to Country, while wondering what is gained by a museum's retention of this object.

One way in which museums and galleries that hold stolen or disconnected objects are called to recognize the potential of Schlunke's 'forces of becoming and belonging' is through efforts to decolonize collections and institutions, which I define here as a shift from an imperialist approach to one that takes into account and engages with first nations peoples.[56]

[54] Katrina Schlunke, 'One Strange Colonial Thing: Material Remembering and the Bark Shield of Botany Bay' (2013) 27 Continuum 18.

[55] ibid 27.

[56] Linda Tuhiwai Smith, *Decolonizing Methodologies: Research and Indigenous Peoples* (2nd edn, Zed Books 2012); Jodi A Byrd, *The Transit of Empire: Indigenous Critiques of Colonialism* (University of Minnesota Press 2011).

Decolonization and Return: Recent Shifts

In recent years, there have been some critical shifts in how GAMs are changing how they think about access to objects taken during genocide. As observed in the introduction to this chapter, these shifts include the understanding of how an object can be used to redress past trauma and how memory institutions might be decolonized. Objects can be used by GAMs to redress past trauma in three main ways: reparations, access, and repatriation.

Firstly, in mobilizing objects for reparations, objects once used to facilitate genocide are mobilized to address transgenerational trauma and redress losses suffered. Sue McKemmish, Shannon Faulkhead and Lynette Russell write of this role that archives can play:

> In Australia, there is, however, recognition of a duality to these records in that, whilst they have in the past been instruments of oppression and the construction of a negative view of Australian Indigeneity, they can in the present and future play an important reconciling role in recovering identity and memory, reuniting families, seeking redress, and in the reconciliation process between Indigenous and non-Indigenous Australians.[57]

As part of a research project into practices of withholding wages from Aboriginal people living on missions and reserves in the nineteenth and twentieth centuries in Australia (Stolen Wages), I conducted archival research in the archives of the Victorian Government Reserves and Mission Stations.[58] Stolen Wages is the term given to the control of the wages earned by and owed to Indigenous people by the Australian government and agencies during the nineteenth and twentieth centuries. The control (withholding, inequality, and theft) of wages was part of the broader Australian history of protectionism, which also included the forced removal of Aboriginal and Torres Strait Islander children from their families (the Stolen Generations). These archives contain many objects that were not only used to withhold wages but to dispossess Aboriginal people from family and country: memorandums, letters, ledgers, and transcripts, all documenting the various decisions made about Aboriginal people and how they would live by colonial settlers. Through research such the Stolen Wages project, these archival records transform from ledgers of wages paid for planting potatoes and stripping wattle bark into documents that might instead be used to seek redress and reparation.

[57] McKemmish *et al*, 'Distrust in the Archive' (n 3) 218.

[58] Gunstone, 'Reconciliation, Reparations and Rights' (n 41) 301; Andrew Gunstone and Sadie Heckenberg, *The Government Owes a Lot of Money to Our People: A History of Indigenous Stolen Wages in Victoria* (Australian Scholarly Publishing 2009).

Secondly, there is the decision by memory institutions to provide access to objects by the communities from which they were stolen. In her article on stolen art, Kemi Alemoru cites Janet Browne, the African Caribbean Officer at the V&A, on the question of loaning items plundered from Ethiopia during an expedition by the British army, when their return is what is desired:

> It [the offer of a loan] wasn't to shut anybody up. It was to say: 'Well we kind of agree with you and this is what we can do. If you want it, you can put it on display in Ethiopia so people can see it in an institution and continue to campaign for restitution . . . It's not that we as a team don't empathise with Ethiopia. But we can't just pack it up in a box and then give it back because we'd all be sacked. However, we can give long loans where it would be years before we saw the items again.[59]

Though not a return of objects, The *Encounters* exhibition described above is a good example of how museums provide access. There was engagement and consultation with the twenty-five communities from around Australia from which these objects may have originated in order to inform both the British Museum and the National Museum Australia of any sensitivities in the display of objects.[60] There was also an effort made in Australia to ensure access to the exhibition by Aboriginal people. However, providing access through major institutions in capital cities is not truly accessible to most. As Maorigirljojo on Twitter, writing about the 2018 *Oceania* exhibition at the Royal Academy of Arts in London, asks, 'How do you resolve availability of ancestral belongings when many people for which these taonga[61] belong suffer from social, financial and cultural damage caused from the process that took the objects in the first place?'[62]

Thirdly, in redressing the effects of cultural genocide, the repatriation of objects may be requested by the original owners, as with the plea for the repatriation of the Gweagal shield by Kelly. For the last few decades there have been increasing calls from communities to return stolen objects, such as the 2018 call from the Governor of Rapa Nui for the British Museum to return Hoa Hakananai'a ('lost or stolen friend'), a large stone moai statue taken from Rapa Nui by the British during the HMS Topaze expedition in 1868.[63] Examples of the repatriation of

59 In Kemi Alemoru, 'You Can Only Hide the Histories of Stolen art for So Long' (2018) 27 *gal-dem* <gal-dem.com/you-can-only-hide-the-histories-of-stolen-art-for-so-long/> accessed 1 June 2020).

60 Special Broadcasting Service (SBS), 'First Nations Artifacts on Loan for Encounters Exhibition' *SBS* <www.sbs.com.au/yourlanguage/aboriginal/en/audiotrack/first-nations-artifacts-loan-encounters-exhibition> accessed 1 February 2019.

61 Taonga Tūturu are treasured objects of significance to Māori culture, history, or society that have been lost or found.

62 Maorigirljojo (@maorigirljojo), 'How do you resolve available of ancestral belongings . . . ' *Twitter* (7 November 2018 12.55am) <twitter.com/maorigirljojo/status/1060251342529331206> accessed 12 November 2018.

63 British Museum, 'Hoa Hakananai'a (Lost or Stolen Friend)/Moai (Ancestor Figure)' (British Museum, nd) <www.britishmuseum.org/research/collection_online/collection_object_details.aspx?objectId=512302&partId=1> accessed 20 October 2018.

personal objects include the repatriation of a Ghost Dance Shirt to the South Dakota Historical Society by Glasgow City Council in 1999 and the existence of laws such as the 1990 Native American Graves Protection and Repatriation Act, which compels US museums to return objects and remains to their communities.[64] Sometimes, in the case of human remains in particular, offers to repatriate have been made by the institution itself. For example, the bodily remains of Aboriginal people (Ancestral Remains) have been held by European museums since the early days of colonial Australia.[65] When European university collections and museums, in recent years, offered to return some of these remains, little or incorrect information was attached to these people, and the communities to which they were to be returned had to be determined. Deanne Hanchant was Archival Research on the National Skeletal Provenancing Project between 1995 and 1997. This Project, which was based at the South Australian Museum, sought to determine the provenance of Ancestral Remains so that they might be returned to their community for reburial. Hanchant reflected on the necessity for the correct provenancing of Ancestral Remains: '[R]emains listed as being from Nukunu, South Australia, were found actually to have come from an unknown locality in the Northern Territory. While disappointing, the results … ensure that remains are not returned to the wrong community and thus cause unnecessary distress'.[66]

Once objects or remains are provenanced, we are left with questions of ownership versus possession and whether the site of an institution (either the one which holds the stolen object or the one to which unprovenanced objects may be sent for storage) is the proper house for these objects. Ultimately, we are left with the question of how to do the right thing by these objects and these people, and, as seen by the example of the Gweagal shield, how an institution should act once an object has been correctly provenanced.

Beyond the use of objects to redress past trauma, actions aimed at 'decolonizing' memory institutions, in particular, have also been gaining momentum of late. In terms of objects from genocide—and particularly those stolen through genocide—these shifts broadly involve calling for the arrangement and description of objects to correctly reflect their origins and the people from whom they

[64] Neil Curtis, 'Repatriation from Scottish Museums: Learning from NAGPRA' (2010) 33 Museum Anthropology 234.

[65] The remains of these people were largely taken for racialized anthropological and scientific research. See Turnbull, *Science, Museums and Collecting* (n 4); Paul Turnbull, 'Managing and Mapping the History of Collecting Indigenous Human Remains' (2016) 65 The Australian Library Journal 203; Cressida Fforde, 'From Edinburgh University to the Ngarrindjeri Nation, South Australia' (2009) 51 Museum International 41; Cressida Fforde, Jane Hubert, and Paul Turnbull (eds), *The Dead and Their Possessions: Repatriation in Principle, Policy and Practice* (Routledge 2002).

[66] Deanne Hanchant, 'Practicalities in the Return of Remains: The Importance of Provenance and the Question of Unprovenanced Remains' in Cressida Fforde, Jane Hubert, and Paul Turnbull (eds), *The Dead and their Possessions: Repatriation in Principle, Policy and Practice* (Routledge 2002) 312.

were taken and the meaningful involvement of curators who represent the cultural groups from which objects come.[67]

Simply changing the context in which objects are arranged or described is not enough. For example, when the Africa Museum, Belgium reopened in December 2018, having worked to transform a previously pro-colonialist display into a critique of Belgium's colonial genocide in what is today the Democratic Republic of Congo. However, what was found by visitors to the newly reopened museum, such as cultural historian Angela Stienne, was that objects that 'used to be on display for colonial propaganda … now … are on display with no context'.[68] While removing context altogether (and yet keeping objects on display) does not decolonize the museum, nor does providing context always equal an action that demonstrates a moving forward. For example, Alice Procter, who leads 'Uncomfortable Art' tours of museums and galleries in the UK, writes of the labelling of a crocodile reliquary at the Oceania exhibition at the Royal Academy of Arts in London: 'Ah yes a reliquary from Porapora, PNG, which is meant to *only be seen by people with appropriate initiation* LOVE TO PUT SOMETHING WITH CEREMONY AND PROTOCOLS ON OPEN DISPLAY AND THEN TELL EVERYONE IM DISREGARDING CEREMONY AND PROTOCOL'.[69] Here, though information about the context of an object is provided, the knowledge about objects is disconnected from the actions of their display.

Often, efforts by museums to decolonize themselves are viewed as tokenistic. For example, when a set of major British museums announced that they would be working to reassess the provenance of their colonial objects,[70] Procter pointed out that 'museums are colonial institutions, I'll believe this transformation when I see it, I'm glad this is a start but there's a big difference between "yikes we better do some research" and actually refiguring displays/repatriating objects'.[71]

There are, however, encouraging examples. Positive decolonising actions within memory institutions include 'First Peoples', the Australian Museums and Galleries Association ten-year Indigenous Roadmap project launched in 2017, which seeks to address the involvement and representation of and interaction with Aboriginal peoples in Australian museums and galleries, with a particular emphasis on two

[67] Elisa Schoenberger. 'What Does it Mean to Decolonize a Museum' *MuseumNext* (February 2019) <www.museumnext.com/2019/02/what-does-it-mean-to-decolonize-a-museum/> accessed 1 June 2020.

[68] Angela Stienne (@Angela_stienne), 'The first room you see … ' *Twitter* (16 February 2019 5.50PM) <twitter.com/Angela_stienne/status/1096746161657077760 > accessed 18 February 2019.

[69] Alice Procter (@aaprocter), 'Ah yes a reliquary from Porapora, PNG … ' *Twitter* (4 December 2018 6.18PM) <twitter.com/aaprocter/status/1069936462563561473> accessed 10 December 2018 (emphasis in original).

[70] Hannah Furness, 'UK Museums Task Staff with Identifying 'Stolen' Colonial Collections' *The Telegraph* (1 January 2019) <www.telegraph.co.uk/news/2019/01/01/uk-museums-task-staff-identifying-stolen-colonial-collections/> accessed 1 June 2020.

[71] Alice Procter (@aaprocter), 'Museums are colonial institutions … ' *Twitter* (3 January 2019 7.12PM). <twitter.com/aaprocter/status/1080821687703269376> accessed 5 January 2019

way caretaking of cultural material.[72] Another examples is the 2018 The Past is Now exhibition at the Birmingham Museum and Art Gallery ('BMAG') that aimed to reclaim and subvert the colonial narrative that surrounds British Colonial objects on display in British museums through a co-curated mobilisation of BMAG's collection to describe the colonial history of Birmingham and its ongoing impacts together with decolonial narratives.[73] With these shifts, we can not only emphasize how these personal objects came to be collected but can work to dismantle and reconsider the interpretation and presentation of objects and to better understand what stories are not being told. As Sumaya Kassim, one of the curators of The Past is Now, writes: 'And when I walked into the exhibition gallery, it was undeniably moving: objects are properly contextualized as souvenirs of traumatic histories. And those histories are narrativized from our perspective.'[74]

Conclusion

Whether directly mobilized in memory of genocide or disconnected from their history as objects taken through genocide, the material presence of personal objects that remain from genocide persists, traversing time and space. I end here, however, with an absence. With the fact that what so often remains after genocide, beyond the piles of shoes from Majdanek at the USHMM and the Gweagal shield disconnected from Country at the British Museum, is a loss from which there is nothing to recover.

What is held by the museum, gallery, or archive is the material object that has been left behind, collected, stolen, or retained. What has been lost through genocide is not capturable through physical, labelled artefacts, nor chronologically arranged or thematically grouped objects. However, something else is represented and held by the material object. What we find in these material objects is that they have arrived here, from them to us, that they are *still* here, and that they are what remains when nothing remains.

This speaks to the increasing potential for emphasizing how these personal objects came into collections while contributing to the work of reconsidering and dismantling the retention or display of personal objects that reproduces the trauma of genocide. It is through their materiality and their physical persistence that these

[72] Terri Janke, *First Peoples: A Roadmap for Enhancing Indigenous Engagement in Museums and Galleries* (Australian Museums and Galleries Association 2018).

[73] Birmingham Museum and Art Gallery, 'The Past is Now: Birmingham and the British Empire' (*BMAG*, 12 December 2017) <https://www.birminghammuseums.org.uk/bmag/whats-on/the-past-is-now-birmingham-and-the-british-empire> accessed 3 March 2019.

[74] Sumaya Kassim, 'The Museum will not be Decolonised' *Media Diversified* (15 November 2017) <mediadiversified.org/2017/11/15/the-museum-will-not-be-decolonised> accessed 1 June 2020.

objects travel from the time before the genocide, through the event, to us here now in the present moment of postgenocide.

The materiality of the objects and their display in a GAM allows the production of a relationship between the object and the visitor looking at the object. They are at once familiar, not so different from the shoes that we are wearing or the objects we continue to make, and come to us from before. We imagine what it is like to hold and to use the objects and, in so doing, we can imagine something of their original owner as something of that owner travels with the object. In these objects—and in stolen objects disconnected from Country in particular—we find an unbroken connection that has the potential to shift how we can share stories that help us to understand the past and how we might now tell, take care of, and hold these material stories.

10

Indigeneity, Memory, and Postgenocide in Guatemala

The Stillness Power of Local Archives*

Marcia Esparza

Introduction

The existing genocide scholarship has paid insufficient attention to Indigenous peoples worldwide, and in particular to the Indigenous communities of Latin America, an area of research that continues to be overlooked and under-researched. This contribution dwells on Maya Indigenous communities of Guatemala with the aim of shedding light on some aspects of their lived experiences in the course of the civil war (1960–1996) and the genocide in its mist (1981–1983), and how those experiences permutate and affect Mayan efforts to (re)constitute and (re)interpret knowledge of state violence and genocide in their aftermath. Specifically, this chapter highlights the importance of preservation of, and access to, local human rights archives which provide an invaluable source of primary material, which coupled with community testimonies of Indigenous resistance to collaboration in state security forces aiding violence and genocide, elucidate some dynamics of genocide and its aftermath that are rarely examined. Indeed, few studies have focused on the lack of preservation of Indigenous human rights archives in Latin America in the aftermath of Cold War genocide and state-sanctioned violence. Yet, in light of the long tradition of Indigenous people's oral history—passing cultural and political knowledge down from ancestors—the archives are of fundamental importance to preserve Indigenous collective memory of war and genocide.[1]

* I would like to acknowledge the invaluable trustful relationship I cherish with Maya-K'iché human rights activists Angelica Macario, 'don Antonio', Candelaria Pixcar—a survivor of one of the early 1980s Chontolá community massacre, and non-Maya Amilcar Mendéz whom have been pivotal in gaining knowledge about Cold War local Indigenous archives. I thank Samuel Neylon for reading a draft of this chapter.

[1] In a recent report, the United Nations Department of Economic and Social Affairs (2017, chapter IV) acknowledged that—based on 2010 census data—the Indigenous Latin American population was approximately 45.3 million. This population represents 826 different Indigenous people or communities, and in addition, 200 other communities are estimated to be living in voluntary isolation. See United Nations Economic Commission for Latin America and the Caribbean, <https://www.cepal.org/en/infographics/indigenous-peoples-latin-america> accessed 6 July 2020.

Marcia Esparza, *Indigeneity, Memory, and Postgenocide in Guatemala* In: *Postgenocide*. Edited by: Klejda Mulaj, Oxford University Press (2021). © The Several Contributors. DOI: 10.1093/oso/9780192895189.003.0010

The long aftermath in the region has been marked by the deepening of neo-liberal economic and cultural projects, the revival of militaristic rhetoric criminalizing left-wing political dissent, and a reinvigoration of militaristic and national security practices.[2] Often treated separately, the rise of global and local neo-liberalism is intimately intertwined with the militaristic and repressive Cold War legacies which involve the ongoing squelching of trade unions and student and Indigenous peasant and human rights organizations. But what exactly is the 'aftermath' of genocide? For Nicole Rafter, 'Just as genocide itself is a process, not an event, so too are its ending processes fuzzy endings [with] ragged conclusions.'[3] In fact, there can be multiple 'aftermaths' after massacres, genocide, and wars, and often, these three overlap and fuel each other's legacies. This uncertainty about the end of episodes of extreme forms of violence has been overlooked by Transitional Justice and peace scholars, who emphasize the significance of the signing of the peace accords in inaugurating ill-perceived 'democratic' eras, and as evidence of the end of state violence in the region (such as the more recent case in Colombia, and in Central America more generally).[4]

Scholars focusing on Latin America have overlooked the ways that local Indigenous archives are threatened by old repressive state structures which have been resurrected, and often only superficially restructured, in the aftermath of genocide.[5] Rather than examining in-depth how legacies of militarization are perpetuated in the aftermath period, researchers have all too readily celebrated the end of wars. Therefore, long-term repercussions of state sanctioned violence on local Indigenous localities, and their resistance to it, remain to-date inadequately examined. Local Indigenous human rights archives, which are created and maintained by local communities independent from national collecting institutions,

[2] For studies on Latin American Genocides see: Ernesto Verdeja, *Unchopping a Tree: Reconciliation in the Aftermath of Political Violence* (Temple University Press 2009); Daniel Feierstein, *Genocide as a Social Practice: Reorganizing Society under the Nazis and Argentina's Military Juntas* (New Brunswick, NJ: Rutgers University 2014); Marcia Esparza, Henry R Huttenbach, and Daniel Feierstein, *State Violence and Genocide in Latin America: The Cold War Years* (Routledge 2010); Marcia Esparza, *Silenced Communities. Legacies of Militarization and Militarism in a Rural Guatemalan Town* (New York: Berghahn Books 2017); Beatriz Manz, *Paradise in Ashes: A Guatemalan Journey of Courage, Terror and Hope* (Berkeley: University of California Press 2005); Carlotta McAllister and Diane M Nelson (eds), *War by Other Means: Aftermath in Post-Genocide Guatemala* (Duke University Press 2013).

[3] Nicole Rafter, *The Crime of All Crimes: Toward a Criminology of Genocide* (New York University Press 2016), especially Chapter 8, 'How Do Genocides End? Do They End? The Guatemalan Genocide, 1981-1983', 181 (hereafter Rafter, *The Crime of All Crimes*).

[4] Andrei Gomez-Suarez, 'Perpetrator Blocs, Genocidal Mentalities and Geographies: The Destruction of the Union Patriotica in Colombia and its Lessons for Genocide Studies' (2007) 9(4) Journal of Genocide Research 637–60.

[5] Transitional Justice refers to a broad range of approaches adopted in the aftermath of intra- or inter-state violence in pursuit of accountability for past atrocities, such as: Criminal Tribunals; Truth and Reconciliation Commissions; Disarmament, Demobilization and Reintegration ('DDR'); and Restorative Justice programmes. For a critical appraisal of the Transitional Justice field, see Nina Schneider and Marcia Esparza, *Legacies of State Violence and Transitional Justice in Latin America: A Janus-Faced Paradigm?* (Lexington Books 2015).

museums, and libraries, remain an ignored and hidden archival treasure in contrast with national museums and other national sites of memory. As suggested by archivists, '[c]ommunity archives are powerful forces in communities historically excluded from more formal and well established institutions'.[6]

The term 'human rights archives' includes:

> bureaucratic records that were created during the abuse itself ... created by human rights activists and lawyers after the fact for use in trials, tribunals, and truth commissions; stories recorded by survivors, victims' family members and communities to memorialize the dead and forge collective memory of past injustice; and, increasingly, forensic evidence such as DNA samples ... that establish scientific facts about large-scale violence.[7]

While definitions of community are contextual and shifting, Andrew Flinn and Others defined community as 'any manner of people who come together and present themselves as such'. Moreover, a "community archive' is the product of their attempts to document the history of their commonality'.[8] For archival studies scholars 'human rights archives are always in some degree shaped by the historical and political context in which they emerge and that conflicts over matters of content, mandate, and rules of access, are virtually inevitable'.[9] In the aftermath of genocide and war in Guatemala, for example, powerful forces worked 'to hide and deny their participation in the violence and oppression'.[10]

This chapter highlights the value of local human rights archives to subvert the dominant narratives which are established in the aftermath of peace agreements, and which are memorialized in the official archives. These local community archives shed light on several key genocide and postgenocide dynamics. First, community archives reveal how official denunciation of atrocities often takes place *after* the worst years of state violence have significantly eliminated widespread political opposition leadership. Second, local Indigenous human rights archives help tear down deeply entrenched national and militaristic narratives embedded in Cold War counterinsurgency discourses and practices. These contradictory narratives represented, and continue to represent, the army as the guardian and saviour of communities from communism, when in fact the army was brutally

[6] Michelle Caswell, Marika Cifor, and Mario H Ramirez, '"To Suddenly Discover Yourself Existing": Uncovering the Impact of Community Archives' (2016) 79 The American Archivist 56.

[7] Michelle Caswell, 'Defining Human Rights Archives: Introduction to the Special Double Issue on Archives and Human Rights' (2014) 14 Archival Science 207.

[8] Andrew Flinn, Mary Stevens, and Elizabeth Shepherd, 'Whose Memories, Whose Archives? Independent Community Archives, Autonomy, and the Mainstream' (2009) 9 Archival Science 71–86.

[9] Geoffrey Robinson, 'Break the Rules, Save the Records: Human Rights Archives and the Search for Justice in East Timor' (2014) 14 Archival Science 323, 325.

[10] The Human Rights Defenders Project, <https://defendersproject.org/2020/02/memory-at-risk> accessed 6 July 2020.

assaulting those very communities. Third, local community human rights archives are important to preserve because they shed light on the *ongoing* effects of genocidal violence in its early and long-term aftermath. Indeed, the functions of archives help drive the dynamic highlighted in the Introduction to this book: 'the capacity of the genocide violence for communication and for being a generative force, a mechanism for change',[11] in the context of survival. Fourth, local archives are crucial resources in challenging and decolonizing the official narratives the non-Indigenous state uses to dehumanize Indigenous peoples. As Martine Louise Hawkes discusses in this volume, 'the personal objects of people murdered through genocide and subsequently displayed in galleries, museum, and archives ... are objects of identity, memory, and forgetting'.[12] I argue, however, that Indigenous human rights archives not only memorialize the dead, but they also document organized collective resistance to genocide and its lingering legacies. In the case of El Salvador, for instance, anthropologist Robin Maria De Lugan argues in her book *Reimagining National Belonging* that local museums make Indigenous culture the basis for their efforts to contrast states' rhetoric of an 'homogenous national population influenced by indigeneity but that did not recognize ethnic and racial minority subpopulations'.[13]

One notable exception has been the 2005 discovery and subsequent preservation of the National Police Archives ('AHPN'). A fire inside an abandoned and dilapidated warehouse sparked a local and international investigation into the discovery of stacks of millions of decaying police records documenting the torture and whereabouts of victims found at the detention centre known as *la isla*, or 'the Island'.[14] This chapter sheds light on the importance of locating, preserving, cataloguing, digitizing, and give public access to local Indigenous human rights archives for the purposes of locating knowledge about past state violence and genocide against Indigenous Peoples.

Scholars have called the silence generated from hidden archives 'symbolic annihilation of the community it serves'.[15] This 'symbolic annihilation' and implicit erasures in archives occur, as Michel-Rolph Trouillot suggests, as part and parcel of the four major stages in 'which silences enter the process of historical production' in various ways: the creation of sources, the creation of archives, the assembling of

[11] Klejda Mulaj, in this volume, 'Introduction: Living with Permutations of Genocide Harm' 2.

[12] Martine Louise Hawkes, Chapter 9 in this volume, 'Memory, Identity, and Possession: Personal Objects from Genocide in Galleries, Museums and Archives' 206 (hereafter Hawkes, 'Memory').

[13] Robin Maria DeLugan, *Reimagining National Belonging. Post-Civil War El Salvador in a Global Context* (The University of Arizona Press 2012) 105. For a discussion of the meaning of Indigeneity, see Francesca Merlan 'Indigeneity: Global and Local' (2009) Current Anthropology 50 (3), 303–33.

[14] In 2018, Gustavo Meoño, AHPN Director was terminated by the Culture Ministry and the Guatemalan office of the United Nations Development Programme ('UNDP')—charged with administering international donations to the AHPN. Subsequently, budget and personnel cuts to the archive were made.

[15] Caswell and Others, 'To Suddenly Discover Yourself Existing' (n 6) 56–81.

narratives, and the creation of formal history.[16] The present chapter draws attention to the ongoing process of recovery and preservation of human rights material belonging to the Maya-K'iché human rights archives, the Runujel Junam Council of Ethnic Communities ('CERJ') ('Runujel Junam' meaning 'We are all Equal') that publicly emerged in the province of El Quiché in 1988. By examining Phase I, the step-by-step efforts to rescue and preserve the CERJ material, and Phase II, the process of cleaning and analysing the material, we can trace the larger political and militaristic context in which Indigenous memory of war and genocide resistance is being silenced and, worse, erased by the failure to dismantle Cold War repressive structures.

To examine these footprints, it is best to rely on a postcolonial view which reveals there was hardly a clean break from the state violence and authoritarianism of the past in the first place. This approach allows us to tackle the 'aftermath' not only as a historical time period but more importantly as a process where the state structures of violence and exclusion remain untouched, thus enabling postcolonial repressive continuities which thwart Indigenous organizations' efforts to tell in their own words—and through their own human rights artefacts and particular memories—their account of the violence. As suggested in the Holocaust literature, 'Genocide is bound up with memory, on an individual level of trauma and on a collective level, in terms of the creation of stereotypes, prejudice and post-genocide politics'.[17]

The process of rescuing, cleaning, organizing, digitizing, archiving, and safeguarding such a large collection of documents was nothing short of groundbreaking. Before shedding light to such a process and the value of ensuing knowledge, the next section provides a brief account of the war and genocide and the origins of the CERJ human rights records. The analysis then proceeds to highlight the importance of local archives in acknowledging Indigenous peoples political indigeneity. The next section of the chapter explores Phase I and Phase II that unpack what CERJ records reveal and their significance for tackling the long aftermath of genocide and war where the footprints of militarization and militarism are still alive shaping the recovery of historical and collective memory of resistance. The last part of the chapter emphasizes the social impact of local human rights archives and organizations which preserve them with particular reference to the role of education as well as the contribution of local archives and human rights organizations as enablers of Indigenous communities' solidarity and their mobilization in resisting dominant narratives of state violence and genocide.

[16] Michel-Rolph Trouillot, *Silencing the Past: Power and the Production of History* (Beacon Press 1995) 26.

[17] Dan Stone, *The Holocaust, Fascism and Memory: Essays in the History of Ideas* (Palgrave Macmillan 2013) 3.

The Genocide and the Usefulness of Indigenous Community Archives

In the early 1980s, US-backed state security forces in Guatemala launched bloody counterinsurgency campaigns (military and civilian efforts to defeat insurgencies) in highland areas to eliminate Maya peasants' uprising and support for left-wing rebel forces. As a result, over 600 massacres were committed against unarmed civilians in areas identified as 'red' or communist belligerent. During 1997–1999, in my capacity as field researcher for the United Nations Truth Commission in the province of El Quiché, where half of the state perpetrated massacres against unarmed civilians took place, I conducted face-to-face interviews with victims and eyewitnesses surviving in the context of the internal colonial system.[18] For decolonial scholars examining Indigenous resistance, such as Aymara sociologist and historian Silvia Rivera Cusicanqui, internal colonialism is a structure of domination left in place by colonizers, based on class, ethnic and racial subordination, and perpetuated by white-skinned local elites to keep Indigenous peoples from attaining socio-economic, political, and cultural equality.[19]

In order to carry out its genocidal policy at the village level, the Guatemalan army drew from its preexisting network of reserves, Indigenous recruits, rural police (known as military commissioners), and their auxiliaries, and ordered them to organize into the infamous Civil Self-Defense Patrols ('PACs'). The PACs were a rural auxiliary security force, linked to the army through a strict chain of command, ordered to police their own communities and to carry out sweeps hunting for rebels in nearby mountains and ravines. At least one million Maya peasants, 'one quarter of the adult population',[20] served as security patrols in rural areas. The UN's Truth Commission established that the patrols had participated in 18 per cent of all human rights crimes. Under the August 1996 Supporting Peace Plan,[21] the PACs were formally disarmed and disbanded at public ceremonies celebrated by the army jointly with the United Nations. In the aftermath of the 1996 signing of the Peace Accords, however, grassroots community organizers continued to report

[18] The UN Truth Commission for Guatemala was established in 1997 to clarify violations of human rights perpetrated in the course of the thirty-year Guatemalan Civil War (1960–1996). This Truth Commission operated for a duration of two years, under the direction of three Commissioners. It conducted 7,200 interviews with 11,000 individuals. See United States Institute of Peace, *Truth Commission: Guatemala*, <https://www.usip.org/publications/1997/02/truth-commission-guatemala> accessed 6 July 2020 (hereinafter USIP, *Truth*).

[19] What is the current structure of internal colonialism? De Sousa Santos asks Rivera Cusicanqui. 'Liberalism and neoliberalism reform but [which] do not restructure systems of oppression', Rivera Cusicanqui argues. In Boaventura de Sousa Santos and Silvia Rivera Cusicanqui, *Revueltas de Indignación y Otras Conversas: Conversas del Mundo Bolivia* (Stigma 2015).

[20] Susanne Jonas and Nancy Stein (eds), *Democracy in Latin America: Visions and Realities* (Greenwood Press 1990) 73.

[21] Officially known as the Army's August 1996 Supporting Peace Plan (Plan de Operaciones Apoyando la Paz) Esparza, *Silenced Communities* (n 2) 61.

death threats made by patrol chiefs who had remained in power as Security and Development Committees (part of the local governance of Mayan communities) and kept their loyalty to the nearest army base untouched.

Soon after the signing of the Agreement for a Firm and Lasting Peace between the state and the Guatemalan National Revolutionary Unity ('URNG') on 29 December 1996,[22] a United Nations' Truth Commission: Commission for Historical Clarification (Comisión para el Esclarecimiento Histórico, 'CEH') was set up (in 1997) to investigate the past. Two years later, the Commission concluded that state-sponsored violence had killed over 200,000 people—83 per cent of whom were Mayan, disappeared 45,000 and displaced 1.5 million people, with many seeking refuge in Mexico and in the United States. Acts of genocide had been committed against four Maya groups between 1981 and 1983.[23] The Guatemalan Civil War left profound scars after 'decades of a 'fratricidal war', the Truth Commission unequivocally established.[24]

In remote communities in El Quiché, harrowing testimonies were provided to the Commission in the context of the internal colonialism affecting highland communities. Tending small plots of land growing corn and beans (peasant main staples), malnourished families of four or more lived in single-room clay, dirt floor huts, and with very limited access to public services. These levels of destitution and poverty remain to this day, as infamously high as the levels of malnutrition at the time of the genocide (1981–1983). Both the Catholic Church[25] and the United Nations[26] undertook nationwide research efforts to record the past history of human rights crimes, producing reports which recognized and validated what grassroots organizations had long been denouncing: the state's brutal assault on their poverty-stricken communities to eliminate a Mayan uprising and an armed rebel threat. Nevertheless, while resistance to state violence has been recognized, what needs to be further emphasized is grassroots efforts to organize and to denounce human rights crimes, and the difficulties presented by legacies of state violence endangering the preservation of Indigenous archives in the wake of both the early 1980s genocide and the late 1996 signing of the Peace Accords. Thus, over two decades after the signing of the Accords, rather than stability and prosperity,

22 The Guatemalan civil war was a thirty-six-year internal conflict that took place from November 1960 to December 1996. This final Accord began implementation of the peace agreements signed under the Framework Agreement during the previous ten years of negotiations between the state, rebel forces, and civil society organizations.

23 These four Maya groups are: The 'Q'anjob'al' and 'Chuj' in Huehuetenango; the 'Ixil' and 'K'iché' in El Quiché; and the 'Achi' in Baja Verapaz. This period of the armed conflict is known as *la violencia*. In Guatemala, there are twenty-four Mayan Indigenous groups who make up over 50 per cent of the national population.

24 Truth Commission, 1999, 1 of the Prologue.

25 For the unofficial Truth Commission's the Recovery of Historical Memory Project (REHMI) report (1998) see, 'Guatemala Nunca Más', <http://www.odhag.org.gt/html/Default.htm> accessed 6 July 2020.

26 USIP, *Truth* (n 18).

Indigenous communities, and their *own* human rights archives, have largely been excluded from truth telling processes. Rather than representing simply personal objects, Indigenous human rights archives exhibit the spirit of *collective organized resistance* against state efforts to silence/hide/deny atrocities as well as the political willingness to defy the lingering, violent legacies of militarization and militarism.

Local Indigenous human rights archives contain otherwise hidden memories waiting to be located, identified, preserved, organized, assessed, and ultimately given back to communities for the purpose of collective enrichment. At the same time, archives can provide evidence of genocidal dynamics, as archives contribute to the building of genocide knowledge and, thus, not only legal evidence for the crimes committed. What are the repercussions of revealing this genocide knowledge and for whom? The preservation and public access to Cold War Indigenous human rights archives have the potential to simultaneously work towards a deeper national conversation that might contribute to a shared narrative of the war and genocide, while at the same time these archives can work against intra-community and national reconciliation because they can further divide communities between those who pledged their support to the state's army or the emergent human rights groups in the aftermath of the 1981–1983 genocide. The latter is especially the case in the larger aftermath context of lingering legacies of prolonged militarization. However, the knowledge unpacked by local human rights archives must be appreciated and valued not least for the sake of truth and the Mayan lived experiences of war and the genocide in its mist.

Indigeneity's *political* meaning in relationship to local archives may provide a way to grapple with the complexity of Indigenous peoples as conscientious objectors and resisters, and not only victims. According to Torres Strait Islander scholar Martin Nakata, 'indigeneity involves: Indigenous descent, self-identification, and acceptance as Indigenous, in the community in which they live'.[27] These archives need to be uncovered and preserved because '[i]ndigenous community requires as many stories to be known as possible, in order to appreciate the diversity of Indigenous experience'.[28] This is more so in the context of Guatemala, and Latin America in general, where Indigenous experience as resisters who stood up against the state military is linked to postgenocide narratives which are silenced or obliterated.

Martin Nakata points out that '[m]any Indigenous individuals come under the collective pressure to construct stories of trauma, loss and disadvantage'.[29] It is for this reason, he argues, that 'we need to keep a rolling agenda to ensure that archives are not just storehouses, but access points for quite valuable Indigenous

[27] Martin Nakata, 'Indigenous Memory, Forgetting and the Archives' (2012) 40 *Archives and Manuscripts* 98, 99.
[28] ibid 103.
[29] ibid 101–2.

materials—materials that can make a real difference in individual lives'.[30] For Nakata, archives can contribute to understanding the various experiences of Indigenous peoples, their complexity, and their relationship with the western world. In this way, Indigenous people can 'come to know about the history of colonial administration and intentions, about the rationale of policy, of the absolute absurdities of attempts to define human beings according to degrees of blood admixture'.[31] To this end, of particular importance is the preservation of, and access to, local human rights archives with community testimonies of resistance to collaboration in security forces aiding in the genocide and its legacies, such as militarization and militarism, because it is an aspect of the dynamics of genocide and its aftermath that we rarely examine.

To understand Indigenous human rights archives in Central America, and concretely in Guatemala, the 'stillness' of power is examined, as shown in the recovery and preservation of CERJ archives, because it is linked to the historical struggles of peasant and indigenous decolonization movements. This stillness refers to stories of political resistance that need to be located and preserved because they inform the various responses to war and genocide shaped by preexisting militarization going all the way back to colonial times when Spanish conquistadores ravaged Indigenous territories. This lack of recognition of diversity is prevalent within critical studies of genocide focusing on Indigenous peoples in Latin America, regrettably an area of research overlooked, among other factors, because of the complexity of establishing long-term research trust that needs to be forged between researchers and local Indigenous human rights organizations and, particularly, their leadership.[32] 'On an epistemological level', scholars assert, 'community archives provide empirical evidence for a community to assert its existence in the past . . . to establish their histories through material artifacts'.[33]

What are the processes of genocide than can be revealed in human rights artefacts? What types of human rights records have been kept and what is the significance of this materiality for organized Maya peasants? By raising these questions, this contribution hopes to demonstrate that a postcolonial and critical genocide studies approach can shed light on how local human rights archives may be seen as tools of resistance, because they contradict national narratives based on a complex militaristic rhetoric that viewed (and still does) Mayan peasants as 'backward people', stripped of political agency while simultaneously compelling them to serve in auxiliary forces such as the patrol system.[34] The narratives uncovered by the CERJ archives comprise what historian René Lemarchand terms an 'unpalatable

[30] ibid 103.
[31] ibid 100.
[32] See Chapter one in Esparza, *Silenced Communities* (n 2).
[33] Caswell and Others, 'To Suddenly Discover Yourself Existing' (n 6) 75.
[34] For a critical postcolonial approach, see Chris Cunneen and Juan Tauri, *Indigenous. Criminology* (Policy Press 2017).

truth',[35] that every genocide has, which refers to the fabricated lies genocidal states create and propagate to gain the support of the population in their mission.

Resistance in El Quiché: The CERJ Human Rights Records

This chapter draws on author's long-standing personal and research experiences which started back in the 1990s—before the fieldwork for the Truth Commission—offering a scholarly account that includes historical analysis, ethnography, and 'participatory action research praxis'.[36] The following is an examination of the process of recovery and preservation of the Maya-K'iché human rights archives, the CERJ, that publicly emerged in the province of El Quiché in July 1988, rooted in the previously successful peasants organization which gave rise to the Peasant Unity Committee ('CUC') and peasant leagues in the late 1970s. Created in the immediate aftermath of the genocide, CERJ was one of the postgenocide emerging civil society organizations protesting wide-ranging military assaults as well as promoting the dignity of victims and justice. Central to CERJ's goal was to inform peasants of their rights to refuse the army's orders to serve into the state-sponsored security force, the PACs.[37]

The patrol system's role in the genocide proved crucial in breaking solidarity links amongst peasant Mayans and the elimination of local political leadership, given that Mayans' support for the left-wing rebels, the Guatemalan Revolutionary Unity ('URNG'), was a frightening challenge for the state. The patrols were first created in the province of El Quiché in the early 1980s in Huehuetenango, Sololá, Totonicapán, Chimaltenango, Alta Verapaz, Petén, San Marcos, and Suchitepéquez. Peasants were compelled to patrol twelve- to twenty-four-hour unpaid shifts. When refusing to do so, they were forced to pay a fine to the neighbour who replaced them, go to jail, or worst of all, face a slow death at the hands of other

[35] René Lemarchand, 'Burundi 1972, Genocide Denied, Revised and Remembered', in René Lemarchand (ed), *Forgotten Genocides: Oblivion, Denial and Memory* (University of Pennsylvania Press 2011) 42.

[36] M Brinton Lykes and Amelia Mallona, 'Towards Transformational Liberation: Participatory and Action Research and Praxis' in Peter Reason and Hilary Bradbury (eds), *The SAGE Handbook of Action Research* (SAGE 2008).

[37] Eyewitnesses to the genocide have noted that 'CERJ was dedicated to the enforcement of indigenous peoples' constitutional rights. Articles 66–70 of the country's constitution which address the cultural and ethnic rights of Maya peoples, and Article 34 which prohibits the forced participation in Civil Self-Defense Patrols, have been the main campaigning points to date. Phillip Wearne, *The Maya of Guatemala* (Minority Rights Group 1994), hereafter Wearne, *The Maya*). Amnesty International monitored the signing of the Global Human Rights Accord which allowed for the presence of the United Nations Verification Mission in Guatemala ('MINUGUA') to monitor the human rights situation in the country; the demobilization (in September 1995) of military commissioners—rural Indigenous police—responsible for thousands of human rights violations; and the beginning of the demobilization of the Voluntary Civil Defence Committees, as PACs were renamed in August 1996. Amnesty International, *Amnesty International Report 1996—Guatemala*, 1 January 1996, available at <https://www.refworld.org/docid/3ae6a9f24.html> (accessed 10 July 2020).

patrols, as happened across the highlands. Many horrendous crimes were committed: massacres of old people, women, and children, kidnappings from the home and off the roads, rapes, threats, and robbery. The PACs prohibited free movement, meetings, organizations, and prevented people from going to work on the coast. By March 1992, twenty-five of CERJ's most prominent leaders had been killed or disappeared.[38] Accounts of these atrocities are part of the CERJ archives. From 2003 when the organization ceased to exist, its remarkable human rights history of resisting the patrol system was kept in boxes until early 2012 when recovery of these materials began.

While it is commonly believed that grassroots human rights organizations only emerged to denounce state violence after the signing of the 1996 Peace Accords, these organizations actually emerged in the immediate wake of the genocide in the early 1980s. This is critically important because it shows the enormous risks that neighbours, men, and women, Maya widows and families of the disappeared undertook to organize and publicly denounce the state's military actions while the army was still occupying their villages. By acknowledging this timeline, a story of Mayan-K'iché resilience, resistance, and organizational effectiveness against military power in a postgenocide context is revealed.

An expert witness to the Truth Commission representing the army declared that 'We never promoted violence. I never heard orders to burn villages or kill neighbors.'[39] CERJ human rights material however reveals otherwise. First, this material reveals the story of CERJ's resistance to the army's militarization and organization of the patrols. This resistance is important for reasons that are often overlooked in the diversity of war indigeneity: it can help us understand that despite the army's commanding and enforcing the patrol system, Maya peasants relied upon their past collective organizational and political experience to gather together and organize human rights groups to denounce state repression. Second, these archival materials reveal the long-standing historical struggle of Maya peasants, their families and communities who stood up against the army, and are incredibly valuable for the construction of the Indigenous' memory of resistance. This organized resistance rests on the long history of Mayan peasant activism in El Quiché region in peasant leagues and trade unions demanding fair wages and dignified working conditions in coffee and fruit plantations going back to the 1970s.

Since its emergence, and over the years, CERJ members produced a wealth of primary sources in the form of human rights material: audio-recording, video-recording, photographs, newspaper clips, testimonies, and legal documents presented before the Organization of American States ('OAS').[40] How can this recent

[38] Wearne, *The Maya* (n 37) 31.

[39] HMP Archives, Truth Commission, Key Witness 92.

[40] 'Primary sources are original records created at the time historical events occurred or well after events in the form of memoirs and oral histories. These may include: letters, manuscripts, diaries, journals, newspapers, speeches, interviews, memoirs ...' American Library Association, Reference and User Services, History Section.

history with state violence be reimagined in a way that reveals the political indigeneity of the Mayans, demanding truth, memory and accountability for the wrongs of the past?[41] Understanding the step-by-step rescue process and initial cataloguing of the CERJ artefacts can help us get a glimpse into the lingering effects of fear and repression shaping the recovery of Indigenous human rights archives in the postgenocide setting.

Phase I: Action Research

Efforts to preserve CERJ human rights materials were not a serendipitous event. In my role as founder of the Historical Memory Project ('HMP') and as a former Truth Commission field researcher, I undertook systematic efforts to locate, protect, and disseminate Cold War records of Latin America to a local and global audience. In light of the lack of understanding of how lingering legacies of war and genocide have been kept alive in their aftermath, HMP's scholarly and advocacy role has been essential since 2002. This is more so when one acknowledges the lack of a specific, physical, and online repository further highlighting the importance of access to human rights artifacts by the City University of New York ('CUNY')—which hosts HMP—and larger New York City immigrant and diasporic communities. Indeed, HMP is the only CUNY-based project that acts on the pedagogical urgency to preserve historical memories from Latin America and to make them accessible to global audiences.

Scholars have noted that archival process requires, 'the functionaries who managed them, the archivists who selected them for preservation and make them available for use, and the researchers who use them in constructing accounts of the past'.[42] In the case of the CERJ material, however, at the request of local archivists and organizations involved in its recovery, the process has been shrouded in utmost secrecy. For this reason, most of the names of those involved in the collection of the archive and its location has not been disclosed. Moreover, at the time of this writing, making these resources available to aggrieved communities in El Quiché, where most members of CERJ belonged, or even letting them know of the recovery of the archives, is utterly silenced. This obliteration is in itself dramatic evidence of how lingering fear of reprisals remains to this day, which continues to prevent the full disclosure of HMP's sustained effort at keeping the records in a secure place.

[41] It is worth mentioning that critiques raised against the politics of memory indicate that 'The fact that the rise of the discourse of memory coincided with the rise of neoliberalism ... should lead us to see memory as an epiphenomenon of neoliberalism rather than a mode of resistance to it.' Eugenio Di Stefano, 'From Shopping Malls to Memory Museums: Reconciling the Recent Past in the Uruguayan Neoliberal State' (2012) 4(8) *Dissidences: Hispanic Journal of Theory and Criticism* <http://digitalcommons.bowdoin.edu/dissidences/vol4/iss8/8> accessed 6 July 2020.

[42] Verne Harris, 'The Archival Sliver: Power, Memory, and Archives in South Africa' (2002) 2 Archival Science 63, 65.

The recovery of the CERJ's human rights archives began in 2012 when I returned to Guatemala to carry out further military archival research which led to the publication of *Silenced Communities*.[43] During this time, I met with human rights activists including Amílcar Mendéz, a rural *ladino* teacher who first helped organize peasants to challenge the illegality of the patrol system in southern El Quiché.[44] Reconnecting with Amílcar enabled me to learn about the whereabouts of CERJ material, which were kept in a rural school classroom. While protected from further rain and sunlight, the documentation was moldy, deteriorating, and covered with the fecal droppings of cockroaches. The first step was the hiring of services to disinfect the material and placing it into boxes to move it to an empty apartment in Guatemala City, all this facilitated by former CERJ Maya-K'iché member Angélica Macario. Acknowledging the courage of team members involved in this risky process, Angelica authorized her name to be mentioned in this chapter. The fact that people's names and whereabouts of CERJ archives remain anonymous, is only one expression of the lingering fear to make public the work with archives in the country.[45]

HMP, together with CERJ, became the guardian of twenty-three boxes including a wide array of documentation first found wrapped in cockroach infested bundles. As of January 2018, a further step ensued, with HMP reaching out to an international funder[46] as well as to other local Guatemalan organizations to join in fundraising's efforts to clean, organize, catalogue, and give access to documentation contained in these boxes.[47] In the course of the process of recovery of the records contained in these boxes, a 'post-custodial' approach was followed similar to the one used by the University of Texas aiding in the preservation and digitization of Guatemalan human rights archives.[48] This approach means keeping physical records in the country, which at least in theory, offers 'communities and

[43] Esparza, *Silenced Communities* (n 2).

[44] Amílcar Mendéz is CERJ legal representative, and former congressman for the Frente Democratico Nacional de Guatemala ('FDNG') of Guatemala (1996–2000). Internationally recognized for his advocacy of human rights, Méndez received the prestigious Robert Kennedy Human Rights Award in 1990. See, Robert F. Kennedy Human Rights, https://rfkhumanrights.org/people/am%C3%ADlcar-méndez-urizar> accessed 6 July 2020.

[45] As has been noted, 'archives, and particularly human rights documentation, remain vulnerable due to lack of infrastructure, as well as political threat'. Theresa E Polk, 'Archiving Human Rights Documentation: The Promise of the Post-Custodial Approach in Latin America', *Portal*, 5 August 2016, <https://llilasbensonmagazine.org/2016/08/05/archiving-human-rights-documentation-the-promise-of-the-post-custodial-approach-in-latin-america> accessed 6 July 2020 (hereafter Polk, 'Archiving').

[46] I am indebted to Swisspeace's Archives Dealing with the Past ('DwP') Project for their relentless and professional support in this phase < http://archivesproject.swisspeace.ch> accessed 10 July 2020.

[47] Repeated attempts to obtain funding from 2012 to 2017 failed in the face of a surprising lack of sympathy by international funders for the importance of the CERJ human rights material. Future organizations supporting the work of Indigenous human rights groups (like HMP) need to figure out ways of socializing the idea that the Cold War human rights records are material for Indigenous peoples' shared humanity.

[48] See the University of Texas at Austin. The UT Libraries' Human Rights Documentation Initiative ('HRDI') <https://legacy.lib.utexas.edu/hrdi/about> accessed 6 July 2020.

organizations greater control over selection, description, and access to their documentation, and helps build local capacity to preserve vulnerable collections'.[49]

Phase 2: A Preliminary Assessment of Artefacts of Indigeneity of Resistance

Particularly relevant for an understanding of why these archives can be seen as dangerous to state denials of genocide is the initial analysis of the documentation, which demonstrates sustained and organized collective political action that took place in the immediate aftermath of the genocide in the mid-1980s. From November 2018 to March 2019, a second phase has included the assessment of what is in the twenty-three boxes, or some twenty linear metres of the CERJ material. Initially, a highly trained team of Guatemalan and non-Guatemalan archival specialists was created. Soon after, however, it was decided by HMP and CERJ members to take the opportunity to offer archivist training to young Maya-K'iché close to the work of CERJ. Of pivotal importance was the participation of a Guatemalan non-Indigenous expert archivist who organized the material into broad categories—employment, health, education—and helped stack the material in clean corrugated boxes. After opening five boxes (out of the twenty-three), the material thus far surveyed shows CERJ daily administrative records which evidence the detailed strategic planning of the organization in the early aftermath of the genocide. These records show CERJ formulating short- and long-term goals broken down into different key areas: aiding victims, informing peasants of their constitutional rights to refuse service in the patrol system, the promotion and education of human rights, and fundraising to support the training of teachers.[50] A next phase is to convert the available material into a digital format so that the archives can become 'live archives' to give a worldwide audience access to this unique material.[51]A last phase will be to find a permanent physical space in the province of El Quiché where this historical material can be preserved and made public.

Through this human rights material, CERJ memorialized its activities in defence of human rights—such as forced military recruitment, land issues, personal exhibitions, or *habeas corpus*—as exhibited in various mediums: photographs, testimonies, magazines, newspapers, legal complaints, among others. Throughout this

[49] Polk, 'Archiving' (n 45).

[50] After the initial shallow inventory elaboration, these boxes were reorganized into fifty-five sub-boxes which, although are not 100 per cent archival quality, offer the documents some protection for their long-term preservation.

[51] Final Report Second Stage: Archival diagnosis, shallow inventory, institutional history and preliminary classification chart, CERJ archive, November 2018–March 2019, Angélica Macario, and others. (Informe final Segunda Etapa: Diagnóstico archivístico, inventario somero, historia institucional y cuadro de clasificación preliminar, archivo CERJ, noviembre 2018–marzo 2019).

material, CERJ members expressed personal, political, and collective indigeneity while contributing to historical memory and the pursuit-of-justice efforts in the aftermath of the genocide, particularly in El Quiché, the epicentre of state violence. Archives show that despite the enormous state pressure and coercive violence against themselves, their families and communities, CERJ members resisted the army's rhetoric printed in army pamphlets which instructed communities that 'patrollers' were allegedly needed to protect their families and communities against 'communist' rebels—completely masking other official ulterior motives.

Instead, the narrative that emerges in the CERJ human rights records, is the story of Indigenous peoples' conscientious objectors, resisters who asserted their rights as early as 1988, as the footprints of the genocide lingered in their communities. This organized resistance shows that collective action was possible because of the heightened understanding of the harm brought to communities when the army imposed their own institutional memory as protectors and guardians of poverty-stricken Maya peasants while simultaneously assaulting their communities in the early 1980s. Furthermore, the uncovered archives 'through their materiality and their physical persistence—offer an unbroken connection from the time before the genocide, through the event, to postgenocide; a connection that has the potential to affect the construction of the narrative of genocide and our understanding of such events'.[52]

Political Indigeneity and the Archives: A Testimony

A preliminary analysis of archives documenting military strategies during the genocide and organized resistance in its aftermath are pivotal to resignify community values of solidarity and reciprocity and past memory of strategies of collective action. A testimony found in one of the boxes tells the story of the beginning of CERJ:

> They told me to go back to the canton because there was a need for people to form the patrol. They said those who do not want to participate in the patrol are guerrillas, and they said that it was necessary to [enroll in the patrol]. In 1987, as we resigned, the patrolmen began to threaten us, that is why we organized ourselves at CERJ ... We told Amílcar Méndez all our problems that we wanted to get out of the patrols, we realized that it was of no use to us, only to control the neighbors, to harm the community. He told us that if that was what we wanted to do, then he was going to help us, [and] that we were going to make a memorial on September 13, 1988 ... [and] we were going to leave [the memorial] to the congress and the

[52] Hawkes, 'Memory' (n 12) 207.

> defense ministry, to the detachment of the area of Chupol. When the patrolmen heard that we made a memorial, the patrollers threatened us, and said that we had left because we wanted to organize the guerrillas again. Because of that memorial there was a big problem in the community.

The collection of newspaper clippings was archived by newspaper, date and subject. In the period from 1993–1995, subjects included: attacks, police officers involved, economy, education, peace process, and other topics, such as articles about the Nobel Prize that was awarded to Rigoberta Menchú in 1992.[53] Clipped newspaper articles show how hate-filled state propaganda criminalized political opposition and called on peasants to join the patrol system. One article detailed how '[t]he army will give arms to peasants for their defense'.[54] Another article boasted that '800 peasants from El Petén joined the army by serving into the patrol system'.[55] By keeping newspapers, CERJ material reveals the army's genocidal strategies, but they also show how peasant organizations such as the CUC demanded that children were spared from serving into PACs.[56]

Social Role: Education

In the aftermath of the genocide, as neighbours and families joined CERJ to denounce human rights crimes, this and other similar organizations promoted the right to education. In particular, CERJ's education efforts are shown in the programmatic records for enrolment into elementary schools. In this process, CERJ informed families and communities about the system of exploitation, namely the internal colonialism, designed to benefit the non-Indigenous elite and oligarchy at the expense of their own lives. Through educational funds, CERJ promoted education in several local villages, providing school children in Southern El Quiché with basic literacy while at the same time promoting the strengthening of political abilities. These efforts empowered CERJ members, and show how political indigeneity was not totally crushed by state violence.

The archives contain records of educational promotion in the Quiché, Ixil, and Boca Costa areas along with proposals laying out the execution of programmes such as school registration and pre-registration. They contain also community records showing inauguration and service contracts for an auxiliary technician from the Ministry of Education, based on data forms from the official educational establishments (2000) such as documents of the Education Commission. Scheduled

53 Final Report Second Stage (n 51).
54 HMP Archives, SDC13293, Prensa Libre.
55 HMP Archives, SDC13309, Prensa Libre.
56 HMP Archives, SDC13961, Prensa Libre.

activities including workshops and meetings, gender workshops, names of leaders, and attendance at forums are also part of the CERJ archives.[57]

Showing CERJ concerns about the rights of the uprooted population, the records kept include a Specific Education Plan, which was proposed within the framework of the Agreement on Resettlement of said populations of the abovementioned areas. Great care was dedicated to recording the identification of personnel with education training, including bilingual personnel, to serve as promoters and teachers in the official state schools that served this population.

Solidarity and Mobilization

In the immediate aftermath of the genocide, still shell-shocked from the army's counterinsurgency campaigns, survivors regrouped into human rights organizations and used specific strategies to resist ongoing violence. Because collective *memories* play a pivotal role in gathering people together, grassroots protests in alliance with human rights groups are also recorded through memorandums and audio videos. These include[58] the National Coordination of Widows of Guatemala (*Coordinadora Nacional de Viudas de Guatemala* ('CONAVIGUA')). An interview found in CERJ archives shows that survivors felt courageous when organizing as Indigenous peoples. Fermina Lopez Castro, a CONAVIGUA leader, stated in an interview I conducted in 1994 in New York City:

> How can we, as Indigenous peoples, participate and organize in the Peace Process? How can we make our voices heard? Several times, patrollers came to spy on us but many people still kept on organizing while some people were afraid of reprisals by the patrols. Now that the Peace Accords will be signed, the valor of the community to continue organizing needs to be recognized.[59]

This testimony attests to the Indigenous peoples' resolve to resist state recrimination in the aftermath of genocide and be active participants in the peace process. Demonstrating CERJ members' organizational capacity to establish strong solidarity links, efforts to collaborate with GAM (Mutual Support Group—*Grupo de Apoyo Mutuo*) in search for the forcibly disappeared, are also memorialized in

[57] Final Report Second Stage (n 51).

[58] Documents around CERJ's participation with entities such as, sectors arising from repression and impunity, Unidad de Acción Sindical y Popular (UASP), Consultative Assembly of the Uprooted Populations (ACPD), Civil Society Assembly, documents from Majawuil Q´ij, Mutual Support Group—*Grupo de Apoyo Mutuo* (GAM), the National Coordination of Widows of Guatemala—*Coordinadora Nacional de Viudas de Guatemala* (CONAVIGUA), Family Members of the Detained and Disappeared of Guatemala—Familiares de Detenidos Desaparecidos en Guatemala (FAMDEGUA).

[59] HMP Archives. Fermina López Castro, March 3, 1994. Asamblea Consultiva de la Población Desarraigada.

CERJ archives. More recently, the GAM archives were recovered and made public through a 'post-custodial' collaboration with the University of Haverford that 'aims to aims to preserve and provide access to materials held by Guatemala's oldest human rights organization'.[60]

A CERJ document attests to patrol resisters' level of organization:

> In the years 1993, 1994, 1995 they have not done us any more damage because we are organized. Three organizations are helping us: CONAVIGUA, CERJ, and GAM. Any threat, problem that we have the organizations support us. Even if the government tell us that we are guerrillas and bad people, we meet to support and defend ourselves. That's why we get together and that's why we are not afraid. We have more confidence in organizations because they tell us our rights, that there are laws that defend us.

In the context of organized mobilization amongst the different human rights groups emerging in the aftermath of the 1980s genocide, human rights archives can enable and promote rural community's solidarity links which were broken and severed by state violence. In this process of recovery of these organizations' archives, communities resist and confront official dehumanizing and criminalizing rhetoric, and construct their own narrative and historical memory of the recent past.

Conclusion

State-sponsored violence against political opponents in Guatemala did not stop in 1996 when the war formally ended. Drug and human trafficking, ingrained state corruption, and widespread gang violence and femicides have added yet another layer of widespread violence. In this context, with few exceptions, efforts to preserve local or national archives have been rare. Scholars and activists have examined different aspects of the causes and the process of the Guatemalan genocide, but the aftermath of genocide and its long-term rippling effects continues to be under-represented in the literature. This chapter has tried to close this gap, and has delved into the postgenocide knowledge in Guatemala revealed by CERJ Indigenous human rights archives and their contribution in: (i) destabilizing the state hegemonic discourse on genocide; (ii) challenging official interpretations of Maya identity and their participation in the civil war; (iii) contributing archival knowledge on the postgenocide for the education of younger generations; and (iv) demonstrating the potential of archival knowledge to open up a national

[60] *The Grupo de Apoyo Mutuo (GAM) Digital Archive Project*—A post-custodial digital archive of human rights materials in Guatemala <http://ds.haverford.edu/gam-archive/2017/12/13/introducing-gam> and <https://www.haverford.edu/library/digital-scholarship> accessed 10 July 2020.

conversation that might contribute towards a shared narrative of the genocide and the civil war more broadly and curb genocide denial as well as disrespect of the Maya community.

The invaluable importance of Indigenous community archives in Guatemala enable us to see how the larger political and militaristic legacies of the genocide shape the preservation or erasure of records. Local Indigenous human rights archives, and the CERJ archives in particular, can be best seen as keepers of memory which can serve as vital tools for mobilizing resistance against dominant and racialized narratives and ongoing silence over the role of militarization and militarism in the countryside of Guatemala. More than twenty years after the official end of the war, Indigenous political memories kept in human rights archives are still waiting to be fully located, identified, preserved, organized, assessed by former CERJ members themselves, and ultimately, given access to communities. These archives can help unmask the false gentility that the military extolled to compel peasants to join its auxiliary force. In the aftermath of the genocide and the war, CERJ's contribution to dismantling hegemonic narratives that challenge the binary 'victim' or 'perpetrator' discourse remain hidden, and the powerful history of resistance against state sponsored violence, unrecognized. This lack of attention—and funding—to locate Indigenous community archives can be seen as one of the factors reproducing and keeping alive the legacies of militarization, because by ignoring their existence the national narrative remains largely shaped by the army's hateful rhetoric, masked by the politics of transitional justice.

In the case of Guatemala, until the elimination of the socioeconomic, political, and cultural root causes of state violence, and the internal colonialism affecting Indigenous communities, the genocide and its lingering aftermath cannot truly be considered an event of the past. As criminologist Nicole Rafter asserts, Guatemala has been 'riven by social class and racial hierarchies to develop a sense of national unity'[61] at the expense of the exclusion and marginalization of Indigenous peoples who make up over half of the population. State efforts have utterly failed to bring the country any closer to a democratic nation based on the Indigenous majority—despite the implementation of transitional justice mechanisms. Significantly, Indigenous local archives can account both for the state violence besieged upon the Indigenous communities, and also the latter's resistance to it thus contributing to a more comprehensive understanding of the aftermath of war and genocide in the country.

[61] Rafter, *The Crime of All Crimes* (n 3) 189.

11
Rhetorical versus Substantive Reconciliation After Cultural Genocide in Canada

Maureen S Hiebert

Introduction

Say the word genocide, and Canada is not usually the first country that comes to mind. For most non-indigenous Canadians, Canada is a peaceful, prosperous, and tolerant multicultural society that upholds human rights. Internationally, Canada is seen as a middle, slightly boring inoffensive power that reliably plays by the rules of the post-1945 international order. According to this narrative, Canadians and Canada are 'nice', eschewing violence and repression domestically, resorting to the use of force internationally only in concert with its allies under the auspices of NATO and the UN, preferring to offer its services as peacekeepers and 'honest brokers' instead. It is hardly in the same company as Nazi Germany or Hutu Power Rwanda.

Until very recently, this self-conception produced an understanding of Canadian history that erased the destruction of indigenous peoples before and after confederation in 1867. True, accounts of Canadian history always began with stories of first contact between British and French explorers and colonists with the indigenous nations in what are now Quebec, Ontario, and the Atlantic provinces. But the presence of Canada's first peoples typically dropped out of the narrative once the story turned to the period when the colonists were secure in the northern parts of British North America and New France (later ceded to Britain in the Treaty of Paris after France's defeat in 1759 at the Battle of the Plains of Abraham at Quebec City). From this point onward, Canada's story became about the evolution of a country of immigrants from Europe, labourers from Asia, ranchers and farmers from the United States, and finally, after the end of the 'White Canada' immigration policy in the late 1960s, new Canadians from all over the globe. First Nations, Metis, and Inuit peoples continued to exist in Canada, of course, but they were not included in settler Canada's national story or identity. And little wonder. The genocide of indigenous peoples through the advent and continued existence of settler colonialism, the reservation system, and the forcible removal of

Maureen S Hiebert, *Rhetorical versus Substantive Reconciliation After Cultural Genocide in Canada*
In: *Postgenocide*. Edited by: Klejda Mulaj, Oxford University Press (2021).
DOI: 10.1093/oso/9780192895189.003.0011

children to the explicitly assimilationist Indian Residential Schools starting at the end of the nineteenth century, was a shameful past that simply did not fit within Canada's and Canadians' 'nice' identity. It remained buried, largely unknown, and unacknowledged by most settler Canadians. Even now, with the release of the Truth and Reconciliation Commission's Final Report in 2015 and the apology by the Government of Canada in 2008 that gave rise to the Truth and Reconciliation Commission ('TRC'), government and non-indigenous Canadians are at best willing to acknowledge past—not present—wrongdoing and embark on the least costly aspects of reconciliation.

The question underpinning this chapter is what does post-(cultural) genocide reconciliation really look like in a longstanding democratic, peaceful, liberal, settler democracy? I argue that reconciliation in Canada is certainly under way, but it has focused on rhetorical/ideational issues while largely leaving aside or taking only very preliminary steps to address substantive/material policies that would produce a more thorough-going form of reconciliation, or rather decolonization, and materially improve the conditions of indigenous peoples on and off reserve. My central claim is that government and many (but not all) non-indigenous Canadians have elected to pursue the rhetorical/ideational aspects of postgenocide reconciliation because doing so bolsters Canada's 'nice guy' multicultural, rights-affirming self-conception. Meanwhile, substantive/material steps towards reconciliation/decolonization have lagged, because they are a decidedly uncomfortable fit with the very logic and material structures of Canada's settler colonial system.

Rhetorical/ideational measures are seen from the non-indigenous side as largely win-win, since they involve relatively low-cost or cost-free changes in discourse that enhance Canada and (non-indigenous) Canadians' reputation for being inclusive and magnanimous. Rhetorical/ideational acts have included political apology and an explicit reframing of the relationship between indigenous and non-indigenous Canada as no longer hierarchical, but nation-to-nation. Substantive/material reconciliation measures such as settling land claims, meaningful indigenous control over resource extraction, and other economic activities on their land, comprehensive criminal legal reform, and self-government continue to be resisted, because they are perceived as zero-sum losses for the settler state and society. The reluctance to engage in substantive reconciliation and decolonization has, ironically, been supported by the emergence of a legal regime surrounding Aboriginal rights and title codified in the Constitution Act 1982. While recognizing that the advent of British sovereignty did not extinguish Aboriginal title, Supreme Court of Canada jurisprudence has, nonetheless, privileged settler economic interests over the consent of indigenous communities over the use of their lands. Gaining consent and establishing a true nation-to-nation relationship would at least in part involve the redistribution of important material resources and powers from the Crown (the Canadian state), other levels of government, and ordinary non-indigenous Canadians to First Nations, Metis, and Inuit peoples.

This 'harder' form of reconciliation gets at the materiality of the settler-indigenous relationship, but it would also take seriously the Crown's treaty obligations to indigenous nations.

Such redistributive policies have been a feature of some postconflict/postgenocide societies elsewhere, but unlike many of these other societies, the beneficiaries of settler colonialism and cultural genocide in Canada remain firmly in place. Postgenocide reconciliation in Canada is marked by the fact that there has been no postgenocide regime change to democracy because Canada already was an established liberal democracy, at least for the non-indigenous majority. There has been no removal of *genocidaire* from the halls of power as explicitly cultural genocidal policies occurred in the past. There has been no subjugation of populations that supported genocidal policies,[1] and no flight of the survivors into permanent resettlement elsewhere. The 96 per cent of Canadians who are settlers are not going anywhere. Non-indigenous and indigenous Canadians are going to have to coexist on Turtle Island (North America) permanently.

I begin my analysis with a brief review of settler colonialism and indigenous genocide in Canada. Here I draw on Patrick Wolfe's notion that settler colonialism is grounded in a 'logic of elimination', particularly concerning European settler conceptions and practices of the 'proper' ownership and use of the land and understandings of indigenous peoples as unadaptable to modernity.[2] Focusing on Western Canada, I will show that this logic gave rise to the removal of indigenous peoples from much of the land to enable the permanent settlement of Europeans via the creation of indigenous reservations in a situation of induced food scarcity and widespread illness among Plains Indigenous nations. This already destructive process was intensified with the creation and operation of the Indian Residential Schools from 1879 to 1996, and was followed by the 'Sixties Scoop' (the policy of placing foster and adopted indigenous children with non-indigenous families from the 1950s to the 1970s). All of these policies were not only underpinned by a genocidal logic of elimination, they were also executed through federal and provincial legislation that was duly passed under constitutional laws affording the Canadian state sweeping legal powers over indigenous peoples. As such, the law, deployed by a fully democratic state in strict conformity with liberal legal conceptions of the rule of law, was used self-consciously throughout the genocidal process as a principal tool of destruction.

I will then cover the steps towards reconciliation taken by the Canadian federal government since the mid-2000s, focusing on the government's apology, the Truth and Reconciliation process and report, and efforts by the current Liberal government to craft what it calls a new 'nation-to-nation' relationship with First Nations,

[1] Rosemary Nagy, 'The Truth and Reconciliation Commission of Canada: Genesis and Design' (2014) 29 (2) CJLS 211–13 (hereafter Nagy, *The Truth and Reconciliation Commission of Canada*).

[2] Patrick Wolfe, 'Settler Colonialism and the Elimination of the Native' (2006) 8(4) JGR 387–409.

Inuit, and Metis peoples. As noted, I will show that these efforts, while important in reconceptualizing the relationship between indigenous and non-indigenous Canada, embrace the least materially costly ideational/rhetorical aspects of reconciliation. These measures have made little headway towards true decolonization. Finally, I examine the relative lack of progress on the more foundational decolonizing material/substantive aspects of reconciliation by focusing on two issue areas: land claims and disputes over resource development on indigenous land. Here I will show that despite their rhetorical embrace of reconciliation, government continues to cleave to the legal requirement of only consulting indigenous communities over economic and resource development projects on indigenous lands while eschewing the transfer of land back to indigenous communities or gaining consent for the use of indigenous lands.

Genocide and the Settler Colonial Project in Canada

Pre-contact, the northern half of Turtle Island was home to a wide variety of indigenous nations with distinct ways of being and knowing, and sophisticated legal, political, and economic systems from the North Atlantic to the Pacific, the forests of the vast Canadian Shield, the Prairies, the foothills of the Rocky Mountains, and the far north beyond the Arctic Circle.[3] The arrival of the French in the seventeenth century in what is now Ontario and Quebec initially gave rise to a more or less equal relationship between the British and French European nations, often in conflict with each other in North America and Europe on the one hand, and local indigenous nations—principally the Iroquois and the Huron—on the other. Indigenous peoples were conceptualized by the Europeans as nations akin to other states in the emerging Westphalian international system. This was largely due to the extremely precarious nature of early British and French settlement which included very small numbers of colonists, explorers, and traders with little familiarity with the land or capacity to physically sustain themselves under harsh conditions. The colonists were also economically dependent on trade with local First Nations for their economic survival and as allies in their struggles with each other over supremacy in the so-called 'New World'. But once British North America and New France took hold and began to attract a large number of colonists, the demographic balance began to irrevocably shift in favour of the colonists. The colonies became self-sustaining. Gone was the need to rely on local indigenous nations for sustenance and protection. With the defeat of the French at the Battle of the Plains of Abraham in 1759 during the Seven Years War and the ceding of New France to Britain in the Treaty of Paris 1763, colonial authorities in British North America

[3] John Borrows, *Canada's Indigenous Constitution* (University of Toronto Press 2010).

and the metropole decisively moved away from a conception of Indigenous peoples as nations and instead towards seeing and treating them as children and as a 'problem' that impeded Western expansion, nation-building, and modernization.

The narrative of Indigenous peoples as problems emerged from a belief that 'the native' could not make the transition to a modern Canadian (ie, settler) life. This construction flowed from racist conceptions of indigenous identity and the desperate circumstances in which First Nations found themselves by the mid-nineteenth century.[4] Seen by their very nature to be alternatively innocent or sinister 'savages', unbelieving and immoral heathens, and lacking in the capacity for the 'industriousness' necessary for life in the new settler society and economy, indigenous people supposedly evinced in most aspects of their lives a deviance that obstructed the settler project. The material conditions of life for First Nations prior to, during, and after the treaty-making process, particularly in the West, served to reinforce the conception of indigenous peoples as unable to cope with the transition to modernity. These harsh conditions, of course, were not of their own making, but the outcome of colonial economic policies, the creation of under-resourced reserves without sustainable economic foundations or adequate food and medicines, and population flows involving the movement of Indigenous nations and European settlers. The knock-on effects of these dynamics were severe, including the near extinction of the bison on the Western plains, repeated exposure first to smallpox and later tuberculosis (including bovine TB from newly introduced cattle), influenza, and other communicable diseases that preyed on what had become immunosuppressed populations.[5] The putting of Indigenous peoples and their lands under government control, the community's regulation through the Indian Act, and finally the Indian Residential School system, was seen by some government officials as a benevolent exercise in preventing the extinction of Canada's Indigenous populations. As historian John Milloy notes, officials believed that the settlement of the West left Indigenous populations 'destined ... to die off' unless, as one official put it, 'special measures' were taken 'to force a change in his [the Indian's] conditions'.[6]

The extinctionist view of Canada's Indigenous and Metis populations existed alongside a more sinister construction of Indigenous peoples as threats to the new settler society. The ongoing 'Indian Wars' in the late nineteenth century just across the border in the northwestern American territories,[7] the hardships wrought by

[4] Andrew Woolford, 'Ontological Destruction: Genocide and Aboriginal Peoples' (2009) 4(1) GSI 82–86.

[5] James Dashuk, *Clearing the Plains: Disease, Politics of Starvation, and the Loss of Aboriginal Life* (University of Regina Press 2013).

[6] N.A.C. RG 10, Vol. 3647, File 8128, MR C 10113, M.A. Macrae to Indian Commissioner, Regina, 18 December 1886; quoted in Milloy, *A National Crime: The Canadian Government and the Residential School System* (University of Manitoba Press 1999) 27 (hereafter Milloy, *A National Crime*.

[7] Andrew Woolford, Jeff Benvenuto, and Alexander Laban Hinton, *Colonial Genocide in Indigenous North America* (Duke University Press 2014); Russell Thornton, *American Indian Holocaust and Survival: A Population History since 1492* (University of Oklahoma Press 1990).

the extinction of the bison and the resulting lack of economic opportunity, food insecurity, and illness that went with it, coupled with the Riel Rebellion of 1869–1870, caused great concern among the non-Indigenous population and leadership. The Davin Report that set the foundations for the Indian Residential School system reported that in the prairie city of Winnipeg it was evident that '[the Metis are] thoughtful if not anxious regarding the Government's intentions regarding them, [and] among the Indians there is some discontent'. Such concerns 'bespoke not a feeling of self-assured superiority in the face of Aboriginal culture but a fear of the unknown Other and of its disruptive potential'.[8] To neutralize this threat, Davin recommended the federal government create a country-wide system of industrial residential schools that would alleviate the desperate living conditions of indigenous children as well as instill in them the requisite level of modern industriousness which would overcome the threat of further rebellion by preparing indigenous youth 'to meet the necessities of the not too distant future; to welcome and facilitate ... the settlement of the country; and to render its government easy and not expensive'.[9]

The most significant obstacle to this grand programme of deconstructing and reconstructing indigenous youth rest with an even more fundamental manifestation of indigenous 'deviance': the supposedly pernicious influence that Aboriginal parents, family members, and communities had on their children. Widespread among non-Indigenous officialdom, both governmental and religious, was the notion that indigenous adults, as the Khmer Rouge said in a different context, 'could not be corrected'. They were relics of the past who were simply too wedded to their ways to be effectively assimilated. Worse, their insufficiently modern modes of being would inevitably undo the good work of the European-style industrial education of the younger generation, thus fatally undermining the entire assimilative project. For the destruction of the Indian child and the communities from which they came to be permanent, the intimate parent-child bonds, and those of the wider family and community, had to be severed for much of the child's formative years (six to sixteen years of age). The re-education of Indigenous youth could only take place in residential schools far from home wherein the churches and the Canadian government directly assumed the roles of teacher and parent.

All of this occurred in a fully fledged democracy. As first a set of colonies and territories within the British empire in British North America and then a self-governing dominion in 1867, Canada legally and politically became a constitutionally governed federally structured settler democracy bound by the rule of law. Legal scholarship and constitutional jurisprudence has established that the preamble to the Constitution Act 1867 set out these features of the Canadian political

[8] Milloy, *A National Crime* (n 6) 31.
[9] N. A. C. MG 26A, Sir John A. Macdonald Papers, Vol. 91, *Report on Industrial Schools for Indians and Half-Breeds*, 14 March 1879, 35428-45, p 10; quoted in Milloy, *A National Crime* (n 6) 32.

and legal system in the rather generally worded phrase '[w]hereas the Provinces of Canada, Nova Scotia, and New Brunswick have expressed their Desire to be federally united into One Dominion under the Crown of the United Kingdom of Great Britain and Ireland with a Constitution similar in Principle to that of the United Kingdom'.[10] Further, section 91(24) granted the federal government 'exclusive Legislative Authority of the Parliament of Canada' over 'Indians, and Lands reserved for the Indians'.[11] Beyond constitutional law, ordinary legislation governing almost all aspects of life for indigenous peoples, including the legal definition of who is a status and non-status Indian, the use of reserve lands, and the education of indigenous children, was codified in the federal Indian Act of 1876 and subsequent versions of the act up to the present day.

Government's conception of indigenous adults as deviant, non-modern, and potentially hostile, and of indigenous children as in need of saving and modernization was constitutive of, and reinforced by, the laws governing indigenous peoples in Canada generally and the legal regime that created and governed the functioning of the residential school system specifically. This regime, and the program of genocidal destruction it put in train, existed within a robust commitment of the rule of law and democratic constitutionalism, thus ensuring that the law would be the main facilitating structure underpinning cultural genocide. As such, government and other officials considered that what they were doing was right because it was lawful. The Canadian government deepened its legal paternalism in the most direct and intimate way possible: assuming control over the education and raising of indigenous children. This project was consciously assimilationist and, therefore, genocidal in its intent and outcome since it was designed to 'kill the Indian in the child' such that no 'Indians' would be left in future versions of completely Canadianized indigenous communities.

Decades after investigations into the deplorable conditions in the schools were first conducted in the early twentieth century,[12] and amidst an emerging post-war human rights revolution, the Canadian government began to think about winding down the Indian Residential Schools ('IRS') system in the late 1940s. Two decades later, residential schools began to close. But instead of opening schools on reserves staffed by indigenous educators teaching an indigenous-centred curriculum, children living on reserves were 'integrated' into non-indigenous schools in nearby

[10] Preamble, *Constitution Act 1867*. A Consolidation of the Constitution Acts 1867 and 1982, Department of Justice Canada, Her Majesty the Queen in Right of Canada, represented by the Minister or Public Works and Government Services, 2012 <http://laws.justice.gc.ca/en/const/> accessed 21 June 2020.

[11] Section 91, s 24, Constitution Act 1867.

[12] P H Bryce (1907). Report on the Indian Schools of Manitoba and the North-West Territories, Department of Indian Affairs (Ottawa: Government Printing Bureau), Canadian Pamphlets <https://archive.org/details/reportonindiansc00bryc> accessed 21 June 2020; P H Bryce, *The Story of a National Crime: Being an Appeal for Justice to the Indians of Canada* (James Hope and Sons, Ltd [1922] 2009); Dr F A Corbett was similarly commissioned to inspect the Ermineskin residential school in Hobbema, Alberta in 1922, see Milloy, *A National Crime* (n 6).

communities. Off-reserve students attended local schools in the towns and cities in which they lived. The aim was to offer Indigenous children exactly the same education as their settler counterparts while allowing them to live with their families in their home communities. Although this new approach to Indigenous education was framed as an exercise in equal access to quality education, and thus the integration of indigenous youth into mainstream Canadian society on equal terms, it was in fact a continuation of a process aimed at the assimilation of indigenous children into settler society. It was not until the 1980s and 1990s that dogged advocacy by indigenous communities finally led to the devolution of indigenous on-reserve education to indigenous communities focused on culturally relevant content, including the revival of indigenous languages.

Assimilation was also pursued through a parallel policy of adopting indigenous children out to middle-class white settler families in what is now known as the Sixties Scoop. Falling under provincial administrative jurisdiction and family law, this policy involved approximately 20,000 indigenous children from the late 1950s into the 1980s.[13] It was motivated by the same specious concerns about indigenous parenting that underpinned the creation of the residential schools while ignoring the role the schools played in family breakdown. The schools had destroyed indigenous ways of being and knowing, languages, traditions, and economic capacity while simultaneously providing such an inferior Western education that survivors had no usable training to allow them to succeed economically on and off reserve. Extreme levels of neglect and abuse at the schools where children were raised for years without their families and communities traumatized many students for life. Chief Bev Sellars of the Xats'ull Cmetem' First Nations (Soda Creek Band) in British Columbia, noted in a speech in 1991 that the effect of the schools on survivors had been devastating, including 'the alcoholism, the very low self-esteem of our people, sexual abuse, family breakdown' and 'loss of parenting skills'.[14] Dian Million argues that the schools deadened the emotions of Indigenous children, turning them into 'automatons' during their years at the schools and after. As adults, many survivors were unable to express the trauma they had experienced. They 'frequently became ineffective adults or parents, because they had been removed from parenting roles and could not cope with the force of their own feelings or others'.[15] Their children were often seized by provincial child protection agencies because of parental neglect and substance abuse. In many cases the children needed protection, but little to no attempt was made to keep them in their home communities with families or Indigenous foster parents. Like their parents and grandparents before them, they

[13] Ernie Crey and Suzanne Fournier, *Stolen From Our Embrace. The Abduction of First Nations Children and the Restoration of Aboriginal Communities* (D&M Publishers Inc. 1998); Margaret Philip, 'The Land of Lost Children' *The Globe and Mail* (Toronto, 21 December 2002) F4.

[14] Quoted in Dian Million, *Therapeutic Nations: Healing in an Age of Indigenous Human Rights* (University of Arizona Press 2013) 79.

[15] ibid 79.

were taken away from their 'deviant' families and communities to settler towns and cities to be raised by mostly white families that provincial family law and policies deemed 'acceptable' parents who embodied the mainstream of settler Canadian society.

The Possibilities and Limits of Reconciliation in Canada

Sheri Rosenberg argued that genocide is a 'social phenomenon' which should be understood 'as a process rather than as the outcome of a process' or event.[16] The genocidal process in Canada featured largely indirect forms of destruction grounded in the eliminationist logic of settler colonialism manifested in the removal of indigenous peoples from much of the land to often remote and marginal reserves, the serial reneging by the federal government for over a century of its treaty obligations vis-à-vis indigenous nations, the forcible removal of children to the residential schools, and later, via out-group fostering and adoption, and involuntary assimilation through all of these processes with the intention of exterminating indigenous languages, cultures, and ways of being and knowing. The legacies of this process have been, and continue to be, highly destructive for many indigenous people and communities. Because of the diffuse, mostly (but certainly not entirely) non-violent, and legalistic nature of the genocidal process, it is difficult to say when or whether it has come to an end, although we can say that official policies of child removal and forced assimilation are no longer in place for the most part. This does not mean, however, that the destructive logic and consequences of settler colonialism is no longer at play. I now turn to my discussion of postgenocide reconciliation with the full knowledge that the boundary between the genocidal process and its aftermath in Canada is blurred and contested.

Political Apology and the Canadian Truth and Reconciliation Commission

The Canadian government issued a formal apology for its role in the Indian Residential Schools in 2008 and created the Truth and Reconciliation Commission a year later. This did not happen out of benevolence or the federal government's own volition, but because it had to. Indeed, the apology and the TRC were not undertaken solely by the state as has occurred in other cases, but as part of an agreement between the state and other parties. They were provisions in an agreement between the federal government, indigenous groups, and lawyers representing

[16] Sheri Rosenberg, 'Genocide Is a Process, Not an Event' (2010) 7(1)1 GSI 17.

IRS survivors to head-off a multi-million-dollar class action lawsuit that the Government of Canada was sure to lose. The lawsuit was the latest in a series of litigations over the harms caused by the residential schools. These cases unfolded in the 1990s in parallel with government and indigenous-led inquiries into various aspects of the political and legal regime surrounding the treatment of indigenous peoples and conditions on and off reserve.

The first major attempt by the federal government to grapple with the plight of indigenous peoples in Canada was the Royal Commission on Aboriginal Peoples ('RCAP'), which issued its final report in 1996.[17] The commission was requested by the Chief Justice of the Supreme Court of Canada, Brian Dickson, and implemented by the government of Prime Minister Brian Mulroney in response to heightened domestic and international awareness of indigenous issues stemming from a confrontation a year earlier between local Mohawk and the town of Oka, Quebec over the proposed expansion of a golf course. [18] Seeking to address the underlying tensions that had led to the Oka crisis, the RCAP was mandated by the federal government to carry out an in-depth examination of Aboriginal (the term used at the time) health, education, governance, the north, the Métis, urban issues, and Elders. During the first two years of its operation (1991-1993) the commission interviewed thousands of indigenous and non-indigenous people in rounds of hearings, followed by an extended period in which commissioners tried to reconcile what they had learned from indigenous witnesses with current indigenous policy (1993-1996).[19] Running to 4000 pages and 435 policy recommendations, the final report called among other things for a concerted process of reconciliation guided by the principles of mutual respect, reciprocity, responsibility, and sharing.[20] A truth and reconciliation process was urged, along with substantive steps towards self-government based on the recognition of indigenous peoples as constituting nations with a right to self-determination. Despite the crisis that spawned its creation, the far-reaching involvement of indigenous peoples in the commission, and its groundbreaking recommendations, the RCAP did not have much of an impact on government policy, including reconciliation.

Frustrated with the lack of government response to the RCAP, survivors of the IRS began to sue the federal government for the harm done to them at the schools.

[17] *Report of the Royal Commission on Aboriginal Peoples*, Library and Archives Canada <https://www.bac-lac.gc.ca/eng/discover/aboriginal-heritage/royal-commission-aboriginal-peoples/Pages/final-report.aspx> accessed 21 June 2020 (hereafter *Report of the Royal Commission on Aboriginal Peoples* (n 17)).

[18] Dale Turner, 'Reconciliation in Contemporary Aboriginal Politics' in Jennifer Henderson and Pauline Wakeham (eds), *Reconciling Canada: Critical Perspectives on the Culture of Redress* (University of Toronto Press 2013) 102.

[19] ibid 102–03.

[20] *Royal Commission on Aboriginal Peoples Final Report*, vol 1 chapter 16 (n 17) <http://data2.archives.ca/e/e448/e011188230-01.pdf> accessed 21 June 2020.

This included the *Blackwater* and *Cloud* class action lawsuits in the late 1990s and early 2000s. Not all of the claims in these cases were successful, but their certification paved the way for the *Baxter* class action which represented 80,000 survivors and their descendants and claimed $100 billion (CND) in damages.[21] The threat that *Baxter* too might be certified, and in the face of an additional eleven class action lawsuits, 15,000 individual claims in various stages against the government and churches, and 5,000 Alternative Dispute Resolution cases, the federal government agreed to settle out of court.[22] Nagy shows that the Indian Residential Schools Settlement Agreement ('IRSSA') that was eventually reached in 2007 was a direct response to mounting legal actions that through dialogue and negotiations produced a hybrid solution that brought together the Assembly of First Nations' demands for accountability and the creation of a public record of what happened at the schools, and a more community-focused approach of grass-roots survivor organizations that emphasized reconciliation.[23]

A detailed agreement, the IRSSA included three major components. The first was the creation of a two billion-dollar fund out of which the Government of Canada would disperse Common Experience Payments of varying amounts to survivors depending on their experiences at the schools. Second, was a formal apology to be delivered on the floor of the House of Commons by the federal government. And finally, a truth and reconciliation process that would culminate in an official report detailing the abuses at the schools, the historical context in which they occurred, their legacies, and a set of recommendations. I will focus my comments here on the apology and TRC specifically.

The apology was delivered on the floor of the House of Commons by Conservative Prime Minister Stephen Harper on 11 June 2008. The Prime Minister began by identifying the moral wrongness of the ideas that underpinned the eliminationist project of the schools. Without identifying this project as genocidal, Harper condemned the removal of children from their parents and communities based on 'the assumption [that] Aboriginal cultures and spiritual beliefs were inferior and unequal'.[24] Noting that the students were often 'inadequately fed, clothed, and housed', and 'deprived of ... care and nurturing', the Prime Minister catalogued the negative experiences and outcomes of the schools for many students. He lamented the 'tragic accounts of the emotional, physical and sexual abuse and neglect of helpless children' and the death of some children at the schools, and those who 'never returned home'.[25]

[21] Nagy, *The Truth and Reconciliation Commission of Canada* (n 1) 205.
[22] ibid 206.
[23] ibid 206–11.
[24] Statement of Apology—to Former Students of Indian Residential Schools, 11 June 2008, Ottawa, Ontario <https://www.aadnc-aandc.gc.ca/eng/1100100015644/1100100015649> accessed 21 June 2020.
[25] ibid.

The saying sorry part of the apology was framed in morally relative, rather than morally universalistic, terms. A contrast was drawn between what the government now knew to be wrong, and for which it was sorry, versus an unstated position that the governments that put the IRS policies into place operated in a different moral universe. Thus, the Prime Minister repeatedly used the phrase 'the Government of Canada *now* [italics added] recognizes' that 'it was wrong to forcibly remove children from their homes ... to separate children from rich and vibrant cultures', that these removals 'undermined the ability of many to adequately parent their own children'. The listing of these wrongs was followed each time by the phrase 'for which we are sorry'.[26]

Having named the moral wrongs committed, aided, and abetted by the Canadian government and offered an apology for them, the Prime Minister concluded his statement by claiming that the apology and the Indian Residential School Settlement Agreement was an integral part of the emerging process of reconciliation generally and 'healing ... and resolution of the sad legacy of the Indian Residential Schools'. As for the yet-to-begin Truth and Reconciliation Commission, Harper linked its work to a broader educative function in Canadian society. The TRC would facilitate reconciliation by 'educating Canadians on the Indian Residential Schools', which would in turn generate a new ideational understanding of the relationship between Indigenous peoples and the wider Canadian society informed by 'knowledge of our shared history, and respect for each other'. The commission would also give rise to a key element of conservative political ideology: 'a renewed understanding that strong families, strong communities and vibrant cultures and traditions will contribute to a stronger Canada for all of us'.[27] This last part of the apology unambiguously tied the moral wrongness of the IRS system to the sanctity of the nuclear family and traditional family values championed by the Conservative Party. By invoking these values and the role the apology, the financial settlement for survivors, and the TRC would play in constructing 'a stronger Canada for all of us' based on 'respect for each other', the Conservative government sought to allay fears among their supporters (not known for their sympathy for Indigenous peoples) that reconciliation through these mechanisms would not be a one-way street to the benefit of indigenous peoples and communities. Instead, the government explicitly framed the process as something that would be in the majority's interest as understood through a conservative ideological lens, and would require indigenous peoples to show due respect for the non-indigenous majority. The interests and concerns of the settler population were still to be front and centre as always.

Although the beginning of the truth and reconciliation process was supposed to immediately follow the federal government's apology, it got off to a rocky start

[26] ibid.
[27] ibid.

and took longer than originally anticipated to get underway. Conflicts among the first panel of commissioners led to their resignation and a reconfiguration of the panel with new members and a new chair, Justice Murray Sinclair, a well-respected Indigenous judge from the Court of Queen's Bench in the province of Manitoba. Part of the difficulty in reaching a consensus on the scope and operation of the TRC was that it was not possible to simply replicate similar processes that had taken place in the Global South. Canada had not emerged from a period of armed conflict, authoritarian rule, or lack of development. As such, established processes of transitional justice, although not irrelevant, needed to be reformulated to suit the reality of Canada's situation as a longstanding, peaceful (for settlers), wealthy democracy in which cultural genocide had been part and parcel of its creation and continued function as a settler society. The commission did not need to address how to construct a new political, economic, or other systems in the aftermath of war and despotism or to foster economic development. Nor was the TRC a judicial body empowered to engage in a formal judicial inquiry including the subpoenaing of witnesses and evidence, rendering verdicts, or recommending criminal charges. Rather, it was tasked with fashioning a strategy for laying bare the interplay between Canada's development as a nation through immigration and territorial expansion, the removal of indigenous peoples from much of the land, and their forcible cultural destruction through the Indian Residential Schools and other processes. It also had to craft a relevant and achievable set of recommendations that would substantively address the legacies of the IRS while tacitly acknowledging that the colonial settler system that gave rise to the schools would largely remain intact. But like other TRCs in South Africa and elsewhere, all those involved recognized that survivors, perpetrators, and beneficiaries (for that is what most non-indigenous Canadians are) would continue to live together.

The Truth and Reconciliation Commission held hearings from 2009 until early 2015 and issued its final report in June 2015. The commission was mandated to 'reveal to Canadians the complex truth about the history and the ongoing legacy of the church-run residential schools' by documenting individual and collective harms in a way that 'honours the resilience and courage of former students, their families, and communities'. The TRC would 'guide and inspire a process of truth and healing, leading toward reconciliation' within indigenous families and communities and between indigenous survivors and their communities with the 'churches, governments, and Canadians generally' with the goal of renewing relationships 'on a basis of inclusion, mutual understanding, and respect'.[28] The commission travelled throughout the country (no small feat given that Canada is the

[28] *Honouring the Truth, Reconciling for the Future: Summary of the Final Report of the Truth and Reconciliation Commission of Canada* (Library and Archives Canada Cataloguing in Publications (2015) 24 <http://nctr.ca/assets/reports/Final%20Reports/Executive_Summary_English_Web.pdf> accessed 21 June 2020.

second largest country geographically), holding National Events in the cities of Winnipeg, Inuvik, Halifax, Saskatooon, Montreal, Vancouver, and Edmonton between June 2010 and March 2014. Roughly 155,000 individuals visited these events and over 9,000 IRS survivors registered to attend. Supplementary Regional Events were held in Victoria and Whitehorse, and local hearings took pace over 238 days in seventy-seven communities across the country.[29]

A process of trial and error, innovation along the way, and catharsis, the commission heard mostly from IRS survivors. Some witnesses opted to give their testimony in private as they were still too traumatized by their experiences to speak publicly and had in many cases not told their families or communities about their abuse. For those who spoke publicly, their shocking testimony revealed to non-indigenous attendees and the press, often for the first time, the extent of the abuses visited upon them during their time at residential school and how the teachers, principals, and other staff systematically denigrated their cultures, spirituality, and languages. As part of the forcible assimilation process, students were prevented from speaking their own languages even among themselves and were severely punished for doing so. One Inuit IRS survivor from Nunavut recalled that when she failed to follow instructions after her arrival at the residential school in Pangnirtung because she did not know any English, she was slapped on the hands. 'That's how my education began', she told the commissioners. Another survivor from the same school was 'smacked … in the mouth with the ruler four times' for speaking to a friend in Inuktitut.[30] Encapsulating the experience of many survivors and the 'success' of the policy of language assimilation, Rose Dorothy Charlie told the commission, '[t]hey took my language. They took it right out of my mouth. I never spoke it again'.[31]

In the end the TRC process focused on two key ideational/rhetorical functions: truth-telling and finding ways to reconceptualize and talk about the history of, and current relationship between, indigenous and non-indigenous Canadians. The first function was concerned with lifting a veil of ignorance and secrecy about the residential schools, both in terms of the genocidal intent behind their creation and the nature of the process of destruction at the schools. Given the relative ignorance or indifference of many settler Canadians, the truth-telling process was a matter of speaking truth to a dominant society that hitherto had been uninterested or unwilling to hear about the residential schools and the subjugation of indigenous peoples in Canada generally. In terms of the process, truth-telling about the reality of the schools before the TRC was, as noted above, a largely one-sided affair, with the vast majority of witnesses being IRS survivors. Very few former staff members were willing to publicly share their experiences and perspectives.

[29] ibid 25.
[30] ibid 82.
[31] ibid 84.

Those who did participate were largely greeted with hostility as they were seen by survivors as trying to justify their actions, deflect responsibility, and minimize the harm they caused to students in their care. As a result, the commissioners were not faced with knitting together competing narratives about what happened at the schools as has been the case with TRCs in the aftermath of atrocities elsewhere. Instead, the public events were more of an opportunity for the commissioners and the wider public to hear the stories of the survivors and to bear witness to their victimization and suffering. These stories and other materials were used by the commissioners to craft a historical record of the IRS system contained in the first part of their final report and the personal, communal, and intergenerational legacies of trauma and dysfunction the schools unleashed.

The second half of the final report emphasized restorative ideational frames such as healing among the survivors, 'settler knowledge acquisition through learning'[32] about the schools, and the fostering of a new respectful relationship between indigenous and non-indigenous communities. Drawing on these frames, the TRC offered ninety four calls to action, just over half of which, commissioner Paullette Regan notes, focused on: reconciliation in Indigenous-Crown relations; the integration of Indigenous law into the larger legal order and specifically the justice system; the revival of religion and spirituality; greater financial support for, and indigenous control over, education in their communities; fostering public memory through art, commemorations, and dialogue; and the recognition by non-indigenous Canadians that settlers and Indigenous peoples are all treaty peoples.[33]

Rhetorical/Ideational Elements of Reconciliation in Canada

Ultimately, the apology and TRC process were supposed to be about building a mutually reinforcing relationship between settler acknowledgement of past wrongs, greater indigenous self-determination and resurgence, and building a true nation-to-nation relationship between Canada and indigenous nations. Together and separately these are all laudable goals that have the potential to effect substantive reconciliation and decolonization. To date, however, settler government and societal institutions have embraced the 'easier' rhetorical or ideational aspects of reconciliation.

As I have noted, the federal government's 2008 apology acknowledged wrongdoing but it was also steeped in conservative political values designed in part to reassure non-Indigenous Canadians that they would not be the losers in any

[32] Matt James, 'Changing the Subject: The TRC, Its National Events, and the Displacement of Substantive Reconciliation in Canadian Media Representations' (2017) 51(2) JCS 379.

[33] Paullette Regan, 'Reconciliation and Resurgence: Reflections on the TRC Final Report' in Michael Asch, John Borrows, and James Tully (ed), *Resurgence and Reconciliation: Indigenous–Settler Relations and Earth Teachings* (University of Toronto Press 2018) 214 (hereafter *Resurgence and Reconciliation*).

reconciliation process. Further, by limiting the apology to the Indian Residential Schools, Prime Minister Harper carefully avoided acknowledging, or having the federal government accept responsibility for, the genocidal foundations and effects of settler colonialism and decades of other discriminatory policies unrelated to the schools. The focus on the IRS also firmly harnessed the apology to past wrongs; that is, to a policy that was no longer in place at the time of the apology. As such, the apology drew a hard line under the oppression of indigenous peoples by signalling that these practices should be seen as firmly in the past. In the years that followed the apology, members of the Conservative government either tacitly or explicitly argued that by offering an apology and establishing the TRC and compensation processes, the federal government (and by extension Canadians) did not have to continue to feel guilty or to work in substantive ways towards decolonization. When confronted with legitimate demands by indigenous communities for meaningful support to ameliorate harsh conditions (for which federal underfunding and neglect were largely responsible) or push-back against state interference in indigenous education and governance, the Conservative government fell back on the apology and the then-underway TRC to blunt these criticisms or to evade taking action. '*It's all in the past ... We've said we're sorry so let's all move on now and stop complaining*', was the not-so-subtle subtext.

During the 2015 federal election, the opposition Liberal Party under Justin Trudeau ran on a platform that included a promise to take reconciliation seriously. After securing victory in part with the support of indigenous voters, the new Prime Minister and his government embraced reconciliation with alacrity. Reconciliation and the implementation of the TRC's calls to action—specifically the creation of a new nation-to-nation relationship—were reframed as top government priorities and as wholly consistent with the Party's conception of Canada as a progressive, rights-bearing, multicultural society.

Adopting a 'whole-of-government' approach, all ministers, regardless of portfolio, were issued mandate letters from the Prime Minister outlining their ministry's role in their core area of responsibility as well as the reconciliation process. The fact that ministers had each received these letters and that they all contained requirements for the new ministers to facilitate reconciliation was widely publicized by the new government. Two new ministries were created out of the old ministry of Indian and Northern Affairs: Crown-Indigenous Relations and Northern Affairs, and Indigenous Services. An illustrative example of the rhetorical/ideational approach to reconciliation by the Liberal government is contained in the mandate letter to Minister of Crown—Indigenous Relations, Dr Carolyn Bennett. We see in this letter a commitment to the ideational reframing of the relationship between indigenous peoples and the rest of Canada on a more equal basis and a willingness to acknowledge past wrongs and their contemporary legacies. We also see, however, an emphasis on process and the persistent privileging on non-indigenous Canadian's interests as understood by the Liberal government.

Minister Bennett's letter instructs her and her ministry to work with Indigenous Services, other ministries, the Official opposition, the public service, civil society, business and labour, and other 'stakeholders' to forge a new relationship with indigenous communities to implement the calls to action of the TRC and effect reconciliation generally:[34]

> As Canada's first Minister of Crown—Indigenous Relations and Northern Affairs, you will accelerate the work you have already begun to renew the nation-to-nation, Inuit-Crown, and government-to-government relationship between Canada and Indigenous Peoples. You will also modernize our institutional structure and governance so that First Nations, Inuit, and Métis Peoples can build capacity that supports implementation of their vision of self-determination. This new relationship must be based on the recognition of rights, respect, co-operation, and partnership.[35]

The minister was tasked with fully twenty-two specific tasks including 'develop[ing] and lead[ing] consultations as we adopt machinery of government changes to renew the relationship with Indigenous Peoples', 'lead[ing] a whole-of-government approach to the renewal of a nation-to-nation, Inuit-Crown, and government-to-government relationship with Indigenous Peoples' including 'Indigenous representatives in meaningful ways in Canada's federal-provincial-territorial dialogues'. The letter also required the minister to engage in a dizzying array of actions including consultation and development of policies around resource development projects, northern development and food security, a new fiscal relationship between the Crown and indigenous peoples (to be established alongside the Minister of Finance), legal reform (in conjunction with the Minister of Justice/Attorney General), confronting the problem of missing and murdered indigenous women, 'work[ing] with Indigenous Peoples to support them in their work to rebuild and reconstitute their nations, advancing self-determination, and, for First Nations, facilitating the transition away from the Indian Act and toward self-government'. The ministry and Government of Canada was also charged with further supporting 'the necessary process of truth-telling and healing' which itself requires working 'with provinces and territories, and with First Nations, Inuit, and the Métis Nation, to drive progress on implementation of recommendations of the Truth and Reconciliation Commission'.[36]

This very long to-do list sounds promising. However, the letter does not mention indigenous matters in a sustained way until paragraph 9. The first part of the

[34] Minister of Crown-Indigenous Relations and Northern Affairs, the Honourable Carolyn Bennett, Mandate Letter: <https://pm.gc.ca/eng/minister-crown-indigenous-relations-and-northern-affairs-mandate-letter> accessed 21 June 2020.
[35] ibid.
[36] ibid.

letter replicates other government goals that are clearly aimed at living up to campaign promises made to non-indigenous voters in the 2015 election and securing non-indigenous Canadians' interests. Although the Prime Minister declares near the beginning of the letter that '[n]o relationship is more important to me and to Canada than the one with Indigenous Peoples' and that now 'is the time for a renewed nation-to-nation relationship … based on recognition of rights, respect, co-operation, and partnership',[37] the rest of the introduction focuses squarely on the new government's key constituency: Canada's 'middle-class'. A representative paragraph states that the Liberal Party 'made a commitment to grow our economy, strengthen the middle class, and help those working hard to join it. We committed to provide more direct help to those who need it by giving less to those who do not. We committed to public investment to spur economic growth, job creation, and broad-based prosperity'.[38] By stating these larger imperatives first, Trudeau makes clear that a renewed relationship with indigenous peoples needs to fit comfortably within the promises made to 'the middle class'. This will be done by avoiding substantive concessions with First Nations over the return of land or economic control over resource extraction, for example. While the 'self-government' label appears repeatedly, there is no discussion of what this should look like. Similarly, the mandate letter does not mention the harder task of returning some land to indigenous nations. And while it talks about the need to consult indigenous communities over economic development and resource extraction, there are no instructions about the necessity of gaining these communities' consent.

Absence of Substantive/Material Reconciliation (Decolonization)

Now, of course, one mandate letter should not be used as the index for reconciliation in Canada post—apology, the TRC, and the election of the Liberal government. But if we look at the current political, economic, social, and legal conditions of Indigenous peoples on and off reserve, not much substantively has changed. There are many areas we might examine, but I will restrict my analysis to two closely related foundational issues: land claims settlements and consultation over the use of indigenous lands for resource extraction, and the transportation of resources to market. The seizure of land is foundational to settler colonialism and the genocide it spawned as I have described earlier. The transfer of some lands back to indigenous control would equally be the foundation for many of the substantive/material changes identified by many indigenous groups as critical to true reconciliation and decolonization. It is also one of, if not the most, difficult issues to resolve since it has a very tangible zero-sum quality to it. The issue of consultation/consent

[37] ibid.
[38] ibid.

is only marginally less controversial since it involves having indigenous communities participate in substantive ways in deciding how the lands they currently control, or have not ceded to the Crown, can be used for economic purposes. However, as I will discuss later, a series of Supreme Court of Canada rulings in which the court established a 'duty of consultation' in most cases and of consent under limited circumstances has meant that indigenous groups do not have an equal say over how their own lands can be used within the larger economy. Governments have taken a fairly strict interpretation of the duty to consult while avoiding the harder, and more constraining, policy of gaining consent.

Since the submission of the Truth and Reconciliation final report, no lands have been transferred from the Crown back to indigenous peoples. Indigenous nations have not, and are not, asking for the return all of the landmass of Canada to indigenous nations. Instead, the goal is to settle outstanding disputes over un-ceded territory—called 'comprehensive land claims' or modern treaties—and disputes over land covered by existing treaties—or 'specific land claims'. To be sure, there have been significant comprehensive land claims settlements between indigenous nations and the Canadian government and some provincial governments, mostly British Columbia where the vast majority of unceded territory is located. Similar to the James Bay and Northern Quebec Treaty of 1975[39] (the first modern treaty since 1920), the federal and provincial government of British Columbia have completed important modern treaties including with the Nisga'a in 2000,[40] and more recently the Tsawwassen First Nation Final Agreement in 2009.[41] The latter two treaties upheld Supreme Court of Canada rulings since the 1980s that historic treaties with the Crown did not fully extinguish Aboriginal title. Although the specific details of these treaties differ, they did grant fee-simple Indigenous land ownership over at least some of the lands they had long claimed were theirs. The modern treaties took decades to complete and were either agreed to or near completion by the time the TRC process began. Since the beginning of the TRC, no new comprehensive land claims have been agreed to and thus no land has been transferred from the Crown to indigenous communities. This is despite the current government's pledge to work in close partnership with indigenous communities to settle outstanding comprehensive land claims as part of the reconciliation process.

When we look at the situation concerning specific land claims disputes over the same period, progress has been similarly slow. As noted, these land claims do not include the prospect of transferring land to indigenous nations, but rather claims that the Crown has failed to uphold its existing treaty obligations. These claims are much more numerous than comprehensive land claims and are just as important

[39] *James Bay and Northern Quebec Native Claims Settlement Act* S.C. 1976-77, c. 32 <http://www.laws-lois.justice.gc.ca> accessed 12 February 2019.

[40] Nisga'a Final Agreement <http://www.nisgaanation.ca> accessed 12 February 2019.

[41] Tsawwassen First Nation Final Agreement <http://aadnc-aandc.gc.ca> accessed 12 February 2019.

because they deal with the ability of indigenous communities to use their land according to their own needs and ways of being and knowing in areas such as education, self-governance, and the development and use of resources. Citing a 2016 Canadian government Auditor General's report, the Assembly of First Nations has noted that '[f]ewer than 15 percent of [specific land] claims from 2007-2016 resulted in settlements—the vast majority of claims were either "rejected" or simply "closed"' by the federal government.[42] The Auditor General's report[43] itself shows in detail that a new process adopted by the Department of Indigenous and Northern Affairs Canada under the Conservative government in 2007 called Justice at Last: Specific Claims Action Plan ('JAL'), and the Specific Claims Tribunal Act passed by parliament a year later establishing the Specific Claims Tribunal, has not substantively improved the land claims settlement process for indigenous communities. The Auditor concluded that from 2007 to 2016, the department failed to realize the objectives of the JAL because it 'did not adequately manage the resolution of First Nations specific claims'. The implementation of the 2007 reforms in practice 'introduced barriers that hindered First Nation's access to the specific claims process and impeded the resolution of claims'. Barriers included 'certain practices that did not encourage negotiations, cuts to funding for claims preparation and negotiation' that were supposed to be made available to First Nations claimants, 'and limited information sharing between the Department and First Nations'. The investigation further revealed that 'the Department was aware of First Nations' concerns about these barriers, but was unable to demonstrate that it had a formal process to gather, monitor, and respond to information and feedback about these concerns and make required improvement'.[44]

The issue of resource extraction, development, and transit on or over First Nations' treaty lands has been a similarly consistent, and urgent, issue over the last two decades. While land claims are critically important for the reasons I have suggested, the process is usually lengthy and behind the scenes. Indigenous participation in economic activities on their lands that affect the wider economy and society, by contrast, are very public affairs. Competing interests and claims made by indigenous and non-indigenous communities—often including cross-cutting alliances and contestation—as well as governments and industry, combine together to produce protracted disputes over economic opportunities, benefits, environmental impacts, and how they will be shared, restricted, or managed.

[42] Land and Claims, Specific Claims, Assembly of First Nations <https://www.afn.ca/policy-sectors/lands-claims/> accessed 12 February 2019.

[43] Report 6—First Nations Specific Claims—Indigenous and Northern Affairs Canada, 2016 Fall Reports of the Auditor General of Canada, Office of the Auditor General of Canada <http://www.oag-bvg.gc.ca/internet/English/parl_oag_201611_06_e_41835.html> accessed 12 February 2019.

[44] Section 6.17, Report 6—First Nations Specific Claims—Indigenous and Northern Affairs Canada, 2016 Fall Reports of the Auditor General of Canada, Office of the Auditor General of Canada <http://www.oag-bvg.gc.ca/internet/English/parl_oag_201611_06_e_41835.html> accessed 12 February 2019.

The courts have been a central venue for the processing of some of these disputes. Because Canada has a common law legal system in which judicial decisions by the apex court (the Supreme Court of Canada) make law, decisions concerning the assertion of Aboriginal rights and Aboriginal title have largely produced the legal regime that defines Indigenous rights and land use. These decisions decisively moved away from earlier judgments that indigenous land title was permanently extinguished by the pre-Confederation and Numbered treaties because indigenous peoples were too 'primitive' to hold land title.[45] Nonetheless, decisions since the 1970s have reinforced that land and especially resources are to be shared, with indigenous communities granted the right to be consulted, and to provide their consent only in limited circumstances.

A critical case was *Delgamuukw v British Columbia*, heard by the Supreme Court of Canada in 1997. Gitksan and Wet'suwet'en hereditary chiefs claimed at trial that their nations had ownership of their traditional territories in British Columbia and, therefore, jurisdiction over it. The Supreme Court reinterpreted the chiefs' claim on appeal as a matter of Aboriginal title under section 35(1) of the Constitution Act 1982.[46] The task for the court was to define what constitutes Aboriginal title and whether and how the Crown may violate it. Writing for the majority, Chief Justice Lamer ruled that the source of Aboriginal title is *sui generis* as it 'arises from the prior occupation of Canada by aboriginal peoples' before the assertion of British sovereignty.[47] Aboriginal title 'encompasses the right of exclusive use and occupation to the land held pursuant to that title'[48] which 'confers the right to use land for a variety of activities' by indigenous peoples 'not all of which need to be aspects of practices, customs, and traditions which are integral to the distinctive cultures of aboriginal societies' (ie, they do not need to be strictly traditional or pre-contact in nature).[49]

The capacity to exercise exclusive land use is, however, balanced against the sovereignty of the Crown. Citing the court's prior jurisprudence, Lamer determined that Aboriginal rights and title 'are not absolute' and 'may be infringed by both the federal and provincial governments'.[50] While infringement 'must be in furtherance of a legislative objective that is compelling and substantial', Aboriginal rights and title 'are a necessary part of the reconciliation of aboriginal societies with the broader political community of which they are a part'.[51] Here Lamer was not conceptualizing reconciliation as a confrontation with, and recovering from, genocide and colonialism, but rather as reconciling the 'prior occupation of North

[45] *St. Catherine's Milling and Lumber Company v. The Queen* (1887) 13 SCR 577 18887-06-20.
[46] *Delgamuuku v. British Columbia* [1997] 3 SCR 1010 para 7.
[47] ibid para 114.
[48] ibid para 116.
[49] ibid para 111.
[50] ibid para 160.
[51] *Gladstone* [1996] 2 SCR 723 para 73; quoted in *Delgamuuku v. British Columbia* [1997] para 161.

America by aboriginal people with the assertion of Crown sovereignty'. Indigenous peoples were thus recognized by the court as 'distinctive societies' but which exist in 'a broader social, political, and economic community'. As such, development of various sectors of the economy (forestry, mining, agriculture, hydroelectric power, oil and gas), environmental protection, and the continued settlement of immigrants to Canada 'can justify the infringement of aboriginal title'.[52] When Aboriginal rights and title are justifiably infringed, government must uphold its 'duty of honour and good faith' and provide 'fair compensation' to the indigenous communities affected.[53] To confront the reality of modern settler colonialism in Canada, the chief justice concluded, we must acknowledge the situation in which we collectively find ourselves: 'Let us face it, we are all here to stay.'[54]

Despite the commitment of the current federal government to live up to the recommendations of the TRC, ongoing disputes over infrastructure projects on indigenous lands demonstrate that the material imperatives of the settler economy remain paramount for government, industry, and Canadians employed in the oil and gas sector. The duty of consultation, rather than a duty to gain consent, has informed how both government and the courts have dealt with these cases to date.

A representative case is the long-running conflict over a pipeline expansion project originally begun by Kinder Morgan, a pipeline company based in the oil-rich but landlocked province of Alberta (the federal government purchased the pipeline in 2018, several years into the planning of the project). The company planned to extend its existing Trans Mountain oil pipeline from just outside of Edmonton, Alberta, to the lower mainland coast of British Columbia at the Westridge Marine Terminal near Burnaby. For the provincial government in Alberta and its oil sector, the increase in pipeline capacity is seen as an absolute necessity since Alberta's primary and tertiary economy is tied to oil and gas. Royalties and tax revenues from the sector also fund important provincial public services including healthcare and education. Following federal National Energy Board ('NEB') rules for the approval of infrastructure projects that span provincial boundaries and cross Indigenous lands, Kinder Morgan engaged in a series of consultations beginning in 2012 with indigenous communities along the expansion route. The company claimed to have 'sought to meaningfully engage with indigenous communities in Alberta and British Columbia' in Treaty 6 and 8 territory, the Metis Nation of Alberta (Zone 4), and '15 First Nation Reserve lands' in British Columbia; a process that resulted in 'more than 30,000 points of contact'. Emphasizing the mutual benefit of the pipeline expansion, Kinder Morgan asserted that 'the Project presents a special opportunity to enhance existing relationships with Indigenous communities

[52] *Delgamuuku v. British Columbia* [1997] para 165.
[53] Ibid para 169.
[54] Ibid para 186.

along our pipeline corridor, while also opening the door to new relationships, including coastal Indigenous communities with respect to marine transportation and safety'.[55]

Following the consultation process, and the completion of other environmental assessment requirements, the NEB approved the project on 29 May 2016. The Prime Minister followed suit on 29 November of the same year through an Order in Council. The granting of the Order in Council itself involved an additional round of consultations with affected indigenous communities by the federal government during the so-called Phase III of the approval process. This is based directly on the Supreme Court's 'duty of consultation' requirement concerning the infringement of Aboriginal title set out in *Delgamuuku* and other rulings. Citing the violation of Aboriginal title and the potential for severe environmental damage due to possible oil spills along the pipeline and inland waters near the Westridge Marine Terminal, several municipalities and First Nations along the route filed a lawsuit against the company and the federal government. The Federal Court of Appeal quashed the federal approval for the Trans Mountain project on 30 August 2018. The court found in part that the Government of Canada 'fell well short of the mark set by the Supreme Court of Canada' by failing to engage in 'two-way dialogue' that was 'deep' and 'meaningful', and which grappled 'with the real concerns of Indigenous applicants so as to explore possible accommodation of those concerns'. 'The duty to consult', the court concluded, 'was not adequately discharged'.[56] The court did not, however, say that the building and maintenance of the pipeline would constitute an unacceptable infringement on Aboriginal title or that the federal government needed to gain the consent of First Nations along the pipeline route. Instead, the justices called on Canada to hold a more thorough and interactive round of Phase III consultations that must include 'deep' and 'meaningful' dialogue. After a second round of consultations, the project received final approval on 18 June 2019 and construction has now begun against the continued objection of some indigenous communities along the route. Although the project had been delayed by the court case and additional consultations, the legal capacity of settler governments and industry to override a lack of indigenous consent remained intact and thus significant settler control over the use of indigenous lands in this case continues largely unchanged.

Frustration with the disconnect between the official rhetoric about reconciliation and the lack of willingness to move beyond a duty of consultation to substantive consent is palpable in indigenous communities. Responding in January 2019 to the use of the Royal Canadian Mounted Police ('RCMP') by the government of British Columbia to break-up protests by hereditary chiefs opposed to

[55] Kinder Morgan, Trans Mountain Expansion Project <by https://www.transmountain.com/indigenous-peoples> accessed 15 February 2019.

[56] *Tsleil-Waututh Nation v. Canada* (Attorney General) [2018] FCA 153, at para 6, 508–47, 575–97.

a liquified natural gas project on Wet'suwet'en territory, the Union of BC Indian Chiefs ('UBCIC') accused the provincial government of taking an overly narrow view of the duty to consult. Grand Chief Steward Phillip, president of UBCIC, dismissed the notion that consultation is sufficient. 'We need to be talking about consent', he insisted.[57] Chief Phillip then connected what he termed the unacceptable use of force by the RCMP against peaceful protesters to a violation of 'meaningful reconciliation'. Addressing the issue of indigenous consent over resource projects on indigenous territory, he vigorously rejected 'the racist notion of veto perpetuated by industry and government, which falsely implies that Indigenous Peoples demand a unilateral final say on decisions that impact them'. Instead indigenous peoples in Canada 'want to have an equal say and have our perspectives respected and upheld' which stands in stark contrast to the Crown which has '[had] a veto over almost every aspect of our lives' historically and currently, including the BC government's use of the RCMP to shut down the Gitimd'en protest camp. Judy Wilson, Secretary-Treasurer of the UBCIC noted that the lack of willingness to give indigenous communities an equal say over the substantive/material development of economic projects on their land extended to the federal government, despite the latter's oft-stated commitment to reconciliation. 'Prime Minister Trudeau continues to defend Canada's support for the Trans Mountain pipeline expansion despite a lack of consent from Indigenous people impacted.'[58] Here we see a demand for reconciliation to be substantive in process and outcome as well as a rejection of a zero-sum approach that would pit indigenous and non-indigenous communities against each other.

Final Observations

Reconciliation since the apology and the release of the Truth and Reconciliation Commission's final report has been a priority for the current federal and the more progressive provincial governments, but only at the rhetorical and ideational level. Substantive material changes have been slow in coming although there has been some additional funding made available to indigenous communities when compared with previous governments. What has been done aligns with the current government's understanding of Canada's identity as a nice guy nation—a nation that now knows its own sad history, that accepts responsibility, that wants to talk about a new relationship of mutual respect. But these rhetorical/ideational stances have not been matched by material change with respect to land and other matters

[57] 'UBCIC Statement of Clarity in Response to Premier Horgan's Comments on Unist'ot'en' *Alberta Native News* (Edmonton 10 January 2019) <http://www.albertanativenews.com/ubcic-statement-of-clarity-in-response-to-premier-horgans-comments-on-unistoten/> accessed 15 February 2019.
[58] ibid.

that would involve settler society, its institutions and governments, businesses and the like giving up real things.

In critiquing this lack of substantive progress, I am not endorsing the 'settler futurity' thesis in which decolonization through substantive material reconciliation is equated with the removal of settlers from the land in whole or in part. As I have noted, indigenous scholars, leaders, and communities are not asking for this. While there are some First Nations scholars and activists who advocate for separation, others offer nuanced and creative ways of rethinking the relationship between indigenous and non-indigenous peoples. This includes how we share the land and how to conceptualize and implement existing treaties in ways that could produce substantive material change but in mutually beneficial ways. To do this, some indigenous scholars such as Starblanket and Kiiwetinepinesiik Stark,[59] have begun to reconceptualize settler-indigenous politics and interrelationships as grounded in kinship and indigenous resurgence. Seeing each other as kin would allow for a more robust understanding of the obligations we owe each other—particularly that owned by the Crown to indigenous nations—shorn of settler colonialism's logics of hierarchy, oppression, and elimination. As members of the same family living in the same house, so to speak, non-indigenous Canadians could move beyond simply saying 'nice' things and feeling guilty about our past while simultaneously refusing to take real steps towards the redistribution of land and other resources that settlers believe is now theirs. Sharing the land and its resources, economic opportunity, access to high-quality culturally-grounded education, substantive justice regardless of identity with kin would rescue reconciliation from devolving into words without actions or actions that create conflict and recriminations on all sides. Chief Justice Lamer was right, Indigenous and non-Indigenous Canadians 'are here to stay'. If we are to leave behind our history and legacies of cultural genocide and achieve substantive reconciliation and decolonization we must create a genuine partnership among all peoples living on Turtle Island.

[59] Gina Starblanket and Heidi Kiiwetinepinesiik Stark, 'Towards a Relational Paradigm—Four Points for Consideration: Knowledge, Gender, Land, and Modernity' in *Resurgence and Reconciliation* (n 33) 175–208.

12
Conclusion
Further Agendas for Postgenocide Research

Christopher P Davey

Opening Remarks

In many ways preceding chapters in this volume have questioned whether the concept of genocide—as defined in the Genocide Convention—is fully capable of classifying particular instances of massive violence in the contemporary world, particularly in terms of the actors and processes involved. Contributions in this volume have advanced the idea that there are scholarly and policy benefits to be had from paying close attention to genocide effects in its aftermath, not least in terms of being more effective in living with the loss and suffering incurred, processes of rebuilding affected societies in postgenocide, efforts to identify early warning signs of genocide and ultimately be effective with prevention. Fully aware that the preceding chapters open up research matters that cannot be exhausted by one single volume, this concluding chapter offers reflections on additional related themes which complement the postgenocide agenda.

In light of growing concerns about climate change and the potential that—in very aggravated forms—climate change might be a factor in the occurrence of genocide, this chapter suggests that the claim of 'climate genocide' might be a useful benchmark to query the relevance of the common conception of genocide. Michael Klare describes climate genocide with this implication:

> failing to halt the advance of climate change … [which] means complicity with mass human annihilation.… [and which] is clearly going to be a process of climate genocide. How can those of us in countries responsible for the majority of greenhouse gas emissions escape such a verdict?[1]

[1] Michael Klare, 'Climate Change as Genocide: Inaction Equals Annihilation,' (*openDemocracy* 21 April 2017) <https://www.opendemocracy.net/en/north-africa-west-asia/climate-change-as-genocide-inaction-equals-annihilation/> accessed 29 March 2019. Klare cites the cases of Yemen, Nigeria, Sudan, and Somalia as harbingers of these cataclysms.

Christopher P Davey, *Conclusion* In: *Postgenocide*. Edited by: Klejda Mulaj, Oxford University Press (2021). © The Several Contributors. DOI: 10.1093/oso/9780192895189.003.0012

This apocalyptic modification of genocide is used to stimulate awareness and action in the face of contemporary resource conflicts, and violence around famine and drought.

Deployments of Raphael Lemkin's neologism after this manner tend to lurch towards the dramatic and test present limitations placed on the concept's use.[2] Klare's proposition demonstrates an activist logic in his use of the term 'genocide'. Similarly, individual and state responsibilities are positioned as key to ameliorating the violent effects of climate change. However, invocations of climate genocide implicate most of us broadly in a total destruction of all life, or omnicide, reminiscent of literature around nuclear war. In this vein, the ramifications on identity and its deployments are similarly beyond the current framing of genocide. Such uses also reflect the wide adaptation and co-options of the term itself. In the face of possible climate genocide it is all too easy to fall into the overused simplifications of genocide, such as 'perpetrator' and 'victim'. Or in another sense, perpetrator and victim seem to become synonymous with (respectively) the global north and the global south. This is not sufficient to capture the dynamic uses of violence globally where not only climate change, but massive inequality, poverty, resource conflict and exploitation, and violent non-state actors overlap. This chapter uses the term 'postgenocide' to assess these intersecting trends.

In response to this growing need to understand climate-related and other contemporary incarnations of mass violence, this chapter considers the convergences of resource scarcity and exploitation, warlordism, the geopolitical ordering of states, and climate change. This is done in the context of postgenocide in our contemporary age, or the Anthropocene, where humanity is considered to be the prevailing influencer of the climate and environment, by relying on existing discussion of these elements and specific cases. Postgenocide presents a conceptual evolution which accounts for genocidal impacts on groups where the traditional, legally defined approaches appear fractured, and the key role of the state or intent to destroy is ambiguous. Further, and in line with prior chapters, postgenocide is discussed here in terms of identities in these convergences. This approach takes the view that identities are generally fluid and performative, and crucially so in both genocide and postgenocide.

Proposed usage of the postgenocide term aims to take the creative imaginary out of environmental security literature, and considers these convergences from the perspective of genocide studies. The chapter will first recap a note on this field, and then discuss postgenocide and its constituent elements, before moving to consider repercussions for identities in the context of postgenocide. The chapter,

[2] As further demonstrated by Adam Jones' brief assessment of arguments framing poverty as genocide, see Adam Jones, 'Genocide and Structural Violence: Charting the Terrain,' in Adam Jones (ed), *New Directions in Genocide Research* (Routledge 2012) 136 (hereafter Jones, 'Genocide and Structural Violence').

therefore, is a reflection on the scope of postgenocide and its applicability to violence in what is known of the Anthropocene. Various cases are used, some from those in this volume and others from contemporary and historic instances of post/genocidal processes.

Climate Violence Debates and the Evolution of Genocide Studies

Environmental security and 'climate wars' literature portray a bleak view of the future and vividly articulate the end times. Extreme weather, water and food shortages, and drought all point towards an escalation of what US military analysts have called 'threat multipliers'.[3] Existing, or traditional threats, are worsened by the destructive potential of these dynamics. According to this literature, these dangers point to a series of genocides, ecocides, or omnicide. Some authors vividly articulate cataclysmic events: resources' wars for survival and nuclear destruction.[4] This literature has warranted a strong response from more critical and quantitative perspectives, especially from political ecologists and climate historians. The consensus here seems to be that environmental security literature tends to be alarmist and catastrophist, and encourages hasty action or a mis-popularization of violence that does not exist at present. Causal chains between climate change, water shortages (and drought in particular), and violence are consistently identified as missing links.[5] Popular environmental security literature involves an imagining of genocide(s) that is provocative and lacks grounding in evidence and existing theory.

[3] This chapter will refer to climate change as the broad labelling of the effects of global warming. It is further understood that outside simple technical differences there are distinct political and ethical nuances to using either term, see Stephen Gardiner, 'Ethics and Global Climate Change,' in Stephen Gardiner *et al* (eds), *Climate Ethics: Essential Readings* (OUP 2010) 4–5; CNA Military Advisory Board, *National Security and the Accelerating Risks of Climate Change* (May 2014) <https://www.cna.org/cna_files/pdf/MAB_5-8-14.pdf> 2, accessed 12 April 2019.

[4] Anthony Barnosky and Elizabeth Anne Hadley, *End Game: Tipping Point for Planet Earth* (HarperCollins Publishers 2015); Gwynne Dyer, *Climate Wars: The Fight for Survival as the World Overheats* (Oneworld Publications 2011) (hereafter Dyer, *Climate Wars*); Harald Welzer, *Climate Wars: What People will be Killed for in the 21st Century* (Polity 2017).

[5] Idean Salehyan, 'Climate Change to Conflict? No Consensus Yet?' (2008) Journal of Peace Research 45, 315–26; Salehyan and Cullen Hendrix, 'Climate Shocks and Political Violence' (2014) Global Environmental Change 28, 239–50; Jürgen Scheffran *et al*, 'Climate Change and Violent Conflict' (2012) Science 336, 869–71 (hereafter Scheffran *et al*, 'Climate Change'); Jürgen Scheffran, Tobias Ide, and Janpeter Schilling, 'Violent Climate or Climate of Violence? Concepts of Relations with Focus on Kenya and Sudan' (2014) International Journal of Human Rights 18, 369–390 (hereafter Scheffran, Ide, and Schilling, 'Climate Violence'); Bruno Tertrais, 'The Climate Wars Myth' (2011) The Washington Quarterly 34, 17–29; Ole Magnus Theisen, Helge Holtermann, and Halvard Buhaug, 'Climate Wars?: Assessing the Claim that Drought Breeds Conflict' (2011/2012) International Security 36, 79–106 (hereafter Theisen, Holtermannm and Buhaug, 'Climate Wars?').

In trying to account for the positions of this debate, it is worth considering what is contained within the theory and historical annals of genocide studies that can fill this gap, in order to offer a broader view on a context of contemporary forms of genocidal violence. Given the prevalence of mass violence, the context in which such violence occurs is important. It is the argument of this chapter that this context is sufficiently unique in the contemporary age to warrant a reconsideration of the conceptual framework of mass violence.[6] Alex Alvarez has argued that the assessment of the impact of climate change on violence should be viewed through situational, ideological, and psychological lenses. He further claims that climate change creates a political environment where people 'react to changes, insecurity, and anxiety by exploiting and manipulating pre-existing prejudices'.[7] A critique of this position is the assumption that claims of direct causal connections between climate change and violence lack broader contextualization. It is the contention of this chapter that postgenocide can be used to identify these convergences.[8]

Genocide studies is simultaneously a growing, fragmented, and innovative field.[9] Being drawn from the invention of Lemkin and his work—both in *Axis Rule in Occupied Europe* and in his later unpublished manuscripts on colonialism as a broader collection of case studies—genocide is a unique classification of mass violence. Derived from early Holocaust studies, genocide studies have recently evolved out of definitional struggles into assessing application and relational perspectives.[10] In other words, we have developed the ability to discuss genocide without having to obsessively or avariciously reinvent Lemkin's term in every article or book. This edited book itself is an example of this matured ability to reconsider genocide without having to reassert self-justification for such an exploration. Contributors in this volume have suggested that there is a need to reconsider genocide on a variety of fronts. A crucial point has now also been reached where

[6] Damien Short, *Redefining Genocide: Settler Colonialism, Social Death and Ecocide* (Zed Books 2016) 37, 67 (hereafter Short, *Redefining Genocide*); Jones, 'Genocide and Structural Violence' (n 2) 147. This is further demonstrated by Zygmunt Bauman in a piece that contrasts 'globalizing wars' waged in the name of an international community and 'globalization-induced wars' as an extension of the ordering of global capital, ie, who benefits and conforms and who does not, see Zygmunt Bauman, 'Wars of the Globalisation Era' (2001) European Journal of Social Theory 4, 11–28. For a contrasting view where climate crises and violence may well unify and strengthen the globality of the community under the banner of humanitarianism, see Gregory Kent, 'Crystallisations of the Global Western State in the Era of Climate Change' (2014) International Journal of Human Rights 18, 320–35.

[7] Alex Alvarez, *Unstable Ground: Climate Change, Conflict and Genocide* (Rowman and Littlefield 2017) 70–73 (hereafter Alvarez, *Unstable Ground*).

[8] Mark Levene, 'Predicting Genocide in an Age of Anthropogenic Climate Change: An Interim Report' (*Crisis Forum* 2019) <http://www.crisis-forum.org.uk/publications/Levene_genocide_climate.doc> accessed 16 April 2019.

[9] See in this volume Klejda Mulaj, 'Introduction: Postgenocide: Living with Permutations of Genocide Harms', (hereinafter Mulaj, 'Introduction').

[10] Alexander Laban Hinton, 'Critical Genocide Studies' (2012) Genocide Studies and Prevention 7, 4–15; Samuel Totten, 'The State and Future of Genocide Studies and Prevention: An Overview and Analysis of Some Key Issues' (2011) Genocide Studies and Prevention 6, 212–16. See a similar approach taken in Chapter 6 by Mnatsakanyan in this volume on relational processes of denial.

analysis need not be limited to the legalistic identification of intent at the expense of robust analysis of genocidal processes and their ensuing legal and other effects as shown throughout this volume. In particular, as demonstrated in the chapters of the third part of this volume, genocide carries deep and devastating structural violence, impacting materiality and narrative.[11] This suggests that mass killing is not the only element of genocide.[12] Recent studies have sought to capture the evolution of the concept of 'ecocide' linking devastation of the environment and detrimental impact on humans. They suggest a 'genocide-ecocide nexus' where the impact of acts of aggression produce, or are integral to, the destruction of a group.[13] Genocide studies is then poised, in part, to address the challenges of climate change and connected patterns of violence in more innovative ways. Yet, it requires further tools to do so.

Postgenocide Elements

As noted in the introduction to this volume, in the same way that post-colonial periodic classification and postcolonialism differ, so too does postgenocide differ from post-genocide as a temporalism.[14] Postgenocide can be considered as a possible evolution of Lemkin's concept for the contemporary era. Using 'genocide' as a heritage, the postgenocide categorization of mass violence and framing of violent processes can help leverage a qualitative and reflective approach to the problems of assessing mass violence in the contemporary age. Mark Levene described postgenocide as:

> a nightmare scenario which is not genocide but rather post-genocide. Mass killing beyond the state: beyond the specificity let alone intent of destroying communal group targets. Committed by two or possibly many more communal or sub-state players. Without logical goals or boundaries. And without end.[15]

Of greatest significance is the attention that postgenocide can give to existing or recent conflicts, where the convergences of global capitalism and climate change are being felt, and are interacting with instances of violence.

[11] See Chapter 9 by Martine Hawkes, Chapter 10 by Marcia Esparza, and Chapter 11 by Maureen Hiebert in this volume.

[12] Scheffran, Ide, and Schilling, 'Climate Violence' (n 5) 370.

[13] Short, *Redefining Genocide* (n 6) 38–67; Scheffran *et al*, 'Climate Change' (n 5) 376; Garry Leech, *Capitalism: A Structural Genocide* (Zed Books 2012) 85–93 (hereafter Leech, *Capitalism*).

[14] Mulaj, 'Introduction', (n 9) 4–5.

[15] Mark Levene, 'A Dissenting Voice: Part II' (2004) Journal of Genocide Research 6, 436 (hereafter Levene, 'Dissenting Voice'). Levene includes a hyphenation of this term 'post-genocide'. As discussed in the Introduction, the hyphen has been dropped in this volume for both the sake of consistency and conceptual development.

It is not that violence and climate change are not related; it is that there is a shallow evidence base and emerging interpretive connections. Jürgen Zimmerer, leading a groundbreaking issue of *International Journal of Human Rights* on climate change, environmental violence, and genocide, acknowledges the convergence of genocide studies and climate change by realizing:

> the simple truth that climate change is already taking place and is already affecting the lives of millions of people seems to have been lost. It might be the tragedy of climate change research that the potentially truly apocalyptic character of climate change in the future obscures the view of the ground-level suffering occurring today. The fact that this suffering predominantly takes place – at least at this moment – in the global south might be a further explanation for this deficiency.[16]

This view takes a midpoint between the literature decrying a violence-ridden future and losses already occurring in the present. Likewise postgenocide should not irresponsibly propagate the imaginary of pending apocalypses, just as much as genocide studies should not replicate interpretations of primordialist tribal conflict. It is a juncture wherein the convergence of global warming, resource exploitation and scarcity, warlordism, and geopolitical ordering may offer a more developed framing of mass violence in the contemporary age, bringing insights into identities formed around such direct and structural violence. Whereas 'genocide' is typically grounded on agency and intent, and underpinned by legal and historical case work, postgenocide is presented here as contextualized in structure and identity-forming processes, with a world systems view of the present and near-future.

Whilst climate change is a massive challenge to human flourishing and survival, it is still considered by most to be a secondary driver of contemporary mass violence.[17] Yet, it should be no surprise that climate change is taken up as the starting point for discussions on mass violence.[18] Levene, for instance, describes postgenocide as a reflection of the failures of liberal peace and neoliberalism. He articulates a global systems and political economy view of global capitalism, and attempts to identify the resultant impacts of physical and structural violence.[19] An example used by Levene on more than one occasion is that of the Chittagong Hill Tracts ('CHT') in Bangladesh.[20] In a postcolonial conflict stretching from the

[16] Jürgen Zimmerer, 'Climate Change, Environmental Violence and Genocide' (2014) International Journal of Human Rights 18, 266 (hereafter Zimmerer, 'Climate Change').

[17] Danny Dorling, *Inequality and the 1%* (Verso 2014) 69–70.

[18] Levene's work centred on the establishment of the *Crisis Forum*, where in collaboration with others, he convened a series of lectures on climate change and violence. The forum was intended to draw together academics, practitioners, activists, and others to consider a more total approach to change in the face of contemporary crises, see (*Crisis Forum*, 2019) <http://www.crisis-forum.org.uk/about_us/index.php> accessed 10 April 2019.

[19] Levene, 'Dissenting Voice' (n 15) 433–37.

[20] Levene, 'The Chittagong Hill Tracts: A Case Study in the Political Economy of "Creeping" Genocide' (2010) Third World Quarterly 20, 339–69 (hereafter Levene, 'Chittagong Hill Tracts').

1970s to the present, several Indigenous groups have organized themselves politically and militarily, most notably the Jumma, to resist the post-independence Bengalization of the region. These groups distinctly identify apart from the national Bengali majority in language and religious and cultural practices. The latter features in the CHT have been subject to measures of Bengali homogeniation.[21] Violence in this period has been characterized as genocidal, including the mass rape of women.[22]

Despite a 1997 peace accord, conflict over CHT identities and resources continues. Although fertile CHT agricultural land is limited, it is perceived as plentiful by the Bengali state.[23] An aggressive Bengali settlement programme, hallmarked with further sexual violence and abuses of several CHT Indigenous groups, has cast further doubt over peace and security in the region. Since the 1970s the Bengali military has had a significant presence in the CHT. Additionally, the increase of settler campaigns has led to the growth of pro-Bengali paramilitary groups committing at least a dozen massacres across three decades.[24] These attacks have continued into the present, accompanied by Bengalization measures.[25] Bangladesh, itself as a state in crisis, offers a deeper context to this seemingly straightforward case of oppressive minority violence and genocide. As of 2017 Bangladesh's international, or external, debt sits at $35 billion (USD), this country being the leading borrower in the World Bank's International Development Association.[26] CHT, despite being a highland in a region likely to be increasingly impacted by rising sea levels, is subject to flooding due to Himalayan glacier melt, cyclones, landslides, and even drought.[27] These stresses on water resources and traditional agricultural methods are made harder to mitigate against in the above described conflict scenario, especially with continuing Bengali settlements schemes. The crises in Bangladesh are only worsened by the influx of Rohingya refugees seeking safety

[21] Bhumitra Chakma, 'The Post-Colonial State and Minorities: Ethnocide in the Chittagong Hill Tracts, Bangladesh' (2010) Commonwealth and Comparative Politics 48, 283, 285 (hereafter Chakma, 'The Post-Colonial State'); Levene, 'Chittagong Hill Tracts' (n 20) 340.

[22] Amnesty International (AI), *Hidden Bangladesh: Violence and Brutality in the Chittagong Hills Tracts* (*AI*, 22 October 2015) <https://www.amnesty.org.uk/groups/wirksworth-and-district/hidden-bangladesh-violence-and-brutality-chittagong-hill-tracts> accessed 10 April 2019 (hereafter *AI*, Hidden Bangladesh).

[23] Zahid ul Arefin Choudhury and Md Rafiqul Islam Fahim Durrat, 'Historical Background of CHT and Introduction to the Study' in Choudury (ed) *Mapping Conflict in Chittagong Hill Tracts 1997-201* (Adarsha Books 2017) 15–16.

[24] Chakma, 'The Post-Colonial State' (n 21) 293.

[25] ibid 295; *AI*, Hidden Bangladesh (n 22) 2015.

[26] International Monetary Fund (IMF), *Bangladesh: Staff Report for the 2018 Article IV Consultation—Debt Sustainability Analysis* (*IMF*, 10 May 2018) <https://www.imf.org/external/pubs/ft/dsa/pdf/2018/dsacr18158.pdf> 2, accessed 10 April 2019; World Bank Group (WBG), *International Debt Statistics 2019* (*WPG*, 2018 <https://openknowledge.worldbank.org/bitstream/handle/10986/30851/IDS2019.pdf?sequence=5> 8–9, accessed 10 April 2019.

[27] Bernhard G Gunter, Atiq Rahman, and A F M Ataur Rahman, 'How Vulnerable are Bangladesh's Indigenous People to Climate Change?' [2008] Bangladesh Development Research Working Paper Series, 12–19.

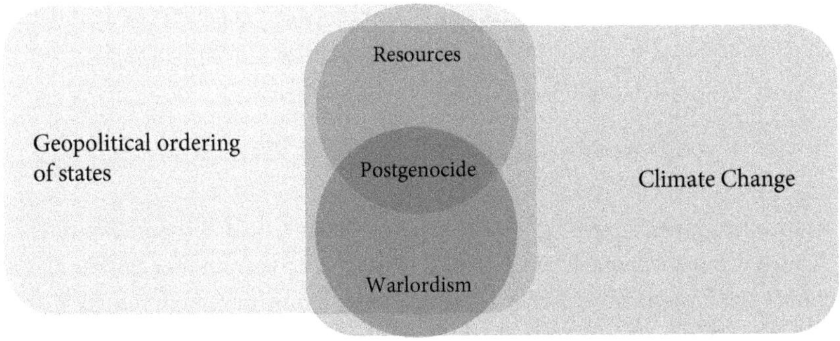

Figure 1 Postgenocide elements diagram

in the Cox's Bazar area of the CHT, as discussed in Jobair Alam's Chapter 5 in this volume. The flow of refugees having a possible contagion effect in spreading conflict is addressed below. Given the above identity, resource, and state crises in Bangladesh, the presence of these refugees fleeing genocide in Myanmar, poses a serious threat to increasing tensions in the CHT.[28]

This view of the CHT broadens the structural culpability, as environmental security literature tends to do, and as recommended by Zimmerer above.[29] Postgenocide then may be characterized as violence without direct intent, and beyond the traditional state, although the state is not absent in this assessment. Similarly, Scheffran *et al* articulate a nexus of climate change, natural resource demand and exploitation, human (in)security, and societal stability. They argue that this nexus connects the more direct elements that may cause violence as well as the longer-term impacts.[30]

As indicated in Figure 1, the convergences of postgenocide centre on climate change and geopolitical ordering as larger structural elements. Resources and warlordism are more immediate and actor-connected. All four elements can be paired as background and foreground: geopolitical ordering and warlordism, and resources and climate change. The intersections of all four elements demarcate a convergence where postgenocide violence may be detectable. As part of this exploratory argument, these convergences represent a space where active drivers of postgenocide violence can be examined. It must be noted, though, that only a

[28] Md Shahriar Islam, 'Communal Peace in Bangladesh after Rohingya Crisis: An Assessment of Different Approaches to Community Development' [2019] Journal of Prevention & Intervention in the Community, 1–16.

[29] Mark Levene and Daniele Conversi, 'Subsistence Societies, Globalisation, Climate Change and Genocide: Discourses, Vulnerability and Resilience' (2014) Journal of International Human Rights 8, 283 (hereafter Levene and Conversi, 'Subsistence Societies'); Jones, 'Genocide and Structural Violence' (n 2) 133–34.

[30] Scheffran, Ide, and Schilling, 'Climate Violence' (n 5) 372.

broader contextualization and analysis of elements of postgenocide can identify such correlations. The following section discusses these convergences.

Climate Change

The last Intergovernmental Panel on Climate Change ('IPCC') report was released in 2014, with the next due in 2022. This UN body is a focal point of climate change literature, with many other fields drawing from it. Some have highlighted the political nature of the negotiations of IPCC publications influencing modest conclusions compared to those advocated by some experts.[31] The 2014 synthesis report indicates that by the end of the twenty-first century there will be an average of a 2°C increase in global temperature along with rainfall increase in already subtropical dry regions and rainfall decrease in already wet tropical regions.[32] These changes are then predicted to see a decrease in useable water in subtropical regions, resulting in drought. The opposite effect will be felt in higher latitudes. Disruptions to food production will be significant and adaptation difficult to mobilize.[33] Human health will likewise be negatively impacted. Such events and precedents would include 'more intense heat waves and fires, increased risks from foodborne and waterborne diseases and loss of work capacity and reduced labour productivity in vulnerable populations'.[34] Diseases, particularly 'vector-borne' ones will vary; increase in temperatures will reduce some diseases in certain areas, however, with overall warming diseases are predicted to increase 'due to the extension of the infection area and season'.[35] On violent conflict the report emphasizes that the impacts and damages will be harder to recover and recoup from due to climate change.[36] Similarly, efforts at reducing poverty will be hampered and harder to ameliorate.

The recent 2018 IPCC report on the 1.5°C temperature increase between 2030 and 2052 revisits the 2014 predictions and findings. It makes this statement:

> Populations at disproportionately higher risk of adverse consequences with global warming of 1.5°C and beyond include disadvantaged and vulnerable populations, some indigenous peoples, and local communities dependent on agricultural or coastal livelihoods (high confidence). Regions at disproportionately higher risk include Arctic ecosystems, dryland regions, small island developing states, and

[31] Dyer, *Climate Wars* (n 4) 14.
[32] IPCC, *Climate Change 2014: Synthesis Report. Contribution of Working Groups I, II and III to the Fifth Assessment Report of the Intergovernmental Panel on Climate Change* (IPCC, Geneva, Switzerland 2014) 10–11.
[33] ibid 70.
[34] ibid 69.
[35] ibid.
[36] ibid 54, 87, 89.

> Least Developed Countries (high confidence). Poverty and disadvantage are expected to increase in some populations as global warming increases.[37]

This predicted set of conditions is seen as an intermediate step between the wider variances of the end of the twenty-first century. Environmental security literature has taken the predictive drive of the IPCC further into threat projection. Here language of tipping points and nonlinear change has also gained currency.[38] Yet, analysis of existing civil wars and drought data indicates that there is no strong positive correlation between these phenomena. It is claimed by the critiques of environmental security literature that there is no direct causation.[39] What the enquirer of postgenocide is left wondering is whether existing data is so disconnected and is therefore quite unrelated to the possible, broad assessment and predictive drives of the IPCC. Recent flows of migrants from both Africa and South America into (respectively) Europe and the United States have both been pegged on the effects of climate change, although this is not likely to be as massive as implied (positively or negatively) by some Western politicians or alarmist commentators.[40] Africa will be particularly affected by rising sea levels where a population of 250 million live in low-lying coastal areas.[41] According to the International Organisation for Migration, the most significant reasons for migration is work, with many finding their way to high-income countries. Yet, the rate of international displacement as a result of violent conflict is at a record high of 22.5 million, of which many African countries serve as departure points. As of 2018, 82 per cent of people internationally displaced by violent conflict originated from Syria, Afghanistan, South Sudan, Myanmar, Somalia, Sudan, Democratic Republic of the Congo ('DRC'), Central African Republic, Eritrea, and Burundi.[42] This is where the challenge of manoeuvring massive data sets becomes apparent. The top ten countries at most risk of extreme and climate related weather disasters (as of 2016) do not immediately overlap with top ten migrant points of origin.[43] This set of climate risk countries are

[37] IPCC, *Global Warming of 1.5°C An IPCC Special Report on the Impacts of Global Warming of 1.5°C Above Pre-industrial Levels and Related Global Greenhouse Gas Emission Pathways, in the Context of Strengthening the Global Response to the Threat of Climate Change, Sustainable Development, and Efforts to Eradicate Poverty* (IPCC, Geneva, Switzerland 2018) 11.

[38] For a nuanced assessment using this approach see Andreas Exenberger and Andreas Pondorfer, 'Genocidal Risk and Climate Change: Africa in the Twenty-First Century' (2014) International Journal of Human Rights 18, 362 (hereafter Exenberger and Pondorfer, 'Genocidal Risk').

[39] Critical views of the direct causation argument can be found here: ibid 354–55; Theisen, Holtermann, and Buhaug, 'Climate Wars?' (n 5) 88–89. For a view on the possible direct and indirect correlation of climate change and violence see Jon Barnett and W Neil Adger, 'Climate Change, Human Security and Violent Conflict' (2007) Political Geography 26, 639–55.

[40] Jean-Michel Severino and Oliver Ray, *Africa's Moment* (Polity 2011) 22–23.

[41] ibid 196–197.

[42] International Migration Organisation (IMO), *World Migration Report 2020* (*IMO* 2019) < https://publications.iom.int/system/files/pdf/wmr_2020.pdf > 39–40, accessed 26 June 2020.

[43] David Eckstein, Vera Künzel, and Laura Schäfer, 'Global Climate Risk Index 2018: Who Suffers Most From Extreme Weather Events? Weather-related Loss Events in 2016 and 1997 to 2016' (*Germanwatch* November 2017) <https://germanwatch.org/sites/germanwatch.org/files/publication/20432.pdf> 6, accessed 12 April 2019 (hereafter Eckstein, Künzel, and Schäfer, 'Global Climate').

also found in areas most vulnerable to climate change, or what Christian Parenti labels the tropic of chaos.[44]

Geopolitical Ordering of States

For Levene the global order in which states exist acknowledges the structure and agency within the geopolitical order of the capitalist world broadly divided by three tiers.[45] States that form the first tier propagate and operate within the Washington Consensus and persisting structures of global capital accumulation and regulation, the International Monetary Fund ('IMF'), and the World Bank. The structural violence purveyed by these systems is widely documented and articulates conflict around resources; resources that vary from land and energy, to crops and traditional medicines.[46] This grouping sets the pace for the following tiers utilizing political and economic power relations to administer flow between the tiers. As discussed in Kevin Aquilina's Chapter 2 in this volume, state-level accountability for international crimes is still wanting.

The second tier is composed of those states that compete in the global capitalist market and are influenced by instruments like currency valuation and international development loans. This is popularly described by Naomi Klein as conformity under the 'shock doctrine' to neoliberal economic and political norms and are set as the standard of functionality and survival of many states.[47] Tier two states may feel the pull of development and display its successes. However, they will also experience the stresses and pressures of this competition. Zimbabwe, under Mugabe, and still in the immediate post-Mugabe era, demonstrates the scale of structural violence present in loosely capable states where human deaths and suffering are widescale.[48] Narratives around colonialism or corruption should not be

This top ten at-risk list includes in descending order Haiti, Zimbabwe, Fiji, Sri Lanka, Vietnam, India, Chinese Taipei, North Macedonia (formerly the Republic of Macedonia), Bolivia, and the United States. The below discussion of Haiti as a case tier-three state impacted by climate crises also indicates the presence of violence in this world systems view, without a comparable flow of conflict refugees. The presence of Zimbabwe at number two in the *Germanwatch* at-risk list, when considered in the context of the political turmoil of Mugabe's exit, ominously foreshadows the crises in 2018 and 2019.

[44] Christian Parenti, *The Tropic of Chaos: Climate Change and the New Geography of Violence* (Nation Books 2011) (hereafter Parenti, *Tropic of Chaos*).

[45] This model was similarly posited in Immanuel Wallerstein, *World-Systems Analysis: An Introduction* (Duke University Press 2004).

[46] Peter Prontzos, 'Collateral Damage: The Human Cost of Structural Violence' in Adam Jones (ed), *Genocide, War Crimes and The West: History and Complicity* (Zed Books 2004), 300–30; Leech, *Capitalism* (n 13) 13–15.

[47] Naomi Klein, *The Shock Doctrine: The Rise of Disaster Capitalism* (Penguin Books 2007); Jones, 'Genocide and Structural Violence' (n 2) 137–38.

[48] ibid 140.

relied on as single explanations of disorder and violence. It is the purpose of the notion of postgenocide to then take a broader view, considering cases such as this, particularly as evidence of tier-two states.

The third tier is populated by states that are the refuse of this world system. More often than not this occurs within or at the peripheries of the global south. States fall further into modes of crisis and conflict, of which Bangladesh, as discussed above, and Haiti serve as examples. In 2010 an earthquake killed over 200,000 people and brought to the fore, again, the impoverished and embattled position of the island state. Prior to the earthquake Haiti was already occupying the third tier, with a colonial legacy of socio-economic race and class divides.[49] The legacy of the Duvalier period was that of proliferation of militias and reinforced collaboration with the US—a militarized presence surrounding Haiti, overlapping with spikes of conflict that prevented Haitians from fleeing the island.[50] The violent abolition of slavery set Haiti on a path of indebtedness to international powers, with US occupation prior to the rise of the Duvalier family dictatorship in 1957. Generally speaking a lack of robust institutions and political stability continually puts Haiti at mercy of powerful neighbours like the US.[51] External debt has nearly tripled since 2000, reaching the 2.6 billion USD mark at the end of 2017, despite IMF debt relief programmes.[52] Haiti also found itself highly ranked on the climate risk index, surrounded by geological fault lines below and severe tropical storms from above. These stresses are unbearable from the socio-economic view. Dramatic changes in precipitation increase flooding, impacts soil quality, deepen soil erosion, and desertification. Deforestation is increasing as a result of population density and the business of small-scale charcoal manufacturing.[53] As a tier three state, Haiti is plagued with the worst expressions of this condition, with legacies of violence and genocidal moments throughout its history.[54]

[49] Robert Fatton Jr, *Haiti: Trapped in the Outer Periphery* (Lynne Rienner Publishers 2013) 55.

[50] ibid 61.

[51] *Council on Foreign Relations*, 'Haiti's Troubled Path to Development' (*Council on Foreign Relations*, 12 March 2018) <https://www.cfr.org/backgrounder/haitis-troubled-path-development> accessed 13 April 2019.

[52] *IMF*, 'Haiti: Debt Statistics and IMF Support' (*IMF*, 27 January 2010) <https://www.imf.org/external/np/country/2010/012710.htm> accessed 13 April 2019; *Index Mundi*, 'Haiti External Debt' (*Index Mundi*, 20 January 2018) <https://www.indexmundi.com/haiti/debt_external.html> accessed 13 April 2019.

[53] Eckstein, Künzel, and Schäfer, 'Global Climate' (n 43). Recent research on this domestic and emerging larger scale industry in East Africa documents the dual impacts of anthropogenic climate change and informal violence. See Adam Brancha and Giuliano Martiniello, 'Charcoal Power: The Political Violence of Non-Fossil Fuel in Uganda' (2018) Geoforum 97, 242–52.

[54] Philippe Girard, 'Caribbean Genocide: Racial War in Haiti, 1802–04' (2005) Patterns of Prejudice 39, 138–61; Jean-Philippe Belleau, 'Killing the Elites: Hatred and Mass Violence in Haiti, 1812-1964' paper presented at the Sixth Global Conference on Genocide by the International Network of Genocide Scholars at Medical Faculty of Aix-Marseille University (France), 4 to 7 July 2018.

It should be caveated that tiers in this schema are not terminal destinations; it is possible and demonstrated that states move between tiers as a result of conformity to the rules of the system. Postgenocide Rwanda—along with various other research on the dynamics of memory and nation-building—attests to mobility around the second and third tiers. Indeed statehood itself demonstrates an undergirding of perpetual crises.[55] Presently operating in tier two, abiding and attempting to compete within global and regional economic regimes, Rwanda has successfully risen from the events of 1994, and subsequent border conflicts up to the present.[56] Some scholars, however, have evidenced climate change and global economy causes at the roots of the 1994 genocide. This includes unsustainable population growth and environmentally damaging agricultural practices, which were further intensified by the collapse of international commodity prices.[57] Yet, politicized memory favouring Tutsi-led economic and political elites simmers the potential for future conflict regionally and within the Rwandan diaspora, along with resource limitations.[58]

Stratification of tiers also shows the connections between climate change, crises, and warlordism (see Figure 1), and internal displacement or creation of refugee flows.[59] Levene and Alvarez go as far as to describe the 'contagion' effect of refugees. Those fleeing can bring a 'flow of weapons, combatants, and ideologies supporting violence'.[60] Studies show a strong link between conflict and migration, as noted above and in some cases even a positive correlation between environmental degradation and violent conflict.[61] However, looking for these direct connections, again, will unlikely produce causal chains. What is discernible from the data is that environmental refugees are only likely to grow in number, and flow between tiers where the mobility exists to do so.[62]

[55] Christopher P Davey, *A Vortex of Genocide: Banyamulenge Identity Formation in Pursuit of the Genocidaire, Zaïre (1996–1997)*, University of Bradford PhD Dissertation, February 2019, 137–51 (hereafter Davey, *Vortex of Genocide*).

[56] Refer in this volume to Chapter 8 by Andrew Wallis, 'Politics of the Inter/National Denial of the Genocide Against the Tutsi in Rwandan' (hereinafter Wallis, 'Politics').

[57] Alvarez, *Unstable Ground* (n 7) 78, 107; Issac A Kamola, 'Coffee and Genocide' (2008) Transition 99, 54–72; Amy K Richmond and Francis A Galgano, 'The 1994 Rwandan Genocide' in Francis A Galgano (ed), *The Environment-Conflict Nexus: Climate Change and the Emergent National Security Landscape* (Springer 2018) 155–65;

[58] Wallis, 'Politics' (n 56); Susanne Buckley-Zistel, 'Remembering to Forget: Chosen Amnesia as a Strategy for Local Coexistence in Post-Genocide' (2006) Rwanda Journal of the International African Institute 76, 131–50.

[59] Scheffran, Ide, and Schilling, 'Climate Violence' (n 5) 374.

[60] Levene, 'Dissenting Voice' (n 15) 436; Alvarez, *Unstable Ground* (n 7) 129.

[61] Nils Petter Gleditsch, Ragnhild Nordås, and Idean Salehyan, *Climate Change and Conflict: The Migration Link* (*Coping with Crisis Working Paper Series*, May 2007) 5; Jean-Marie Guéhenno, 'Conflict is Key to Understanding Migration,' (*Carnegie Europe*, 13 May 2016) <https://carnegieeurope.eu/strategiceurope/63578> accessed 22 July 2019.

[62] Parenti, *Tropic of Chaos* (n 44) 130–31.

Warlordism

Military groups on a scale of private and professional to local and informal can be directed from the tier one, but operate and thrive in the third tier. As noted in the introduction, such violent non-state actors are not covered by the UN Genocide Convention. This leaves a further gap in our current definitional thinking. Warlord literature broadly defines this phenomenon as armed groups within decentralizing states, exerting power through control of fixed or moveable assets, and using personal networks and violence to maintain that power.[63] In zones of lawlessness, mercenaries are often flown in where a domestic military is unable, unwilling or non-existent. More specifically, private military contractors ('PMCs') might also represent the interests of first and second tiered states in the third.[64] These constitute a conscious order in a context of seeming chaos. Typically, militarized or armed actors in tier three are often characterized as the epitome of lawlessness. However, examples from the Great Lakes conflicts demonstrate a similar representation of outside interests.[65] In this case and others, armed groups are often directly representative of sponsoring second tier states, perhaps even eventually connected to first tier economic accumulation of international organizations. Armed groups and militias establish a local economy of benefit through enforced, but informal, taxation or territory control around resources.[66]

The post-Cold War era saw a realignment of non-conventional forces. Martin Shaw describes this as 'loosely democratic national-liberationist ideologies and authoritarian practice ... in a repressive direction in many new irregular armed forces'.[67] This transition from revolutionary violence to more contemporary expressions has resulted in continuance of counterinsurgency methodologies of civilian casualties and destruction of property where power is less guaranteed by a backing state, but built through terrorization of civilian populations and maintenance of a political economy. Furthermore, the veneer of ideological rebellion or liberation masks a commodification of low-intensity conflict and violent

[63] Kimberly Marten, 'Warlordism in Comparative Perspective' (2006/2007) *International Security* 31, 47–48. See also Troy S Thomas, Stephen D Kisser, and William D Casebeer, *Warlord Rising: Confronting Violent Non-State Actors* (Lexington Books/Rowman & Littlefield 2005).

[64] The Wagner Group is a current example of an international PMC, but with significant links to Russian interests internationally, significantly in tier three states with resources, see Neil Hauer, 'Russia's Favourite Mercenaries' (*The Atlantic*, 27 August 2018) <https://www.theatlantic.com/international/archive/2018/08/russian-mercenaries-wagner-africa/568435/> accessed 30 March 2019; The Inquiry, 'What is the Wagner Group' (*BBC World Service*, 25 March 2019) <https://www.bbc.co.uk/programmes/w3cswqvs> accessed 25 March 2019.

[65] Filip Reyntjens, *The Great African War: Congo and Regional Geopolitics, 1996–2006* (CUP 2009) 114–17, 224–31.

[66] John MacKinlay, 'Defining Warlords' (2000) 7(1) International Peacekeeping 48, 55; P W Singer, 'Private Military Firms: The Profit Side of VNSAs' in Klejda Mulaj (ed), *Violent Non-State Actors in World Politics* (Columbia University Press 2010).

[67] Martin Shaw, *War and Genocide: Organised Killing in Modern Society* (Polity 2003) 153 (hereafter Shaw, *War and Genocide*).

livelihoods.[68] Examples from the 1990s into the present include a host of armed groups, where conventional militaries detach or fragment into informal groups operating outside the accountability of the state and international norms. Specific cases include: Iraq and Syria in iterations of the so-called Islamic State (IS) and earlier in the Mahdi Army; West Africa in the Sierra Leone and Liberia conflicts, featuring the Revolutionary United Front, and in East-Central Africa with the Rwandan Patriotic Front ('RPF'), *Forces Armées Rwandaises* and *Interahamwe* in the Rwandan civil war and genocide, and the subsequent RPF-led conglomeration of rebel factions in the *Alliance des Forces Démocratiques pour la Libération du Congo* to topple Mobutu.[69]

Participation in these groups is varied and difficult to relegate to broad generalizations. It is the local context and perceptions of actors that serve as primary factors in mobilizing individuals not only to take up arms, or be compelled or forced to do so, but the perpetuation of such as a livelihood. Kieran Mitton's study of participation in militia groups in Sierra Leone reveals an array of factors that could be portable to other cases. Many of the young men in these groups joined or were abducted into service. Variations of agency resulted in a complex matrix of rationality, shame, disgust, and brutalization.[70] This complicates the view of warlord groups as fallout from the breakdown of the controlling barriers of the state.[71] Stathis Kalyvas has argued that there are 'endogenous' logics of participation derived from an array of interests and motivations. A scholarly reliance on ideology to explain any kind of participation is ignorant at best, and irresponsible at worst.[72] Understandings of actor involvement in violence is necessarily varied. Postgenocide attempts to bring this broader sense of how participation in violence, and even genocidal violence, is experienced by actors within the context of the larger structural and often local underpinnings.

Resources

The scarcity and exploitation of resources serves as a direct connection to the political economy of tier three states. However, this element is embedded in the structure of climate change for the purpose of postgenocide. Natural resources,

[68] Mary Kaldor, *New and Old Wars: Organised Violence in a Global Era* (Polity 2012) 103; Justine Brabant, "*Qu'on Nous Laisse Combattre, et la guerre finira*" (La Decouverte 2016) 94–99.

[69] Shaw, *War and Genocide* 154 (n 67). For the Mahdi Army see *Mapping Militants* (*Centre for International Security and Cooperation*, May 2019) <http://web.stanford.edu/group/mappingmilitants/cgi-bin/groups/view/57> accessed 5 April 2019.

[70] Kieran Mitton, *Rebels in a Rotten State: Understanding Atrocity in the Sierra Leone Civil War* (Hurst 2015) 6–18.

[71] Alvarez, *Unstable Ground* (n 7) 73–74.

[72] Stathis Kalyvas, 'The Ontology of "Political Violence": Action and Identity in Civil Wars' (2003) 1(3) Perspectives on Politics 475, 482; Stathis Kalyvas, *The Logic of Violence in Civil War* (CUP 2006) 22 (hereafter Kalyvas, *Logic of Violence*).

their demand, availability, and extraction are deeply connected to the variances in climate and the environment. Levene notes how tier one of the geopolitical order directly or indirectly benefits from the resources held in tier two and three states. This may even occur via the involvement of PMCs or local militias.[73] Global resource demand is ever increasing, with methods of resource extraction likely to become more invasive and extreme.[74] Indeed, the issue of mass complicity in climate change and even postgenocide is relevant here as the economies of dominant consumerism, markets, development, and productivity are in detrimental competition with nature. This nexus also has a catastrophic and destructive impact on Indigenous groups.[75] The linkages between genocidal processes and resources are perhaps understated in genocide studies. The case of First Nations groups in Canada as subject to continuing forms of violence in Maureen S Hiebert's Chapter 11 in this volume, demonstrates this. Currently, in the Canadian province of Alberta, tar sands extraction increasingly encroaches onto historically stolen land, leaving vastly negative health and social impacts, in a province already subject to forest fires, only likely to increase with rising and variable temperatures. Resources are being consumed through a process of paternalistic destruction, underpinned by a narrative of progress and development.[76]

West Papua is an example of the deadly combination of resource scarcity and exploitation in postgenocide (see Figure 1). This is another case of postcolonialism in the mix of postgenocide. After independence and into the 1980s, Indonesia followed the Dutch (as the former metropole) model of treating West Papua as a *terra nullius*, perceptibly rich in resources that have been exploited to both social and environmental detriment. The population has equally been viewed as vessels for resource extraction, including oil, minerals, and timber.[77] Indonesia, during its occupation, also opened up the area to multinational corporations' exploitation, particularly from logging by Australian and Canadian companies.[78] The disruptions of these occupation and extraction activities have resulted in massive flows of refugees. However, it would be disingenuous to characterize West Papuans as passive receptacles of colonial and neo-colonial oppression. As brutal as the Indonesian military has been, Indigenous people have engaged in their own violence as a separatist movement with various motivations.[79] West Papua has not avoided the

[73] Levene, 'Dissenting Voice II' (n 15) 437–38.
[74] Short, *Redefining Genocide* (n 6) 53.
[75] Levene and Conversi, 'Subsistence Societies' (n 29) 283.
[76] Short, *Redefining Genocide* (n 6) 159–84.
[77] Kjell Anderson, 'Colonialism and Cold Genocide: the Case of West Papua' (2015) 9(2) Genocide Studies and Prevention 12–13.
[78] *Cultural Survival*, 'West Papua: Forgotten War, Unwanted People' (*Cultural Survival*, June 1991) <https://www.culturalsurvival.org/publications/cultural-survival-quarterly/west-papua-forgotten-war-unwanted-people> accessed 10 March 2019.
[79] Stuart Kirsch, 'Rumour and Other Narratives of Political Violence in West Papua' (2002) 22(1) Critique of Anthropology 53–79; Esther Heidbüchel, *The West Papua Conflict in Indonesia: Actors, Issues and Approaches* (Johannes Herrmann Verlag 2007) 112–58.

impact of climate change as a likely tier three candidate. It is part of the trend of malaria encroachment into highland areas previously free of the disease.[80] Land clearing for large-scale palm oil production is likely having a deleterious effect on the water table of West Papua, although further study is needed to ascertain the full impact.[81]

The value of postgenocide is that it takes an intersectional approach to these converging elements identified by Levene. This helps bridge the gap within popular environmental security literature while responding to the corresponding critique of this literature: a contextual view of so-called climate violence. Genocide studies' inclination towards qualitative sociological and historical analysis also adds to this perspective what the climate wars narrative fails doing. The field can also carry a sensitivity towards violence that does not abuse visceral accounts made in the name of emotive narratives of genocide.[82]

There are some additional caveats to be considered in attempting to evolve this concept. Shaw warns against the conceptual proliferation within the field. It was noted above as to why postgenocide is analytically helpful including in developing Levene's initial offering. The use of this concept is less directed at broadening the historical cannon of genocides, but rather proposes a distinct categorization. Further, a measured caution should be applied in the use of this term. There are likely many cases of mass or localized violence fitting into one or more elements of postgenocide. The cited examples above may, indeed, reflect these elements across the areas of Figure 1, with some more clearly visible than others. If the above schema of elements is not rigorously applied to particular cases, postgenocide may then be used by environmental security literatures activist and imaginary discourse to evoke 'genocide'. It is therefore crucial to retain this kind of broader world systems approach in order to avoid missing structural and even local complications of using a postgenocide lens.

Postgenocide Identities

This section takes into account the above mentioned relational developments in genocide scholarship and highlights some congruence between them and the notion of postgenocide. Genocide studies' relational turn posits that identities in

80 Newsdesk, 'Climate Change and Infectious Disease: A Dangerous Liaison?' (2008) 8 The Lancet 92.

81 Irina Comte and Others, 'Agricultural Practices in Oil Palm Plantations and Their Impact on Hydrological Changes, Nutrient Fluxes and Water Quality in Indonesia: A Review' (2012) 116 African Affairs 71–124.

82 For instance, Linda Melvern, *A People Betrayed: The Role of the West in Rwanda's Genocide* (Zed Books 2009) or, Judi Rever, *In Praise of Blood: The Crimes of the Rwandan Patriotic Front* (Random House 2018).

genocide are both performative and fluid.[83] The destruction of identities, along with their symbolic and physical expressions, is at the core of genocide. The fatal disruption of social figurations of a group results in permanent fracturing, whilst also violently constructing new ones.[84] Agency and action for all types of actors involved in genocide is performative on many levels. Yet, actors are often neatly divided and categorized as victims and perpetrators in much of the literature. The subaltern perspective of many actors engaged in perpetration of mass violence is demonstrative of this relational identity, as noted in the Haitian example.[85] In this scenario, the Other is identified based on a perceived threat or vulnerability, which can only worsen in violence prone environments such as perceived enemy identity and territory, refugee camps, or frontlines.[86] Such threat perceptions remain active in the reconceptualization of identities in postgenocide, as shown in contributions in Parts II and III of this volume.

Performing Violent Identities

The fluidity and performativity of identities is reflected in experiences of multiple cases of genocide and perceptions of the latter. Such cases take on a subaltern relation between actors and engender a specific performativity. Omar Bartov introduced this idea in *Mirrors of Destruction* by tracing the post-First World War perceptions that built into the animosities exploited by totalitarian regimes in the 1920s and 1930s. A group sensing their own victimization and constructing a narrative of this identity does so in relation to the threatening Other.[87] As seen in the Hutu-power response to the threat of civil war in early-1990s Rwanda, the violent Othering of the so-called dangerous Tutsi saw a similar development of this logic. Scott Straus, in the case of Rwanda and other African conflicts, notes that states who engage in genocide or mass violence are embedded with a 'domination-vulnerability paradox' perspective.[88] He claims that political power often comes with the burden of constantly creating, and then fending off, enemies at the gate. This dynamic of performative identity and power is also prevalent in settler

[83] Performativity here is broadly defined using Judith Butler's discussion of gender identity, that identity finds substance in its performance, see Judith Butler, *Gender Trouble: Feminism and the Subversion of Identity* (Taylor and Francis 1999) 11.
[84] Claudia Card, 'Genocide and Social Death', (2003) 18(1) Hypathia: A Journal of Feminist Philosophy 66 (hereafter Card, 'Genocide').
[85] The dynamic of layered victim and perpetrator experiences in the Haitian experience is reflected in the story of a torturer and soldier of a past regime, see Edwidge Danticat, *The Dew Breaker* (Knopf Doubleday Publishing Group 2007).
[86] Kalyvas, *Logic of Violence* (n 72) 85.
[87] Omer Bartov, *Mirrors of Destruction: War, Genocide, and Modern Identity* (OUP 2000) 137–38.
[88] Scott Straus, *Making and Unmaking Nations: The Origins and Dynamics of Genocide in Contemporary Africa* (Cornell University Press 2015) 56 (hereafter Straus, *Making and Unmaking Nations*).

genocide. Settlers engage in genocidal violence and enact destructive structures in order to preserve or maintain the viability of colonies and newfound livelihoods, responding to perceived (or constructed) existential threats on the frontiers of empire.[89]

Connected actor or group experiences in genocide and mass violence have a strong formative impact on actors, shaping perceptions of the Other and the Self.[90] English soldiers who brutally colonized Irish peasants during the second half of the sixteenth century, took their perception of the Other, grounded in a frontier environment, into the so-called New World.[91] There they drew on these perceptions and performatively reacted with overwhelming violence against Pequot and neighbouring peoples' resistance to the colonial logic of resource accumulation and exploitation. The results can be characterized by the one-sided conflict wherein many Pequots were massacred in 1637 at Mystic Fort. In this instance a village was surrounded and burned by Connecticut soldiers. Any Pequots trying to escape were shot.[92] Prior to this episode, Massachusetts militia performed a retaliatory attack against a Narragansett settlement on Block Island. This same Narragansett people then participated in the Pequot village attack as a result of existing animosity and ongoing conflict.[93] This complex layering of participation and agency underscores the weak utility of perpetrator and victim tropes.[94] Within the framing of postgenocide, actors can be thought as varied but generally labelled as militarized, although not always with a state-based authorization. Thus, taking the above relational approach, in the postgenocide framework actors are seen as fluid and layered between victim and perpetrator experiences. Postgenocide therefore might helpfully complicate simplistic appeals to victim and perpetrator categories.

Furthermore, recent studies are seeking to make larger-scale connections between the massive depopulation of the Americas and the impact on the climate and macro-carbon capacity due to the shift in land use.[95] Within the Americas,

[89] Refer to Martine Hawkes' Chapter 9 in this volume; also Dirk Moses (ed), *Empire, Colony, Genocide: Conquest, Occupation, and Subaltern Resistance in World History* (Berghahn Books 2009) 31.

[90] Christopher P Davey, 'A Soldier's Journey: Banyamulenge Narratives of Genocide' (2020) Journal of Interpersonal Violence 16–19 (hereafter Davey, 'Soldier's Journey').

[91] Michael Freeman, 'Puritans and Pequots: The Question of Genocide' (1995) 68(2) The New England Quarterly 282–84 (hereafter Freeman, Puritans and Pequots'); Ronald Dale Karr, '"Why Should You Be So Furious?": The Violence of the Pequot War' (1998) 85(3) The Journal of American History 878–79.

[92] Freeman, 'Puritans and Pequots' (n 91) 288–89.

[93] David Stannard, *American Holocaust: The Conquest of the New World* (OUP 1992) 112–15. Stannard continues to describe how during King Philip's War, both the Narragansetts and Wampanoags were obliterated by English colonists.

[94] This dynamic is further documented across more than one generation in colonial Arizona. As a result of multi-generational experiences of violence, as both perpetrators and victims, Anglo-Americans, Mexicans, Tohono O'Odham Indians, participated in the execution of 150 unarmed Apaches. From underneath the apparent chaos of this event Jacoby draws out the narratives and structures at play in this case, Karl Jacoby, *Shadows at Dawn: An Apache Massacre and the Violence of History* (Penguin 2009).

[95] Alexander Koch and Others, 'Earth System Impacts of the European Arrival and Great Dying in the Americas after 1492' (2019) 207 Quaternary Science Review 13–36.

just south of what became New England, the mass disruption of life realigned identities and power relations as a result of social, economic, and military upheaval and crises.[96] More recently, and within the contemporary age, was the realignment of identities in Eastern Congo in the lead up to the First Congo War (1996–1997). The presence of a million refugees and thousands of *genocidaire* Hutu forces in camps in North and South Kivu disrupted and reoriented localized conflict around anti-Tutsi narrative within a nexus of Zairian state crisis, humanitarian disaster, and massive environmental degradation as a result of the refugee camps. This coincided with Zaire/DRC entrenching its tier-three status.[97] Postgenocide, therefore, is closely intertwined with performing identities, and restructuring and spatialization of power.

Resource Wars, Wars of Survival

The narrative of resource wars, whether deployed in the imaginative exploration of climate violence or expressed in the voices of perpetrating actors, conjures a hyper-identity conflict based on existential crisis and a fight for survival. One conclusion of the critical analysis of environmental security literature is that ethnicity becomes commodified and leveraged in conflicts. It is possible that identities in future climate wars gain higher currency in a nexus of survival and resource ownership. Even if the more nuanced views in this perspective are to be given credence, like that of Parenti, such conflicts are now and will be oriented around dynamics of resource control and survival, as well as the militarization and securitization of borders and resource access.[98] Easy parallels can then be drawn with the above discussed colonial conflicts where European actors, removed from the metropole perceiving themselves cornered in foreign frontiers may respond with overwhelming violence. This is done both for survival and the viability of the colonial enterprise.[99] In some cases the perceived, inevitable extinction of Indigenous peoples as races that would not survive into the modern era further enabled and created extinctionist discourses that gave way to exterminatory violence.[100] Although

[96] Robbie Franklyn Ethridge and Sheri Marie Shuck-Hall, *Mapping the Mississippian Shatter Zone: The Colonial Indian Slave Trade and Regional Instability in the American South* (University of Nebraska Press 2009).

[97] Davey, *Vortex of Genocide* (n 55) 122–33.

[98] Parenti, *Tropic of Chaos* (n 44) 147–57.

[99] Mark Levene, *Genocide in Age of Nation State: v. 2: Rise of the West and the Coming of Genocide* (I.B. Tauris 2005) 258–59 (hereafter Levene, *Rise of the West*); Tom Lawson, *The Last Man: A British Genocide in Tasmania* (I.B. Tauris 2014) 47–52 (hereafter Lawson, *Last Man*). A fuller example of the logic of colonial viability at the expense of colonial subject is found in the conscious choice to continue exports in the face of El Nino induced famine in India, see Mike Davis, *Late Victorian Holocausts: El Nino Famines and the Making of the Third World* (Verso Books 2002).

[100] Lawson, *Last Man* (n 99) 41–42; Benjamin Madley, *An American Genocide: The United States and the California Indian Catastrophe* (Yale University Press 2016) 185–86.

removed by the past, these set a threshold for perceptual development and survival in new frontiers, such as future competition over resources. In past colonial conflicts, identity was leveraged or weaponized against Indigenous groups, or those that resisted the tide of progress. The Other was not fit for the future either as a result of the capacity of the emerging order, or the Other's ontological contradiction to the future. It is not unreasonable to assume the recurrence of these dynamics in upcoming conflict settings.

Indeed, resource related conflicts in our contemporary age echo some of the above trends. Violence in these scenarios is more likely where recourse to nonviolent political mechanisms is limited or perceived to be absent.[101] Marginalization from the state and the absence of democratic processes are then key drivers of conflict. The frontiers of the Sudanese state, both in the West and in the South, have resulted in this kind of violent conflict for decades. The centralized Arab-Islamic identity constructed by the National Islamic Front has been mobilized in the preservation of the state in back-to-back crises since independence.[102] Exclusion was pursued along ethnic group lines, but with deep historical, colonial, and socioeconomic underpinnings. Darfur, as a frontier land of Sudan, was demarcated by nomadic pastoralism and more stable farming, with a heritage of Arab-slave trading.[103] Broadly speaking, there are dozens of self-identified grouping that crisscross the Arab heritage, non-Arab heritage, and pastoralist and sedentary divides.[104] The most recent iteration of conflict in this part of Sudan, and most violent, came at the convergence of drought, famine and regional war from the 1980s into the 1990s. By the beginning of the 2000s, after decades of marginalization and exposure to these factors, stress on traditional socioeconomic structures and the increased availability of weapons the ground was ready for genocide in Darfur.[105] Emerging Fur, Zaghawa, and Masalit non-Arab rebel groups mobilized against the state in order to have access to power and therefore preservation and protection. They were tipped into action by the utility of past uprisings in response to the above dynamics and their exclusion at the negotiating table at the end of the North-South civil war.[106]

Whilst scholars warn against Darfur in the 2000s as a clear-cut case of climate violence, it stands apart in a postgenocide framing. Both war in neighbouring Chad and other parts of Sudan and climate change had eroded literally and figuratively the capacity of the state to locally mitigate and manage conflicts.

[101] Exenberger and Pondorfer, 'Genocidal Risk' (n 38) 355.
[102] Straus, *Making and Unmaking Nations* (n 88) 234–26; Amir H Idris, *Conflict and Politics of Identity in Sudan* (Palgrave Macmillan 2005) 12–13.
[103] ibid 24–32.
[104] Julie Flint and Alex De Waal, *Darfur: A New History of a Long War* (Zed Books 2009) 6–9 (hereafter Flint and De Waal, *Darfur*); Straus, *Making and Unmaking Nations* (n 88) 247.
[105] Gerard Prunier, *Darfur: The Ambiguous Genocide* (Hurst & Company 2005) 54–80 (hereafter Prunier, *Darfur*); Straus, *Making and Unmaking Nations* (n 88) 248–50.
[106] ibid 250.

Violent armed actors on various sides of the conflict emerged, whether Justice and Equality Movement or Janjaweed, to exploit resources or destabilize the region.[107] The Janjaweed militias, growing in presence, armaments, and impunity, were unified from previously divided North and South Darfur factions into a force able to respond to swift violence against non-Arab uprising.[108] Identities within the rebellious Darfur groups are complex and range across intersecting scale of an incorporation of Islam (political and religious), African, black, and Bedouin, embracing the universalism of Islam to the chagrin of the powerful Arab-Islamism of the centre in Khartoum.[109] Decades of regional environmental stress and conflict, and spread of Arab nationalism fed into the composite complexity of ethnic identity in Darfur.[110] Ideologies that accompanied the power being handed out from the centre to the periphery came with loaded weapons and ideology. Both enabled the interpretation of this complexity and conflict over resources' access (pasture and arable land). Ethnic identities of Arab and non-Arab, or black African, or so-called slaves, were mobilized and leveraged to exploit and explain the conflict. Labelling the genocidal processes against the perceived non-Arab frontier peoples as a drought war or racially polarized tribal conflict is equally misleading.

In response to the claims of drought and ethnicity causing conflict, the Darfur case demonstrates that perceived tribalesque ethnic conflict actually involves the mobilization of ethnicity and identity as alternative power structures and networks adopted by groups competing for resources.[111] In the postgenocide framework, identities become the tools of conflict at a nexus of threat and survival. Other elements of postgenocide are also detectable in this case (see Figure 1). Funding the ability of the Sudanese state to sponsor its proxies in Darfur was the continued sale of oil and maintenance of competition on the global market.[112] US involvement in the region had long revolved around the perceived Islamist threat and oil markets, utilising sanctions and IMF withdrawal as tools of discipline in the region.[113] This conflict for survival and resources escalated and still perpetuates at the peripheries of a tier two state of Sudan, where events in Darfur started representing that of a tier three state.

The dire nature of such circumstances only further radicalizes the claims of who belongs politically and who deserves resources, and therefore ultimate survival.

[107] The Janjaweed groups are discussed below, but for discussion of rebel group actions see Samuel Totten and Eric Markusen (eds), *Genocide in Darfur: Investigating the Atrocities in the Sudan* (Routledge 2013) 12, 19.

[108] Flint and De Waal, *Darfur* (n 104) 56–70.

[109] James Christian Patrick, 'Darfur—Ground Zero for Africa's Crises of Identity: A Psychohistoriography of Tribes in Conflict' (2013) 6(1) African Security 14–15, 19.

[110] Prunier, *Darfur* (n 105) 162–64.

[111] Alvarez, *Unstable Ground* (n 7) 77.

[112] Hamid E Ali, 'Estimate of the Economic Cost of Armed Conflict: A Case Study From Darfur' (2013) Defence and Peace Economics 24, 507.

[113] Prunier, *Darfur* (n 108) 51–52; Luke Anthony Patey, 'State Rules: Oil Companies and Armed Conflict in Sudan' (2007) 28(5) Third World Quarterly 997–1016.

If an ontopological framing and narrative means forming a polity out of a violent past, this creates further inclusion and exclusion as well as construction of memory and denial. Postgenocide scenarios demonstrate the *extremis* of identity in contemporary violent conflict.[114] Within the experiences of crises occasionally felt in tier two states, but the norm in tier three states, nation building or consolidation of groups of belonging tends towards violence. The disintegration of such political projects hinge on the construction and preservation of identities.[115]

Mobilizations of Identity

Actor typologies can expand to include a variety of traditional and non-traditional actors as party to ongoing climate violence.[116] Identity beyond victims and perpetrators is not just deconstructive, but a recognition of the complex layers and fluidities of identity. Agentic actors in postgenocide then pop up across the macro, meso, and micro layers of social relations. The institutions acting as caretakers and operators of the international system, underpinning the earlier observed tiered system of states, stand out as possible perpetrating organizations, including, as mentioned above, the IMF, and World Bank. However, they are deeply connected to the many links in global economic systems benefiting and therefore perpetuating these structures. This connectivity takes us right down to the warlord actors exploiting resources and civilians (see Figure 1) who are then participating in global markets through sponsor states, PMCs, and environmentally exploitative corporations. This should then convey the gravity of relational and interdependent actors, institutions, and structures as players in this global system.[117] However, given a qualitative analysis of cases, the mobilization and leveraging of identity can be deciphered. The perception and portrayal of migrants, armed actors (both local and PMCs), political actors, civilians, and other categories can be parsed out of any case, whether through micro-level qualitative research, or more macro-level analysis of structures. Identity categories within postgenocide are inherently broad and far-reaching.

Already highlighted in this chapter is the uncertainty of intent in postgenocide. This is rooted in the same phenomena of interconnected actors and structures.

[114] Klejda Mulaj, 'Violence of War, Ontopology, and the Instrumental and Performative Constitution of the Political Community' (2018) 44(1) Review of International Studies 65–66.

[115] Levene, *Rise of the West* (n 99) 160.

[116] Levene and Conversi, 'Subsistence Societies' (n 29) 282; Zimmerer, 'Climate Change' (n 16) 277. Both these pieces refer to how genocide scholars themselves, mostly resident in the global north, are engaged in lifestyles with high carbon footprint.

[117] Christopher Powell, 'What do Genocides Kill? A Relational Concept of Genocide' (2007) 9(4) Journal of Genocide Research 528; Nick Crossley, *Towards Relational Sociology* (Routledge 2011) 125–28, 140–44 (hereafter Crossley, *Relational Sociology*); Jones, 'Genocide and Structural Violence' (n 2) 134.

A relational concept of genocide supports a structural approach, suggested by Shaw as, 'a recurring pattern of social conflict, characterized by particular kinds of relationships between actors, and with typical connections to other conflict structures in society'.[118] Relations are then decipherable between actors and groups in a nexus of interactions across networks.[119] As postgenocide re-conceives of this nexus through the above described elements, the potential for the lethal harm of genocide grows. The sources of unintentional destruction can be multifaceted, but simultaneously complicit through violent and destructive acts from climate altering resource extraction to climate and resource-based group violence.[120]

As noted in the above examples, particularly that of Darfur, ethnicity has a fluid and violently mobile character. In violent contexts, especially where the state is in crisis or caught in the tier three trap of institutional breakdown, identity can be ascribed and subscribed for means of survival and as an expression of changing power relations. Indeed, part of the challenge that is addressed in geo-political ordering of states is that the very perception and use of identities from tier one down into tier three states varies greatly.[121] The establishment of the IS across Iraq and Syria further illustrates the elements of postgenocide, as well as a particular application and misunderstanding of identities in places of crisis.[122]

War and massive destabilization in Iraq and the overwhelming regime response to popular resistance in Syria both fuelled the rise of IS, albeit for a brief period. Syria in particular saw a period of drought reducing food production and in turn increasing urbanization and rural impoverishment between 2006 and 2011.[123] IS drew in the disenfranchised and vulnerable from across the region and even globally. Unemployment and a lack of opportunities can be cautiously framed as of the universal mobilizers at stake here for would-be IS fighters.[124] A digital and mobile recruitment campaign successfully recruited people globally to fill the ranks of IS, some of whom had already experienced mass violence in different contexts, including South East Europe. Young men from Bosnia, Kosovo, and North Macedonia who experienced wars of dissolution of the former Yugoslavia as children in the 1990s, but lived in the present framed by their violent past and marginalized through unemployment and poverty became pray of IS recruitment

118 Shaw, *War and Genocide* (n 67) 97.
119 Crossley, *Relational Sociology* (n 117) 33.
120 Card, 'Genocide' (n 84) 70–71.
121 Alvarez, *Unstable Ground* (n 7) 51–52.
122 For the IS refer to Christopher P Davey, 'ISIS—Becoming Armed, Dangerous and a Participant in Mass Violence' (*Transconflict*, 17 November 2014) <http://www.transconflict.com/2014/11/isis-becoming-armed-dangerous-participant-mass-violence-171> accessed 19 April 2019 (hereafter Davey, 'ISIS'); Alyssa Chassman, 'Islamic State, Identity, and the Global Jihadist Movement: How is Islamic State Successful at Recruiting "Ordinary" People?' (2016/17) 9 Journal of Deradicalization 205–59 (hereafter Chassman, 'Islamic State').
123 Alvarez, *Unstable Ground* (n 7) 93–94.
124 Davey, 'ISIS' (n 122); Chassman, 'Islamic State' (n 122).

strategy.[125] What needs to be emphasized here is the performative scale of interaction across multiple experiences of mass violence and genocide. IS actors came from or identified with violent, conflict-driven backgrounds, whether in Europe or the Middle East, where there was a perception of marginalization and disadvantage. Layered exposure and performativity of power through committing further atrocities is key for this mobilization and participation in genocide processes.[126]

Performativity in postgenocide is then particularly destructive and is imbued with exponential potential, depending on responses to climate change and even to making the global economic system less burdensome for its most vulnerable subjects. Although distinct intent may not necessarily be present or clearly discernible, postgenocide demarcates a disruption of social figurations that is detrimental. As noted earlier by both Levene and Zimmerer, performative perpetration is bound up in multiple spaces captured by the elements of postgenocide: global consumerism, international financial institutions, routes of resource trafficking or exploitation, and empowering violent non-state actors, but not necessarily beyond state interests. Identities in postgenocide can then serve as lenses to these dynamics, whereas the traditional tools of the study of genocide, such as intent and agency, are more diffuse on this broader scale. As observed in the introduction of this volume, transferability is key: '[T]ransferability of the material power of genocide—not least death and suffering—to (contests over) memory, remembrance and laws of genocide and, crucially, re-imagining, re-understanding, re-experiencing political community in the postgenocide setting.'[127] Transferability indicates varying power dynamics demonstrating the reverberations of any genocide, upsetting conventional legal norms of perpetrator and victim as connected to the political community. The ascription, subscription, leveraging, and mobilization of identity can be traced as golden threads.

Departing Thoughts

Postgenocide can be conceived as an approach that expands and complements existing genocide scholarship in terms of processes, actors, identities, and narratives. Use of postgenocide is not an attempt to broadly redefine Lemkin's work, but to adjust it to the contemporary age. It highlights an emergent approach where legal and historical views on genocide are insufficient in capturing this concept's

[125] According to a recent report, more than 1,000 adult male fighters, women, and children from the Western Balkans have spent time in the latest conflicts in Syria and Iraq, and around half of them remain there. Refer to Adrian Shtuni, 'Fighters and Homegrown Jihadis: Trends and Implications' (2019) *Combating Terrorism Centre at West Point* 12 <https://ctc.usma.edu/western-balkans-foreign-fighters-homegrown-jihadis-trends-implications> accessed 25 March 2019.

[126] Davey, 'Soldier's Journey' (n 90) 13–15.

[127] Mulaj, 'Introduction' (n 9) 14.

intersections, and takes into account recent debates including those in climate violence research. In doing so the concept of postgenocide is illuminated and could be applied to other conflicts involving mass violence beyond formal states. What has been identified here, using the work of genocide scholars labouring at the peripheries of their field—including contributors in this volume—is a nexus of violence where the geopolitical ordering of states, climate change on a larger scale, resources scarcity or exploitation, and warlordism on a smaller scale, produce a violence not unlike genocide but devoid of the traditional markers. The diagram above (Figure 1) is an initial attempt at visualizing these convergences, demonstrating an array of ways in which postgenocide violence may occur or seem likely. Future analysis of postgenocide should seek to examine emerging and historic cases, as well as map out the pattern and processes of identity formation within its identified elements.

It is apt that a volume such as this which attempts to recast existing conceptions and approach(es) to genocide ends with a solemn but confident appeal to hope and meaningful prevention—a hope in reducing genocide and generating a more robust response to atrocity. This message of hope intentionally or unintentionally reinforces or defends use of Western liberal and neoliberal institutions. However, in the case of postgenocide, this would be disingenuous at best. This is because it is this same collection of liberal institutions and orientations that perpetuate geopolitical ordering, resource exploitation and scarcity, climate change, and warlordism, or at least as variances of beneficiaries or sponsoring connections. Perhaps, what is more appropriate at this juncture is an appeal to sense or see identities, their politics and conflict, as an avenue to understand emergent patterns of postgenocide in the contemporary age.

Consciously or not, our own complicity in postgenocide through some of the spaces mentioned above should not deter us or promote a fatalistic outlook from genocide scholars or human beings generally. As we reach the height of the Anthropocene, adaptation should be the order of the day. Before us now, more than ever, is an opportunity to adapt existing observations of a type of violence already embedded in a world system seemingly bent on self-destruction. Remaking our conceptual approaches is a fitting accompaniment to marking our impact on the planet and humanity.

Index

For the benefit of digital users, indexed terms that span two pages (e.g., 52–53) may, on occasion, appear on only one of those pages.